Strategic Social Media Management

Karen E. Sutherland

Strategic Social Media Management

Theory and Practice

Karen E. Sutherland
University of the Sunshine Coast
Sippy Downs, QLD, Australia

ISBN 978-981-15-4657-0   ISBN 978-981-15-4658-7 (eBook)
https://doi.org/10.1007/978-981-15-4658-7

This Palgrave Macmillan imprint is published by the registered company Springer Nature Singapore Pte
Ltd.
The registered company address is: 152 Beach Road, #21-01/04 Gateway East, Singapore 189721,
Singapore

Foreword

Social media is in a constant state of growth, change, and innovation. We are entering a time where updates are happening every second of every day. New tools are being introduced and applied in campaigns and global practices on a regular basis. Some of the platforms we have grown accustomed to have either changed dramatically or have disappeared from the face of the earth (RIP Meerkat, Vine, etc.). For the modern social media professional in the industry, it is quite challenging to manage all of the changes, expectations, and duties of the profession while harnessing the skills needed to be successful and sustainable in the field. This is a delicate balance of understanding the creative aspects of the field with the strategic mindset, but it is one that is a growing skill for social media professionals to master.

However, we need to be aware and prepare for these growing changes that are occurring in the industry and technology landscape. Instead of being reactive and waiting for trends to happen, it is important to understand the strategy that goes into identifying these trends, crafting creative and innovative pieces of content, and sharing relevant points of information for communities to help foster a stronger relationship amongst key audiences. With all of these advances, social media education and the book market have also had to keep up with the changes in the field. Most books cover the basics of each platform or view social media through one lens to evaluate, examine, and apply the principles and practices online.

The integration of all of these factors in a coherent and relevant manner have been lost until now. This book by Dr. Karen Sutherland comes into play in addressing a huge gap in the social media landscape.

Karen Sutherland's *Strategic Social Media Management: Theory and Practice* will provide you with a comprehensive guide to the dynamic realm of social media management and support you to apply these principles and practices into real world scenarios. As you move forward in this book, you will see that social media management is not just for public relations or advertising, but it really is multidisciplinary and global in nature. In addition, the book presents a clear vision and pathway to fully integrate both research and industry best practices into strategic social media management. Along with sharing relevant best practices, case studies, and insights into strategic social media management, another unique feature of the book are the interviews from global leaders and experts across all areas in strategic social media management. This book provides a comprehensive, global, and diverse representation of the areas in the industry as well as the leaders who are helping shape the field as we know it in the twenty-first century.

The mark of a true successful and industry changing book is not only the information and best practices that is being shared and presented, but also looking at the person who wrote the book. Dr. Karen Sutherland is one of the leading experts in social media management both in and out of the classroom. Dr. Sutherland has successfully integrated and executed these same practices with her students as well as in her consulting efforts. If you need evidence or proof, all you have to do is look on social media at the global impact she has created with her work with her students and the mentorship she has provided for educators and professionals alike.

Strategic Social Media Management: Theory and Practice will not only be a book you will enjoy reading and using, but it will be one you will have at the forefront of your bookshelf filled with post it notes and highlighted marks. This is a book for students, professionals, and educators alike to have as part of their growing social media library.

I wish you all the best of luck as you enter this exciting journey in reading *Strategic Social Media Management: Theory and Practice*. You are in good hands with Dr. Karen Sutherland as your guide, mentor, and supporter in this journey.

Karen Freberg, PhD
Louisville, KY, USA

Preface

Why This Text Is Different

This guide adopts a multidisciplinary approach to social media management to focus on three key functions of social media practice – marketing, advertising and public relations – and will be useful for:

Students

This text will provide students with the theoretical grounding involved in strategic social media management and the knowledge and skills to support its practical application. Students will learn about the cycle of managing social media for a business or nonprofit from both a macro and micro level acquiring practical skills in strategy development, content curation and creation in the process.

Educators

For educators, this text will provide a detailed framework that can support the delivery of content-rich social media classes that bridge the divide between theory and practice. Each chapter contains helpful pedagogical features such as further reading, questions for critical reflection and practical activities that can be used in the classroom. Furthermore, the division of the book into three related but distinct parts enables educators to apply the part/s most relevant to their courses.

Practitioners and Business Owners

This book is the perfect reference guide for Social Media Managers. It provides practical advice on social media strategy development and delivery as well as content-based tactics that connect with target audiences. Also included are links to helpful tools, templates, further information and online courses that support the further development of social media skills.

Social Media: The Only Constant Is Change

The only constant aspect of social media is that it is constantly changing, yet this text will provide readers with the theoretical principles, core concepts and practical skills from marketing, advertising and public relations disciplines that will maintain their relevance throughout this evolution. The fundamental principles will continue to apply, only the window-dressing changes and this book will help readers to keep moving along with the advancements in technology. For those managing social media, the only way to keep up is to ensure that you have a sound knowledge of the three key functions of social media technology: marketing, advertising and public relations.

Further to achieving competency in these three essential disciplines, this book has been divided into three vital practices relating to social media management: social media strategy development, strategic social media content curation and strategic social media content creation. Each of these important practices are explored from marketing, advertising and public relations perspectives for effective social media management. The goal of this book is to provide readers with a complete view of the tasks and knowledge required to be a successful social media manager. It may sound complex, but that is because being responsible for managing a business' or organisation's social media presence is a multi-faceted role. This text will provide a realistic, practical and comprehensive perspective of the entire process of social media management.

It is recommended to read the chapters of this book in order on the first way through to gain a solid understanding of the social media management process, then to use this text as a reference guide to assist with specific topics during their practical application. This introductory chapter includes a brief description of each part of the book and its chapters to provide an overview of what you can expect on this journey into the world of strategic social media management.

Part 1: Social Media Strategy Development

Part 1 demonstrates the importance of taking a strategic approach to social media management. The aim of this part is to guide you through the process of social media strategy development and provide a sound basis of knowledge for you to progress through the next two parts of the book.

Chapter 3: Let's Start from the Beginning – Understanding Your Audience

This chapter teaches you what strategy is, why it is important and what it looks like in actuality. Furthermore, the chapter will focus on the importance of thorough research as the first (and most integral) stage of strategy development. It provides you with practical advice on what, where and how to research at the beginning of the social media strategy development process. A key focus of this chapter is the importance of audience research and the development of personas to understand the customer journey on social media.

Chapter 4: Managing Reputation, Ethics, Risk, Issues and Crises

This chapter focuses on the fundamental considerations for Social Media Managers, how to behave ethically and how to navigate the issues of risk, privacy, consent, issues and crises to protect client/organisational reputation. The legalities and ethics surrounding the development of client contracts, effective social customer service and influencer marketing are also featured.

Chapter 5: The Foundational Components of Strategy

► Chapter 5 focuses on the importance of articulating strategic goals, SMART Objectives and key messages as fundamental components that underpin a social media strategy. This chapter also focuses on negotiating a budget with your client or organisation to support the development, implementation and evaluation of a social media strategy.

Chapter 6: Stop Selling, Start Helping: Prescribing Tactics to Win over Target Audiences

► Chapter 6 strongly focuses on the shift from push marketing to providing valuable and interesting content that shares brand stories to engage with target audiences. This chapter explores a wide range of social media tactics, including paid promotional content (such as advertising and boosted posts), influencer marketing, competitions, events, games, etc. It also demonstrates why all tactics must be underpinned by quality storytelling to connect with target audiences.

Chapter 7: Social Media Monitoring, Measurement, Analysis and Big Data

► Chapter 7 focuses on how to measure the performance of a social media strategy and why it is important to do so. The chapter also provides advice on how to gather, report and analyse data to formulate recommendations for continual improvement of social media performance. It explores techniques such as sentiment analysis and netnography. This chapter also focuses on social media monitoring, social listening, the analysis of social media data and the benefits and best practice for Social Media Managers working with Big Data.

Chapter 8: Social Media Scheduling and Account Management Platforms

► Chapter 8 focuses on the practice of strategic scheduling of social media posts and advertisements and how Social Media Managers can manage multiple accounts using account management platforms. While the range of scheduling and account management platforms continues to increase, this chapter will explain the key things to consider when choosing and applying these technologies.

Part 2: Strategic Content Curation

Content curation is the practice of sharing worthwhile content (created by others) across social networks. However, there are many ethical, legal, theoretical and practical considerations involved with the content curation process. Part 2 provides guidance through this process. There is also a strong emphasis on finding accurate content that is of value to target audiences. Furthermore, this section demonstrates a range of techniques to showcase curated content in ethical and useful ways that engage quality storytelling and support strategic goals and objectives.

Chapter 10: Ethical Content Curation

This chapter explores the history of content curation and how it applies in a social media context. ▶ Chapter 10 will investigate the theoretical underpinnings of content curation and the difference between content curation and content aggregation. This chapter also focuses on the steps to curate content in an ethical and legal way with a strong focus on sourcing accurate information to avoid issues such as: copyright breaches, plagiarism, legal proceedings, reputational damage and loss of social media followers.

Chapter 11: The Content Curation Process

▶ Chapter 11 provides step-by-step instructions regarding how to undertake the content curation process to source content that supports strategic goals and objectives. As there are many tools now available that can automatically curate content on specific topics, this chapter will also explore the benefits and disadvantages between manual and automated content curation.

Chapter 12: Techniques to Share Curated Content to Engage with Target Audiences

▶ Chapter 12 provides a range of techniques to help you when presenting curated content on mainstream social media platforms to communicate key messages and appeal to target audiences. There is more to content curation than pressing 'share' on someone else's post. This chapter demonstrates different approaches to ensure that your posts remain fresh and interesting to target audiences.

Part 3: Strategic Content Creation

Part 3 guides readers through the process of creating social media content that demonstrates quality storytelling and helps to achieve strategic goals and objectives. The chapters explore the production process relating to a range of content including written copy, photos, graphics and video.

Chapter 14: Writing for Social Media

► Chapter 14 focuses on the process and techniques to write engaging content for the major social media platforms such as: Facebook, LinkedIn, Twitter, Instagram, YouTube, Weibo, Tik Tok, blogs and chatbots. This chapter also provides advice on how to manage complaints written on social media profiles.

Chapter 15: Creating Compelling Images, Graphics, Memes and Infographics

► Chapter 15 explores the process of ethically capturing compelling digital images with tools such as smartphones and digital cameras. It includes topics such as composition and lighting to guide you through the process of editing digital images for mainstream social media platforms. This chapter also explores filters and geofilters, the history of memes and the effectiveness of presenting data using infographics. Finally, this chapter draws on semiotic theory and Gestalt Principles to provide guidance through the process of creating graphical content that conveys key messages and connects with target audiences.

Chapter 16: Producing Social Media Videos that Pop

► Chapter 16 guides readers through the process of producing and editing engaging social media videos for a range of platforms. This chapter presents current debates surrounding vertical versus horizontal video, native versus linked video, etc. This chapter also explores the use of smartphones versus digital video cameras to capture footage. It also explains the process of pre-production to ensure footage and sound captured allows for quality digital storytelling to target audiences. ► Chapter 16 also investigates the phenomenon and production of live video for platforms such as Facebook, Twitter, YouTube and Instagram and video conferencing tools such as Zoom and Facebook Rooms.

Chapter 17: Conclusion: Social Media – The Only Constant Is Change

This chapter sums up the previous topics covered and revisits the core principles of strategic social media content curation and creation. This concluding chapter will also provide readers with advice regarding how to keep their knowledge and skills current in the ever-changing landscape of social media as well as strategies for self-care in what can be a high-pressure profession.

Additional Helpful Features

In addition, this text offers a range of other helpful information, tools and templates to assist you in practically applying the knowledge that you will gain from each chapter.

Interviews with Social Media Managers and Experts from Around the Globe

Each chapter concludes with an interview with a social media expert discussing the topic of the chapter and sharing their knowledge and experience working within the field. Collectively, the interviews provide readers with international perspectives on social media management with industry professionals interviewed from: Australia, the UK, Hong Kong, Mexico, South Africa, Sweden, the USA and India. These will further assist readers by providing context and practical advice on how the knowledge gained can be of assistance in the real world of social media management.

Templates

The appendix of this book contains a range of templates to assist you with all facets of social media strategy, content curation and creation processes. You will find the following:
- Complete Social Media Strategy Template, including:
  - Customer Persona/s
  - Customer Journey
  - Content Pillars
  - Tactics Plan
  - Social Listening, Monitoring and Measurement Frameworks
  - Budget
  - Content Calendar
- Social Media Video Shooting Script

Plus other tools that will assist you with social media management.

Useful Links

Throughout the book you will also find useful links relating to each chapter topic. These links will allow you to source further information and helpful tools and follow experts to assist you in further developing your skills and knowledge.

Practical Exercises

Each chapter also includes practical exercises so that you can really hone your skills in social media strategy development, content curation and creation. These exercises enable you to increase your proficiency and confidence before sharing them with the world via social media platforms.

Employability Advice

Also embedded within each chapter are nuggets of information and advice relating to careers in social media management and the types of skills valued by employers. This information is based on the findings from a recent study that I conducted with 398 employers to investigate the most valued social media skills and what are considered to be the most unprofessional social media behaviours. This information will assist you by ensuring that any skill gaps or any unprofessional social media activities are identified to provide you with the opportunity to increase your employability as a Social Media Manager when seeking clients and/or employment at a business or nonprofit organisation.

This book is a comprehensive guide to the process of social media management. It will provide you with a solid foundation of knowledge and practical skills from the three fundamental perspectives of marketing, advertising and public relations. While the journey sounds challenging, it will also be interesting and a lot of fun. Social media management is an exciting process and one that I feel deeply honoured to be able to share with you.

You can contact me any time on my social media channels or via email if you have any questions or would like to share your thoughts with me. My details are below. I wish you every success in your social media journey.

Dr. Karen Sutherland
F: /drkarensutherland/
T: @kesutherland777
I: @karenesutherland
L: /karenesutherland
W: drkarensutherland.com
E: drkaren@drkarensutherland.com

P.S. I would also like to thank my social media inspirers: Associate Professor Karen Freberg from the University of Louisville; Dennis Yu from Blitzmetrics; Madalyn Sklar, Social Media Coach; Leo Morejon from Build and Inspire; Mireille Ryan, CEO of the Social Media Marketing Institute; and Lisa Harrison, Digital Sociologist for encouraging me on my social media journey.

Contents

Introduction

Contents

© The Author(s), under exclusive license to Springer Nature Singapore Pte Ltd. 2021
K. E. Sutherland, *Strategic Social Media Management*, https://doi.org/10.1007/978-981-15-4658-7_1

Congratulations. Your interest in social media management is extremely timely. We are part of a digital revolution and by learning more about the approaches and tasks required to manage social media, you will be able to use it to your (and your business' or clients') greatest advantage. Social media technology has become such a pervasive, and often necessary, part of the everyday lives for so many that social media proficiency is now considered to be one of the top five skills sought by employers (Deloitte, 2018). And more specifically, in a recent study of 396 Australian employers, public relations and customer service expertise were ranked as the most important social media skills above skills such as content production (Sutherland, Freberg, Driver, & Khattab, 2020). As you will learn through this book, social media has grown in more than popularity; it keeps maturing, and so must our approaches to the way that we manage it.

In the past 15 years, social media has evolved from a fun way for college students to connect online to an essential tool for businesses and nonprofits to support the achievement of organisational goals and authentically connect with their customers and communities.

1.1   Social Media Growth Has Been Consistent and Steady

Overall, the rapid and widespread adoption of social media has been consistent and steady over the past decade without any real indication of slowing down. Even serious data and privacy breaches such as the Facebook Cambridge Analytica scandal (BBC, 2018) was not enough for social media user numbers to decline; on the contrary, numbers continued to grow (Al Jazeera News, 2018). Reports of "people leaving social media in droves" (Hsu, 2018) do not stack up with user data. At the time of writing, we are now in a place where the number of social media users has reached 3.81 billion globally and for many in the developing world, their very first experience with the internet will be via Facebook (We Are Social, 2020; Mirani, 2015). The discussion shifted long ago from whether social media is just a fad (Tuarob & Tucker, 2013). The conversation has ceased to be about *whether* organisations should use social media. Instead it is focused on *how* they can use it to support the achievement of their business goals; and the landscape keeps changing. The COVID-19 Pandemic demonstrated what a lifeline social media can be in connecting businesses, customers, nonprofit organisations and communities on a global scale in response to social distancing requirements (Baker, 2020; Gianotto, 2020).

1.2   Social Media Technology Continues to Grow in Complexity

Social media technology continues to grow in complexity for business owners, marketers, advertisers and public relations professionals seeking to use it to connect with prospective and existing customers. Gone are the days when it was enough to post on Facebook a few times per week without any real strategic approach. To stay relevant, organisations and individuals are advised to function like a media company and produce worthwhile content for their followers. As Gary Vaynerchuk (2013) recommends, "It literally doesn't matter what business you're in, what industry you operate in, if you're not producing content, you basically don't exist." However, social media evolves rapidly, and this continual change is influenced by developments in technology, consumer demands, competition between platforms and other environmental factors. This requires organisations to be nimble, flexible, strategic and relevant. The era of the set-it-and-forget-it marketing approach is over.

1.3 Social Media Is More Than a Marketing Tool

Social media can no longer be viewed as an inexpensive and simple marketing tool (Radick, 2014). As a technology, it provides a multitude of functions and services to a wide range of users. It is this multidimensional aspect of social media that can often leave business-owners, marketers, advertisers and public relations professionals confused. Approaching social media management through the lens of one perspective is highly problematic. However, this seems to be the norm with many of the social media guides currently available. There are a multitude of social media texts on the market, but many provide advice from a single disciplinary perspective, which neglects the multidisciplinary and multi-functional characteristics involved with social media management.

Over time, social media has developed to be more than a marketing tool. Indeed, it is an effective way to promote an organisation's products and services, yet, traditional above-the-line marketing techniques have proven to be less effective with social media users (Traphagen, 2018). Marketers have been required to rethink their approach when using social media as part of their promotional mix. Blatant organisational trumpet-blowing can turn social media users away (Macnamara, 2010).

1.4 Social Media Involves More Than Advertising

Social media has also become more than an advertising tool; however, its power in targeting (and retargeting) specific groups through their purchasing journey cannot be denied (Lee, Hosanagar, & Nair, 2018). In 2017, Facebook made $40 billion in advertising revenue alone, which indicates its preference and widespread use by advertisers (Statista,

2019). Furthermore, social media advertising has overtaken advertising on traditional channels such as television, newspapers and radio which has had a detrimental effect on the ability for these legacy media outlets to continue to operate (MDG Advertising, 2018). Yet, while the use of social media advertising is growing, users have indicated their disdain when they are bombarded with too much advertising (Mattke, Müller, Maier, & Graser, 2018). It is a line that advertisers must tread carefully. Social media advertising must be relevant to the audience it is targeting, and a carefully nurtured relationship can be the most effective way to ensure that this is the case.

1.5 Social Media Is an Effective Long-Term Relationship Management Tool

Furthermore, the two-way functionality of social media has also positioned it as an effective relationship management tool for public relations and communication professionals (Cade, 2018). Social media allows for online conversations, private and public, and this opportunity for two-way exchanges help an organisation to build relationships (positive or negative) with users who may be current or future customers. It is this aspect of social media that is often overlooked and instead, social media is approached as a tool to broadcast information instead of one to nurture long-term and meaningful connections (Grunig, 2009). To date, the focus of social media texts has largely been on how to use the technology as a marketing tool. Some texts exist focusing on the ways that social media can be used for strategic communication and relationship-building. However, this publication is different. It provides a comprehensive multidisciplinary and multidimensional perspective of the realities of social media management practice.

References

Al Jazeera News. (2018). *Number of active Facebook users increased despite scandals*, viewed: 03/02/2019: https://www.aljazeera.com/news/2018/04/number-active-facebook-users-increased-scandals-180426073628185.html

Baker, E. (2020). *Online groups keeping people connected during the coronavirus crisis*, viewed 09/05/2020: https://www.abc.net.au/news/2020-04-05/online-groups-keep-people-connected-in-covid-19-crisis/12115680

BBC. (2018) *Facebook scandal 'hit 87 million users'*, viewed: 03/02/2019: https://www.bbc.com/news/technology-43649018

Cade, N. L. (2018). Corporate social media: How two-way disclosure channels influence investors. *Accounting, Organizations and Society, 68–69*, 63–79.

Deloitte. (2018). ACS *Australia's Digital Pulse - Driving Australia's international ICT competitiveness and digital growth*, viewed: 03/02/2019: https://www.acs.org.au/content/dam/acs/acs-publications/aadp2018.pdf

Gianotto, S. (2020). *How can COVID-19 help businesses grow using social media?* Viewed 09/05/2020: https://blog.retail.org.au/newsandinsights/how-covid-19-can-help-business-grow-using-social-media

Grunig, J. E. (2009). Paradigms of global public relations in an age of digitalisation. *PRism, 6*(2), 1–19.

Hsu, T. (2018). For many Facebook users, a 'Last Straw' that led them to quit. *The New York Times*, viewed: 03/02/2019: https://www.nytimes.com/2018/03/21/technology/users-abandon-facebook.html

Lee, D., Hosanagar, K., & Nair, H. S. (2018). Advertising content and consumer engagement on social media: Evidence from Facebook. *Management Science, 65*(11), 4967–5460.

Macnamara, J. (2010). Public relations and the social: How practitioners are using, or abusing, social media. *Asia Pacific Public Relations Journal, 11*, 21–38.

Mattke, J., Müller, L., Maier, C., & Graser, H. (2018). Avoidance of social media advertising: A latent profile analysis. In *Proceedings of the 2018 ACM SIGMIS conference on computers and people research* (pp. 50–57). ACM.

MDG Advertising. (2018). *How social media has changed the Ad game*, viewed: 03/02/2019: https://www.mdgadvertising.com/marketing-insights/infographics/how-social-media-changed-the-ad-game-infographic/

Mirani, L. (2015). Millions of Facebook users have no idea they're using the internet. *Quartz*, viewed: 03/02/2019: https://qz.com/333313/milliions-of-facebook-users-have-no-idea-theyre-using-the-internet/

Radick, S. (2014). Why social media is getting even more expensive. *PR Daily*, viewed: 03/02/2019: https://www.prdaily.com/why-social-media-is-getting-even-more-expensive/

Statista. (2019). *Facebook's advertising revenue worldwide from 2009 to 2017 (in million U.S. dollars)*, viewed: 03/02/2019: https://www.statista.com/statistics/271258/facebooks-advertising-revenue-worldwide/

Sutherland, K., Freberg, K., Driver, C., & Khattab, U. (2020). Public relations and customer service: Employer perspectives of social media proficiency. *Public Relations Review, 46*(4), 101954.

Traphagen, M. (2018). Social media in 2018: Time to grow up or get out. *Marketingland*, viewed: 03/02/2019: https://marketingland.com/social-media-2018-time-grow-get-236162

Tuarob, S., & Tucker, C. S. (2013). Fad or here to stay: Predicting product market adoption and longevity using large scale, social media data. *ASME. International Design Engineering Technical Conferences and Computers and Information in Engineering Conference, Volume 2B: 33rd Computers and Information in Engineering Conference* ():V02BT02A012. https://doi.org/10.1115/DETC2013-12661.

Vaynerchuk, G. (2013). Every single one of you is a media company. GaryVaynerchuk.com, viewed: 03/02/2019: https://www.garyvaynerchuk.com/every-single-one-of-you-is-a-media-company/

We Are Social. (2020). *Digital around the world in April 2020*, viewed: 08/05/2020 https://wearesocial.com/blog/2020/04/digital-around-the-world-in-april-2020

Social Media Strategy Development

Contents

Social Media Strategy Development

Contents

© The Author(s), under exclusive license to Springer Nature Singapore Pte Ltd. 2021
K. E. Sutherland, *Strategic Social Media Management*, https://doi.org/10.1007/978-981-15-4658-7_2

2

Developing an evidence-based strategy is the first action that a business or nonprofit organisation should take in relation to their social media presence (Freberg, 2018; Kim, 2016; Quesenberry, 2018). Without conducting in-depth research that informs social media activities, Social Media Managers are merely guessing as to what will work for their organisation or clients. It is a rare business or organisation that has an unlimited supply of funds, time and staff to support such guesswork.

Developing a research-based social media strategy not only guides and informs actions relevant to the audiences trying to be reached, it also saves time, money and effort by reducing the margin for error through the use of data. While nothing is ever 100% certain where social media management is concerned, developing an evidence-based strategy from the outset certainly allows Social Media Managers to take more calculated risks.

Part I of this text will guide you through the vital processes and activities involved with developing a social media strategy. ▶ Chapters 3, 4, 5, 6, 7, and 8 each focus on an essential strategic component that works together as a map to guide a client's or organisation's social media activities through the strategic stages of preparation, implementation and evaluation.

However, before embarking on ▶ Chap. 3. It is important to clearly define what a strategy, its fundamental components and how the process of their implementation aligns with the content presented in this section.

The words 'strategy' and 'strategic' can be bandied around with gusto without deeper explanation or qualification for their use. Remember, that just because someone describes something as strategic, it does not mean that it automatically is.

By its simplest definition, a strategy is "a plan of action designed to achieve a long-term or overall aim," (Lexico, 2019). Moreover, a strategy is an overarching plan that identifies and analyses opportunities in a contested environment and adapts resources to take advantage of them in order to achieve a specific goal.

In a nutshell, strategies take measurable objectives (that support business or organisational goals) and express how they will be achieved. Therefore, when an action or activity is described as 'strategic', it means that it has been researched, selected and implemented because it aligns with organisational or business goals and is appropriate and relevant to the audience being targeted.

To plan effectively, Social Media Managers must conduct in-depth research to accurately inform the actions to be included in (and excluded from) that plan. In a Higher Educational environment, there is a strong focus on research, its methods and its benefits. However, in industry, the perception of research as a priority can sometimes weaken due to time pressures and resource scarcity. Yet, basing a strategy on estimation and assumptions could be described as the antithesis of strategic. It is closer to gambling. Research can improve a strategy's probability for success, and essentially, this is what all Social Media Managers should be aiming for.

2.1 The Stages Involved in Developing a Social Media Strategy

◘ Figure 2.1 below demonstrates the stages involved when developing and implementing a social media strategy. Part I focuses on each of these steps. In line with Stage 1, the planning stage, ► Chap. 3 focuses on audience research. Understanding the people a client or organisation is trying to connect with is the most important part of not only the strategy, but with any form of communication.

► Chapter 4, also part of the planning phase, is devoted to understanding the rules around ethical and legal requirements in relation to social media strategy development including how to manage issues, crises and organisational reputation in a social media context. This is an essential part of planning to ensure that all necessary legal and ethical requirements are in place before a strategy is implemented.

► Chapter 5 also aligns with the planning stage. This chapter will provide guidance on how to identify and develop strategic goals and objectives that will underpin all actions employed as part of strategy implementation. What is essential to remember with a social media strategy is that it must be part of and support the goals and objectives of a broader marketing and communication plan. Furthermore, the social media strategy and the broader marketing and communication strategy must align directly with the goals of the organisation or business and every action must help to achieve them in some way.

A 'strategy' is not strategic if it does not support the overall goals of the business or organisation it belongs to.

► Chapter 6 combines both the planning and implementation of social media tactics to inform Social Media Managers on how to select the correct approaches, actions and activities to achieve its goals and objectives.

► Chapter 7 investigates the evaluation phase featuring a strong emphasis on how powerful the practice of gathering and analysing data can be in informing decisions and promoting continuous improvement.

Part I then ends with ► Chap. 8, relating to the implementation and evaluation stages, exploring social media scheduling and account management platforms and how they can be used to support the implementation of a social media strategy.

2.2 The Components of a Social Media Strategy

◘ Figure 2.2 illustrates the vital components of a social media strategy, which are included in the template in Appendix 1.

The components listed in ◘ Fig. 2.2 are aligned with the stages of social media strategy development. It is thorough research as

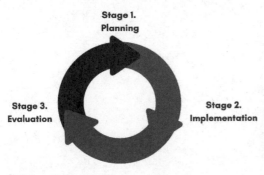

◘ **Fig. 2.1** Stages in social media strategy development

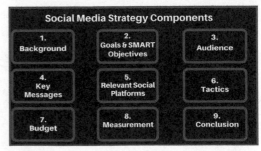

◘ **Fig. 2.2** Social media strategy components

2

the very first step that will help to accurately inform all of the components included in the rest of the strategy.

By the end of ▶ Chap. 8 you will have gained a deep understanding of the stages, processes and components involved when designing a strategy for a client, organisation or your own business. Furthermore, a strategy template is available in Appendix 1 that can assist you when practically applying what you learn in this first section. After Part I, you will then be well-equipped to tackle Part II Strategic Content Curation.

Before we reach that stage, let's progress to: ▶ Chap. 2.

References

Freberg, K. (2018). *Social media for strategic communication: Creative strategies and research-based applications*. Los Angeles, CA: SAGE Publications.

Kim, C. M. (2016). *Social media campaigns: Strategies for public relations and marketing*. New York: Routledge.

Lexico. (2019). Definition of strategy in English, Lexico.com *Powered by Oxford*, viewed 23.08.2019: https://www.lexico.com/en/definition/strategy

Quesenberry, K. A. (2018). *Social media strategy: Marketing, advertising, and public relations in the consumer revolution*. Lanham, MD: Rowman & Littlefield.

Let's Start from the Beginning: Understanding Audiences

Contents

© The Author(s), under exclusive license to Springer Nature Singapore Pte Ltd. 2021
K. E. Sutherland, *Strategic Social Media Management*, https://doi.org/10.1007/978-981-15-4658-7_3

By the End of This Chapter You Will:

- Understand why audience research is an essential first step of the social media development process.
- Gain an insight into a range of research approaches and methods to assist with audience research.
- Learn the six key steps to audience research and how to implement them.
- Understand why customer personas and customer journeys are fundamental when developing a social media strategy.

TLDR

- Audience research is the most important part of social media strategy development because it informs all other strategic decisions and can help with leveraging the algorithms of social media platforms.
- A triangulated approach to audience research involves using a range of research methods is effective in gaining an in-depth understanding.
- A mixed-method research approach using a combination of quantitative and qualitative methods also adds greater rigour when researching audiences.
- Primary research involves directly gathering data from audiences such as through a survey. Secondary research involves analysing other people's data such as an industry report.
- It is important to assess the credibility of secondary research before using it to inform strategic decision-making.
- The five key steps to audience research are: Client Research > Social Media Audit > Competitor Analysis > Audience Analysis> Creating Customer Personas > Tracking the Customer Journey

3.1   Introduction

Understanding your audience is the most important factor in effective communication, which is why the topic takes prominence as the first chapter in this text (Freberg, 2018; Young, 2016). A Social Media Manager may understand social media platforms inside and out and have extensive expertise in advanced marketing and advertising techniques, but all of this knowledge will be pointless if they cannot connect with their target audience.

Guessing what will work with an audience is very much a hit and miss affair unless you are trying to target people who have similar characteristics as you. As a Social Media Manager, this is rarely the case. This is why research also plays a fundamental role at the beginning of social media strategy development (Freberg, 2018; Kim, 2016; Quesenberry, 2018). As you will learn in this chapter, understanding your audience involves much more than learning about their favourite platforms, it also involves learning about a client, organisation and their competitors.

Using more than one method to gather information on the same topic, also known as triangulation, can provide a much deeper understanding than using only one method alone by providing "opportunities for convergence and corroboration of results that are derived from different research methods," (Almalki, 2016, p. 291). This is the recommended approach when conducting research as part of social media strategy development. Relying on one source of information about an audience is almost as risky as making assumptions about them or basing decisions on stereotypes.

For a social media strategy to resonate with a target audience, it is worth the time and effort to conduct robust research to truly understand this group of individuals before developing any other parts of the strategy (Information Resources Management

Association, 2018; Thomas, 2018). This chapter will provide guidance for Social Media Managers on different research types and methods plus the different facets of audiences that should be investigated.

It can be tempting to perceive audiences, customers, publics and stakeholders as a homogenous faceless mass, but this is a perilous approach to take. While there are groups of people who share similar characteristics and interests, Social Media Managers must remember that these groups are composed of multidimensional individuals. This is why it is essential to learn as much as possible about the particular characteristics, wants and needs of the individuals within the audience groups with whom you are trying to connect through the development and implementation of a social media strategy.

This chapter adopts a practical approach to guide you through the six key steps involved with audience research as the vital first stage of social media strategy development.

3.2 Research Approaches and Methods

First, it is essential to understand more about research practice, because there are many different types of research approaches and methods. Yet, there are some overarching categories that help to simplify and understand them. Firstly, the type of research that you can conduct is either Primary Research or Secondary Research.

Primary Research is the data that you gather firsthand (Croucher, 2019; Kenett & Shmueli, 2016). For example, conducting surveys or focus groups for a client. Secondary Research is the analysis of data that already exists (that you did not gather). This is also called 'desk research' and can include analysis of industry reports as an example. Primary and Secondary Research are explained in much greater depth below.

3.2.1 Primary Research

As defined, Primary Research involves Social Media Managers directly gathering and analysing data on behalf of their clients or organisation. This means that instead of reading a report on the general viewing habits of YouTube users and using only that information to inform your decisions, you would base your decisions using direct analysis of the Channel Analytics of your client or organisation's YouTube channel. The difference is that you are conducting an analysis of a relevant audience rather than on data gathered by someone else about a general audience. Secondary research can also be helpful, as will be discussed, but Primary Research will be of most value to you as a Social Media Manager as it will provide an in-depth insight into the specifics of a target audience.

Primary Research can also be further categorised under two broad categories: Quantitative and Qualitative (Clark & Ivankova, 2015; Sarstedt & Mooi, 2019). Both types of research are extremely helpful when investigating audiences because they provide very different yet complementary perspectives.

3.2.2 Quantitative Research

Quantitative Research is largely focused on numbers, counting and statistics (Kolb, 2017; Malhotra & Malhotra, 2012). For example, analysis of numerical survey data or social media analytics from Facebook Insights. Analysis of quantitative research can assist in identifying relationships and trends on a large scale. However, while qualitative research is useful in identifying trends in large data sets, it is also very restricted in delving more deeply into the reasons behind why trends exist. Facebook Insights can show the days and times when most followers are online, yet it cannot explain why most followers are online at that time. This is where qualitative research is required.

3.2.3 Qualitative Research

Alternatively, Qualitative Research focuses on gathering non-numerical data to gain a deeper understanding of the meanings and underlying reasons and factors behind why particular issues and phenomena occur (O'Reilly & Kiyimba, 2015). Examples of qualitative research can be semi-structured interviews, focus groups and observation. These methods gather data that is much more abstract in that it can delve into people's personal motivations and feelings regarding products, brands and social media use. Following on from the previous example, interviewing Facebook followers regarding their social media habits, why they use particular platforms at certain times would provide a much deeper understanding of their motivations behind their social media use.

While qualitative research can provide deeper understanding, it can be very time consuming and it is not uniform in the same way that quantitative research is, meaning that broad assumptions cannot be made unless a large and representative sample is being analysed (Aurini, Heath, & Howells, 2016).

◾ Table 3.1 provides a list of research methods that can be categorised as generally quantitative or qualitative, but sometimes they can be a mix of both. For example, surveys are largely quantitative research methods, but they can contain qualitative elements such as fields for participants to leave open comments which must be analysed using qualitative methods.

Furthermore, the method of content analysis can also contain both quantitative and qualitative elements. Content Analysis can be used to analyse social media content through the identification of a particular code within the selected content. However, only counting the number of times the code appears is a quantitative approach. Yet, delving deeper and analysing the underlying contexts for the occurrence of the code in social media content is a qualitative practice

3.2.4 A Mixed-Methods Approach

A highly recommended research approach is to use a combination of quantitative and qualitative methods (Clark & Ivankova, 2015). In academic research this is called a mixed-methods approach and aligns with triangulation because each method increases rigor with its strengths while counteracting the deficiencies of the other (Creamer, 2017).

Quantitative and qualitative each have their strengths and weaknesses but used together they are a powerful research approach. For example, my PhD research investigating social media and nonprofit organisations began with a survey of the general population (quantitative research). Analysis of the survey data highlighted areas that required further investigation and these findings were used to develop interview questions.

Interviews were then conducted with employees responsible for social media at a sample of nonprofit organisations plus donors and volunteers associated with those organisations (qualitative). Finally, content analysis was used to compare what the nonprofits' social media practitioners were really doing compared with what they said they did in the interviews (quantitative and qualitative).

Clearly, as a Social Media Manager, it is not viable in terms of time and expense to

◻ **Table 3.1** Quantitative and qualitative research methods

Quantitative research methods	Qualitative research methods
Surveys	Interviews
Questionnaires	Focus groups
Polls	Observation
Statistical modelling	Content analysis

undertake audience research at PhD levels, however, this example demonstrates how using a range of approaches can provide a much greater insight than using only one source or even less effective, basing decisions on guesswork without doing any groundwork at all.

3.2.5 Secondary Research

As previously defined, Secondary Research refers to the analysis of existing research that has been gathered by someone else (Largan & Morris, 2019; McQuarrie, 2015). Secondary Research is definitely helpful, particularly in the early stages of audience research and social media strategy development, because it can provide Social Media Managers with a general snapshot of the industry and population specific to a client's or organisation's strategic goals.

This form of research is often referred to as 'desk research' because it can be conducted via the internet without leaving your desk. This type of research can be extremely helpful for the following reasons:

- *It can help Social Media Managers learn about unfamiliar topics and audiences* in the first instance. This knowledge can then be used to guide more relevant and specific audience research. For example, The Social Mango, a social media agency in Mumbai, India has a wide range of clients including a dental agency. The Social Media Managers at the Social Mango do not have any formal qualifications or experience in dentistry apart from being a customer. Therefore, it is important for them to conduct desk (primary) research about the dentistry industry to help provide accurate information throughout the strategy development and content creation processes.
- *It can be less expensive and more convenient than undertaking primary research.*

There are many free industry and government reports and academic research papers and articles written by experts that are available for free and can be found through a simple Google search.

However, there are also some disadvantages for Social Media Managers if relying solely on Primary Research data for audience research:

- *The data may not be specific enough to a target audience.* For example, if the social media strategy being developed is aimed at musicians in the local area from a particular age range, only looking at an industry report about the ages of platform users may not be specific enough. Research should be sourced about the social media platforms used by musicians.
- *The data may be outdated.* Social media moves extremely quickly which means secondary data can soon become stale. It is unwise for a Social Media Manager to base their strategic decisions on general audience data that is more than 12 months old.
- *The data may only be relevant to a specific geographical region.* Try to find secondary data sources that apply to the region where target audiences are located otherwise you may base decisions in terms of platforms and tactics on inaccurate data. There can be variation between countries and even cities in relation to the social media habits and behaviours of its residents, so it is important never to assume that every geographical region uses social media in the same way.

For example, in the U.S. Twitter is used much more extensively than it is in Australia. A recent report found that 35% of U.S. social media users regularly engage with Twitter yet only 20% of Australian social media users prefer the platform (We Are Social, 2018a, 2018b).

Furthermore, in Australia Twitter is generally used for very specific purposes such as to participate in conversations around popular television programs, to keep abreast of news and to share commentary at events, rather than for general chit chat. If a Social Media Manager used the U.S. secondary data to make decisions on an Australian audience, their strategy and tactics would fall flat because they would be unaware of these cultural nuances.

Just as it has been recommended to use a mixed methods and triangulated approach to primary audience research, it is also suggested that Social Media Managers use a combination of Primary and Secondary research when investigating their target audience at the beginning of the strategy development phase. Both types of research can complement each other. Secondary research should be conducted first and helps Social Media Managers build their knowledge and identify research gaps that can then be addressed by primary research.

◘ Table 3.2 provides a list of possible sources for secondary research.

◘ Table 3.2 Secondary research sources	
Industry reports	**Peer-reviewed journal articles**
Government report	Newspapers
Magazines	Official organisational websites
Public records	Market research reports
Annual reports	Newspapers
Business directories	Encyclopedias

3.2.6 Five Key Questions to Ask to Assess the Relevance of Secondary Research Sources

Below is a checklist to determine whether a primary research source is relevant to specific audience investigation and strategy development.

1. *Currency:* When was this data collected? Is it still relevant?
2. *Geography*: In what country and state was this data collected? Does it align and apply to the location and the habits of my target audience?
3. *Specificity:* Is this data too general for my target audience? Are there any other sources that are of greater relevance to the characteristics and preferences of my target audience?
4. *Exclusivity:* What doesn't this source tell me about my target audience?
5. *Credibility:* How was this data collected? Who collected it? How large was the sample and who was in it?

As we will explore in Part II in relation to curated content, it is important to assess the credibility and accuracy of any information to use as content and research sources on which to base strategic decisions. Never assume that Secondary Research is correct, purely because it is easily accessible online. It is better to gather Secondary Research data from credible sources such as the few examples listed in ◘ Table 3.2. Secondary research is more than only gathering sources, it also requires critical analysis of those sources.

Yet, best-practice in conducting audience research would be to allow ample time to undertake solid primary and secondary research to properly inform a social media strategy. However, in reality, Social Media Managers can be expected to propose a

3

strategy in a reduced time period resulting in ample research being close to impossible.

In such cases, it is up to the Social Media Manager to work with the time and resources that they have available to them, but to advise their clients and organisation against risking damage to organisational reputation, time and money on tactics that have not been properly researched.

Solid research in the beginning of strategy development saves time and money in the longer term. Furthermore, approaching research in a systematic way can also increase efficiency, as outlined in the six key steps outlined in the rest of this chapter.

3.3   The Six Key Steps Involved with Audience Research

There are six key steps involved with conducting audience research, and the first three involve investigating a client or organisation and their competitors. This approach may seem unorthodox, because surely audience research should be focused on the audience from the outset.

However, it is essential for a Social Media Manager (and a client or organisation) to reflect internally as a first step to gain as much knowledge and understanding of their performance and practice in reality, before seeking answers externally.

For example, if a client, who is a gym owner, who would like to use social media to attract more female members, yet the gym is clearly not equipped for women to train there, beginning with researching the social media habits of women interested in fitness is not going to be very helpful.

As a Social Media Manager, you might develop a highly successful campaign to bring women through the doors of that gym, but chances are they will not stay very long.

> 66 Consider client and competitor research as getting your own house in order before inviting people over to visit. 99
>
> Dr Karen Sutherland

The same steps should be completed even when working in-house. Social Media moves rapidly so it is important to have current and realistic organisational knowledge at the beginning of strategy development.

3.3.1   Step 1. Client Research

Researching a client will provide an in-depth insight into their story and their perceptions of current and prospective customers (Tasso, 2017). As mentioned, conducting both primary and secondary research will be most beneficial in informing a sound social media strategy.

It is recommended that Social Media Managers conduct primary research to answer the topic questions listed below and visit their client in their working environment (if geographically possible. If not use Zoom or Skype) to interview them on the same topics to see if any gaps can be identified in data gathered using both methods.

One of the best ways to research an audience is to put yourself in their shoes. Understand the type of customer experience a client is trying to offer and immerse yourself in it to see if it stacks up in reality.

3.3.1.1 Client Research Questions

1. When and why did you start your business?
2. What are your products and services?
3. What are your business goals?
4. What is your greatest challenge in achieving those goals?
5. What are the best and most challenging things about your industry?
6. Who are your customers? Who would you like them to be?
7. How would you rate the customer experience and service that you currently offer?
8. How would (and have) your customers rated their experience with your business?
9. What are some of your common customer complaints?
10. What are some of your customers' common questions?
11. Who are your direct competitors?
12. Do you have branding guidelines? If so, may I please have a copy?
13. What are your current social media activities?
14. What has been successful and unsuccessful for you on social media?
15. What do you want social media to do for your business?

The answers to these questions will not only provide important information about a client and their business, they will also give an insight into a client's attitude in relation to their customers, competitors and current social media practices.

The way in which a client answers these questions will help to determine how switched on they are in terms of their business and how connected they are to their customers. Do they know their customers well? Do they love to serve their needs, or do they find their customers a hindrance?

It is definitely better to ask these questions in an interview situation rather than via email. Body language, nonverbal cues and long pauses before answers can also add deeper meaning to your investigation that could never be communicated via email (Hair Jr & Lukas, 2014; Saldaña & Omasta, 2017).

Interviewing a client is an essential first step, however, as is recommended that Social Media Managers take a triangulated mixed-method approach to audience research as the first important step in strategy development, the next step requires a thorough audit of a client's social media activities.

This will assist you in comparing the client's responses with the data from their social media platforms to see if there are any gaps or differences. After interviewing a client, it is essential to conduct some independent research on their social media presence in the form of an audit.

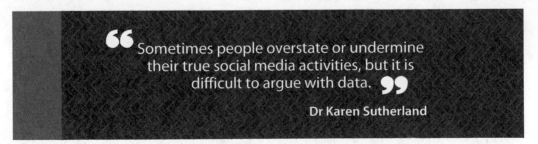

66 Sometimes people overstate or undermine their true social media activities, but it is difficult to argue with data. **99**

Dr Karen Sutherland

3.3.2 Step 2. Social Media Audit

A social media audit involves a complete analysis of a client's social media activities and performance (Quesenberry, 2018; Tuten & Solomon, 2017). It is essential to have a thorough understanding of a client's social media presence (e.g. what is working and what is not working) before a Social Media Manager can begin to make any recommendations.

▶ Chapter 7 provides much deeper insight into social media listening, analytics, monitoring and measurement. However, analysing a client's historical social media data is an important part of researching their audience because it provides an understanding of who the audience is, what they respond to (and more importantly) what they will not respond to in terms of content. An audit such as this will also demonstrate how engaged an audience is and more importantly, how engaged a client is with their customers.

These are the vital items that must be assessed as part of conducting a social media audit for a client.

- **Social Media Platforms**
- Find all of the social media platforms on which a client's business has a presence even if they are inactive.
- **Social Media Profiles**
- Next, find all of the profiles that a client has on each platform. You may discover multiple (and similar) profiles for each brand where a staff member left with the log-in details or the owner forgot their log in details and created another profile for the business. This can also be a common occurrence within non-profit organisations. For example, a non-profit Coast Guard organisation on Australia's Sunshine Coast functions solely due to the work of volunteers. However, volunteers can be transient in nature. A volunteer set up this organisation's Facebook page and attracted more than 1000 followers before moving on and taking the passwords with them. They were the only Admin and Facebook would not provide access to anyone else. The Organisation set up another page and began again.

It is extremely important to know about all created profiles (and their history) to be able to make informed decisions as part of the strategy development process and to implement processes to

- Avoid such duplication from happening again.

3.3.3 The Visual Representation of the Brand on Each Social Media Profile

How is a client visually representing their brand on each of their social media profiles? Individually are they using:
- The correct logo?
- The correct brand colours?
- Images that adhere to the size specifications of the specific social media platform?
- Images that are of high enough resolution?
- Using copyright free and royalty free images?
- Visual imagery that looks professional and is clearly identifiable as their brand?

3.3.4 The Textual Representation of the Brand on Each Social Media Profile

It is equally important to closely audit the text that is being used to represent a client's brand on their social media profiles. If a client is on point with their visual branding, but the accompanying text is of low quality, it will dilute any impact and potentially cause reputational damage with current and prospective customers.

While social media is currently a very visually focused medium, text still plays an important role and therefore must be scrutinised in the following ways:
- Are the bio sections on each profile populated?
- If so, is the company information up to date?

- Does the company info leverage the features of the platform? For example, does it include a link to the company website, or relevant hashtags etc.?
- Is the current text free from errors in spelling, grammar and punctuation?
- Does the text truly capture the organisation's brand voice?
- Has the bio been written with the target audience in mind? For example, does it use language and terms that will resonate with the people a client is trying to reach? This will come more apparent the further you work through the audience research process, so be sure to revisit this part of the social media audit when you have greater knowledge regarding the audience.
- What text is missing from social media profiles that could help the target audience learn more about a client's business?

3.3.5 Previous Social Media Activity

As outlined in ► Chap. 7, each social media platform on which a client's business has a presence will provide analytics of some form from which you can analyse a client's social media activities and performance.

It is paramount that clients provide access to their analytics during the audience research process otherwise you will not be able to make informed decisions when developing their social media strategy.

Avoid being overwhelmed when viewing a client's analytics. At this stage of the social media audit, the key areas to focus on are:

- *Frequency of posts.* How regularly is the client posting on their social channels and how does this information fit in with what is recommended for each platform?
- **Days and times content is being posted.** *Gathering this information will assist* you in matching what you client is doing compared to what the audience analytics are suggesting.

- *Types of content posted.* Is the client posting only textually based content or are they also posting images and videos?
- *Quality of content posted.* How would you rate the quality of the content being posted? Does it look professional or amateur?
- *Relevance to the platform.* Does the content being posted meet the specifications of the platform? Is the client posting across platforms, for example, posting directly from Instagram to Facebook resulting in too many hashtags on Facebook and tags that do not work?
- *Originality of content.* Is the client creating their own original content or only sharing curated content? We explore more about curated content in Part II of this book.
- *Alignment to brand and brand voice:* Does the content posted previously align with the client's brand and align with their business' brand voice?
- *Relevance to the audience:* Again, this will become clearer the further you get with the audience research, but does the content posted seem like it would be of interest to the audience that you client is trying to attract?

3.3.6 Social Media Performance

Gaining a thorough insight into how a client is performing on social media will also provide valuable knowledge about their target audience.

Analysing performance data from each platform's analytics such as Facebook and Instagram Insights or using a third-party tool, will demonstrate whether a client's content is currently resonating with followers or falling short.

While ► Chap. 7 will provide an in-depth insight into the analysis of social media performance data, at the audit stage it is important to determine the following metrics:

3

3.3.7 Vanity Metrics (Indicators of Content Interaction)

- *Number of Followers and page likes:* This will provide a sense of the size of the audience.
- *Reach:* This will provide an insight into the number of people who are potentially seeing a client's social media content on their feed.
- *Engagement:* This refers to the metrics relating to when the audience interacts with a client's content such as with likes, reactions, comments and shares (Kerpen, Greenbaum, & Berk, 2019). However, be thorough when analysing engagement, because sometimes all is not what it seems.

For example, if a post generates 100 comments it may seem like an excellent engagement rate. However, if 99 of those comments are complaints, then this is definitely not a positive result for your client. It is a similar situation with reactions on Facebook and shares. It is important to analyse sentiment (qualitative) as well as the number of times a reaction occurs (quantitative).

A share can be a mixed result depending on the commentary being shared along with the content. It is also important to measure how quickly a client responds to direct messages on their social media platforms to assess the level of customer service that they are currently providing.

- *Content generating the greatest audience response:* The aim of understanding this is to identify what works (and what does not) to gain an insight into what resonates with this particular audience so that tactics and content can be created to achieve a similar positive response and avoid negative responses.

It is important here to analyse the type of content that has been most effective in terms of video, photographs, graphics, curated pieces as well as a deeper analysis of the topics covered in each piece. What themes seem to resonate most with this particular target audience? If there is limited or no engagement at all, this is also very telling. It means that a client's posts are not inspiring their followers enough to interact with them.

3.3.8 Conversion Metrics

(Tangible business outcomes from social media content)

- Conversion metrics track tangible actions undertaken by social media users as a result of social media activity (Charlesworth, 2017; Rishi & Bandyopadhyay, 2017). For example, a Facebook ad that drives traffic to a product page in an online store. We will explore this in greater detail in ▶ Chap. 7.

It is also important to ask your client about conversion metrics as part of the social media audit. Some business owners are very organised in relation to measuring the tangible impact of their social media activities, but more commonly, business owners are at a loss as to how to do this.

Some conversion metrics to ask from a client are:

- *Google Analytics Data:* more specifically Acquisitions and Conversions to track how effective social media channels have been in driving traffic to the website and whether people are converting when they get there. However, with Facebook's 'Clear History' function, users can prevent data being gathered on their activities from other websites and sent to Facebook (Hern, 2019).
- *Social Media promotions converting to in store sales:* Ask the client if they track the success of a social media promotion in terms of it being redeemed in store.

- *Facebook Pixel Data:* This information can show whether people are converting as a result of Facebook and Instagram paid ads and boosted posts which is also reliant on whether the target audience has 'Clear Facebook History' function switched on (Yurieff, 2019).
- *Event Attendance as a Result of Social Media Promotion:* Does the client track social media's impact not only on ticket sales but also on event attendance?
- *Social Media Driving Online Registration:* Has your client used social media to drive the completion of an online registration or membership form? Have they collected how well this worked?
- *Social Media to Attract Donations and Volunteers:* If the client is a nonprofit organisation, do they track social media's performance during donation and volunteer drives?

These are only a few ideas in relation to conversion and they will be different for every client. When conducting the social media audit for the client, it is essential for Social Media Managers to be thorough and to ask as many questions as possible. This will provide you with the most comprehensive view of what has happened in the past and what is currently occurring so that you can make informed choices for the future.

Think of yourself as a detective. You are investigating what is working for your client in terms of their social media, but more importantly, what is not working.

It is essential to find out how well social media is supporting the achievement of a client's business goals. If there are deficiencies, the best time to identify them is at the very beginning of the strategy development process rather than being surprised while it is being implemented. This is why the social media audit is such an important component of audience research.

Having an in-depth insight into your client's social media presence, activities, habits and attitudes only presents part of the overall picture. Another important part of the research process is to learn about other brands and businesses with whom they are competing for the target audience's attention and custom.

3.4   Step 3. Competitor Analysis

The next stage of audience research involves analysing a client's main competitors to understand exactly the options currently available to the target audience.

If a client's goals is to increase sales, as it is for many business owners, the aim will be to use social media in a way that resonates with prospective customers so that a client's brand will be top-of-mind the next time they need the particular product or service that the client has on offer.

Furthermore, a competitor analysis also allows a comparison between a client's social media activities and those of their competitors. The aim is to uncover what may be attracting customers to choose a competitor instead of a client.

A competitor analysis uses similar steps to those when conducting a social media audit, but without access to social media performance data directly from the platforms. Other third-party tools are recommended for this analysis as listed further in this chapter.

Important components of a competitor analysis are:

- *Social Media Platforms used by each competitor:* Are they active and have a large engaged following on a social media platform that your client does not use?
- *Social Media Profiles:* Do they have more than one on each platform? Are there sub-profiles? Checking competitors' websites for links to social media profiles will help to track them down.

3

- *Page likes and Follower Numbers across platforms:* This is important to compare audience sizes with those of your client to see who has the larger following.
- *Visual and Textual Representation of Brand on Social Media Profiles:* This should be audited this in the same way as a client's profiles. Check on the branding, the look and feel and the textual components. Do a client's competitors represent their brands on social media more professionally than your client? Is the look and feel of their social media present attracting prospective customers away from your client? Is the client's social media presence up to the competition?
- *Social Media Activity:* How often are competitors posting and on what times and days? How does this information compare with the client's activities?
- *Types of Content:* Does the client's competitors create their own content, or do they rely on curated content? Do they use video extensively? Does live video feature and what is the quality of the graphic elements that they use in their posts? What topics are their posts about? How do these compare with the client's posts? This information will assist greatly in understanding the intended approaches to social media by competitors.
- *Audience Engagement:* While you will not have access to competitors' native platform analytics, it is possible to examine audience engagement using tools such as:
  - *The Pages to Watch Function* at the very bottom of the Overview page on your client's Facebook Insights allows a direct comparison of the number of Facebook posts, following growth, post engagement and the posts each week that generated the greatest engagement.
  - *Phlanx* can calculate Instagram audience engagement of any public profile.
  - *There are a range of tools available* such as SocialBakers and Nacho Analytics that can also assist in analysing and comparing competitor audience engagement data from a range of social media platforms.

The key when analysing the audience engagement of competitors is to identify successes and failures.

You are advised against blatantly copying the successful posts of competitors. Instead, use these successful posts to gain an insight into the types of content that resonates with the target audience that a client is aiming to reach.

Analyse competitors' content that does not generate engagement as a warning of what to avoid.

- **Share of Voice Analysis (SOV):** SOV measures publicly available social media content to measure which brand is being mentioned online the most and the sentiment (positive, negative and neutral) in relation to what is being posted (Kim, 2016).

This type of analysis helps to compare what current and prospective customers are saying about a client's and their competitor's brands to determine which brand is dominating the online conversation. Tools such as BrandWatch and Meltwater offer SOV functionality.

With a thorough understanding of a client, their competitors and a comprehensive social media audit conducted this knowledge can be applied in the collection and analysis of audience data. Steps 1–3 were important because they provided context for a greater understanding of the target audience to be achieved in Step 4.

3.5   Step 4: Audience Analysis

The final stage of audience research is an extensive analysis of a client's target audience. Depending on the business and organisation and their strategic goals, this group generally consists of existing and prospective customers (or donors, volunteers, etc.).

The people with whom a client has an existing relationship and the people with whom a client is trying to connect. It is essential to gain an in-depth insight into both groups to understand who the client's supporters are and what resonates with them so that you can use this knowledge to foster relationships with new people to continue to build a client's target audience.

The first three key steps will provide Social Media Managers with valuable information about what is on offer to the target audience from a client and their competitors. The next stage of research will identify any gaps between what the client is offering and the wants and needs and attitudes of the target audience.

3.5.1 The Aim of Audience Analysis

The aim of this stage of audience research is to understand as much as possible about the people that a client is trying to connect with. Doing so helps social media to be used as a tool to develop strong relationships with the target audience on behalf of a client, and to facilitate the evolution of a community around your client's brand.

Social media has the ability to connect people "...with shared commonalities such as geographical proximity, brand loyalty, usage characteristics, demographics, politics and religion," (Gangadharbatla, 2012, p. 408). By understanding these characteristics and attributes, a Social Media Manager will know what inspires, excites and resonates with a target audience. Understanding a target audience to evoke these positive reactions and foster strong relationships is a highly beneficial outcome arising from thorough audience research, which can also result in leveraging the algorithms of social media platforms.

3.5.2 What is an Algorithm?

In a social media context, an algorithm is a set of coded instructions by which a platform determines which content is displayed on a user's newsfeed (Ismail, 2018). While there is extensive speculation regarding how algorithms work on each platform (and the suggestion they are ever-changing), it seems relevance is the common measure by which social media content is prioritized (Barnhart, 2017). Hence, it is suggested that users will be presented with more of the types of content and from users they interact with positively (e.g. like, share, comment, and message). For example, a social media user is likely to see more video on their feed if they regularly interact with video (Cinelli et al., 2020). Furthermore, users will see more from a business page if they frequently engage with its content. Also, a post that is receiving a high level of engagement may be prioritized and given greater reach even if the user does not regularly engage with its content creator. This is because the platform deems this content to be valuable based on the volume of engagement from other users.

It is this automated prioritization of content and its impacts that have been defined in the literature as algorithmic culture theory. Strehovec (2013) suggests that "...algorithmic culture points to the fact that contemporary cultures are more and more influenced by the software applications of the information." This theory suggests a social media user's worldview may be shaped by the content they are presented with on their newsfeeds. Thus, content is selected using the platforms' automated mechanisms based on what it deems to be of relevance to the user's preferences. This can result in an 'echo-chamber', where information from different sources never reaches the user's newsfeed to challenge this algorithmically developed world-view (Cinelli et al., 2020).

3.5.2.1 Leveraging the Algorithm

Yet, from marketing, advertising and public relations perspectives, the goal is to create social media content that resonates positively with the target audience, encouraging regular engagement, so that social media platforms prioritise it on their newsfeed. Thorough audience research helps to create content that cuts through and connects with the target audience to prompt positive engagement and leveraging the algorithm of the platform. The ability to leverage the algorithm can be another valuable outcome of comprehensive audience research.

3.5.3 Target Audiences are People Too

Marketers, Advertisers and Public Relations professionals bandy around terms such as market segments, target audiences, publics and stakeholders to denote the groups of people that they are trying to reach and inspire (or convert) to perform a desired behaviour such as purchasing a product or registering to be a volunteer.

While it is easier to view audiences as a homogenous mass, Social Media Managers must remember that any group is comprised of individual people with their own wants, needs and preferences.

It is important to recognise the differences between the people you are trying to reach and to identify their similarities. It is the common ties that bind a target audience that can be used to strengthen their connection with each other and a brand.

There are five important components to include when analysing any audience.

1. *Demographic Information*
   The word 'demographic' refers to the ways in which a population is structured (Oxford Dictionary, 2019). These are the statistical facts and/or details about who a person is, where they live and how much they earn etc. This information helps a Social Media

Manager to understand the factual details about their audience so that they target the most appropriate group correctly.

For example, targeting the services of a wedding planner at married couples would be ineffective. Similarly, trying to connect with retirees using terms popular with teenagers would be unsuccessful. This is why it is essential for Social Media Managers to know the demographic details of the people with whom they are trying to connect.

Understanding the demographic information of an audience also assists when running paid advertisement on platforms such as Facebook, Instagram and LinkedIn as this information assists in accurate targeting. Please refer to ► Chap. 6 for more information about paid advertising tactics for social media.

Important demographic categories to research about a target audience are:
- Age
- Gender
- Cultural Background
- Nationality
- Marital Status
- Number of Children (if any)
- Education Level
- Occupation
- Annual Income
- Living Status (homeowner, renting etc.)
- Religion
- Languages spoken
- Disabilities
- Political Affiliation

3.5.4 Methods to Gather Demographic Information

There are a range of primary and secondary research methods that can assist Social Media Managers to gather demographic data.

- *Social Media Analytics* such as Facebook and Instagram Insights can provide information such as age, gender, location, country, city and language. Clearly this demographic data relates only to the people currently interacting with a client's social media profiles.
- *Population Statistics* from Census data. For example, the *Australian Bureau of Statistics (ABS)* is a wealth of information on the demographic makeup of the Australian population. Its website has countless reports that can assist in the audience research phase and its helpline has extremely knowledgeable statisticians to assist. Many countries have similar governmental bodies in charge of gathering data on the nation's population.
- *Industry Reports* can also contain valuable information about target audiences in each sector. Identify the professional bodies relevant to a client and search their websites for up-to-date audience information.
- *Surveys and Focus Groups* with current and prospective members of a client's target audience can return comprehensive insights and can allow for deeper psychographic research at the same time.

3.5.5 Psychographic Information

Where demographic information is factual information about people's lives, psychographic is focused on their personal characteristics in terms of their thoughts, opinions, preferences, attitudes and lifestyle (Grewal et al., 2017).

A group of people may all live in the same town, therefore, they have the same demographic information in relation to that specific fact, yet their psychographic information will be very different.

Psychographics are a form of market segmentation (Green & Warren, 2019) and are extremely important in the context of

Social Media Managers representing brands, because it can often be a group's common interest or opinion about a particular cause or topic that will be most important when attempting to build a relationship with them on behalf of a client.

There are definitely instances when demographic data is used in a similar way, such as Emergency Services using social media to alert people in a specific geographical area about an impending emergency.

However, as the name suggests, psychographics rely on appealing to the certain psychological characteristics of a target audience. Important psychographic characteristics to research a target audience are:

- Personality
- Personal Values
- Interests and Hobbies
- Attitudes
- Lifestyle
- Preferences and Dislikes

These areas are as important to understand a client's audience as demographic information and at times they can influence each other.

For example, someone who is interested in surfing may choose to live close to the beach and a person's income level and influence their lifestyle. Understanding these characteristics about a client's target audience will assist you when developing Customer Personas as part of the audience research process that we will explore later in the chapter.

3.5.6 Methods to Gather Psychographic Information

Again, there are a range of primary and secondary research methods that can be used to gather psychographic data. While secondary sources can reduce time and expense, they may not be specific enough to a client's business to gain an in-depth insight into the people that you are attempting to connect

3

with. This is where primary research methods can return much deeper insights, such as:

- *Interviews* can allow Social Media Managers to delve deeply into specific topics. However, they can take a long time and can return skewed results unless numerous interviews are conducted to ensure the sample size is valid.

- *Surveys* can provide a snapshot of an audience's broad characteristics. As a research method, online surveys can be easy and inexpensive to produce and disseminate. This method is good to gain some insight into audience psychographics but is more effective when coupled with a qualitative method, such as interviews and/or focus groups.

- *Focus Groups* are a great way to explore topics with several members of a client's target audience where participants bounce ideas off each other. Group dynamics and the facilitator can have a huge influence on the success of this research method, but it can really help to better understand the wants, needs, preferences, dislikes and habits of a client's audience.

- *Social Media Analytics* can greatly assist in identifying audience activity (or lack of it) on a client's social media channels. While this will be covered in ▶ Chap. 7, similarly to the client and competitor analyses reviewing social media analytics can provide a deep understanding into the content types and topics that prompt engagement from the audience.

On Facebook, it is important to also review the types of reactions people are leaving, because they are not always positive. Furthermore, reviewing the comments and direct messages on each platform will provide an in-depth understanding of customer attitudes, feedback and commonly asked questions.

This type of qualitative data is gold as it has been provided organically and without being prompted by deliberate survey questions or similar.

> ❝ Remember, counting the number of comments is not an accurate measure of engagement.
> Analysing the tone of those comments is. ❞
>
> **Dr Karen Sutherland**

It is a similar case with reviews. Are the reviews being left on social media channels (and on Google) positive or negative? What are they actually saying about the product, brand, and/or service. Also, analysing the analytics of paid ads are crucial to better understanding how (or if) they are performing to achieve strategic goals.

- *Website Analytics* can show what people are looking at on a client's website, how long they are staying, the social media channels that are sending them there, and the pages that make them want to leave. All of this information can provide an insight into the wants, needs, likes and dislikes of the client's target audience.

— *Appointing a Market Research Company* can be a much simpler option if your client has the budget. Many Market Research Companies have access to large panels of people from demographic and psychographic groups that may be of interest to your client and can conduct research activities such as focus groups, interviews and surveys on your client's behalf. However, using this option can be expensive.

— *Industry Reports* can provide some level of detail about the psychographic information about the customers in a specific industry sector, which can be helpful, but this information may be too general on which to base decisions about a client's social media activities.

It is worth keeping this information in mind when developing customer personas, but always compare it against the primary research being conducted on the target audience.

This is why adopting a triangulated approach to audience research is helpful when understanding target audiences.

3.5.7 Social Media Habits

When trying to connect with a specific group of people on social media it is essential to understand how and why they use the technology. As a Social Media Manager, you will need to build a strategy and tactics around a target audience's social media habits if you are hoping to achieve a client's strategic goals.

It is surprising how often businesses can get this wrong, building their social media activities on false assumptions and their own platform preferences rather than allowing the data to inform their decisions. Important information to gather regarding target audience social media habits:

— *Social Media Platforms* most commonly used. This is the most important factor to take into consideration. It is pointless to try to engage with an audience on a social media platform if they do not use it.

For example, using Snapchat to reach retirees would be a waste of time and effort, because it is a social media platform predominantly used by people under 34 years of age (Noyes, 2019). Know the main platforms that a client's target audience uses and limit activity to those platforms.

It is better to use one or two social media platforms well and develop an ample following there than trying to have a less effective presence on a range of platforms.

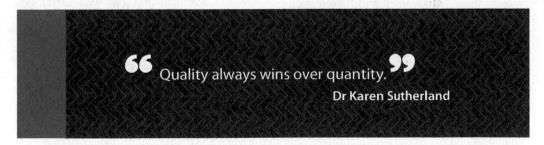

66 Quality always wins over quantity. **99**

Dr Karen Sutherland

— *Time of day the audience uses social media:* Understanding when a client's target audience uses social media helps to inform the best times of day to post to reach the greatest number of people.

— *Devices used to access social media:* Knowing how a client's target audience is accessing social media can also assist you when developing content.

3

For example, Dennis Yu recommends only using 1-minute vertical videos on Facebook if the majority of a target audience accesses social media on their mobile phones to achieve the greatest amount of reach (Yuzdepski, 2018).

There are many other facets in relation to audience social media habits, but these are the three key areas that must be taken into consideration above all others.

The industry reports mentioned below also offer a wide range of interesting data in relation to better understanding the ways that target audiences use social media.

3.5.8 Methods to Gather Data on Audience Social Media Habits

Data about audience social media habits can be gathered using a range of primary and secondary research methods as listed below.

- *Interviews, Surveys and Focus Groups* are generally an effective way to gather data but may be problematic because they require audience members self-reporting about their personal social media usage (Rosenbaum, 2017). Self-reporting can sometimes be inaccurate particularly when a research participant feels embarrassed about their social media use.
- *Social Media Analytics* such as Facebook and Instagram Insights can provide data that identifies the times when the majority of followers are online.
- *Social Media Platforms* also have general information about audience consumption that may be useful.
- *Industry Reports and Websites* can provide relevant information regarding target audiences. While these are also quite general, this data is helpful in the sense that it can provide information about prospective target audiences from

a range of demographic and psychographic groups and their findings are usually based on large samples suggesting a decent level of research rigour.

It is always recommended to examine the methods used in gathering any data that you plan to base decisions regarding a client's social media activities.

Below is a list of worldwide resources with some Australian references. The links to these resources are at the end of this chapter. Please check for country-specific resources because social media is used in different ways around the world (◘ Table 3.3).

Any data is meaningless unless it is used to inform decisions. Step 5 synthesises the data gathered in Steps 1–4 to create a customer persona that will guide important decisions throughout the planning and implementation processes of social media strategy development.

3.6 Step 5. Creating Customer Personas

Steps 1–4 in the audience research process explored thus far has involved gathering a significant amount of data about target audiences.

In its current form it may seem extremely challenging to use this information in a useful way to inform meaningful strategic decisions for a client. One of the key approaches to research is to cast the net wide in the initial stages and then refine it to synthesise the data in a way that will empower effective decision-making. As a Social Media Manager creating customer personas is a helpful way to achieve this.

A Customer (or Buyer) Persona is a technique that involves creating a profile of the demographic and psychographic characteristics of a client's typical target audience member.

Table 3.3 Social media industry reports and websites

Resource	Description
▶ Statista.com	A statistics portal that contains data from 600 industries and 50+ countries. It is an excellent resource for global social media usage data
▶ SocialMediaNews.com.au	A website containing monthly Australian social media usage data
▶ WeAreSocial.com	WeAreSocial collaborates with Hootsuite to produce reports on worldwide digital and social media trends and usage that include country-specific reports. This is an extremely helpful resource for Social Media Managers when conducting audience research in a range of geographical regions
▶ Zephoria.com	Digital marketing agency, Zephoria, regularly shares valuable statistical information regarding specific platforms which can be a useful inclusion when researching target audiences
Australian Bureau of Statistics (ABS)	As mentioned previously in the chapter, the ABS (or the equivalent in your country) can be an extremely valuable resource when researching social media usage habits and device ownership
▶ Brandwatch.com	The 'Resource' section of the Brandwatch website is a treasure trove of valuable information, particularly the 'Reports' page that provides in depth insights into demographic, psychographic and social media user habits
Yellow Social Media Report	The Yellow Social Media Report provides an interesting and useful snapshot in the social media usage habits of Australian users. The information included ranges from demographic data (age, gender, location) in terms of platform usage to where people are using social media platforms (while watching television and even when on the toilet.)

Using this technique can assist you as a Social Media Manager to imagine the audience in a much more personalised and multifaceted way (Taylor, 2017).

Being able to visualise and experience a real sense of knowing and understanding who you are trying to communicate with can greatly assist when developing social media content and interacting with audiences on social media.

As mentioned, seeing a target audience as a homogenous faceless mass will result in creating dull, ineffective social media content because it will not resonate with individual people. Creating Customer Personas helps to humanise target audiences and bring them to life. It is much easier (and effective) to communicate with someone that you feel that you know than with a complete stranger. Taking this approach supports crafting customised communication that speaks directly to people within that group.

3

> **66** Remember, if you try to speak to everybody, you will not speak to anybody. **99**
>
> **Dr Karen Sutherland**

Based on the depth of the research conducted during this first stage of the strategy development process, it is advisable to create more than one Customer Persona.

As a first step, it is worth creating two different categories of Customer Personas, one for existing target audience members that a client has an existing relationship with (current customers, volunteers, donors, etc.) and the other for the target audiences that a client is attempting to connect with. The data gathered may also indicate that there are several sub-categories within each persona.

Revisit the client's strategic goals before creating these categories to keep you on track in terms of the outcomes aiming to be achieved. It can be tempting to become distracted by creating too many personas based on the data gathered rather than checking that they will actually support the overall goal of the strategy.

It is important to identify the audience groups that it is vital to connect with to achieve a client's strategic goals and focus only on those.

Newberry (2018) recommends that the following categories be included when creating a Customer Persona. Populate these fields using the data gathered through the audience research process in Steps 1–3 inclusive. Here you are creating the profile of an average target audience member based on the analysis of your research.

Persona Name   Give this person a name to help to bring them to life in your mind as a real person. This may not be a real name, but

more of a character. Newberry (2018) suggests *"Jogging Jane"* when developing a customer persona for a female sportswear brand.

- **Age**
- **Location**
- **Language**
- **Job title**
- **Average income**
- **Buying behavior**
- **Interests & activities**
- **Life stage**
- *Customer Pain Points 1–4:* List the four common problems that this person experiences. Draw on your analysis of the reviews, comments, direct messages and client research to identify them.
- *Customer Goals 1–4:* List four common goals that this person is trying to achieve. Again, use the data that you have gathered to guide you in identifying them.
- *Ways a Client's Business/Products Can Help 1–4:* With this person's pain points and goals identified, clearly articulate four key ways that a client's business, products and/or services can directly assist this person to solve their problems and achieve their goals.
  Remember to *explain the benefits* to this person. Avoid jargon and industry specific. Never expect a target audience to join the dots because they will rarely go to that effort.

Now that you know who the target customer is, it is also important to understand where they are going and how they will get there in the process of becoming a customer. Step 6 involves plotting out this journey to gain a deeper understanding of the target audience as they transform from social media users to loyal brand advocates.

3.7 Step 6. Tracking the Customer Journey

With the in-depth insight of the target audience gained through steps 1–4, it is essential to understand the journeys that each takes as they begin from first becoming aware of a client's business or product to becoming a customer.

Businesses often make the mistake of trying to blatantly sell their products to people with whom they do not have any type of relationship. In ► Chap. 5 we will explore this in much greater depth.

Imagine walking up to a stranger on the street and asking them to marry you. This is essentially the same thing. A strategy and supporting content must be focused on building a relationship with the target audience, building trust through the development of problem-solving content and respectfully guiding them through the stages to where they are keen to become a customer.

Asking people to convert into a customer when they are only just getting to know a client's brand is usually asking too much too soon. Gary Vaynerchuk (2013) recommends giving three times before asking the audience for anything, which helps to build trust, credibility and the overall relationship.

It is worthwhile to attempt to track the specific customer journey for each of the customer personas that you have created, but as a general rule, people go through the following stages when they first become aware of a brand or product until they reach the point of making a decision and taking action.

The Hierarchy of Effects is a theoretical model used to explain this process appears in advertising and marketing literature and has also been borrowed by public relations (Lavidge & Steiner, 1961). According to the model originally developed by Lavidge and Steiner (1961), audiences must move through three key stages before acting (◘ Table 3.4).

The Hierarchy of Effects Model was later adapted in the advertising literature by Barry and Howard (1990). to become the A.I.D.A model, that represents the following stages (◘ Table 3.5):

◘ Table 3.4	The hierarchy of effects model
Stage	**Definition**
1. Cognitive	**1a. Awareness:** target audience member first learns about a business/brand/product/service
	1b. Knowledge: target audience member builds further understanding about the business/brand/product/service
2. Affective	**2a. Liking:** target audience member begins to develop approval for a business/brand/product/service
	2.b Preference: target audience member strengthens their support for a business/brand/product/service
3. Conative	**3a. Conviction:** target audience member decides that they will act in relation to a business/brand/product/service
	3b. Action: target audience member undertakes the desired action of conversion in relation to a business/brand/product/service

3

Stage	Description
Table 3.5	The A.I.D.A model
Awareness	When someone first learns about the existence of a business/brand/product/service
Interest	When the same person identifies that the business/brand/product/service may be able to help them to solve a problem and/or achieve a goal
Desire	When the person learns that this business/brand/product/service is definitely one that they would like to try
Action	When the person takes the action to purchase a product or service

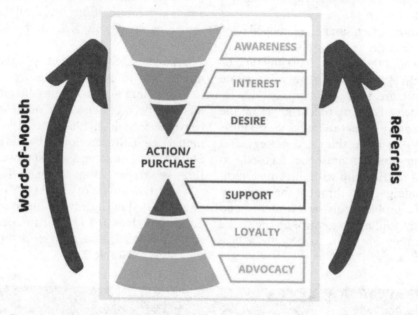

Fig. 3.1   Reworked AIDASLA model (Landis, 2019)

While the Hierarchy of Effects and the AIDA Model can be effective in better understanding the customer journey, they neglect to map what happens after the desired action is undertaken.

Just because a member of the target audience has converted to a customer does not mean that this will happen again, especially if they have had a negative experience.

This is why a further development of the AIDSLA model can be extremely helpful in tracking what happens after conversion to ensure that as a Social Media Manager, you are not only using social media to encourage the target audience to become customers, you are inspiring them to become repeat customers and brand advocates.

As demonstrated in ▪ Fig. 3.1 the three additional stages added to the AIDA model are: Support, Loyalty and Advocacy.

Support is already a component of the Hierarchy of Effects model and can result in repeat purchases, but also engagement with a brand's social media content as a gesture to show this backing. However, Loyalty and Advocacy are new additions.

Trust is the most important component of any relationship and a customer must experience a high degree of trust in a business/brand/product or service before they will shift from the support to the loyalty stage.

Loyalty suggests that not only are they a repeat purchaser, but that they will remain steadfast and will not be tempted by any other brands. Positive brand experiences over time on social media and offline are the keys in building this trust.

The final stage of the customer journey according to ◙ Fig. 3.1 is Advocacy. This is the most beneficial stage for your client because it means that the customer loves and trusts the brand so much that they would recommend it to people that they know; essentially placing their own reputation on the line in the process. The AIDASLA Model (Landis, 2019) has been further finessed for this text by adding arrows to demonstrate the cyclical nature of the customer journey. The arrows signify advocacy behaviour in the form of referrals and word-of-mouth that can help to instigate the customer journey for customers, existing and new.

Word-of-mouth is still the most effective form of marketing and social media has only increased its impact, positive or negative (Li et al., 2018).

Your aim as a Social Media Manager is to guide a client's target audience through to this final stage, but it takes time and care in relation to the social media content and tactics used to get them there. Social Media can be a long game, but the rewards are worth the effort.

Conclusion

This chapter explores why audience research is an essential first step of the social media development process and presented a range of research approaches and methods to gather valuable audience insights. Four key steps were suggested when researching audiences: Client Research, Social Media Audit, Competitor Analysis, Audience Analysis, Customer Personas and Tracking the Customer Journey to provide Social Media Managers with an in depth understanding of the target audiences with whom they are trying to connect on behalf of their client or organisation.

3.7.1 Interview: Gemma Donahoe - Social Media Manager, Seven Network, Australia

1. **Please tell me about your current role.**
   I'm currently the Social Media Manager for Seven News Queensland. At the moment, my team consists of myself and three other social media producers. We run social media pages from Cairns all the way down to the Gold Coast. We're on Twitter, Facebook, Instagram and YouTube. We manage more than 20 profiles in total. We have both a Twitter and Facebook account for every region. We also have a couple of YouTube accounts and just one Instagram for Seven News Queensland.

2. **What do you enjoy most about working with social media?**
   I love social media because it's very fast paced and it's fun and it's always changing. You never have the same week or the same month. There are always new trends or new apps or new platforms coming out, so we're always trying to try all the new ones first and see where everyone is at and where everyone likes to get their news. So, it's always very exciting.

3. **What are the greatest challenges?**
   I find that because it's always changing, that is also the most challenging thing. When new trends or new apps come out, you don't necessarily know what will work best, so we try them all. We try to get on top of things as soon as

3

they come out because sometimes, they work really well, especially for our audience in particular. But other times they fail, and sometimes it feels like you can waste time when you're trying our all the new apps and all the new platforms.

4. **How did you come to work in social media? Please tell me your career story.** I studied journalism, majoring in public relations at the University of the Sunshine Coast.

And from there, I had to do an internship and chose my internship with Seven News.

And one day, it was a bit more of a quiet day and the social media girl came over to me and she said, "Hey, come sit at my desk for a little bit."

I sat at her desk with her and I realised how much I loved social media. A few months later, I kept going in for a bit more work experience at the social desk and then I got a job as a casual Social Media Producer.

After about three months as a casual Social Media Producer, I got the full-time gig in Brisbane, working in Brisbane. And then a year later, I became a Social Media Strategist before my boss left and I took the role as Social Media Manager. I've been in all the social roles so far, but I'm loving it.

5. **What do you think are the three most important things for Social Media Managers to consider about audience research when developing a social media strategy?** The first thing is knowing your audience. Building an online audience is impossible without understanding the communities that you're trying to reach out to. That can be demographics, that can be interests or even education. And so, it's just really important to know your audience and who you're trying to reach out to.

For example, our news bulletins that go to air every night, it's generally for an older demographic. We not only want to reach the older demographic, but we also want to try and reach out to the younger people as well. That's where social media becomes really handy because more and more people are getting on board and we can actually reach out to everyone.

The second thing I would say is knowing where your audience is, so what platforms they are on. And that can be hard sometimes because you do need to try out every platform and see where they are and where you are receiving the most engagement.

The third thing is understanding what your audience wants. It's really important to know that because otherwise, you will not be receiving the amount of engagement you want on your platforms. And engagement is the number one thing you want online, on social media, for your business or for your company to succeed.

6. **What do you think are the benefits of audience research?** The benefits are that you don't have to waste time on certain platforms or apps to try and figure out who's using what the most, or what your audience wants to see your company on the most, or business. The research behind it is really, really important because you can hit the nail on the head the first few goes and just really get it out there.

7. **What are the challenges of audience research?** Finding out where your audience is and what they use. You really do need to find out where the audience you want to target is online. And that's why the research is so important because you can just go down so many different avenues until you figure out where you can find them and where you can stay.

8. **How does thoroughly researching your audience help the people that you are trying to connect with on social media?**

It benefits the audience because you will give them what they want. It is very easy these days for people to continue to scroll and not look. If you understand your audience and you can give them the correct content that they want to see, they will engage, and your pages will do better.

9. **What are your favourite tools, methods and approaches to conduct audience research and why?**

Most platforms that we use actually offer statistic pages, and we also sign up to a couple of other pages. For example, CrowdTangle, where we will get reports which show us and our competitors on a leaderboard. We can go further into those stats and kind of see what posts are performing well in particular, what aren't doing so well and if our competitors are beating us or not. There are a couple of tools that you can use to find out these things, but usually on the platform you're using, you should be able to see the statistics as well.

10. **What do you think of the current landscape of social media management as a profession?**

It's definitely growing. I don't think when I was in uni, I really didn't know that many job opportunities. Social media is definitely a profession that has just soared within the last five years. I think every single company; every single business needs it. I think sometimes people are a little reluctant to go into it just because they think it's an on the side thing, but now it's not. Everyone is on social media and everyone needs to be on social media.

11. **Where do you think the profession and social media is heading in the future?**

Social media management, it's very important. You can't just have 10 social media producers working on one thing because there are so many higher levels of social media that you need to look at in regard to audience research and looking at statistics and everything like that. Social media management is very important for every business, every company to really get on the right track and because everything is constantly changing, you need someone to be looking at that all the time.

12. **What advice would you give to someone who is trying to begin a career in social media?**

You can never stop learning with social media, because everything is constantly changing. Just stay updated. There are jobs in social media everywhere. It's a very promising career to have. Everybody needs it. I think just go for it and you won't regret it.

It's a lot of fun.

13. **What has been the best piece of advice that you have been given?**

My previous boss, before she left, she said, "I have the simplest piece of advice that I can give any manager, whether it be social media or not." And she said, "Be a good person. It all just sort of comes back to that."

❓ Questions for Critical Reflection

1. Why is it important to use a range of research approaches and methods when researching audiences?

2. What are the differences between quantitative and qualitative research methods and what are the benefits of using them together?

3. Why is it important to research your client and their competitors as part of the audience research process?

4. What are the risks of developing a social media strategy without first conducting an audit of your client's social media presence?

5. What is a Customer Persona and why are they useful when creating strategic social media content?

6. Explain the customer journey and why Social Media Managers need to understand it when developing a social media strategy and content?

▷ Practical Exercises

1. Using the steps outlined in this chapter, conduct a social media audit on your own social media presence. What does it tell you about the way that you present yourself on social media? What are your strengths? In what areas do you require further development?

2. Using the steps outlined in this chapter, pick your favourite brand and conduct a competitor analysis on their social media presence. Explain the key findings that you have learned from this process. What can it tell you about their customers?

3. Think about the very last product that you purchased. Using the AIDASLA Model, track your purchasing journey back to the first time that you learned about the product. How did you move through the stages from the AIDASLA Model? At what stage would you consider yourself to be now? Please explain your answer.

References

Almalki, S. (2016). Integrating quantitative and qualitative data in mixed methods research – challenges and benefits. *Journal of Education and Learning, 5*(3), 288–296.

Aurini, J. D., Heath, M., & Howells, S. (2016). *The how to of qualitative research: Strategies for executing high quality projects*. Los Angeles: Sage.

Barnhart, B. (2017). *Everything you need to know about social media algorithms*, viewed 09/05/2020. https://sproutsocial.com/insights/social-media-algorithms/

Barry, T. E., & Howard, D. J. (1990). A review and critique of the hierarchy of effects in advertising. *International Journal of Advertising, 9*(2), 121–135.

Charlesworth, A. (2017). *Social media marketing: Marketing panacea or the emperor's new digital clothes?* New York: Business Expert Press.

Cinelli, M., Brugnoli, E., Schmidt, A. L., Zollo, F., Quattrociocchi, W., & Scala, A. (2020). Selective exposure shapes the facebook news diet. *PLoS One, 15*(3), e0229129.

Clark, V. L. P., & Ivankova, N. V. (2015). *Mixed methods research: A guide to the field* (Vol. 3). California: Sage Publications.

Creamer, E. G. (2017). *An introduction to fully integrated mixed methods research*. California: SAGE Publications.

Croucher, J. S. (2019). *Quantitative analysis for management*. Sydney: McGraw Hill Australia.

Freberg, K. (2018). *Social media for strategic communication: Creative strategies and research-based applications*. California: SAGE Publications.

Gangadharbatla, H. (2012). Social media and advertising theory. *Advertising Theory*, 402–416.

Green, M. C. K., & Warren, J. (2019). *Global marketing*. London: Pearson.

Grewal, D., Levy, M., Mathews, S., Harrigan, P., Bucic, T., & Kopanidis, F. (2017). *Marketing* (2nd ed.). Sydney: McGraw-Hill Education Australia.

Hair Jr., J. F., & Lukas, B. (2014). *Marketing research* (Vol. 1). Sydney: McGraw-Hill Education Australia.

Hern, A. (2019). Facebook launches 'clear history' tool – But it won't delete anything. *The Guardian*, viewed: 25.08.2019. https://www.theguardian.com/technology/2019/aug/20/facebook-launches-clear-history-tool-but-it-wont-delete-anything

Information Resources Management Association. (2018). *Social media marketing: Breakthroughs in research and practice*. Pennsylvania: IGI Global.

Ismail, K. (2018). *AI vs. Algorithms: What's the Difference?* Viewed 09/05/2018. https://www.cmswire.com/information-management/ai-vs-algorithms-whats-the-difference/

Kenett, R. S., & Shmueli, G. (2016). *Information quality: The potential of data and analytics to generate knowledge*. Chichester: Wiley.

Kerpen, D., Greenbaum, M., & Berk, R. (2019). *Likeable social media, third edition: How to delight your customers, create an irresistible brand, & be generally amazing on all social networks that matter: How to delight your customers, create an irresistible brand, & be generally amazing on all social networks that matter*. McGraw Hill Professional.

Kim, C. M. (2016). *Social media campaigns: Strategies for public relations and marketing*. New York: Routledge.

Kolb, B. (2017). *Marketing research: A concise introduction*. Califorina: SAGE.

Landis, T. (2019). How to automate your marketing and generate referral business. *OutboundEngine*, viewed 28.05.2019. https://www.outboundengine. com/blog/automate-marketing-generate-referral-business/

Largan, C., & Morris, T. (2019). *Qualitative secondary research: A step-by-step guide*. SAGE Publications Limited.

Lavidge, R.J. & Steiner, G.A. (1961). A Model for Predictive Measurements of Advertising Effectiveness. Journal of Marketing, 25 (4), 59–62.

Li, P., Yang, X., Yang, L. X., Xiong, Q., Wu, Y., & Tang, Y. Y. (2018). The modeling and analysis of the word-of-mouth marketing. *Physica A: Statistical Mechanics and Its Applications, 493*, 1–16.

Malhotra, N. K., & Malhotra, N. K. (2012). *Basic marketing research: Integration of social media*. Boston: Pearson.

McQuarrie, E. F. (2015). *The market research toolbox: A concise guide for beginners*. London: Sage Publications.

Newberry, C. (2018). How to build a buyer persona (includes free template). *Hootsuite*, viewed 28.05.2019. https://blog.hootsuite.com/buyer-persona/

Noyes, D. (2019). The top 10 valuable snapchat statistics – Updated July 2019. *Zephoria*, viewed: 26.08.2019. https://zephoria.com/top-10-valuable-snapchat-statistics/

O'Reilly, M., & Kiyimba, N. (2015). *Advanced qualitative research: A guide to using theory*. Los Angeles: Sage.

Quesenberry, K. A. (2018). *Social media strategy: Marketing and advertising in the consumer revolution*. Maryland: Rowman & Littlefield.

Rishi, B., & Bandyopadhyay, S. (Eds.). (2017). *Contemporary issues in social media marketing*. New York: Routledge.

Rosenbaum, J. E. (2017). *Constructing digital cultures: Tweets, trends, race, and gender*. Maryland: Lexington Books.

Saldaña, J., & Omasta, M. (2017). *Qualitative research: Analyzing life*. Los Angeles: Sage Publications.

Sarstedt, M., & Mooi, E. (2019). *A concise guide to market research. The process, data and methods using IBM SPSS statistics - third edition*. Germany: Springer.

Strehovec, J. (2013). Algorithmic culture and e-literary text semiotics. *Cultura, 10*(2), 141–156.

Tasso, K. (2017). *Growing your property partnership: Plans, promotion and people*. New York: Estates Gazette.

Taylor, D. (2017). Buyer personas can help you understand customer perceptions. *Central Penn Business Journal, 33*(33), 12. Retrieved from https://search-proquest-com.ezproxy.usc.edu.au/docview/1937665406?accountid=28745

Thomas, M. (2018). *Financial times guides: Social media strategy: Boost your business manage risk and develop your personal brand*. Harlow/London/New York: FT Publishing, Financial Times.

Tuten, T. L., & Solomon, M. R. (2017). *Social media marketing*. California: Sage.

Vaynerchuk, G. (2013). *Jab, jab, jab, right hook: How to tell your story in a noisy social world*. New York: Harper Business.

We Are Social. (2018a). Digital in 2018 in the United States. *We Are Social*, viewed 31.05.2019. https://www.slideshare.net/wearesocial/digital-in-2018-in-the-united-states-86861659

We Are Social. (2018b). Digital in 2018 in Australia. *We Are Social*, viewed 31.05.2019. https://wearesocial.com/au/blog/2018/02/2018-digital-report-australia

Young, R. O. (2016). *Persuasive communication: How audiences decide*. New York: Routledge.

Yurieff, K. (2019). Facebook finally rolls out privacy tool for your browsing history. *CNN Business*, viewed: 26.08.2019. https://edition.cnn.com/2019/08/20/tech/facebook-clear-history/index.html

Yuzdepski, Z. (2018). Dennis Yu's 3×3 video grid strategy for local businesses. *Vendasta*, viewed 28.05.2019. https://www.vendasta.com/blog/dennis-yu-facebook-video-marketing

Further Reading

Freberg, K. (2018). Chapters Five and Eight. In *Social media for strategic communication: Creative strategies and research-based applications*. SAGE Publications.

Miller, G. (2014). How to use the Facebook pages to watch to track competitors, social media. *Examiner*, viewed 31.05.2019. https://www.socialmediaexaminer.com/facebooks-pages-to-watch/

Newberry, C. (2018). How to define your target market: A guide to audience research. *Hootsuite*, viewed 28.05.2019. https://blog.hootsuite.com/target-market/

Porteous, J. (2018). Target audience analysis: Everything digital marketers need to know. *Social Bakers*, viewed 28.05.2019. https://www.socialbakers.com/blog/target-audience-analysis-guide-everything-digital-marketers-need-to-know

Quesenberry, K. A. (2016). Chapters Seven, Eight and Nine. In *Social media strategy: Marketing and advertising in the consumer revolution* (pp. 85–137). Maryland: Rowman & Littlefield.

Helpful Links

Audience Engagement Measurement Tools

BrandWatch: https://www.brandwatch.com
CrowdTangle:https://www.crowdtangle.com/
Meltwater: https://www.meltwater.com

Nacho Analytics: https://www.nachoanalytics.com/
Phlanx: https://phlanx.com/engagement-calculator
SocialBakers: https://www.socialbakers.com/

Secondary Audience Research Sources

Australian Bureau of Statistics (ABS): https://www.abs.gov.au/

SocialMediaNews.com.au: https://www.socialmedia-news.com.au/
Statista.com: https://www.statista.com/
WeAreSocial.com: https://wearesocial.com
Yellow Social Media Report: https://www.yellow.com.au/social-media-report/
Zephoria.com: https://zephoria.com/insights/

3

4

Managing Reputation, Ethics, Risk, Issues and Crises

Contents

© The Author(s), under exclusive license to Springer Nature Singapore Pte Ltd. 2021
K. E. Sutherland, *Strategic Social Media Management*, https://doi.org/10.1007/978-981-15-4658-7_4

By the End of This Chapter You Will

- Know what ethical social media practice involves and the fundamental role it plays in reputation and risk management.
- Understand why reputation management is a key priority when managing social media for a client or organisation.
- Learn how to manage social media risk through preventative processes, such as when working with clients and influencers.
- Distinguish the difference between an issue and a crisis.
- Identify how poor social customer service can create issues and crises.
- Learn how to provide superior social customer service and manage customer complaints.
- Understand the key steps involved to manage an issue or a crisis in a social media environment.

TLDR

- Social media poses reputational, legal, financial and operational risks to a brand, business or organisation.
- Social media risks can be managed through the implementation of ethical practices, superior social media customer service delivery, a relationship management approach, proactive governance and social media influencer risk reduction strategies.
- Social listening must be a daily practice to identify issues before they become crises.
- An issue is a trend or condition that if left to continue can have a detrimental impact on the function and reputation of an organisation.
- A crisis threatens the existence of an organisation.
- An issue can be managed proactively. A crisis is managed reactively.

- The three stages of a crisis are: Pre-Crisis, Acute Crisis and Post-Crisis.
- A current, specific and well-practiced crisis management plan is essential for a Social Media Manager to prepare with their clients.
- A social media crisis management plan must be initiated within 1 hour of a crisis being detected.
- A post-mortem must be conducted at the end of every crisis as a practice promoting continuous organisational improvement.

4.1 Introduction

With audience research established as an essential first stage of social media strategy development, ► Chap. 4 explores another crucial component of social media management: ethical practice. While behaving ethically as a Social Media Manager may seem obvious, there are many nuances to the role that must be deconstructed and explained.

As the title of this chapter conveys, risk, reputation, issues and crisis management are additional key focuses. A significant proportion of this chapter will investigate proactive measures to help avoid issues and crises from occurring.

Employing ethical practices from the outset can greatly minimise the risk that issues and crises will eventuate from a client or organisational level. Keeping one's side of the street clean is the best form of reputation management and frees attention to focus on achieving strategic goals. Doing so can take a range of processes ranging from only posting accurate information to having legally binding contracts with clients and social media influencers; all practices detailed in this chapter.

Life is not foolproof. Issues and crises can still arise when dealing with external publics and stakeholders. Social Media Managers must have the expertise to address

4

issues and crises in a measured, ethical and professional way on behalf of their clients and representative organisations. Techniques on how to manage issues and crises are analysed towards the end of the chapter.

First, it is important to understand what risk is in a social media context and how it can impact businesses and organisations.

4.2 What Is Risk?

At its very core, risk relates to the possibility of loss or change that can negatively affect a business or organisation. Aven and Renn (2009) define risk as.

» ...uncertainty about and severity of the consequences (or outcomes) of an activity with respect to something that humans value.

The unpredictable and uncontrollable nature of social media can pose many risks to businesses and organised. In the early days of social media, it was not uncommon for public relations professionals and marketers to be hesitant about using social media on behalf of their clients and organisations due to this unpredictability.

One of the greatest risks posed in the beginning (and today) is that social media is a two-way communication channel and that users can not only speak publicly to organisations, users could speak to each other and share their experiences ▢ Fig. 4.1. Explains how information flowed before and after social media.

In the early days of social media, this fear of two-way communication with the audience resulted in organisations using social media to broadcast information in the same way that most traditional media are used. Sometimes, businesses and organisations turned off the comments functionality on their social media profiles, not to control the risk, but to remove it altogether.

Grunig (2009) refers to these risk eradication practices as an "illusion of control". Grunig (2009) suggests assertions that public relations practitioners could ever control the flow of messages before digital technologies are incorrect and attempting to control social media conversations is equally misguided.

As explored in this chapter, turning off commenting functionality or negative comments will not stop them. The conversation will only move elsewhere. Businesses and organisations can greatly reduce risks associated with social media by behaving transparently and engaging in challenging conversations, not trying to avoid them in an attempt to prevent risk.

4.3 Social Media Risks

If not approached strategically and proactively, social media can pose the following risks to businesses and organisations:

— **Reputational Risks**
  Reputation can be defined as the opinion or belief that is held about a per-

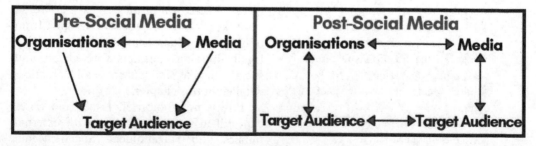

▢ **Fig. 4.1**   Information Flow Before and After Social Media

son, brand, organisation or other entity (Roberts, 2009). In public relations literature, reputation is defined as an intangible asset that is the result of an individual, business or organisation's past actions (Mahon, 2002; Fombrun, 1996). While reputation can be described as intangible, its influence can significantly impact the health of a business or organisation. A negative reputation can result in a loss of trust, customers and profits. While it can take years to develop a positive reputation, it can be severely damaged through one unethical action and can take years to rebuild. For example, reports in the UK of Starbucks paying minimal taxes while returning substantial profits attracted widespread criticism and resulted in its #spreadthecheer campaign being hijacked and reputational damage eventuating (Sisson & Bowen, 2017). A positive reputation must be earned. It cannot be bought, is highly subjective and can be formed on the premise that perception is reality. Social media is an amplifier of the positive and the negative (Yu, 2014). A business or organisation that employs ethical and legal practices to assist their target audience and the wider community via social media will undoubtedly build trust with their customers. Its positive reputation will be well-known. However, a business or organisation that behaves unethically and unlawfully will have a challenging time developing trust with their customers and community. Social media will amplify these practices through their actions, but also through the online conversations of the people who know about them. See ▶ Chap. 7 for more information about the impacts of online conversations. Reputation management is a core function of public relations practice. To achieve this, professionals in the field are vigilant in protecting organisational reputation through transparent, ethical and legal practices.

This approach must also extend to social media practice to take a proactive approach to reputation management.

— *Legal Risks*

Contravening the law can result in irreparable loss to reputation and the creation of major crises that can threaten the health of an organisation. From the perspective of a Social Media Manager it may be challenging to know how other parts of a business or organisation function when they are outside the scope of day-to-day activities. However, it is the responsibility of a Social Media Manager to know and understand the law that governs the requirements of their role. According to Gilmore (2014) there are legal landmines in relation to business and organisational use of social media that must be considered and addressed to avoid issues and crises from eventuating.

Ignorance of the law is not a valid excuse. Instead, it is best-practice for a Social Media Manager to be aware of the legal implications within the countries they are operating and in any others they may be strategically targeting. It is also recommended to seek professional legal advice to assess that tactics are lawful before their implementation.

As laws vary between countries it is impossible to explore them all within the scope of this text. Unpacking the general areas that require legal attention will be of much greater benefit. Researching the laws specific to your region in relation to the following areas is highly recommended.

— *Copyright breaches:* Using other people's content without permission and vice-versa. This topic is explored in much greater detail in ▶ Chap. 10 and includes an interview with Ethan Law, Attorney at the Social Media Law Firm.

— *Defamation:* Communicating inaccurate information about a person, business or organisation to a third party

4

resulting in reputational damage. It is essential that any information is checked for accuracy before being shared on social media. ▶ Chapter 10 provides steps on how to assess the accuracy of information.

– *Advertising Fraud:* "A type of online fraud where a fraudster deceptively makes an advertiser pay for low quality and fake traffic" (Carr, 2018; Sizmek, 2014). This illegal practice can take many different forms and can be carried out by or to a Social Media Manager. Please check the Helpful Links section at the end of this chapter for information on preventative practices.

– *Non-Disclosure and Misrepresentation in Advertising:* Not disclosing when content is a paid advertisement (for example when working with influencers, explored later in this chapter) or overstating benefits or misrepresenting products in advertising can also have legal implications in some countries as well as being highly unethical. For example, using stock images and suggesting that they are genuine representations of a product or service is unlawful and unethical.

– *Non-compliance e.g. General Data Protection Regulation (GDPR):* Many regions of the world have their own compliance requirements. The GDPR applies to individuals living in the European Union (or the greater European Economic Area) providing new rights to access and control their data on the Internet (GDPR.edu, 2019).

While the GDPR governs the use of EU residents' data, this law has impacted countries worldwide who interact with EU residents online. It is essential for Social Media Manager to have a working knowledge of the GDPR and links to learn more are in the Helpful Links section at the end of this chapter.

– *Competitions and Promotions:* Laws around competitions and promotions differ between countries, but these gener-

ally regulate games of chance (Gilmore, 2014). There are different types of competitions and promotions with different laws for each that must be researched before being included in a social media strategy (or implemented).

Different social media platforms also have their own rules around competitions and promotions so these must also be complied with. It is essential to research these when even toying with the idea of including a competition or promotion as a tactic.

– *Social Media Spam:* Many countries now have laws to prevent the sending of unsolicited emails, also known as spam. In a social media context, spam can also include unsolicited direct messages or even automated messages, using an excessive number of unrelated hashtags, hijacking the comments of another user's post to share links to products or tagging people unnecessarily in a post to promote a product or service (Kalner Williams, 2017; Schaefer, 2017)

There are many methods of spamming, and while the law may not cover some of these practices yet, they are highly unethical and counterproductive. It is much more effective to build positive relationships over time than to repel someone as a first impression.

– *Privacy and Data Breaches:* Again, laws differ between countries, but businesses and organisations have the responsibility of ensuring that any data gathered from customers or social media users is strictly confidential, is not shared with any other party and personal details are never identified, particularly online.

This is in line with the GDPR, but it is advisable to have a business or organisational policy and process around the management of personal data to avoid any privacy breaches. Privacy and data risks can also relate to the following:
  – Exposure of confidential information via social media.

- Data breaches (company and customer).
- Social media profile hacking.
- Phishing via email or direct messages
- Brand impersonation through the creation of unauthorised profiles.
- Password insecurity.
- *Financial and Operational Risks*
- *Costs:* A common misconception still exists with some business owners and organisational decision makers that social media management is free (Neisser, 2013). However, to approach it in a professional way it takes time, expertise and resources. Sometimes business and organisations do not factor this cost into their budgets leaving them out-of-pocket when they discover the true cost of professional social media management.
- *Reduced productivity due to employee distraction:* Research has indicated that personal social media use at work can have a negative impact on productivity and performance as a result of the digital distraction of employees (Cao & Yu; 2019; Javed et al., 2019). A reduction in productivity can have a detrimental impact on a business or organisation's bottom line. A study by Teamlease found that unrestricted social media usage can decrease productivity by 13% (Khosla, 2016).
- *Human error when social media advertising:* Usually social media advertising accounts for business or organisations for platforms such as Facebook, Instagram, YouTube, Twitter and LinkedIn etc. are linked to a corporate credit card. An error when setting up an advertising campaign can result in exorbitant (and unplanned) advertising costs if the mistake is not identified and rectified quickly.
- *Poor selection of social media influencers:* As explored later in this chapter, the poor selection of a social media influencer can result in wasted finances and a damaged reputation. For example, an influencer

campaign called #girlsmakeyourmove cost Australian taxpayers $600 k and was initiated by the Government's Health Department.
- The campaign was supposed to encourage girls to become more active. However, the influencers selected for the campaign were not screened properly and it was later discovered that they had posts promoting unhealthy activities such as binge drinking alcohol and racist comments (Sweeney, 2018). This resulted in considerable backlash and widespread negative media coverage.

4.4 Social Media Risk Management

While some risks cannot be avoided entirely, there are certain measures that can be undertaken to reduce the risks associated with social media management. Five key practices to mitigate social media risks are: ethical behaviour, superior social customer service delivery, a relationship management focus, proactive governance and social media influencer risk reduction strategies. Using these five practices together can result in a business or organisation having stronger relationships with internal and external stakeholders and reducing the risk of issues and crises occurring due to transparent and proactive processes as explained below.

4.4.1 Risk Management Practice 1: Ethical Practices

Behaving ethically is one of the most effective ways to reduce the likelihood of issues and crises from occurring. A Social Media Manager may not be able to control the ethical practices of a client or within a broader organisational context, but they can provide guidance and lead by example through their own conduct.

First, it is important to understand exactly what ethics are, particularly in relation to social media practice. Ethics have been defined as moral standards of behaviour and conduct (Kim, 2016; Luttrell, 2018).

In a social media context this extends further than purely practicing within the law.

> 66 Social media ethics requires honesty, transparency and genuineness in all interactions, practices and processes. 99
> Dr Karen Sutherland

Examples of unethical social media practices to be avoided are:

- *Not obtaining consent* before using other people's content or posting images of others, particularly children.
- *Running bogus competitions* to increase followers where nobody wins a prize.
- *Non-disclosure on sponsored posts.* Transparency is essential for organisational reputation. Many countries now have laws or guidelines regarding this such as the Ad Standards guidelines for influencers in Australia (AdStandards, 2018).
- *Buying followers and likes* is dishonest and will prevent the accurate measurement of genuine engagement from a target audience. While having a large following may seem to be impressive to others, this is purely a vanity metric (see ► Chap. 7). Having a fake following will actually impede the achievement of conversion and strategic goals.
- *Fake reviews and recommendations* are also pointless and can result in backlash and reputational damage when the truth is revealed. Genuine feedback (positive and negative) and your response to it is what can build a business as will be explained in *Risk Management Practice 2*.
- *Posting fake negative reviews on competitors social media profiles* is also a highly

unethical practice that will result in reputational damage when the truth is exposed.

- *Posting inaccurate information* is also highly unethical and ignorance is not a valid excuse. All information must be checked for validity before posting. (See ► Chap. 10 for information).
- *Sharing offensive, damaging, defamatory and discriminatory information* (racist, sexist, homophobic etc.) will damage more relationships with a client's target audience than it will resonate with them. Remember, social media is a powerful way to bring people together and should not be used to injure and/or attempt to create division.

4.4.2 Risk Management Practice 2: Superior Social Customer Service Delivery

An important risk mitigation strategy (and simply excellent business practice) is to provide superior customer service experiences using social media. Also commonly referred to as "social customer service" providing customer support through social media channels has become more than a common practice, but a necessary business function (Hill-Wilson & Blunt, 2013).

If a brand or organisation has a social media presence, customers expect to be able to interact with it in a timely way, a phenomenon that Hill-Wilson and Blunt (2013, p. 2) describe as the "I want it now world". Social media has provided a tool for customers to communicate with brands and organisations in a much more convenient and accessible way than in the past through phone calls and written channels such as letters and emails.

4.4.3 The Power of the People

Today, every customer has the power at their fingertips to share their positive or negative experience with the rest of the world through social media. Baer (2016, 63.) describes social customer service as a "spectator sport". Baer (2016, p.63) describes this with the statement:

> » Imagine that every time that you chatted with a customer, hundreds of other people were watching and listening to the conversation. This is what happens on social media.

The way that a staff member responds to (or ignores) one person on social media can directly impact the buying decisions of many other current and prospective customers. In fact, in a study of social customer service, Bazaarvoice (2019) found that responding to negative customer feedback in particular can increase intention to purchase from the business or organisation.

Often community management and social customer service responsibilities can fall within the scope of social media management functions. However, it is clear to have these tasks clearly allocated from the outset so that service quality does not become an afterthought.

In larger organisations, training existing customer service specialists in proficient use of social media to communicate with customers can be a logical step. After all, cus-

tomer service professionals are already highly informed about their company and how to provide quality service, it is applying that to a social media environment that may require guidance.

However, if undertaking social customer service responsibilities as a Social Media Manager, please consider the following aspects of this practice:

- *Social customer service is amplified.* Interactions with customers can feel like high-pressure situations because they are generally witnessed by a large audience (or can be if something goes wrong). This is very different to a one-to-one exchange in person, on the phone or via email.
- *Interactions can spread quickly.* Customer exchanges can become viral particularly if the incident is perceived to be one of poor customer service. Word-of-mouth remains a powerful marketing tool and electronic word-of-mouth can be particularly potent in damaging brand reputation because it can spread across the globe extremely quickly.
- *Social Customer Service is an essential skill* for anyone who manages a public social media profile for a brand, business, non-profit or service. Understanding how to engage with customers in a calm and helpful way is a necessary part of social media management when engaging with customers, but clients too.

  A survey of 398 Australian employers ranked social customer service and public relations expertise as the most valuable social media skills of university graduates (Sutherland et al., 2019, in-press).
- *Complaints are an opportunity* to turn the situation around in real-time in front of an audience. Baer (2016) suggests that it is important to "hug your haters" to seize the opportunity of converting an unhappy customer into a brand supporter.

  Doing so can improve positive brand associations with the complainant as

4

well as other social media users who witness the exchange (Bazaarvoice, 2019). Baer (2016, p. 68) stipulates that, "hugging your haters doesn't mean the customer is right; it means the customer is answered." Often being heard and acknowledged can turn a negative into a positive.

– *Social media provides customer insights and opportunities to improve* that were not accessible before without market research. Before social media a business owner may have never learned about a negative customer experience.

Instead, a customer can tell an average of 16 people about a negative incident, but the business being oblivious did not provide any opportunity to improve. While social media has enabled customers to communicate their experiences publicly, it also provides businesses an opportunity to learn about them, make amends and enhance their customer service processes.

Kamleitner (2016), Bazaarvoice (2019) and Gunarathne, Rui and Seidmann (2018) suggest the following social customer service practices:

1. *Respond quickly to positive and negative comments and reviews.* All customers want to be listened to and acknowledged regardless if their experience was positive or negative

2. *Complaint responses should not be copy-and-pasted and generic* asking the customer to contact the organisation. Instead, each response should be customised to the customer's complaint and contain helpful advice on how to rectify the specific issue. Using generic complaint responses can decrease intention to purchase by nearly 30% (Bazaarvoice, 2019).

3. *Customer complaints can contain calls-to-action that can provide insights for continuous improvements.* For example, complaints or reviews that include terms such as: "if only", "I wish" or "one change" can provide helpful feedback from the customer perspective (Bazaarvoice, 2019).

4. *Maintain the same professional, friendly and helpful tone in response to positive and negative comments.* Never let your tone shift to frustration or anger.

5. *Use social listening to proactively respond to negative and positive comments before they become issues or crises.* As explained in ▶ Chap. 7, social media listening and monitoring can help to identify and respond to unhappy customers by taking a proactive approach.

6. *Ensure that everyone in the organisation is trained in social customer service.* All employees need to know how to communicate and engage with customers online and only regular training can achieve this.

7. *Keep nurturing customer relationships even after a complaint has been resolved.* Check in to see how a customer is even after they seem satisfied with the outcome. This demonstrates an exceptional level of customer care on behalf of the brand or organisation rather than hoping the customer will go away and be quiet once a resolution has been reached.

66 Social customer service is about ongoing relationship management. **99**

Dr Karen Sutherland

4.4.4 Risk Management Practice 3: A Relationship Management Focus

Adopting a relationship management approach to social media can assist in reducing risk because the focus is placed on developing positive connections instead of how to capitalise from the target audience. As discussed in ▶ Chaps. 3 and 5, without a solid relationship with a target audience, achieving strategic goals and objectives will be extremely challenging.

Social media is a long-term relationship management tool for business and nonprofits. It is important for Social Media Managers to remember that their main aim is to build trust through the cultivation of long-term positive relationships with individual people on behalf of their clients or organisations. Relationships take work, effort, attention and understanding. They can never be automated.

Sutherland (2015) and Sutherland and Mak (2017) suggest that engaging with target audiences on social media should be approached using a blend of relationship management theory developed by Ledingham (2003) and dialogic theory developed by Kent and Taylor (1998) gleaned from the public relations literature.

The rationale behind this blend of theories when approaching social media is to remind Social Media Managers that for relationships to function positively, two-way communication (e.g. dialogue) must play an integral part.

▪ Figure 4.2 demonstrates the blend of components from the two theories and ▪ Table 4.1 explains the significance of each component in the context of social media management.

The relational and dialogic components explored in ▪ Fig. 4.2 and ▪ Table 4.1 are all underpinned by the consistent need to approach social media through employing ethical behaviour, allowing and participating in honest discussions and demonstrating a commitment to fostering long-term relationships on behalf of clients or organisations.

4.4.5 Risk Management Practice 4: Proactive Governance

The risks associated with social media management can also be significantly reduced

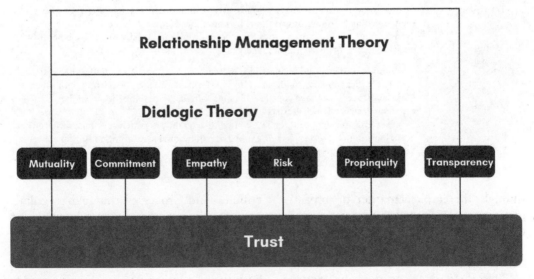

▪ **Fig. 4.2** Blend of Relationship Management and Dialogic Theories (Sutherland, 2015; Sutherland & Mak, 2017)

4

Table 4.1 Components of the blend of relationship management and dialogic theories (Sutherland, 2015; Sutherland & Mak, 2017)

Theoretical component	Description
Mutuality	The willingness for two parties to be connected and their efforts to make the other party feel like an equal member of the relationship (Augur, 2010; Kent and Taylor, 2002). This can equate to a member of a target audience following a social media profile and the owner of that profile responding to comments in a timely and respectful way.
Commitment	Being genuine, transparent, committed to engaging in conversation and to making the effort to understand the other party involved in the relationship are the key requirements for a functional relationship on social media (Kent & Taylor, 2002). A Social Media Manager will not build positive relationships if they are not interested in making time to undertake these tasks.
Empathy	Showing support, acknowledgement and understanding of the other party is also integral for a functional relationship (Auger 2010; Kent & Taylor, 2002). A Social Media Manager who maintains a cold, corporate persona when interacting with target audiences will find it challenging to build solid relationships.
Risk	There is risk inherent in any dialogic exchange. However, for true dialogue to take place, there should be space available for both parties to share their beliefs, opinions and ideas (Stewart & Zediker, 2000; Theunissen & Wan Noordin, 2012). Of course, if the other party becomes abusive in their responses or demonstrates troll-like behaviour, it is better not to continue with the dialogue.
Propinquity	Detailed in great depth in Chap. 5, propinquity requires both parties of a relationship to be available to discuss issues as part of the decision-making process, a commitment to the history, currency and future of a relationship and a willingness to actually engage (Kent & Taylor, 2002). In a social media context it requires both parties to want to be involved in discussing issues and an investment that the relationship is ongoing.
Transparency	The free flow of accurate information between a brand and its target audience rather than impeding two-way conversations by not allowing comments etc. Transparency requires both parties to be honest, open and trustworthy, all elements of ethical practice for social media managers.
Trust	"Without trust there is no relationship," (Welch, 2006, p. 140). Essentially, all social media activities should be undertaken to build trust between a client's brand and their target audience. It can take considerable time for trust to develop, but it can be extremely beneficial once it exists. However, trust must be continually nurtured like tending a garden and must never be taken for granted. Trust is the most valuable reputational asset an organisation can have and must be treated accordingly.

through the implementation of proactive governance. As a practice, governance can be defined as: "as a set of processes and structures for controlling and directing an organization," (Abdullah & Valentine, 2009, p. 88).

Therefore, in a social media management context, governance refers to the policies and processes that can regulate how people working within a business or organisation use social media, promoting a risk mitigation approach to social media activities. Table 4.2 provides details of initiatives relating to proactive governance.

Table 4.2 Proactive governance initiatives to reduce social media risk

Governance	Description
A social media policy	A social media policy can ensure employees understand what is considered acceptable and unacceptable social media behaviour in their workplace, and the consequences for not behaving appropriately. Resources to support social media policy development are included at the end of this chapter. The communication of a social media policy must be delivered in an engaging way to capture the attention of employees. For example, the Salvation Army Australia promoted their social media guidelines to internal stakeholders using an animated YouTube video (Salvation Army Australia, 2013).
Regular social media audits	Audits help to determine who currently has access to a business or organisation's social media accounts. This will identify if there are any unauthorised people with access to social profiles, such as former employees, to reduce the risk of unapproved content from being posted.
Social listening	Already explored in this chapter and in Chap. 7, social listening can help to identify and manage issues before they become crises.
Customer service processes and procedures	These ensure consistency of customer experience and help to guide staff on how to engage and interact with customers via social media.
An issues and crisis management plan	Explored in greater depth later in the chapter, having a plan as a map to guide responses to issues and crises can ensure that such situations are addressed in a calm, sensitive and strategic way as a method of diffusion. Without a plan in place, panic can compel a reactive approach that may escalate an issue into a crisis or further exacerbate a crisis causing irreparable reputational damage.
Regular and clear internal communication	Internal stakeholders such as employees cannot uphold policies and processes if they do not know what they are, why they are important to the function of the business org organisation and why they are specifically relevant to them. Just as audience research is the first fundamental step of social media strategy development (see ▶ Chap. 3), the same applies to internal communication. One message and one channel will not reach everyone equally. Thorough research of internal audiences will inform the most effective way to connect with them.
Frequent training	Regular training around policy and processes and their implementation, and social media developments can reduce the risk of employees not following procedures due to confusion around what to do. It is essential to make any social media training a positive and engaging experience to encourage buy-in and support from employees in attendance.
Consequences for process and policy breaches	Research has indicated that some of the best social media policies are for naught if consequences for breaching them are not followed through (Sutherland, 2015). A social media policy or process will not be effective or taken seriously by employees if consequences do not follow its flagrant flouting. Remember that social media can pose enormous risks to organisational reputation if used in an unethical or damaging way and such behaviour must be taken seriously.

4

For Social Media Managers working as sole operators or who have their own agencies, the following risk mitigation initiatives are recommended:

- *Professional Indemnity Insurance*
Social Media Managers operating as sole traders (or who have their own agencies) are strongly encouraged to purchase Professional Indemnity Insurance (also known as Professional Liability Insurance (PLI) or Errors and Omissions (E&O) in other parts of the world).

  Even the best Social Media Managers can make errors in their actions, judgement and/or advice. Professional Indemnity insurance provides protection against any claims for loss or damage made by clients and can cover items such as civil liabilities, public relations costs and expenses involved with investigating the issue (CGU, 2019). In terms of risk management for strategic social media management, insurance of this type is imperative.

- **Client Contracts**
A further risk mitigation strategy relating to social media management is to develop a client contract that is signed by both parties before any work begins. This is to clarify from the outset exactly the social media management services will involve, the timeframe within which they will be delivered and most importantly, the cost.

  Not itemising and communicating this information at the beginning of the social media management process can result in disappointment, legal action, negative reviews and word-of-mouth with potential reputational damage as a consequence.

  Never rely on a verbal agreement with any client. Managing client expectations is an essential part of social media management and this must occur from the start. A signed contract is the best way to guard against issues later.

Examples of client contracts have been included in the Helpful Links section at the end of this chapter. It is paramount that any contracts and contract templates are reviewed by qualified legal professionals before being used. This is another method to reduce risk.

Key points to cover in a client contract are (Butler, 2019):

- *Details of both parties* at the beginning of the contract.
- *Timeframe*. When the contract begins and when it ends.
- *Itemise the scope of the work* to be undertaken and within what timeframe. Also include process information such as how many rounds of revisions are included, the approval process for content, access to social profiles etc. Be as specific as possible.
- *Budget and payment terms.* Include the itemised costs for each item and the hourly rate etc. Please see ▶ Chap. 5 for more information on budget. Also include when payment must be made by, penalties for late payment and the refund process just in case.
- *Termination information,* how this would be communicated and notice required.
- *Breach of Contract* and how this will be managed.
- *Copyright.* Which party owns the work that is produced.
- *Confidentiality Agreement or Non-Disclosure Agreement* to prevent any communication of clients to others.
- *Professional Indemnity Insurance,* explain cover.

Above all, ensure that specificity is a priority in any client documents to avoid grey areas, ambiguity and misinterpretation that could create an issue later.

4.4.6 Risk Management Practice 5: Social Media Influencer Risk Reduction Strategies

Working the social media influencers has become a commonly used social media tactic over the past few years (Abidin, 2016). While working with influencers can be beneficial, doing so can also pose many risks to brands, businesses and organisations if not approached cautiously.

To completely understand the risks associated with engaging with social media influencers as a tactic, it is essential to understand what influence is and its theoretical underpinnings.

4.4.7 What Is Social Media Influence?

Social media influence describes the level of power an individual has to affect the opinions, preferences, decisions, choices and behaviours of fellow social media users. Theories abound as to what exactly constitutes influence in a social media context. Traackr (2019) suggests that influence is the result of three key factors merging, as demonstrated in ◘ Fig. 4.3.

Reach refers to the size of the audience to whom the 'influencer' can expose their content.

Relevance indicates that the content being produced by the 'influencer' is applicable for and of interest to the audience being targeted.

Resonance suggests that not only is the 'influencer's' content of interest to their target audience, it inspires them on an emotional, psychological, physical or intellectual level.

Therefore, the combination of these three factors: Reach, Relevance and Resonance is what creates influence; the mixture of exposure, interest and inspiration. Yet, this is only one theory.

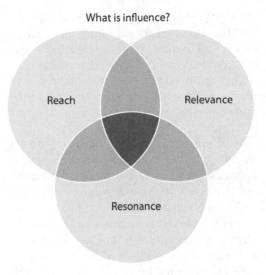

What is influence?

Reach   Relevance

Resonance

◘ **Fig. 4.3** The Components of Influence (Traackr. com, 2019)

Describing the ingredients of influence as a concept can be as challenging as attempting to pinpoint why a piece of content becomes viral. If the exact recipe was known, every social media user would be an influencer who posts only viral content. Any theories should be only understood as a possible explanation.

Next, it is important to explore the concept of what a social media influencer is.

4.4.8 What Is a Social Media Influencer?

A Social Media Influencer is a Key Opinion Leader and is often referred to as a KOL in Asian markets such as Hong Kong and China (Zou & Peng, 2019; Hung, 2019). In simple terms, a social media influencer or KOL is an individual with the power and ability to affect other social media users. They embody the three elements of influence as proposed in ◘ Fig. 4.3 (reach, relevance and resonance) with their social media content to build a powerful rapport with those users who follow.

De Veirman et al. (2016, p. 1) defines influencers as "people who built a large net-

4

work of followers and are regarded as trusted tastemakers in one or several niches". It is this status as "trusted taste-makers" that can be highly attractive to clients, organisational decision-makers and social media managers when trying to promote a product or service to a specific target market.

Cutting through the clutter of social media noise has resulted in an economy of attention to which social media influencers are perceived to have a voluntary captive audience (Franck, 2019).

Social media influencers or KOLs are often associated with having significant celebrity status such as Kim Kardashian with 145 million followers (Instagram, 2019) or Kakakaoo is 9.8 million fans on Weibo (Weibo, 2019). However, marketers are now engaging with a wider range of social media influencers or KOLs with smaller audience sizes in a bid to reach more engaged and targeted audiences and to achieve more with limited budgets.

For example, Kylie Jenner can charge up to $1.2 million per Instagram post (Hanbury, 2019) with 3.9% of her followers engaging with her content, which equates to approximately 5.6 million people (Phlanx, 2019).

For Social Media Managers, a budget that could collaborate with the likes of Kylie Jenner is rare, but there are other categories of social media influencer or KOL that are more commonplace to work with. The specific audience sizes of the social media influencer categories listed below are often speculated, but they provide a general guide of the different ranges.

Categories of Social Media Influencers:
- **Mega Influencers:** Celebrities and other high-profile people.
- **Macro Influencers:** Between 100,000 and 1 million followers.
- **Micro Influencers:** Between 1000 and 100,000 followers.
- **Nano Influencers:** Less than 1000 followers, but strong influence within a particular community.

The cost per post is suggested to increase according to the number of social media followers an influencer has. However, influencers with fewer followers can have greater engagement rates can be perceived as being more trusted by their audience because their relationship with them can be stronger. In some cases, micro and nano influencers may be local personalities, who may not be known outside of their region, but have strong personal relationships with other social media users within their local area.

The strength of these relationships has become of greater relevance to marketers as a measure of influence than a celebrity with millions of followers that they have never met. This is especially the case for local businesses such as bricks-and-mortar clothing boutiques and restaurants that aim to connect with local residents as their core target market.

4.4.9 Two-Step Flow Theory

The process of social media influence can be described using a variation of the Two-Step Flow theory by Katz, Lazarsfeld and Roper (2017) as highlighted in ◘ Fig. 4.4 The theory of Two-Step Flow is a communication theory that is often used in the public relations literature (Theaker, 2016; van Ruler, 2018).

Two-Step Flow suggests that receiving information from an opinion leader has greater impact in shaping public opinion than it if it was received directly from an organisation or from a traditional media outlet in a similar way that the public relations, marketing and advertising industries have paid for celebrity endorsements to communicate messages and to sell products for decades. However, the prevalence of social media has now given rise to a new category of celebrity (or micro-celebrity), the social media influencer or KOL (Khamis, Ang, & Welling, 2017). In the context of

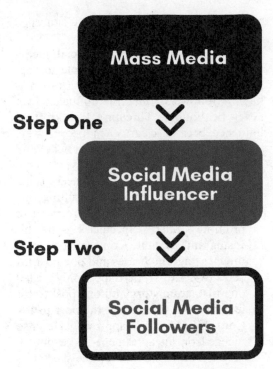

Fig. 4.4 Two-step flow: The power of influence

social media, an opinion leader can be defined as a blogger, YouTuber, Instagram Influencer or TikTok star etc.

As ◘ Fig. 4.4 demonstrates the information is first shared from a media outlet or organisation to a Social Media Influencer or KOL as the first step. The second step involves the Social Media Influencer or KOL communicating that information to their audience on behalf of the media outlet, organisation or brand. The premise being that the audience will be more receptive and will pay attention to the information being communicated if delivered from a trusted person of influence.

4.4.10 Brand Benefits

Before exploring the risks associated with working with social media influencers, it is also important to investigate the benefits to make a balanced decision on whether to include KOL collaboration in a social media strategy.

Benefits working with social media influencers include:

- *Positive brand associations:* The positive opinions, thoughts and feelings that the target audience already has for an influencer can be transferred to a brand or product as a result of collaboration (Juhlin & Soini, 2018).
- *Leveraging an influencer's reputation:* If an influencer or KOL is trusted by their audience, the products or services are also assumed to be credible (Lou & Yuan, 2019).
- *Amplifying message to a wider network:* Working with influencers can provide access and exposure to new and larger networks of people.
- *Increasing relevance within a target market:* Sometimes a brand or product may not be top-of-mind to a target audience until a compatible social media influencer or KOL provides that relevance through their endorsement and/or publicised use of the product or service.
- *Enhanced word-or-mouth:* Collaborating with a social media influencer is essentially paying for the initiation of positive word-of-mouth. The influencer or KOL begins the conversation with their followers continuing through comments, shares and user-generated content.
- *Social proof:* Based on the theory of "normative social influence" that suggests people will behave in ways similar to those that they admire to feel more accepted by their peers (Burnkrant & Cousineau, 1975).
- *Expert endorsement:* This works extremely well when an influencer has expertise in a particular field because it suggests to the target audience that an expert has deemed this particular related product or service as credible. For example, make-up YouTubers using a particular brand of cosmetics in a video tutorial (Ananda & Wandebori, 2016).

4

These benefits provide Social Media Managers, clients and organisational decision makers with attractive incentives to work with influencers. However, while the benefits can be vast, at the other end of the scale, the risks and potential reputational damage that can arise from working with influencers and KOLs can be severe.

4.4.11 Potential Risks and Reputational Damage when Working with Social Media Influencers and KOLs

- *Overstating Influence:* Influencers can inflate their follower numbers, and buy fake followers to misrepresent themselves (Graham, 2019). Instagram no longer allowing likes to be visible has also made it more challenging for brands to ascertain engagement (BBC News, 2019).

4.4.11.1 Threatin - the European Tour Based on Lies

Threatin a heavy metal 'band' based in Los Angeles, USA used unethical tactics to manipulate venue owners across Europe into booking the band for an international tour.

To achieve this, Jered Eames, the band's frontman, bought followers to suggest to

venue owners that they had a large and loyal fan base across Europe, when the opposite was actually the case.

Eames also featured in a promotional video showing the band performing, but shots of the crowd were not included suggesting that these performances were all to an empty room; which was the exact scenario once the European tour was underway. Nobody showed up to their gigs and the Eames' backing band quit halfway through the tour. Venues and promoters were out of pocket as a result and the last few dates of the 10-city tour were cancelled (Kushner, 2018).

This case highlights that social media influence can be reasonably simple to suggest online through unethical tactics such as buying followers, but true influence can never be bought. Threatin's lack of true influence became clear when people were not making the effort to pay for a ticket and attend their gigs.

- *Failing to Influence:* Influencer Luka Sabbat was sued by PR Consulting Inc. for failing to live up to an agreement to promote Snap Spectacles on his Instagram account. Contracted to post three Instagram Stories and one post for $60 k ($45 k up front) Sabbat only posted one Instagram story and one post to his feed and did not submit the post to PR Consulting for pre-approval. He also reneged on an agreement to be photographed in public wearing the spectacles during the Milan or Paris Fashion Weeks (Eustachewich, 2018).
- *Negative associations:* Logan Paul (18 million YouTube subscribers) posted a video to YouTube that showed a dead body in a forest in Japan known as a locale for suicide.
  YouTube temporarily suspended all ads on his videos and cut him from their web series (BBC News, 2018).
- *Fake sponsored posts:* Micro-influencers are uploading fake sponsored posts to make brands think that they have greater influence than they genuinely have. This may have the opposite effect on companies being aligned with an influencer who may not fit with their brand (Lorenz, 2018).
- *Not following instructions:* Scott Disick did not read instructions regarding sponsored post properly. Cut and pasted everything into an Instagram. Disick damaged his and sponsor's reputation (BBC Newsbeat, 2016).
- *False Advertising:* Influencers can be hired to sell products and services that

do not exist in the same way that they are being advertised. The Fyre Festival is a perfect example of this where social media influencers were used to sell tickets to an event concept rather than the true reality of what was delivered (Richardson, 2017).

4.4.11.2 False Impressions Sell Festival Tickets to Fyre

Influencers were used to sell the event concept of Fyre Festival that was never achieved. Before the logistics of the festival site were confirmed, the organisers took a group of supermodels to the Bahamas for a photo and video shoot to promote the event.

The content from this expedition promoted the festival as a luxury, high quality event to sell tickets before the fundamental components of the event were locked down. Social media influencers were also used to promote the event on their channels to their vast audiences, again selling tickets to an event concept rather than the actual event.

The result: festival attendees were extremely disappointed and inconvenienced when the event was the opposite of the concept presented to encourage ticket sales. They were left stranded and hungry when the festival site was not ready.

The models and social media influencers leveraged their clout to sell tickets to a disastrous event. In a sense, they allowed the organisers of the Fyre Festival to hire their influence to sell event tickets. Should influencers feel responsible for not checking the validity of the event concept before agreeing to take part or are they victims as much as the attendees? (Richardson, 2017).

- *Non-Transparency:* The Australian Association of National Advertisers (AANA) recommends that any sponsored posts on social media should prominently include #ad or #spon. (AdStandardsBlog, 2018). However, these are only guidelines and not legally binding.

- *Posting factually incorrect information* (e.g. health and dietary) Fitness influencers posting dangerous health and nutrition advice that is not based on scientific research. A recent study found that almost 90% of social media influencers share inaccurate health and nutrition information (Forrest, 2019). This was also the case throughout the COVID-19 Pandemic where researchers from QUT Digital Media Research Centre found social media influencers to be 'super-spreaders' of disinformation regarding the virus (Keating, 2020; Turnbull, 2020).

With the potential benefits and risks of collaborating with social media influencers explained, it is essential to learn strategies to minimise possible liabilities.

4.4.12 A Risk Management Approach to Influencer Engagement

- *Define your audience:* The most relevant influencer or KOL is determined by the audience that a social media strategy is aiming to reach. Define the audience first and then search for an influencer who is trusted by that influencer.
- *Discover the right influencers* using tools such as Phlanx, TRIBE or through manual searches.
  - *Evaluate the influencer's social media content.* Does it align well with the product? Is there any content that could damage the reputation of your product or brand? Does their content generate a decent level of engagement from followers?
  - *Does the influencer's follower base align with your client's target audience?*
  - *What brands have they worked with before?* Will previous collaborations complement or negatively affect the

4

reputation of a client's product or service?

- *How much engagement do their posts generate in comparison with their total number of followers?* This is essential. If an influencer has 1 million followers but only averages less than 100 likes per post, it may not be worth the expense of a collaboration. Ask the influencer for access to their analytics such as Facebook or Instagram Insights to make sure the figures are legitimate.

- *Build a relationship over the longer term* by genuinely engaging with relevant influencers' content over time. Understand their values and what resonates with their audience and invite influencers to events relevant to their niche and audience without requesting anything in return. Consider the customer journey as explored in ► Chap. 3. An influencer must also go through the same process when first becoming aware of a client's brand and moving through the stages to become an advocate. Do not ask for too much too soon. Focus on building the relationship first.

- *Monitor Influencers for opportunities:* Follow influencers relevant to a client's or organisation's target market to gauge their social media practices over time.

- *Have a legally binding contract* that details the obligations of both parties. Similarly to a client contract, according to Lasky (2019) and Influencer Marketing Hub (2018), an influencer contract should contain the following:
  - *The names of both parties.*
  - *Deliverables:* The specific details of the content to be posted by the influencer. Number of posts, type of posts (image, video etc.), times and dates of posts, required hashtags including those disclosing the sponsorship (e.g. #sponsored, #paid, #ad). Also, a requirement that these disclosures are

prominent. A specific list of what to include and what to exclude should also be included.
  - *Payment and payment terms* including time frame and method. Also included should be penalties for missing deadlines.
  - *Cancellation:* What happens if either party wants to end the agreement.
  - *Approval Process* for content. Clear instructions on how permissions for content will be obtained before anything is posted.
  - *Confidentiality and exclusivity* requirements. Include whether the influencer can work with other similar businesses and the information that is acceptable and unacceptable to share with other entities.
  - *Have the agreement checked by a qualified legal professional.* It is better to be cautious and seek advice from experts in relation to any legal matters.

- *Check the credibility and accuracy of the information being posted.* This should occur as part of the content approval process. Please refer to ► Chap. 10 for techniques to assess information accuracy.

- *Measure results during and after the collaboration* to gauge return on investment (ROI) and conduct social listening activities to monitor online conversations as a result of the influencer campaign.

Working with social media influencers can be highly beneficial when they are the right fit for a client's brand, but sometimes even the most robust risk mitigation strategies cannot prevent issues and crises from arising. This can be the case with social media management in general.

It is vital for Social Media Managers to have a thorough understanding of what constitutes an issue and a crisis, the steps to help prevent them and strategies to manage them if they ever occur.

4.5 Issues and Crisis Management

While risk minimisation must be part of daily social media management practice, sometimes issues and crises still occur. In larger organisations, a Social Media Manager will often be directed by in-house or external public relations professionals as part of a wider Crisis Management Plan.

It is essential for a Social Media Manager to understand at least the basics about issues and crisis management, particularly when issues can originate through social media channels. As explored in this section, issues can soon turn into crises if left unchecked. However, first it is important to understand the difference between an issue and a crisis, because they are managed very differently.

4.5.1 What Is an Issue?

An issue is defined as a trend or condition that if left to continue can have a detrimental impact on the function and reputation of an organisation (Coombs, 2014). In short, issues are smaller problems that when eradicated, reduce or remove the possibility that they can escalate into a crisis.

For example, Mara Zabala tweeted about her negative experience with AirEuropa when she was denied access because she was in a wheelchair and did not have anyone accompanying her (Antevenio, 2018). AirEuropa did not respond to the complaint and so it went viral via social media influencers with a significant following also sharing Zabala's tweet to their networks. Not responding to this issue when it first came to light resulted in considerable reputational damage for AirEuropa.

An issue occurs when there is a gap between what an organisation does and the public's expectations of the organisation's behaviour and can escalate quickly if this gap is not addressed as soon as an issue is detected.

4.5.2 What Is a Crisis?

A crisis is any situation that can have a destructive impact on an individual, business or organisation. The damage could be reputational, operational or threaten the lives of people associated with the business or organisation. A crisis threatens the existence of an organisation (Sheehan & Quinn-Allan, 2015).

The Domino's Pizza YouTube video where employees blew their nose on pizzas (among other things) is a classic example of a social media crisis. This video had the potential to damage a global brand and diminish trust in the company's hygiene practices (Clifford, 2009).

The fact that this crisis is still fresh in the minds of many demonstrates how powerful social media can be at embedding negative brand incidents within the memories of a target audience.

The key difference between a social media issue and crisis is:

- An **issue** can be **managed proactively.**
- A **crisis** is **managed reactively.**

4.5.3 Risk Assessment to Determine If a Situation Is an Issue or a Crisis

▣ Figure 4.5 is a helpful tool that can guide Social Media Managers in assessing the risk of a situation to predict its impact to a client's brand or organisation. The Social Media Risk Assessment Matrix cross-references the likelihood that a specific crisis could occur against the possible consequences if it eventuated.

- *The green* squares identify a possible issue that will need to be proactively addressed.
- *The yellow* squares indicate an issue that is on its way to becoming a crisis that needs to be managed quickly before it escalates.

4

Likelihood of Spread	**Likely**	**Medium**	**High Risk**	**Extreme Risk**
	Unlikely	**Low Risk**	**Medium**	**High Risk**
	Highly Unlikely	**Insignificant Risk**	**Low Risk**	**Medium**
		Slightly Harmful	**Harmful**	**Extremely Harmful**

Consequences

◧ **Fig. 4.5** Social Media Risk Assessment Matrix

— *The red* clearly indicates a crisis is well underway and action must be taken.

For example, one negative comment on a Facebook post may pose a medium risk when it is detected and can be managed to minimise the risk of damage. However, a disgruntled customer whose post with a photo of a faulty product that tags in your client's brand and has become viral could definitely be identified as belonging to the extreme high-risk category.

4.5.4 How Does an Issue Turn into a Crisis?

Some crises occur like a thunderbolt and without warning. However, the literature supports the notion that the raging fire of a crisis first began as a tiny spark of an issue (Meng, 1992; Sheehan & Quinn-Allan, 2015).

It is wise for Social Media Managers to understand the process of the issue lifecycle so that they know how and where to intervene to extinguish rather than inflame.

◧ Figure 4.6 demonstrates the lifecycle from issue to crisis (Meng, 1992).

◧ Figure 4.6 demonstrates how social media can play a pivotal role in exacerbating an issue to rapidly propel it towards the crisis stage. Traditional media coverage can play an instrumental role.

Both social media and traditional media can leverage coverage of issues and crises from each other, working together to intensify an issue so that it quickly becomes a crisis. Furthermore, while a crisis may enter a dormant phase, social media has the power to begin the life cycle multiple times because previous posts may be engaged with again at a later date resurrecting them to prominence once again or social media users generate their own content to remind their network of the incident.

For example, an Australian charity came under fire when a staff member made a homophobic comment during a radio interview (Duck, 2012). While this incident occurred in 2012, Facebook users continue to remind their networks about the crisis particularly during donation drives causing cyclical reputational damage to the charity.

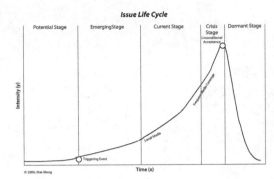

Fig. 4.6 The Issue Life Cycle

Yet, according to Devlin (2007, p107) there are three main stages of a crisis.

— **Pre-Crisis Stage:** An organisation has identified the existence of the crisis, but it is not yet evident to anyone external to that organisation (Devlin, 2007; Khattab, Fonn & Ali, 2017; Jaques, 2009). Acting within the pre-crisis stage to diffuse the situation can eliminate its escalation to a crisis (Khattab, Fonn, & Ali, 2017; Coombs, 2014).

— **Acute Crisis Stage:** A specific event triggers the beginning of the crisis and it becomes visible to external stakeholders and to the wider public. At this stage the crisis is in motion and prevention is no longer an option. Instead damage control measures must be implemented (Devlin, 2007; Khattab et al., 2017; Coombs, 2014).

— **Post Crisis Stage:** Assessment of damage is undertaken along with close focus on stakeholder communication and relationship management (Devlin, 2007; Khattab et al., 2017; Coombs, 2014).

Therefore, with a cyclical social media crisis, these three stages may occur many times. A consistent focus on ethical behaviour, clear communication and relationship management will minimise possible fall-out.

Austin et al. (2012, p.4) suggest that communication of a crisis occurs through the flow of information between an organisation, traditional media and social media (particularly between followers and influencers to inactive users). ◘ Figure 4.7 details the information flow, information type and the relationships that connect them.

A Social Media Manager must consider the communication flow of a crisis more broadly. As ◘ Fig. 4.7 demonstrates there are many channels and players involved in the communication of a crisis and all must be considered when implementing initiatives to manage it. This is why the skills of experienced public relations professionals are often employed during times of organisational crisis.

4.5.5 Planning for an Issue or Crisis

As mentioned numerous times throughout this text, social listening can play a fundamental role in identifying issues before they become crises. However, another vital component of issues and crisis management is having a plan providing specific detail of what to do in the event of a crisis. Often the social media component will be part of a much larger organisational crisis management plan.

Newbury and Dawley (2019) recommend the following components to be included in a social media crisis management plan.

Key Components of a Social Media Crisis Management Plan:
— Guidelines for identifying the type and magnitude of a crisis.
— Roles and responsibilities for every department.
— A communication plan for internal updates.
— Up-to-date contact information for critical employees.
— Approval processes for messaging posted on social media.

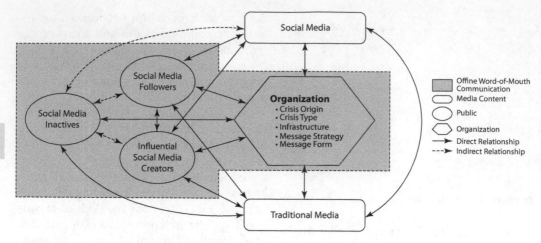

Fig. 4.7   Social Mediated Crisis Communication Model (Austin et al., 2012, p. 192)

- Any pre-approved external messages, images, or information.
- A link to your social media policy.

These components provide step-by-step instructions on the policies and processes that must be undertaken when a crisis is underway. Not having these items up-to-date and prepared ahead of time will result in a crisis escalating because nobody within the organisation will be informed about who or how to respond and precious time will be lost in trying to determine the best course of action.

4.5.6 Practice Makes Perfectly Prepared

Having a plan prepared is not enough. Its implementation must be practiced through simulation exercises by those responsible for crisis management within an organisation (Ashcroft, 1997). Sometimes a plan may look sound on paper, but gaps appear once it is put into practice, and the wrong time for those gaps to appear is in the midst of a crisis. Furthermore, the plan must be approved

by a client or organisational decision-maker well ahead of time to ensure that precious time is not lost on lengthy approval processes.

4.5.7 Managing an Issue or Crisis

There are some fundamental actions to complete when a crisis is underway to attempt to minimise its impact rather and not increase its lifespan. Miller (2015) suggests the following four steps when managing a social media crisis (□ Fig. 4.8).

Additionally, □ Table 4.3 details further specific actions that can greatly assist when managing a social media crisis. It is highly recommended that these actions are included in an organisation's social media management plan accompanying others relevant to the specific business or organisation,

A Social Media Manager should have a working knowledge of how to manage an issue or crisis for their client or organisation but remember to have these plans and processed approved as part of the initial engagement process rather than floundering at the time an issue or crisis occurs.

YOUR SOCIAL MEDIA CRISIS PLAN

BROUGHT TO YOU BY  socialbakers

1. DETECT

Make sure you are listening on all appropriate channels to chatter about your company. If you see something with negative sentiment and a legitimate complaint, act before it goes viral

2. IDENTIFY

Figure out who is involved in the issue, what happened, why it happened, and how you can resolve it.

3. CONSIDER

Does your tone line up with your company and the seriousness of the issue?

Deal with the crisis in a timely but thoughtful manner.

Make sure your response is transparent, both in your apology and in your steps to resolve it

4. RESPOND

Respond on appropriate social media channels (and non-social media channels too!)

☐ Fig. 4.8 Four Steps to Manage a Social Media Crisis (Miller, 2015)

Conclusion

This chapter explored the fundamental role that ethical social media practice plays in reputation and risk management. Common risks associated with social media management were investigated and five key risk minimisation strategies were presented, particularly in relation to social media service and collaborating with influencers.

The difference between an issue and a crisis was defined and actions to address and manage issues and crises is a social media context were also recommended.

4

Table 4.3	Fundamental actions to take during a social media crisis
Actions	**Description**
Implement the crisis management plan within 1 hour.	*"Acting fast is important. More than a quarter of crises spread internationally within just 1 hour. But it takes companies an average of 21 hours to defend themselves in any kind of meaningful way."* (Newbury & Dawley, 2019)
Respond sensitively to every complaint or comment (positive and negative).	This is essential to begin rebuilding relationships that may be damaged in the event of a crisis. Every person wants to be heard. Responding to each comment authentically (not cutting and pasting) is the most genuine way to demonstrate this.
Engage but do not argue.	Some social media users genuinely want answers whereas others are there to troll. A "troll" is defined as social media user who is malicious and aims to cause disruption, aggravation and arguments (March & Marrington, 2019). If a troll appears in a crisis situation (or at any time) remain calm, and present facts. If the person is abusive, defamatory or threatening in their remarks consider blocking them from the profile, but only after listening to their case. Facebook allows page owners to hide specific comments so that the person leaving it (and their friends) can still see it, but nobody else can. There are further resources on how to manage trolls in the helpful links section at the end of this chapter.
Keep listening	Social listening is a constant practice and must be continued throughout and after a crisis to understand what social media users are saying about it.
Stop all scheduled posts.	Allowing scheduled posts can be perceived by the target audience as insensitive and tone deaf. For example, Tesco's scheduled tweet about "hitting the hay" in the midst of a crisis where horse meat was found in its meat products (Hough, 2012).
Ensure account security	Secure all social channels so that only those authorised staff managing the crisis have access.
Communicate internally	Let internal stakeholders such as employees know what is unfolding in relation to the crisis, the steps that will be taken and what they need to do.
Learn from each issue and crisis to keep improving	During the post-crisis stage it is essential to complete a post-mortem on the events that occurred to cause the crisis, how well it was managed when it was underway and the necessary steps going forward to resolve it. Every crisis must be a learning experience.

Case Study: Hong Kong Airlines Avoids Crisis with Social Listening

Hong Kong Airlines recently used social listening tool, Talkwalker to assist them in identifying an issue and managing it before it became a crisis. Initially, the airline did not realise that a ticketing issue resulted in round-trip business-class fares to be advertised on a range of travel websites for the heavily reduced price of $600 (Owen, 2019).

The Social Media Team from Hong Kong Airlines used social listening tool, Talkwalker to gauge the conversation taking place regarding this heavily-reduced ticket price. Customers were extremely excited about the price, but also aware that it may be an error. However, rather than changing the tickets back to their correct price and cancelling and refunding the fares of people who had already purchased the tickets at the reduced price, Hong Kong Airlines used the information gathered through social listening to handle the issue with much greater sensitivity.

The airline followed the steps of Detect (first discovering the issue), Identify (determining exactly what the issue was, where and why it was happening), Consider (analysing the listening data to work out the best way to respond) and Respond (making an announcement soon after the issue was detected).

Hong Kong Airlines' response was well-considered and accepted positively by their customers. As a company they acknowledged their mistake. Although they changed the tick-ets back to their correct price, they agreed to honour all of the fares that have been sold to customers for the lower price of $600. As a result, the airline did not experience the negative sentiment that may have occurred if they responded in an authoritarian way by not admitting their mistake and/or honouring the tickets sold at a reduced rate. Instead, the sentiment was extremely positive (Owen, 2019).

This case highlights the many benefits of social listening in the practice of issues and crisis management. Hong Kong Airlines may have been unaware of the issue for a much longer time period if they were not tuned into the online conversations taking place about its brand. Furthermore, not understanding the sentiment and themes of the conversations taking place may have resulted in a negative backlash if they responded in a very heavy-handed way instead of managing the situation delicately with their customers' best interests as their greatest priority.

Hong Kong Airlines were able to turn an issue into a positive outcome for their customers and their company through the use of social listening.

1. What were the key practices that Hong Kong Airlines implemented to help manage this issue?

2. Why do you think customers responded positively to the way that Hong Kong Airlines handled this incident?

4.6 Interview: Mariana Pérez Díaz, Digital Strategist & Social Media Manager, TERAN\TBWA, Mexico

1. **Please tell me about your current role.**
   I work for TERAN/TBWUA. It's a big agency here in Mexico. I've worked as a Social Media Manager for different types of brands. I have alcohol brands and food brands, other types of brands. I enjoy my work a lot. I focus on doing strategies for big brands and I also do reports for social media. Right now I look after eight brands. I also deal with little ones too. I think that the two biggest ones are the hardest ones.

2. **What do you enjoy most about working with social media?**
   I like to know about users and how they feel about our brands. I also like engaging with them. That's my favourite part of it.

3. **What are the greatest challenges?**
Reaching users. There's a lot of competition right now, so it's hard to give them the best content and to really understand what they're looking for, so that you feel relevant for them.

4. **How did you come to work in social media? Please tell me your career story.**
I've been working in social media for 6 years now. We started as a social media trainee for make-up brands in a little agency. That was my first experience. Before that I studied communications at university. When I went to university, it wasn't a really known field in Mexico, especially. Life took me there and I was already like a heavy user, so it was the perfect job for me.

5. **What do you think are the three most important things for Social Media Managers to consider when preventing issues and crises and also managing them if they arise?**
You need to be honest so people don't mistrust you. That's the first one. You should always be clear. For example, when you're having something where people have to participate, you must clear and super specific to avoid misunderstanding. You also have to be ethical. Don't copy other things that brands are doing. If a user sees this they can comment about it, and this could also lead to misunderstanding or criticism. Be original.

6. **What do you think are the benefits of behaving ethically and managing risks before the turn into issues and crises?**
People trust you and trust your brand. This translates like having a relationship with your users.

7. **What are the challenges in managing risk, issues and crises for Social Media Managers?**
I think trends are a challenge because everyone wants to be part of the hype.

This can lead to copying competitors. There's a fine line between being original and being trendy and doing things that other people are doing and copying. That would be a risk.

8. **What are your favourite tools, processes or practices to manage risk, issues or crises and why?**
We use tools like Radian6 and other social listening programs. When we find something that is a sensitive issue or something that is bothering users, we try to respond proactively to prevent a crisis. We monitor online conversations every day to see if they are healthy and positive or if we find something negative that we need to respond to.

9. **What do you think of the current landscape of social media management as a profession in Mexico?**
It's still growing. Everyone thinks that a Social Media Manager is the same thing as a Community Manager. There are also people who think that a Social Media Manager has to do graphic design or to do other types of things that are far from social media. So it's still growing and there's also a lack of opportunities here in my country, unfortunately.

10. **Where do you think the profession and social media is heading in the future?**
I think that social media has a lot of opportunities and it will become more and more important. I also hope that budgets increase.

11. **What has been the best piece of advice that you have been given?**
Keep studying. Even now I am completing my second Masters degree. This one is in Communication and Digital Humanities. I think studying is key for every professional field. In the digital one, it's super important to keep getting better.

4.6 · Interview: Mariana Pérez Díaz, Digital Strategist & Social Media Manager...

69   **4**

12. **What advice would you give to someone who wants to be a Social Media Manager?**

Learn everything about the digital world. Keep studying, as I said, and look for new trends and to see what they're doing in other countries. Always benchmark competitors and try to be disruptive because new ideas are always welcome.

❓ Questions for Critical Reflection

1. What risks can arise for businesses or organisations from the use of social media? What negative impacts could each have? Please explain your answer.
2. Why is ethical social media practice one of the most effective risk mitigation strategies? Please provide an example or case study to support your answer.
3. Why is social listening an essential risk management practice? What could happen if a business or organisation does not engage in regular social listening activities?
4. What is the difference between an issue and a crisis? Please provide an example of a social media crisis that could have been avoided if addressed early in its lifecycle.
5. Why is having a client contract a vital risk management procedure for Social Media Managers? Provide examples of the issues that may arise when work is undertaken without a contract.
6. What are some of the risks associated with collaborating with social media influencers? How can these risks be minimised?
7. Why should a social media crisis management plan be implemented within 1 hour of a crisis being detected? Please explain your answer.

❯ Practical Exercises

1. Imagine that you have started working as a Social Media Manager at a children's charity that has 50 employees. You identify that your new employer does not have an organisational social media policy. As one of your first tasks in your new role you begin developing one. Please read the social media policy template in the Helpful Links section and consider what you would include in a social media policy for the children's charity.
2. You are the Social Media Manager for a used car hire company. An angry customer has left a negative review on the company's Facebook business page with a photo of bald tyre supposedly from the vehicle that they hired from your company. Using the Social Media Risk Assessment Matrix from this chapter, identify the severity of the review in terms of risk. Is it an issue or a crisis? Please explain your answer.
3. On LinkedIn, one of your client's connections has left abusive and critical comments in response to an update that you posted about your client winning a local business award. Using the knowledge gained from this chapter (and from reading *How to Handle Trolls: A Social Media Manager's Guide* in the Helpful Links section) will you manage this situation? Please explain the rationale for your approach.

References

Abdullah, H., & Valentine, B. (2009). Fundamental and ethics theories of corporate governance. *Middle Eastern Finance and Economics, 4*(4), 88–96.

Abidin, C. (2016). Visibility labour: Engaging with Influencers' fashion brands and# OOTD advertorial campaigns on Instagram. *Media International Australia, 161*(1), 86–100.

4

Ad Standards. (2018). *Ad Standards guidelines for influencers*, viewed 22.08.2019: https://adstandards.com.au/blog/ad-standards-guidelines-influencers

Ananda, A. F., & Wandebori, H. (2016). The impact of drugstore makeup product reviews by beauty vlogger on YouTube towards purchase intention by undergraduate students in Indonesia. *International Conference on Ethics of Business, Economics, and Social Science, 3*(1), 264–272.

Antevenio. (2018). *7 examples of crisis in mismanaged social networks*, viewed 22.08.2019: https://www.antevenio.com/usa/7-examples-of-crisis-in-mismanaged-social-networks/

Ashcroft, L. S. (1997). Crisis management-public relations. *Journal of Managerial Psychology, 12*(5), 325–332.

Auger, G. A. (2010). Using dialogic web site design to encourage effective grantor-grantee relationships. *PRism, 7*, 2.

Austin, L., Fisher Liu, B., & Jin, Y. (2012). How audiences seek out crisis information: Exploring the social-mediated crisis communication model. *Journal of Applied Communication Research, 40*(2), 188–207.

Aven, T., & Renn, O. (2009). On risk defined as an event where the outcome is uncertain. *Journal of Risk Research, 12*(1), 1–11.

Baer, J. (2016). *Hug your haters: How to embrace complaints and keep your customers.* New York: Portfolio/Penguin.

Bazaarvoice. (2019). *The Conversation Index VOLUME 6*, viewed: 06/08/2019: http://media2.bazaarvoice.com/documents/Bazaarvoice_Conversation_Index_Volume6.pdf

BBC News. (2018). *Logan Paul: Outrage over YouTuber's Japan dead man video*, viewed: 22.08.2019: https://www.bbc.com/news/world-asia-42538495

BBC News. (2019). *Instagram hides likes count in international test 'to remove pressure'*, viewed: 22.08.2019: https://www.bbc.com/news/world-49026935,

BBC Newsbeat. (2016). **facepalm* Scott Disick posts ad instructions on Instagram*, viewed: 22.08.2019: http://www.bbc.co.uk/newsbeat/article/36341601/facepalm-scott-disick-posts-ad-instructions-on-instagram

Burnkrant, R. E., & Cousineau, A. (1975). Informational and normative social influence in buyer behavior. *Journal of Consumer Research, 2*(3), 206–215.

Butler, B. (2019). How to write a contract between your agency and a client, *Zen Pilot*, viewed 22.08.2019: https://www.zenpilot.com/happy-client-show/how-to-write-an-agency/client-contract

Cao, X., & Yu, L. (2019). Exploring the influence of excessive social media use at work: A three-dimension usage perspective. *International Journal of Information Management, 46*, 83–92.

Carr, C. (2018). What is Ad Fraud in digital marketing? *PPC Protect*, viewed: 22.08.2019: https://ppcprotect.com/what-is-ad-fraud/

CGU. (2019). *Professional Indemnity Insurance*, viewed: 22.08.2019: https://www.cgu.com.au/business/professional-indemnity

Clifford, S. (2009). Video Prank at Domino's Taints Brand. New York Times, viewed 14.11.2020: https://www.nytimes.com/2009/04/16/business/media/16dominos.html

Coombs, W. T. (2014). *Ongoing crisis communication: Planning, managing, and responding.* California: Sage Publications.

De Veirman, M., Cauberghe, V., & Hudders, L. (2016). Marketing through Instagram Influencers: Impact of number of followers and product divergence on brand attitude. *International Journal of Advertising, 36*(5), 798–828.

Devlin, E. S. (2007). *Crisis management planning and execution.* BocaRaton, FL: Taylor and Francis.

Duck, S. (2012). Salvos apologise for 'gays are evil' remark, *The Courier Mail*, viewed: 22.08.2019: https://www.couriermail.com.au/ipad/salvos-apologise-for-gays-are-evil-remark/news-story/02683ef943031d09ea2fe18ceed97d2f?sv=72a55c948ca0ffd5417f95c99cd0b89a

Eustachewich, L. (2018). Influencer sued for not endorsing Snapchat's glasses hard enough, *New York Post*, viewed 22.08.2019: https://nypost.com/2018/11/01/influencer-sued-for-not-endorsing-snapchats-glasses-hard-enough/

Fombrun, C. (1996). *Reputation: Realizing value from the corporate image.* Boston, MA: Harvard Business School.

Forrest, A. (2019). Social media influencers are dishing out false nutrition and weight loss advice 90% of the time, viewed 22.08.2019: https://www.businessinsider.com/social-media-influencers-give-bad-health-advice-90-percent-of-time-study-shows-2019-4/?r=AU&IR=T

Franck, G. (2019). The economy of attention. *Journal of Sociology, 55*(1), 8–19.

GDPR.edu. (2019). *What does GDPR stand for? (And other simple questions answered)*, 22.08.2019: https://gdpr.eu/what-does-it-stand-for/

Gilmore, G. (2014). *Social media law for business: A practical guide for using Facebook, twitter, Google+, and blogs without stepping on legal land mines: A practical guide for using Facebook, twitter, Google+, and blogs without stepping on legal landmines.* McGraw Hill Professional, United states of America.

Graham, M. (2019). Fake followers in influencer marketing will cost brands $1.3 billion this year, report says, CNBC.com. viewed: 22.08.2019: https://www.cnbc.com/2019/07/24/fake-followers-in-influencer-marketing-will-cost-1point3-billion-in-2019.html

Grunig, J. E. (2009). Paradigms of global public relations in an age of digitalisation. *PRism, 6*(2), 1–19.

Gunarathne, P., Rui, H., & Seidmann, A. (2018). When social media delivers customer service: Differential customer treatment in the airline industry. *MIS Quarterly, 42*(2), 489–520.

Hanbury, M. (2019). The 35 celebrities and athletes who make the most money per Instagram post, ranked. Business Insider Australia, viewed 14.11.2020: https://www.businessinsider.com.au/kylie-jenner-ariana-grande-beyonce-instagrams-biggest-earners-2019-2019-7?r=US&IR=T

Hill-Wilson, M., & Blunt, C. (2013). *Delivering effective social customer service: How to redefine the way you manage customer experience and your corporate reputation*. Wiley.

Hough, A. (2012). Horse meat scandal: Tesco apologises over 'hay' Twitter post, *The Telegraph*, 22.08.2019: https://www.telegraph.co.uk/foodanddrink/foodanddrinknews/9810767/Horse-meat-scandal-Tesco-apologises-over-hay-Twitter-post.html

Hung, E. C. (2019, July). An investigation into the power of digital media in Hong Kong. In *International conference on applied human factors and ergonomics* (pp. 65–70). Cham: Springer.

Influencer Marketing Hub. (2018). *Influencer Contract Template*, viewed: 22.08.2019: https://influencermarketinghub.com/influencer-contract-template/

Jaques, T. (2009). Issue management as a post-crisis discipline: Identifying and responding to issue impacts beyond the crisis. *Journal of Public Affairs: An International Journal, 9*(1), 35–44.

Javed, A., Yasir, M., Majid, A., Shah, H. A., Islam, E. U., Asad, S., et al. (2019). *Evaluating the effects of social networking sites addiction, task distraction and self-management on*. Journal of Advanced Nursing: Nurses' Performance.

Juhlin, L., & Soini, M. (2018). *How do influencer marketers affect brand associations? : a semiotic Instagram study in the sports fashion industry* (Dissertation), viewed: 22.08.2019: http://urn.kb.se/resolve?urn=urn:nbn:se:hkr:diva-18290

Kalner Williams, L. (2017). How to prevent social media spam from damaging your brand, *AgoraPulse*, viewed 22.08.2019: https://www.agorapulse.com/blog/prevent-social-media-spam

Kamleitner, M.(2016). 6 Social Customer Service Best Practices for any Business, *Live Chat Inc.*, viewed: 22.08.2019: https://www.livechatinc.com/blog/social-customer-service/

Katz, E., Lazarsfeld, P. F., & Roper, E. (2017). *Personal influence: The part played by people in the flow of mass communications*. Routledge.

Keating, C. (2020). *'Like a Virus' – Disinformation in the Age of COVID-19*, viewed 09/05/2020: https://research.qut.edu.au/dmrc/2020/04/30/like-a-virus/

Kent, M. L., & Taylor, M. (1998). Building dialogic relationships through the world wide web. *Public Relations Review, 24*(3), 321–334.

Kent, M. L., & Taylor, M. (2002). Toward a dialogic theory of public relations. *Public Relations Review, 28*(1), 21–37.

Khamis, S., Ang, L., & Welling, R. (2017). Self-branding, 'micro-celebrity' and the rise of social media influencers. *Celebrity Studies, 8*(2), 191–208.

Khattab, U., Fonn, S. B., & Ali, S. (2017). Strategic communication Management of Corporate Crises: Case analysis. *e-Journal of Social & Behavioural Research in Business, 8*(1), 15.

Khosla, V. (2016). Social media affecting workplace productivity: Report, *The Economic Times*, viewed 22.08.2019: https://economictimes.indiatimes.com/jobs/social-media-affecting-workplace-productivity-report/articleshow/54915706.cms?from=mdr

Kim, C. M. (2016). *Social media campaigns: Strategies for public relations and marketing*. New York: Routledge.

Kim Kardashian West. (2019). *kimkardashian*, viewed: 22.08.2019: https://www.instagram.com/kimkardashian/

Kushner, D. (2018). The Great Heavy Metal Hoax -How a down-on-his-luck headbanger fabricated a persona, faked a tour, and promoted himself as a hard-rock savior, *Rolling Stone*, viewed 22.08.2019: https://www.rollingstone.com/culture/culture-features/threatin-metal-tour-fake-ticket-sales-hoax-767580/

Lasky, M. (2019). 9 best practices for influencer marketing agreements, *Convince and Convert with Jay Baer*, viewed 22.08.2019: https://www.convinceandconvert.com/social-media-marketing/influencer-marketing-agreements/

Ledingham, J. A. (2003). Explicating relationship management as a general theory of public relations. *Journal of Public Relations Research, 15*(2), 181–198.

Lorenz, T. (2018). Rising Instagram Stars Are Posting Fake Sponsored Content, *The Atlantic*, viewed 22.08.2019: https://www.theatlantic.com/technology/archive/2018/12/influencers-are-faking-brand-deals/578401/

Lou, C., & Yuan, S. (2019). Influencer marketing: How message value and credibility affect consumer trust of branded content on social media. *Journal of Interactive Advertising, 19*(1), 58–73.

Luttrell, R. (2018). *Social media: How to engage, share, and connect*. Maryland: Rowman & Littlefield.

4

Mahon, J. F. (2002). Corporate reputation: Research agenda using strategy and stakeholder literature. *Business and Society, 41*(4), 415–445.

March, E., & Marrington, J. (2019). A qualitative analysis of internet trolling. *Cyberpsychology, Behavior and Social Networking, 22*(3), 192–197.

Meng, M. (1992). Issue life cycle has five stages. *Public Relations Journal, 48*(3), 23.

Miller, W. (2015). 5 things you must have in your social media crisis plan, *Social Bakers*, viewed: 23/11/2019: https://www.socialbakers.com/blog/2100-5-things-you-must-have-in-your-social-media-crisis-plan

Neisser, D. (2013). Wait, social media isn't free? *Social Media Today*, viewed 22.08.2019: https://www.socialmediatoday.com/content/wait-social-media-isnt-free

Newberry, C., & Dawley, S. (2019). How to manage a social media crisis: A practical guide for brands, *Hootsuite*, viewed 22.08.2019: https://blog.hootsuite.com/social-media-crisis-management/

Owen, D. (2019). How Hong Kong airlines increased brand sentiment by 212%, Hootsuite, viewed: 23/11/2019: https://hootsuite.com/resources/how-hong-kong-airlines-increased-brand-sentiment-by-212-percent

Phlanx. (2019). Phlanx.com, viewed 22.08.2019: https://phlanx.com/engagement-calculator

Richardson, D. (2017). Blame the Fyre Festival Fiasco on the Plague of Celebrity Influencers *Wired*, viewed 22.08.2019: https://www.wired.com/2017/05/blame-fyre-festival-fiasco-plague-celebrity-influencers/

Roberts, D. (2009). *Reputation management for education: A review of the academic and professional literature*. London: The Knowledge Partnerships.

Salvation Army Australian. (2013). *Social Media Policy*, viewed 22.08.2019: https://www.youtube.com/watch?v=iDa-4P4wwFw

Schaefer, M. (2017). The difference between social selling and social spamming, *Business Grow*, viewed 22.08.2019: https://businessesgrow.com/2017/12/11/social-spamming/

Sheehan, M., & Quinn-Allan, D. (Eds.). (2015). *Crisis communication in a digital world*. Port Melbourne: Cambridge University Press.

Sisson, D. C., & Bowen, S. A. (2017). Reputation management and authenticity: A case study of Starbucks' UK tax crisis and "# SpreadTheCheer" campaign. *Journal of Communication Management, 21*(3), 287–302.

Sizmek. (2014). Fraud in Digital Advertising, viewed 22.08.2019: https://www.sizmek.com/media/filer_public/eb/13/eb13ee88-972e-441a-a879-8e641609b4c2/casestudy_060514_fraud.pdf

Stewart, J., & Zediker, K. (2000). Dialogue as tensional, ethical practice. *Southern Communication Journal, 65*, 224–242.

Sutherland, K, Driver, C, Freberg K & Khattab, U. (2019). *Employer preferences for social media proficiency in university graduates*, (in-press).

Sutherland, K. E. (2015). *Towards an integrated social media communication model for the not-for-profit sector: A case study of youth homelessness charities*. Doctoral dissertation, Monash University.

Sutherland, K. E., & Mak, A. K. (2017). Blending dialogic and relationship management theories-developing an integrated social media communication model for the non-profit sector. In *New Media and Public Relations* (Vol. 3, 3rd ed., pp. 129–140). Peter Lang Publishing, Incorporated.

Sweeney, L. (2018). Health Minister announces urgent investigation into taxpayer-funded campaign working with Instagram influencers, *ABC News*, viewed 22.08.2019: https://www.abc.net.au/news/2018-07-20/health-department-investigating-instgram-influencer-campaign/10016712

Theaker, A. (2016). *The public relations handbook*. Routledge.

Theunissen, P., & Noordin, W. N. W. (2012). Revisiting the concept "dialogue" in public relations. *Public Relations Review, 38*(1), 5–13.

Traackr.com. (2019). *Discover the Value of Influencer Marketing*, viewed 22.08.2019: https://www.traackr.com/resources/influencer-marketing

Turnbull, T. (2020). *Celebrities 'super-spreaders' of fake news*, viewed 09/05/2020: https://www.aap.com.au/celebrities-super-spreaders-of-fake-news/

van Ruler, B. (2018). Communication theory: An underrated pillar on which strategic communication rests. *International Journal of Strategic Communication, 12*(4), 367–381.

Weibo. (2019). *Kakakaoo*, https://www.weibo.com/u/1927564525?topnav=1&wvr=6&topsug=1&is_hot=1

Welch, M. (2006). Rethinking relationship management: Exploring the dimension of trust. *Journal of Communication Management, 10*(2), 138–155.

Yu, D. (2014). *Dennis Yu answers your toughest Facebook questions*, Tabsite, viewed 22.08.2019: https://www.tabsite.com/blog/dennis-yu-answers-toughest-facebook-questions/

Zou, Y., & Peng, F. (2019, July). Key opinion leaders' influences in the Chinese fashion market. In *International Conference on Fashion communication: between tradition and future digital developments* (pp. 118–132). Cham: Springer.

Further Reading

Baer, J. (2016). *Hug your haters: How to embrace complaints and keep your customers*. New York: Portfolio/Penguin.

Coombs, W. T. (2019). *Ongoing crisis communication: Planning, managing, and responding*. California: Sage Publications.

DiStaso, M. W., & Bortree, D. S. (Eds.). (2014). *Ethical practice of social media in public relations*. Routledge.

Gingiss, D. (2017). *Winning at social customer care: How top brands create engaging experiences on social media*. CreateSpace Independent Publishing Platform.

Mennie, P. (2015). *Social media risk and governance: Managing Enterprise risk*. Kogan Page Publishers.

Stewart, D. (2017). *Social media and the law: A guidebook for communication students and professionals*. Taylor & Francis.

Helpful Links

Ad Fraud Prevention: https://digitalcontentnext.org/blog/2019/04/02/5-steps-to-protect-your-website-from-digital-ad-fraud/

General Data Protection Regulation (GDPR) Information Portal: https://eugdpr.org/

How to Create a Social Media Crisis Management Plan [Free Template]: https://blog.hubspot.com/service/social-media-crisis-management

How to Handle Trolls: A Social Media Manager's Guide: https://socialmediahq.com/how-to-handle-trolls-a-social-media-managers-guide/

How to Write a Social Media Policy for Your Company (Free Template): https://blog.hootsuite.com/social-media-policy-for-employees/

Social Media Client Contract Templates: https://www.socialsamosa.com/wp-content/uploads/2013/10/Social-Media-Contract-Samples.pdf

Social Media Influencer Contract: https://influencermarketinghub.com/influencer-contract-template/

Phlanx Influencer Engagement Calculator: https://phlanx.com

Tribe Influencer Marketing Platform: https://www.tribegroup.co

The Foundational Components of Strategy

Contents

© The Author(s), under exclusive license to Springer Nature Singapore Pte Ltd. 2021
K. E. Sutherland, *Strategic Social Media Management*, https://doi.org/10.1007/978-981-15-4658-7_5

By the End of This Chapter You Will

- Understand what goals are and why they are essential components of a social media strategy.
- Learn how to work with a client or organisation to identify relevant strategic goals.
- Understand what SMART Objectives are and why they are also necessary foundational inclusions in a social media strategy.
- Learn how to craft realistic and relevant SMART Objectives that support the achievement of strategic goal/s.
- Know what key messages are, their strategic function and how to write them
- Understand the impact that client budget can have on the implementation and evaluation of a social media strategy and learn strategies to manage client expectations.
- Learn what to include and how to develop a realistic budget for a social media strategy.

TLDR
- Goals, SMART Objectives, Key Messages and Budgets are the core foundational components of a social media strategy.
- Social media strategies fall within two broad categories: Short Term and Long Term (or ongoing).
- Integrated Marketing Communication (IMC) is a process that combines communication, marketing and advertising practices into a unified and coordinated approach.
- A goal is the most preferred outcome that a social media strategy is aiming to achieve. It is the desired result culminating from focused ambition, effort and activity.
- SMART Objectives must be: Specific, Measurable, Achievable, Realistic and Timely and provide defined and measurable targets to accomplish the strategic goals.
- Key messages are the most important points of information to communicate to the target audience that will inspire them to help to achieve the goals of the social media strategy.
- Key messages relating to the communication of brand qualities or problem solving should employ a *Show Don't Tell* approach.
- Budgets can significantly influence the development, implementation and evaluation of a social media strategy and must be carefully (and sensitively) negotiated to reach an outcome of win/win for both parties.

5.1 Introduction

▶ Chapter 5 is devoted to the exploration of the core foundational components required for a stable social media strategy. These items are truly the epitome of what a strategy is. Without goals, objectives, key messages and any idea of budget social media activities cannot be described as strategic. Instead they would be better described as haphazard, sporadic and random.

▶ Chapter 3 focused on the importance of audience research as the integral first step of strategy development. ▶ Chapter 4 provided advice on how to apply ethical practices from the outset to avoid or address any issues before they turn into crises. The knowledge gained from the previous chapters was preparation for this ever-important strategic phase.

In this chapter you will learn how to articulate:

- What you are aiming to achieve,
- The specific time-bound targets that will help you to get there,
- What you will say to the target audience to make this happen and

— The financial resources that will support the entire process.

These components will determine, guide and underpin the overall course of the social media strategy. By the end of ▶ Chap. 5 these items will be confirmed.

The next stage of strategy development (explored in ▶ Chap. 6) involves the development of the tactics (or actions) that will support the achievement of the core foundational components articulated in this chapter.

5.1.1 A Continual Journey

Social media strategy development is a continual journey, and we are still very much at the beginning. However, before specific components are unpacked, it is important to gain an understanding of the general structure and categories of social media strategies.

The strategy structures and components shared in this book are those of a basic strategy. These can differ slightly depending on the organisation or business, and their components can be referred to by different names. The overall purpose and function of the structure and its components can be described as universal.

5.1.2 An Integrated Approach Is Vital

It must be stated from the outset that a social media strategy should form one part of an overall Integrated Marketing Communication (IMC) strategy (Quesenberry, 2018). It functions as an important cog in a wheel of marketing communication activities.

This integrated approach to social media is vital for several important reasons, namely:

— Social media has greater impact when used in combination with a range of marketing and communication channels (Sutherland, 2015).
— Social media should complement any other marketing communication tactics and channels being used within a business or organisation. Each should work together to achieve a common goal instead of competing to cause confusion.

From this broad explanation IMC involves the combination of different marketing and communications functions, but what does this truly mean in practical terms?

5.2 IMC (Integrated Marketing Communication)

IMC "integrates and aligns strategic and tactical marketing communication decision making (Reid et al., 2005; Schultz & Schultz, 1998; Valos et al., 2016). It is a process that combines communication, marketing and advertising practices into a unified and coordinated approach.

When approaching social media strategy development, it is logical to include aspects of these practices to ensure a holistic approach. ▢ Figure 5.1 demonstrates a

▢ **Fig. 5.1** Integrated Marketing Communication Model

range of activities that can fall within the umbrella of IMC.

However, there is much speculation in the IMC and associated literature about these inclusions (McCloskey, 2018; Percy, 2018).

Each component can directly impact the other. For example, a Facebook advertisement may be highly effective at driving traffic to a client's website, but if the website is difficult to navigate, the target audience will be gone in a flash. All these components must work together to be effective.

While we are focusing solely on social media in this text, the fact that it takes a multidisciplinary approach including concepts, theories and practices from marketing, advertising and public relations further confirms the necessity of taking an integrated approach to social media management.

Social media management does not include only marketing or public relations or advertising. Effective social media management is a combination of disciplines and while we are focusing on the three in this book, there are more. The integration of disciplines and marketing and communications functions will be explored in much greater depth in ► Chap. 6 and Section 6.3.

First, it is essential to develop a solid understanding of social media strategy structure and its components.

5.3 Social Media Strategy Structure

Generally, strategies (social media and otherwise) tend to fall within two broad categories: short-term and ongoing.

■ *Short-Term Strategies*
Short-term strategies are developed to support the social media activities around a temporary episode such as an event, the launch of a business, product or brand, a membership, volunteer or donation drive or a promotional offer running for a limited time. Short-term strategies have a specific end date and usually involve a series of scheduled tactics implemented in the lead up and during the event.

Social media strategies implemented in the short-term are usually contained within a larger integrated marketing communication (IMC) campaign and act as milestones to break up the duration of a longer-term strategy.

■ *Ongoing or Long-Term Strategies*
Ongoing strategies keep day-to-day social media activities on track to support the achievement of overall business or organisational goals. They can provide a strategic overview of social media activities over the course of 12 months but can be longer or shorter depending on client or organisational needs.

Within an organisation, Social Media Managers can be required to provide an annual plan or strategy that maps out activities for the next year, but longer-term strategies such as these need to be revisited regularly due to the ever-changing nature of social media. Furthermore, short-term strategies are positioned within longer-term strategies to provide more targeted and concentrated support throughout the year.

For example, maintaining a social media presence and engaging with target audiences on a day-to-day basis would require a very different strategic approach than promoting an event and inspiring members of the target audience to attend. However, the long-term or ongoing strategy continues to be implemented, particularly in reference to customer service and engagement, even when a short-term strategy is underway. ◘ Figure 5.2 demonstrates how an annual social media strategy can contain several

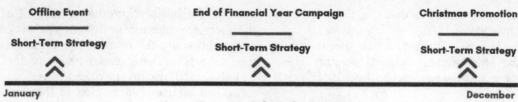

Fig. 5.2 A Long-Term Social Media Strategy with Intermittent Short-Term Strategies

short-term strategies within it to support activities throughout the year.

You will notice that the long-term strategy ticks along even when there is a burst of a short-term strategy within it. During those times it is important for Social Media Managers to review how the ongoing strategy will work in conjunction with the short-term strategy to ensure that the target audience is not inundated with content and competing key messages.

However, the day-to-day community interaction and customer service support should continue as per usual throughout the year.

5.3.1 Social Media Strategies: Integration between Short-Term and Long-Term

Consider you have a nonprofit organisation as a client and every year they have a donation drive before the end of the financial year to encourage current and prospective donors to give so that they can claim the donation in their tax return. During other weeks throughout the year you have a content calendar organised and scheduled where you post once per day on Facebook and Instagram (see ▶ Chap. 8 to learn more about scheduling).

The content varies in type and topic each day according to a client's content pillars and their analytics (more on this in ▶ Chaps. 6 and 7). This scheduled content is developed to support the organisation's strategic goals, objectives and key messages. The short-term strategy to support the donation drive needs to be integrated into the longer-term strategy for a brief period.

A clever way of doing this is to continue to use the same themes and content types but focus them on achieving the goals of the short-term strategy. This way, the target audience is not being presented with additional content and the posts are in line with what generates the greatest engagement with the target audience and with the organisation's content themes.

Furthermore, increasing donations is one of the organisation's long-term goals, but will be focused on exclusively during the implementation of the short-term strategy.

This example demonstrates how short-term strategies can be integrated into longer, day-to-day strategies. The most important thing to consider is that both types are working together to support organisational goals, effectively communicating key messages and accurately engaging with the target audience.

These key components are the building blocks to a highly functional social media strategy as we will explore.

5.4 Structural Components of a Social Media Strategy

Figure 5.3 demonstrates the core components of a social media strategy. Throughout the rest of this chapter we will delve deeply into all except for tactics that has an entire chapter devoted to its explanation (see ► Chap. 6).

You will notice that *goals sit at the peak of the strategic model* presented in ◘ Fig. 5.3. This is because goals are what the strategy is aiming to achieve overall with all other components working together to support their achievement.

Objectives, or more specific *SMART* objectives directly support the strategic goals. These are specific and time-bound targets that focus social media activities to accomplish the goals of the strategy.

Tactics then support the SMART Objectives as they are the specific actions within the social media strategy that target the audience to help them through the different stages of the customer journey (see ► Chaps. 3 and 6) to achieve the objectives and in turn the overall strategic goals.

Supporting all these components is audience research as this will be what informs everything from the key messages, platform selection and the development of relevant tactics that both engage and resonate with the target audience.

Finally, underpinning the entire strategy is the budget, because the funds and resources allocated to the development and implementation of the strategy will greatly influence what can be included within it.

◘ Figure 5.4 demonstrates the challenges Social Media Managers can often experience when managing client expectations in relation to budgets.

With an overview of a social media strategy presented, it is essential to delve deeply into the form, function and purpose of each component so that you can apply this knowledge to crafting your own social media strategies.

◘ **Fig. 5.3** Structural Components of a Social Media Strategy

◘ **Fig. 5.4** Client expectations vs budgetary reality

5.4.1 Goals

At the peak of the strategy structure, a goal is the most preferred outcome that a client or organisation is aiming to achieve. It is the desired result culminating from focused ambition, effort and activity. For example, common goals for a university student are to graduate and begin a career.

There are objectives or mini targets that a student will aim for in the pursuit of those goals such as passing their courses and/or securing an interview for employment. Yet, their actions as a student will either support or obstruct the achievement of those goals.

Within the context of a social media strategy, the goal (or goals) are the results that the overall strategy aims to achieve. As discussed, social media strategies can be developed to support the achievement of either short term or long-term goals.

Suppose that a local hardware store runs an event to teach current or prospective customers basic plumbing skills such as how to change a washer.

A short-term social media strategy may be developed and implemented for this event to achieve the overall goals to:

1. To attract people to the event.
2. To increase sales of plumbing supplies.

You will notice that the goals stated in the example above are very broad statements without detail included, and this is exactly how they should be. Within the context of a social media strategy, goals are succinct, overarching statements that articulate intent.

The details of how the goal/s will be achieved will be present in the other strategic components. The goals in this example relate specifically to the desired impact of the social media activities being implemented to support the success of the event.

Firstly, the social media activities employed must be focused on attracting people to the bricks-and-mortar store to attend the event. Next, the client is keen to use social media activities to help drive sales of the types of products used at the event, in this case plumbing supplies.

Short term goals must align with long-term goals in some way otherwise they are a waste of time and resources and distract attention away from the bigger picture.

The goals of a long-term social media strategy for the hardware store mentioned above could be:

1. To increase sales
2. To increase engagement across social media platforms

Again, these are written as big picture aims and the successful achievement of one can directly influence the other. An increase in engaged social media followers can result in an improvement of sales and a rise in sales can also result in increased social media engagement if approached strategically.

This is because both cases rely on interest from the target audience. Thorough audience research (▶ see Chap. 3) to inform the development of helpful tactics and content (▶ see Chap. 6) to spark and then leverage interest is the momentum required to guide the target audience through the customer journey to achieve both goals.

The short-term goals in this example align directly with the long-term goals presented. The sales-related goal, while specifically targeting plumbing supplies, can result in sales.

Furthermore, attracting people to the event, inviting event attendees to follow the business on social media (if they haven't already), and encouraging engagement through tagging themselves in photos and sharing posts documenting their experience on their own channels also supports the second long-term goal.

This approach to generating social media engagement events is also known as a propinquital approach which will be explored in greater depth in ▶ Chap. 6.

The key thing to remember when identifying goals for any type of social media strategy is:

> 66 The goals of a social media strategy must be aligned with overall business goals. Anything else is counterproductive. 99
>
> Dr Karen Sutherland

As a Social Media Manager, the first questions you must ask a client at the beginning of the social media strategy development phase are:

1. *"What are your business/organisational goals?"*
2. *"Do you have a business/organisational plan, and if so, may I please have a copy?"*

This will ensure that you are on the right track from the beginning and any social media activities bolster what the business or organisation wants to achieve overall.

If a client does not have business/organisational goals or a plan, it is important for them to articulate some overall aim that they are hoping to achieve from social media before going further.

Not having clearly defined goals from the outset is akin to fumbling around in the dark trying to find a light switch.

5.4.2 The Appropriate Number of Goals to Include in a Social Media Strategy

A further vital consideration relates to the number of goals to include in a strategy. For long-term strategies three would be the maximum and no more than two goals for a short-term strategy.

Remember, a social media strategy focuses social media activity to achieve an overall goal. Trying to achieve several goals at once can result in the fragmentation of effort and resources plus the dilution of results.

Fewer goals means more concentrated efforts and greater impact. Often when a client identifies several goals that they hope to achieve, separate strategies are required to support them.

Frequently, what the client is requesting is a mix of long-term and short-term goals, therefore, a long-term strategy interspersed and integrated with short-term strategies is the most logical and efficient approach.

5.4.3 Crafting Goals for a Social Media Strategy

When writing goals to include in a social media strategy please remember the following:

- *Keep it brief.* A goal should be one succinct sentence, a broad statement of what is to be achieved. The detail is included later in the strategy.
- *Make each goal a 'To' statement:* Your goal is something that you are aiming to achieve, so it provides clarity and focus to write it in that way. For example: To increase volunteer numbers, *'To sell tickets'. 'To generate leads'.*
- *Do not include too many.* Less is more. No more than two goals for a short-term

strategy and no more than three for a long-term strategy. Some strategies need only one.

- *Only include one goal in each statement.* A goal that states:

  » 'To increase social media engagement and following' is really two goals and should be written accordingly.

  » Different tactics will be used to increase following compared with increasing engagement. Including both causes confusion when writing the SMART objectives.

  » There are exercises at the end of this chapter to assist you in writing goals for a social media strategy and guidance in the strategy template included in the Appendices.

  » With goals written, relevant SMART Objectives must be developed to support their achievement.

5.4.4 SMART Objectives Explained

While goals are broad statements of what a social media strategy aims to achieve, objectives add specific details to the map of how to achieve them. Objectives serve two key functions.

The first function is to provide defined targets to accomplish the strategic goals. This ensures that all activities implemented as part of the strategy are focused solely on goal achievement.

The second function is to provide a benchmark for evaluation (Belch et al., 2008). The success of a social media strategy can never be truly confirmed without measuring it, a process that will be investigated in much greater depth in ▶ Chap. 7.

Keeping this idea of evaluation in mind, objectives can also be known as Key Performance Indicators or Key Progress Indicators (KPIs) that essentially measure whether a social media strategy has been a success or a wasted effort (Belch et al., 2008; Kim, 2016; Tuten & Solomon, 2017).

However, for objectives to function productively in a social media strategy, they must be SMART.

While there are slight variations in the literature around what each letter in the acronym represents. Some scholars refer to them as SMART Goals. Avoid focusing on the semantics.

All variations of SMART Objectives promote the need to articulate specific targets that can be measured and achieved within a set time period (Belch et al., 2008; Chia & Synnott, 2012; Freberg, 2018; Kim, 2016; Quesenberry, 2015; Tuten & Solomon, 2017).

◘ Figure 5.5 presents what each of the letters in SMART represent: Specific, Measurable, Achievable, Realistic and Timely. Each letter serves its own function in articulating what the objective must accomplish to support the overall strategic goal:

- *Specific:* Articulate exactly what you are referring to e.g. *What and.or who?*
- *Measurable:* State precisely what you will be measuring e.g. *How many?*
- *Achievable:* Ensure that what is being proposed as an objective can be achieved e.g. has anyone else achieved it? Do you have the resources to achieve it?
- *Realistic:* Evaluate whether the objective can really be achieved within the

◘ **Fig. 5.5** SMART Objectives

specified timeframe. This can be contentious when working with clients who have unrealistic expectations and misguidedly believe that social media can return colossal results overnight.

Remember, social media is a long game and it is better to underpromise and overdeliver. Therefore, it is essential to the overall success of a social media strategy to be realistic from the outset about what can be achieved within a specific time period.

— *Timely:* Stipulate the deadline for achieving this objective, e.g. *When*.

SMART objectives are written as one sentence that contain each of these elements. One of the greatest benefits of correctly written SMART Objectives is that they clearly indicate the metrics that need to be included in the Measurement section of the strategy that will be discussed in greater detail in ▶ Chap. 7.

◨ Figure 5.6 provides an example of a SMART Objective with each element identified within the sentence. Please take careful note of the structure and components of this SMART Objective and apply this knowledge when developing your own in the practical exercises at the end of this chapter.

The example presented in ◨ Fig. 5.6 is in line with the scenario presented previously in this chapter about the short-term social media strategy developed to support an event at a hardware store.

The example is very specific and realistic in terms of what is to be achieved. It clearly states on whom the objective is focused, how many of that target audience the objective aims to attract to the event and exactly what and when the event is.

Also, the specificity relating to local followers is included with the intention to encourage repeat business with those who would find visiting the hardware store a convenient option because it is located in their neighbourhood.

Imagine that the Hardware Heaven Facebook page has 3000 page likes or followers. In this instance, attracting 30 people is an achievable number to aim for. However, if the same page had only 40 followers, attracting 30 people from this target audience would be a much more challenging task. This is why it is important to assess how achievable a SMART Objective is when developing it.

Furthermore, setting a realistic timeframe will also have an influence on the likelihood of the objective being met. For example, if the strategy was implemented four weeks from the event date, this is a realistic time period to achieve the objective of attracting 30 Facebook followers to the workshop. If the strategy was implemented

To attract 30 local followers of the Hardware Heaven Facebook page

Specific ⌃ Achievable   ⌃
                              Specific
Measurable ⌃ Realistic

to our Get Your Plumb On Workshop on the 26th of July.

⌃   ⌃
Specific   Timely

◨ **Fig. 5.6** SMART Objective: To attract 30 local followers of the Hardware Heaven Facebook page to our *Get Your Plumb On Workshop* on the 26th of July

two days before the event, the probability of achieving this objective will be considerably reduced.

5.4.5 Be Transparent

SMART Objectives must be crafted in a way that sets the strategy up for success but must not be manipulated in an unethical way to suggest to clients that greater achievements have been attained than what has truly occurred.

Changing SMART objectives at the end of the implementation phase or inflating results by only presenting percentages are both highly unethical behaviours.

Imagine if the goal was to increase Facebook page likes and currently only 10 people like the page. The implementation of the strategy results in only five additional people liking the page. Statistically, that is a 50% increase, which sounds impressive, but in reality, it is only five people and not an extraordinary achievement.

This is why it is extremely important to couple percentage increase targets with the figure this equates to so that the utmost transparency is presented to a client.

5.4.6 The Appropriate Number of SMART Objectives to Include in a Social Media Strategy

SMART Objectives must adequately support the strategic goals. This requirement for support is evident when revisiting ▫ Fig. 5.3. SMART Objectives are positioned directly under the goals with a longer tier to signify the stability they must provide.

Due to this function, it is essential to have two SMART Objectives per goal. This increases the support and probability for the goal to be accomplished by dedicating two streams of social media activity to its achievement. For example, if the goal is:
- **Goal:** To attract people to the event.
  The first SMART Objective is:
- **SO1:** To attract 30 local followers of the Hardware Heaven Facebook page to our *Get Your Plumb On Workshop* on the 26th of July.

A second SMART Objective that supports the goal could be:
- **SO2:** To encourage a minimum of 10 local followers of the Hardware Heaven Facebook page to bring at least one other person with them to our *Get Your Plumb On Workshop* on the 26th of July.

The second SMART Objective in this example leverages the first by encouraging those target audience members who are already interested in attending the event to share the experience with others in their network.

Clearly both SMART Objectives are working together to achieve the same goal but have slightly different focuses.

If only the first SMART Objective was included in the strategy to support the goal and it was not accomplished, the strategic goal would not be achieved. Therefore, it is necessary to have two SMART Objectives working to achieve the goal.

More than two is possible, but this adds another layer of complexity to the strategy and can sometimes result in the SMART Objectives competing against each other instead of working together.

With the goals and SMART Objectives now explained, ▶ Chap. 6 focuses on developing the tactics (or actions) to support the achievement of the objectives.

In ▶ Chap. 6 you will learn that a basic social media strategy structure at least three tactics should support each SMART Objective to also minimise risk if any do not work and increase the probability that the objective will be met, and the overall goal achieved.

Next, it is essential to clearly articulate the key messages that must be communicated through tactics and content that will inspire the target audience to perform the desired actions required to achieve the goals of the strategy.

5.4.7 Key Messages Defined

Key messages are the most important points of information to communicate to the target audience (Badal et al., 2019; Kim, 2016). To be effective, they must be clear, succinct and uncomplicated.

Key messages must also be written using terms and language that the target audience will understand (▶ see Chap. 3) and serve a vital function to the overall success of the strategy. All content (see Sections 3.2 and 3.3) must convey at least one of the key messages for it to be considered strategic.

Remember, that the content and tactics perform the role of the messenger, they are not the message. Sometimes it is easy to become preoccupied with perfecting the content or tactic and lose sight of what each is attempting to communicate.

Key messages, tactics and content must work together to reach the target audience, attract their attention and generate sense-making (Abbas et al., 2018; Quesenberry, 2015). If any of these functions are not fulfilled, the probability of achieving the SMART Objectives and goals will be significantly reduced.

If the content is not reaching the target audience at all, it cannot attract their attention and facilitate understanding. If the content reaches the target audience, but does not attract their attention, sensemaking will not occur.

Finally, if the content reaches the target audience, attracts their attention and the key message/s do not make sense to them this will also result in a lost opportunity.

5.4.8 Core Functions of Key Messages

A Key Message generally aims to fulfil one of the following functions when communicating with a target audience.

Key Messages
- *Inform:* Provide specific details about a brand, product, service, event, etc.
- *Educate:* Increase understanding to build on existing knowledge or to change perceptions about a brand, product, service, event, issue or cause, etc.
- *Establish Empathy:* Demonstrate an in-depth insight and understanding of the target audience's experiences and their need for the brand, product, service, etc.
- *Problem Solve:* Present a solution and/or assistance to help solve a problem or challenge experienced by the target audience.
- *Inspire Action:* Communicate a call-to-action to prompt the target audience to perform a desired behaviour such as visiting a website, calling the business, booking tickets etc.

5.4.9 Crafting Key Messages

The trick when crafting Key Messages is to keep them as clear and simple as possible to increase the likelihood that the target audience will understand them, remember them and comprehend the actions that you want them to undertake.

Sometimes clients want to include too many details within the Key Messages because they feel that the target audience needs to know as much as they can about their business or organisation. Yet, the target audience will walk away at the slightest hint of confusion.

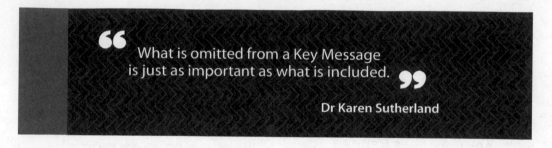

5

Important questions to ask when developing Key Messages are:

1. *What is the most important information that the audience needs to know* to support the achievement of the strategic goals and SMART Objectives?
2. *What doesn't the audience need to know?* What further information can be eliminated from the answer to Question 1?
3. *How will the target audience benefit from the knowledge contained in this Key Message?*
4. *What is the specific problem experienced by the target audience* and how can we provide a solution?
5. *Clearly state the actions that you want the target audience to undertake.* What is the call-to-action?
6. *What will the target audience gain from performing this call to action?*

Establishing the most important information using these questions will greatly assist when further refining the Key Messages for a social media strategy.

In terms of structure, each Key Message should be a succinct, single sentence. If the function of a Key Message was to educate the target audience about the Hardware Heaven brand, a Key Message could be:

Where hardware becomes easy.

Notice how distinct brand values are communicated succinctly.

This Key Message aims to reassure the target audience that shopping at Hardware Heaven will be an effortless experience.

In relation to the *Get Your Plumb On Workshop*, a Key Message might be:

Don't miss out on our Get Your Plumb On Workshop; book your place on our website today.

This example is a clear and direct call-to-action to the target audience. What is important with this Key Message is to ensure that how to book for this event is easy to find on the website ready for when the target audience responds to the call-to-action.

Remember IMC mentioned previously in the chapter. All pieces of the strategy must work together and are best tested from the target audience's perspective before they are implemented and regularly monitored once the strategy is underway (▶ see Chap. 7).

5.4.10 The Appropriate Number of Key Messages to Include in a Social Media Strategy

Less is more, when selecting Key Messages to include in a social media strategy.

Between one and three key messages is recommended to incorporate within a single strategy.

Keeping the number of Key Messages to a maximum of three assists the target audience to remember the most important information. Too many messages will be forgotten or ignored because they will take too much effort to recall.

Therefore, it is essential for Social Media Managers to be extremely discerning when selecting only the most vital pieces of information to convey within a social media strategy. In line with our focus so far and to pre-empt the focus on problem-solving content and tactics explored in ▶ Chap. 6, it can be helpful to include the following Key Message types in a Social Media Strategy:

- *Key Message 1. Brand Info:* A succinct statement of who the brand is and what it stands for. Doing this informs people who are unfamiliar with the brand and reminds those who are. E.g.

  Hardware Heaven: Where hardware becomes easy.

- *Key Message 2. Present assistance or solution to a problem:* Doing this presents the brand in a favourable light to the target audience by establishing an understanding of their challenges and providing a helpful solution. However, the problem must be a legitimate one identified through audience research and the solution or assistance must be genuine. E.g.

  Reduce expensive plumbing fees by attending our Get Your Plumb On Workshop to learn how to complete basic jobs yourself.

- *Key Message 3. Call-to-action:* This is where you encourage and inspire the target audience to act in a way that helps to achieve a SMART Objective and, in turn, a goal.

  Do not expect the target audience to *respond in a particular way without* clearly stating what that is. A call-to-action must be simple, and it must be easily performed in actuality. E.g.

  Don't miss out on our Get Your Plumb On Workshop; book your place on our website today.

Another example is a recent campaign by Monash University where the tagline was a simple call-to-action: "If you don't like it, change it," (Monash University, 2019). This key message was featured with visual content demonstrating some of the key areas where Monash University graduates and researchers are impacting the world. This encouraged people to engage with Monash University if they wanted to make positive change.

Complete the Practical Exercises at the end of this chapter to hone your skills with Key Message writing.

With a solid idea of what Key Messages are and how they should be written for inclusion in a social media strategy, it is also important to consider a range of ways to communicate them to a target audience.

5.4.11 Key Messages: Show Don't Tell

Constantly repeating the Key Messages word-for-word in social media content will bore the target audience extremely quickly. A disengaged target audience is the complete opposite to the outcome a strategy aims to achieve.

To avoid this result, it is important to gauge when a Key Message should employ the storytelling principle of: Show Don't Tell. This means that instead of literally telling the target audience a Key Message, such as:

» *Hardware Heaven: Where hardware becomes easy,*

  Would be demonstrated through storytelling and content that this is the case (Anderson, 2013).

For example, through a customer testimonial or a 'How To' video.

5.4.11.1 Trusted House Sitters Use Customer Testimonials to Show and Not Tell

Building trust is key component in house sitting. The person opening their home to a housesitter must trust the person assigned to look after the home. The housesitter must trust the owner so that they feel safe, comfortable and secure while minding their home.

To build this trust, house-sitting service, Trusted House Sitters, encouraged customers to upload testimonials to their website that could be used across their channels. The company offered prizes for people who uploaded testimonials and made the process of uploading content extremely simple (Stemler, 2018).

As a result, more than 2000 testimonials were uploaded that they could use to communicate their key messages. Rather than telling their current and prospective customers that they were a trustworthy organisation, their existing customers did this for them through their video and image-based testimonials (Stemler, 2018).

Consumers today place less faith in organisations blatantly telling them how good they are and place greater confidence in other sources of information such as online reviews such as those left on Trip Advisor or Facebook (Mumuni, Lancendorfer, O'Reilly, & MacMillan, 2019).

Consumers are searching for evidence that supports the claims a brand makes. The careful development of tactics and content can provide this function to build trust and credibility with the target audience.

It is acceptable to 'Tell' when conveying Key Messages that are focused on the communication of specific details related to calls-to-action, times and locations, etc. to avoid any ambiguity or confusion.

However, when it comes to communicating brand qualities or how helpful a brand or product is, it is much more effective to employ the 'Show Don't Tell' principle. A deep exploration of the application of this principle through storytelling is contained in ▶ Chap. 6.

This Chapter has provided a map to develop strategic goals, SMART Objectives and Key Messages as the foundational components of a social media strategy. Next, we must investigate the importance of budget and how it influences all other components.

5.4.12 How a Budget Can Impact a Social Media Strategy

Budget is positioned on the largest tier of the social media strategy structure because it has the greatest influence over what can be included in its development and implementation. One of the most prevalent misconceptions surrounding social media is that it is free (Freberg, 2018; Kim, 2016; Tuten & Solomon, 2017).

It can most definitely be free for someone using a personal profile, but for businesses it is now a case of pay for play in many respects. If a client does not want to devote much of a budget to their social media strategy, this will have a significant impact on the tactics that can be used to support the achievement of SMART Objectives and strategic goals.

As with many situations in life, social media is also a case of you get what you pay for (Freberg, 2018). Below are only some of the areas of social media management that budget can impact.

5.4.13 Budget Can Impact Content Production

A budget can determine the difference of content being created using free tools and content produced using professional suppliers. For example, as explored in ▶ Chap. 15, quality graphics can be created using free features from tools such as Canva. However, the finished product may not be as compelling as the content produced by a professional graphic designer.

Furthermore, video can be produced using a Smartphone and free online editing tools such as WeVideo. However, if a client is aiming to produce a professional-looking high-quality video showcasing their new product launch, the difference in quality and editing when using a professional videographer will be clear.

It can be the same with photography and copywriting. Factoring quality content production into the strategy's budget is imperative.

It is a similar case when assessing the value of social media management skills, particularly if you have expertise in the content production skills mentioned above.

A client is not paying for the time it takes to produce the content. They are paying for the many years of knowledge and experience that it has taken that have led to this level of expertise.

High-quality content takes time, knowledge and proficiency to produce.

> 66 Quality
> Social Media Management
> is not free. 99
> Dr Karen Sutherland

5.4.13.1 Budget Can Impact Reach

As mentioned previously, social media is now pay for play particularly on platforms such as Facebook and Instagram. This means that businesses must pay the platforms to extend the reach of their content. Reach refers to the number of individual people who view a piece of content (Headworth, 2015; Information Resources Management Association, 2018).

For example, a Facebook post on a business page may reach only 6% of followers if posted organically (not paid). Whereas, paying Facebook to boost the post (paying for specific audiences to see it) or placing the post as a Facebook advertisement in Facebook Business Manager (an interface for the owner of Facebook business pages) will not only greatly extend the reach of the post, specific audiences can be defined, targeted and retargeted using the Facebook Pixel, as long as they have not used Facebook's 'Clear History' feature (Hern, 2019).

If a client or an organisation has a presence on Facebook and/or Instagram and do not allocate any budget for paid advertisements as tactics, they must also adjust their expectations in relation to the number of people who will see their content, particularly if they do not have a larger following.

There are organic tactics that can improve reach, but these are very sporadic in their success and should not be relied upon for the goals and SMART Objectives of a social media strategy to be accomplished.

5.4.13.2 Budgets Can Impact Tools

Budgets can also dictate the tools accessible to develop, implement and evaluate a social media strategy. Quality social media management can be delivered without tools, however having a budget for tools can assist with processes such as social listening, content curation, content creation, scheduling, monitoring and measurement.

When developing a budget, it is important to factor in a percentage to cover preferred tools and platforms to support the overall process of social media management to assist with the delivery of successful results to a client.

5.4.13.3   Budgets Can Impact Time

The adage, 'time is money' is also reflective in relation to social media. A budget means that it is possible to outsource tasks so that they are completed at a faster rate. It can also decide the difference between manually completing tasks and automating them. Sometimes clients can completely underestimate the time that it takes to develop, implement and evaluate a social media strategy.

If a client is not willing to pay for more than a few hours per week to fund the implementation of their social media strategy, it can take a much longer time for the strategy to achieve its goals and SMART Objectives.

It is extremely important not to underestimate the time it will take. As mentioned previously, it is better to under-promise and over-deliver than to cause disappointment by completing the opposite. This takes the careful negotiation and management of client expectations from the outset.

5.4.14   Budget Approaches: Top Down and Bottom Up

There are three main approaches to budgets evident in the marketing, advertising and IMC literature: Top Down and Bottom Up (Belch et al., 2008; Chitty et al., 2011).

Top Down refers to senior management of an organisation or a client setting what the available budget is (or is not) at the beginning of the strategy development phase (Belch et al., 2008; Chitty et al., 2011). A common approach to setting a budget that is Top Down is by building it around the notion of Return On Investment (ROI).

This means that the client or decision maker will set the budget according to the returns that this will generate as a result (Chitty et al., 2011). For example, setting an advertising budget according to how many online sales are made as a result of that advertising.

Bottom Up is when the budget is proposed by the Social Media Manager who estimates all costs associated with the social media strategy (development, implementation and evaluation) and provides a quote to the client or decision maker at an organisation (Belch et al., 2008; Chitty et al., 2011). The client or decision maker accepts the quote with the estimated budget and confirms that the Social Media Manager can begin work on the strategy or does not accept the quote or the budget.

5.4.14.1   What to Include in a Budget

◻ Table 5.1 presents the recommended items to include in a social media strategy as proposed by Quesenberry (2019) who also factors in hours of work spent on delivering each item. This is in line with the public relations literature that also factors in staff hours (Chia & Synnott, 2012).

Quesenberry's (2019) approach to a social media management budget has been further enhanced to include the items that also feature in the social media strategy development and evaluation phases.

◻ Table 5.1 presents a comprehensive list of items to include in a social media strategy budget. However, this is just a guide and should be customised to the specific needs of the Social Media Manager and their client. A copy of this budget template is available in the Social Media Strategy Template in Appendix 1.

Top Down/Bottom Up or *Bottom Up/Top Down* is a combination of both approaches and is the approach most commonly used (Chitty et al., 2011). This approach is much more collaborative and involves a negotiation between both parties (client or decision maker and Social Media Manager) to reach an agreed budget that the client or decision maker can afford, and the Social Media Manager can work with to achieve the results expected by their client. This approach can

Table 5.1 Items to include in a social media strategy budget

Strategic phase budget category	In-house expense (fixed/percent)	Outsource expense (fixed/percent)	Total category (fixed/percent)		
Development Research (Audience Research, Client Research, Industry Research, Social Media Audit, Competitor Analysis etc). Social Media Strategy Proposal	$ per hour per item	$ per hour per item or $ amount for each item.	$	(per item)	%
Implementation *Content curation* Tools Time *Content creation* Writing Graphics Video *Social advertising* (list each platform) *Promotions/contests* (prizes, discounts, promotions etc.) (list each platform) *Social engagement* (time to listen and respond to comments and questions) (list each platform) *Offline tactics* (events etc.) *Software/tools* Monitoring Scheduling Analytics	$ per hour per item	$ per hour per item or $ amount for each item.	$	(per item)	%
Evaluation Measurement and monitoring framework implementation Data analysis Performance report and recommendation development Implementation of recommendations	$ per hour per item	$ per hour per item or $ amount for each item.	$	(per item)	%
TOTAL	$ %	$ %	$		%

vary between the client or the organisational decision maker opening the budget negotiations with the Social Media Manager or vice-versa. This approach is clearly the most logical of the three because it involves two-way conversation, a dialogue to reach a compromise, which is a positive and respectful way to approach setting a budget.

5.4.14.2 Tips to Negotiate a Budget with a Client or Organisational Decision Maker

The Top Down/Bottom Up and Bottom Up/Top Down budget approaches all involve careful negotiation. Reaching an agreement in terms of the costs involved with developing, implementing and evaluating a social media strategy can be a precarious and challenging conversation because both parties want to reach an outcome that is attractive for them.

A client or organisational decision maker wants to receive maximum return on their investment (ROI) and Social Media Manager wants to be paid appropriately for their time and to have adequate financial resources to return the results the client is expecting. The best result of a budget negotiation is that it is a win/win for both parties.

As Sutherland (2015) suggests, social media professionals often need to educate people within their organisations (and external clients) about the realities of social media, in this case the time and costs associated with developing, implementing and evaluating a social media strategy.

Sometimes clients or organisational decision makers have an in-depth knowledge of the costs involved with social media management are trying to negotiate the best deal for them.

However, as social media can be such a new area for many business owners and senior management in organisations there is a high probability that they do not understand the work and costs involved.

When entering a budget negotiation, please consider the following:

- *Avoid using terms such as "costs, price, expense, fees etc."* Instead use terms such as "investment, budget," (Martin & Knoohuizen, 1995, p. 192).

- *Manage Expectations:* This is essential throughout all facets of social media management not only in budget negotiations. Never make promises to a client regarding the results that you plan to achieve for them; unless you can predict the future, you can never know this for sure. The only promises that can be made to clients are in relation to the tangible items that can be truly delivered such as a strategy document, content creation, platform management etc., (see ▪ Table 5.1).

- **Unrealistic Time Frames - Common Client Expectations Requiring Management.**

  A study of 26 digital agencies by Databox to explore issue of management client expectations found that addressing unrealistic deadlines imposed by clients was one of the most common challenges experienced by the sample (Albright, 2018).

  Clients were identified as expecting extensive work within impossible time frames, usually because they did not understand the level of labour and effort particular tasks required.

  Participants of the study also mentioned that some clients did not understand that the timeframe of tasks can change if they do not go as planned.

  Suggestions to manage client expectations in relation to time include educating the client regarding the work involved and the best and worst case scenarios, regular communication relating to how well the original timeline is being adhered to and under-promising and over-delivering (Albright, 2018).

  It is important to estimate the length of time the job will take and then adding at least a third to compensate for things not going to plan and to surpass client expectations if meeting the deadline early.

Ensure that a contract is developed stating what is to be delivered and is signed by both parties at the time when the budget approved (See ► Chap. 4). Be honest and communicate regularly.

Once the strategy is underway and an unexpected cost seems likely, communicate this to a client immediately and seek their approval before adding this to the budget.

— *Be completely transparent and provide detailed explanations with evidence.* On the proposed budget itemise everything involved in the social media management of your client and provide an explanation about each item, exactly what is involved and how long it will take.

Provide evidence to support your explanation to reassure the client that this is commonplace within the industry. Your aim is to build trust with a client by demonstrating to them that you are credible and not trying to exploit them. Use the opportunity to increase their understanding of social media and what is involved.

— *Be flexible.* This does not mean reducing your prices but providing options for each task with different tiers of pricing. For example, if video production is required, the top tier of pricing would include outsourcing to a professional video producer.

However, the lowest tier would involve using a Smartphone and free editing tools where the investment would be related to your hourly rate to produce the video in-house.

— *Ask for more than you want (within reason) to provide room for negotiation.* Most negotiations include a few interactions before the final budget is agreed upon by both parties. If you present your proposed budget in the first instance and the client wants to negotiate it down, you will need to reduce the budget or walk away before any discussions have had the

opportunity to truly begin. However, do not be excessive, because this will also quickly halt negotiations and reduce trust between you and your client. Adding between 5%–10% to the overall cost will allow some room to move.

— *Focus on the relationship.* The aim is to convert the client or organisational decision maker into a repeat customer (Martin & Knoohuizen, 1995, p. 192). Negotiations must be undertaken in a fair and respectful manner. Even if a client walks away from the budget negotiation, it does not mean that this will be the end of the discussion. They may seek additional opinions and quotes and return in the future.

— *Do not be afraid to respectfully walk away.* If a client or organisational decision maker is rigid in budget discussions and asking for an unrealistic amount of work for a heavily reduced price, please do not be afraid to respectfully walk away. Try to accommodate their needs, but negotiations should be win/win.

Underselling your knowledge and experience sets a standard with your client and it will be challenging to ask them to pay more in the future. It also undermines social media management as a profession.

These tips are not foolproof and may not work with every client. However, they are worth considering particularly if budget negotiations are an unfamiliar practice.

Conclusion

This chapter explored the foundational components of a social media strategy. The importance of strategic goals and SMART Objectives were investigated demonstrating how they drive the action and results of a social media strategy.

The functions of Key Messages were also analysed to demonstrate how, when

5

clearly defined, they can inform, educate and inspire the target audience to undertake the necessary actions to support the achievement of goals and SMART Objectives.

Furthermore, this chapter focused on the significant influence that a budget can have on the tactics and content included in a social media strategy. This chapter concluded with focus on what to incorporate in the budget for a social media strategy and provided practical recommendations to manage client expectations and undertake budget negotiations with a client or organisational decision maker.

Case Study: Casper Uses IMC to Launch New Sleep Channel

UK bed retailer, Casper, developed and implemented an integrated marketing communication campaign to launch their new *Casper Sleep Channel*. The *Casper Sleep Channel* was a new offering available on IGTV, YouTube and Spotify that provides users with more than 225 minutes of meditations, bedtime stories and sounds that aim to send listeners off to sleep (Gianatasio, 2019). The channel is an excellent way to position the brand as top-of-mind when people are most likely to want or need Casper products; at bedtime.

The brand used a multi-platform approach to launch this new channel. While the channel itself was available on IGTV, YouTube and Spotify, its promotion used a range of other platforms including Facebook, Instagram and Twitter to drive traffic to the various Sleep Channel locations (West, 2019).

Casper, also used traditional media to promote the channel so that communication would be extended to a wide range of audiences not only in the online space. Cross-promotion was a tactic used throughout the campaign. While the first traditional media push was used to create awareness of the channel, social media was then utilised to move the audience through the customer journey.

While use of the channel is free, the action did not involve the listener purchasing anything to access it, Casper sought channel followers and subscribers to build a community around their brand. This would result in those regularly listening to the channel being exposed to the Casper brand on a regular basis. Furthermore, Casper providing content that can assist people to drift off to sleep (an offline event) could help to generate positive brand associations for listeners and help to build or strengthen brand relationships.

After the promotional launch campaign, Casper continues to use its social media channels to inform followers when new additions are available on the channel, to maintain interest and continue to drive people back to the channel to consume its content. While this campaign did not incorporate all components of IMC it involved quite a few and leveraged its principles to deliver a highly successful campaign. At time of writing, the Casper Sleep Channel has 7.72 k YouTube subscribers (YouTube, 2019).

1. Why do you think the Casper Sleep Channel was so popular?
2. What value did the Casper Sleep Channel offer to its users?

5.5 · Interview: Camilla Billman, Social Media Manager – CB Sociala Medier...

97   5

5.5   Interview: Camilla Billman, Social Media Manager – CB Sociala Medier, Gothenburg, Sweden

1. **Please tell me about your current role.**
    I'm a social media manager in Sweden and I'm just starting out. I've been doing this professionally for about a year and a half now. In my role as a single entrepreneur, I do everything from audits, strategy, scheduling posts on Instagram or Facebook, to coaching small business owners on how to grow their presence on LinkedIn on a small budget.

2. **What do you enjoy most about working with social media?**
    I just, I love watching people and businesses grow. I also love that I learn something new every day. You need to keep on your toes and it just keeps you fresh all the time.

3. **What are the greatest challenges?**
    Well, since I'm in Sweden the market is still too small to have a specific niche, which means I need to become the expert of my customers and I need to learn their business back to front. One of my clients has a water filtering company and I have no idea about water filtering, but I mean you ask me anything and I'm the expert.
    It's also hard to convince the customer that they need to spend money. That's one of the biggest challenges in social media because some think that social media should be free and it's not.

4. **How did you come to work in social media? Please tell me your career story.**
    Well, I originate from the IT business, EVOLVO IT to be specific, as a business analyst of many things. But I've been doing social media for an animal shelter here in Kungsbacka on the West Coast of Sweden for about 4 years and I really, really enjoyed it. I grew their Facebook presence and their Instagram, built up their webpage and I really enjoyed it. Then in 2017, I got the opportunity to restart my professional life and I thought, "What am I going to do?" I wasn't sure.
    I knew I didn't want to travel to Gothenburg and sit in two traffic to commute. Someone said to me, "Well, why don't you start your own business doing social media management for other companies as you've been doing it for free for the last four years." So, I thought, "Okay, yeah, let's try that." That's where I am at the moment.

5. **This chapter is about articulating strategic goals, SMART Objectives and key messages as fundamental components that underpin a social media strategy. What do you think are the three most important things for Social Media Managers to consider when going through this process?**
    I would say number one, understand who your customer is. This will get you far. Understanding your customer needs or their problems. This will get you even further. Then understanding what you want, which is social media, what your goals are to be specific.

6. **What do you think are the benefits of articulating strategic goals, SMART Objectives and key messages?**
    When you've done the groundwork, you have a solid base to stand on and it will be easier to continue your journey, your social media journey and reach your set goals. It will also be a lot easier for you to create the content that will help you achieve this.

7. **What are the challenges of articulating strategic goals, SMART Objectives and key messages?**
    Something that I really wish that companies would consider more is to make sure that everyone in the company is on board with the social media train. Because with your employees, you have

5

the best company ambassadors and the best advertising you can get.

8. **How can you help current prospective customers by articulating strategic goals, SMART Objectives and key messages?**

It generates a greater understanding throughout the company. If everyone is working with it and has it in their mind and a lot of companies are still way behind on this, it's like, "Oh no, you can't say watch LinkedIn during your work." But what if LinkedIn is your work? It's part of your daily chores then, yeah, they should be in on it.

9. **What are your favourite tools or methods to articulate strategic goals, SMART Objectives and key messages and why?**

Insights of the social media channels you're going to use. Hopefully they are on social media and you can see what they've been doing. You can learn a lot about your customers just by looking at the insights. Of course, the Google analytics and the Facebook Pixel. It's outstanding to get data. To make it more visual and to make the customer understand, I use PowerPoint because sometimes when you connect pictures and texts, it makes it easier for them to understand because not everyone is as attuned to social media as the manager is.

10. **What influence does budget have on the development and implementation of a social media strategy?**

It has a lot of influence because it's not free, whatever the customer thinks. It's free for a private person, but for businesses, you need to pay. That's the hard truth. If you have a good social media manager that can create great ads for then even a small amount will get you quite far.

But when Facebook learns your business and you learn how your customers respond to the ads and you see

results that you can put more money in. That's a good thing about online advertising, I think, because you can track everything and you can see exactly where the money goes.

11. **What advice can you provide to Social Media Managers to manage client expectations in relation to budget?**

I think it's important from the start to set the expectation. That the client understands what they're getting, what they're paying for, so they don't have expectations to make something viral, which I hear a lot, "Oh, can you make this viral?" I was like, "It doesn't work like that, and you're selling water filters." It is hard, but just have it in writing what their expectations are and what you can do and what you can do with that budget you have.

12. **What do you think of the current landscape of social media management as a profession?**

It's a profession on the rise, especially here in Sweden. I think it's going on in the US for quite some time and perhaps in Australia too. But in Sweden, it's really starting to grow. We're not there quite yet. Big companies obviously have an intern, or someone working hired to do this. But it's new to have to outsource social media management.

Often here in Sweden, it's Anna at the front desk or something. That works out for the first month perhaps. Then Anna gets busy and then you don't post anything, and nothing shows up and that's not good.

13. **Where do you think the profession and social media is heading in the future?**

Well, there will be challenges, but I think it will continue to grow, especially when companies realise that they don't have to do it themselves. They can outsource it to someone else, a consultant or client or just hire someone part time. But the challenge in the future, I think, since our conversations on social media takes place on the dark social, with the dark social, I mean private messages and private chats and chat rooms and so forth or in groups. So how can we reach these? So that is a challenge for the future.

14. **What has been the best piece of advice that you have been given?**
Well, in social media, know your customers and what problems they have. Because if you can solve their problems, then you really help your customers.

15. **What advice would you give to someone who wants to work as a Social Media Manager?**
Just do it. Start practising on your own channels. Take all the courses you can. There's a lot of free stuff out there if you're willing to look for it and just do it. Life is too short not to enjoy it.

❓ Questions for Critical Reflection

1. Why are goals, SMART Objectives, Key Messages and Budgets the core foundational components of a social media strategy?
2. What is the difference between short-term and long-term social media strategies? When can they be integrated?
3. Why is it important for a social media strategy to have at least one goal? Please explain your answer.
4. What can happen if a social media strategy has more than two goals? Please provide an example.
5. What is a SMART Objective? Please provide an example.
6. What is a Key Message? Why is it important not to have more than three Key Messages in a social media strategy?
7. What should a Social Media Manager remember when negotiating a strategy with a client?

❯ Practical Exercises

Jenny and Tim the owners of an online store called, *Maza*, that sells swimwear for men and women contacts you seeking social media management services. The owners want to increase their brand's social media following in a bid to boost sales in their online store.

They currently have a presence on Facebook and Instagram and their target customer is predominantly female aged between 25–45.

The brand logically has a beachy, Summery feel and prides itself on quality products that don't fade, fast delivery and sizes to fit all body types. With this information in mind, and using the knowledge gained from this chapter, please develop the following:

1. Two goals as identified by the owners of *Maza*.
2. Two relevant SMART Objectives to support each goal.
3. Three relevant key messages that communicate the most important information to the target audience that inspires them to visit and purchase from the online store.

References

Abbas, A., Zhou, Y., Deng, S., & Zhang, P. (2018). Text analytics to support sense-making in social media: A language-action perspective. *MIS Quarterly, 42*(2).

Albright, D. (2018). 26 Agencies on the winning approach for managing client expectations, *Databox,* viewed: 24/11/2019: https://databox.com/managing-client-expectations

Anderson, L. (2013). *Creative writing: A workbook with readings.* Oxfordshire: Routledge.

Badal, H. J., Boudewyns, V., Uhrig, J. D., August, E. M., Ruddle, P., & Stryker, J. E. (2019). Testing makes us stronger™: Evaluating the correlation between exposure and intermediate outcomes targeted by the Campaign's messages. *Patient Education and Counseling, 102*(1), 53–60.

Belch, G. E., Belch, M. A., Kerr, G. F., & Powell, I. (2008). *Advertising and promotion : An integrated marketing communications perspective.* Sydney: McGraw-Hill.

Casper. (2019). Welcome to the Casper Sleep Channel, *YouTube,* viewed: 24/11/2019: https://www.youtube.com/watch?v=0DvlgV3DUUs

5

Chia, J., & Synnott, G. (2012). *An introduction to public relations and communication management.* South Melbourne: Oxford University Press.

Chitty, W., Barker, N., Chitty, B., Valos, M., & Shimp, T. A. (2011). *Integrated marketing communications.* South Melbourne: Cengage Learning.

Freberg, K. (2018). *Social media for strategic communication: Creative strategies and research-based Applications.* Thousand Oaks, CA: SAGE Publications.

Gianatasio, D. (2019). Casper Launched a Sleep Channel of Sounds to Help You Drift Off, *Muse By Clio*, viewed: 24/11/2019: https://musebycl.io/music/casper-launched-sleep-channel-sounds-help-you-drift

Headworth, A. (2015). *Social media recruitment: How to successfully integrate social media into recruitment strategy.* London: Kogan Page Publishers.

Hern, A. (2019). Facebook launches 'clear history' tool – But it won't delete anything, *The Guardian*, viewed: 25.08.2019: https://www.theguardian.com/technology/2019/aug/20/facebook-launches-clear-history-tool-but-it-wont-delete-anything

Information Resources Management Association. (2018). *Social media marketing: Breakthroughs in research and practice.* Hershey, PA: IGI Global.

Kim, C. M. (2016). *Social media campaigns: Strategies for public relations and marketing.* New York, NY: Routledge.

Martin, J. D., & Knoohuizen, N. (1995). *Marketing basics for designers: A sourcebook of strategies and ideas.* New York, NY: Wiley.

McCloskey, D. (2018). *Marketing communications. Ways and Possibilities of Integrated Marketing.* Germany: GRIN Verlag.

Monash University. (2019). If you Don't like it, change it. *Monash University*, viewed: 25/11/2019: https://change-it.monash.edu/

Mumuni, A. G., Lancendorfer, K. M., O'Reilly, K. A., & MacMillan, A. (2019). Antecedents of consumers' reliance on online product reviews. *Journal of Research in Interactive Marketing, 13*(1), 26–46.

Percy, L. (2018). *Strategic integrated marketing communications.* London: Routledge.

Quesenberry, K. A. (2018). Social Media Strategy: Marketing, Advertising, and Public Relations in the Consumer Revolution. Rowman & Littlefield: Maryland.

Quesenberry, K. A. (2019). *Social media budget template.* Rowman & Littlefield, viewed: 28/07/2019: http://www.postcontrolmarketing.com/wp-content/uploads/2018/05/SocialMediaBudget Template.pdf

Quesenberry, K. A. (2015). *Social media strategy: Marketing and advertising in the consumer revolution.* Lanham: Rowman & Littlefield.

Reid, M., Luxton, S., & Mavondo, F. (2005). The relationship between integrated marketing communication, market orientation, and brand orientation. *Journal of Advertising, 34*(4), 11–23.

Schultz, D. E., & Schultz, H. F. (1998). Transitioning marketing communication into the twenty-first century. *Journal of Marketing Communications, 4*(1), 9–26.

Stemler, S. (2018). Case Study: How Trusted Housesitters Collected Over 2,000 Boast Customer Testimonials Using a Contest, *Boast*, viewed: 24/11/2019: https://boast.io/case-study-how-trusted-housesitters-collected-over-2000-boast-customer-testimonials-using-a-contest/

Sutherland, K. E. (2015). Towards an integrated social media communication model for the not-for-profit sector: A case study of youth homelessness charities (Doctoral dissertation, Monash University).

Tuten, T. L., & Solomon, M. R. (2017). *Social media marketing.* Los Angeles, CA: Sage.

Valos, M. J., Haji Habibi, F., Casidy, R., Driesener, C. B., & Maplestone, V. L. (2016). Exploring the integration of social media within integrated marketing communication frameworks: Perspectives of services marketers. *Marketing Intelligence & Planning, 34*(1), 19–40.

West, C. (2019). 6 standout social media marketing examples for 2019, *Sprout Social*, viewed: 24/11/2019: https://sproutsocial.com/insights/social-media-marketing-examples/

Further Reading

Social Media Strategy

Freberg, K. (2018b). *Social Media for Strategic Communication: Creative strategies and Research-Based Applications.* SAGE Publications.

Kim, C. M. (2016b). *Social media campaigns: Strategies for public relations and marketing.* Routledge.

Quesenberry, K. A. (2015). *Social media strategy: Marketing and advertising in the consumer revolution.* Rowman & Littlefield.

Defining Goals

Chenn, J. (2018). How to create achievable social media goals, SproutSocial.com, viewed 29/07/2019: https://sproutsocial.com/insights/social-media-goals/

Newberry, C. (2019). How to set and reach social media goals (+ 10 types of goals to Track), Hootsuite.com, viewed 29/07/2019: https://blog.hootsuite.com/smart-social-media-goals/

SMART Objectives

Bjerke, M. B., & Renger, R. (2017). Being SMART about writing SMART objectives. *Evaluation and Program Planning, 61*, 125–127.

Heinze, A., Fletcher, G., Rashid, T., & Cruz, A. (2016). *Digital and social media marketing: A results-driven approach*. Routledge.

Key Messages

Harrison, K. (2019). How to create compelling key messages, Cuttingedgepr.com, viewed 29/07/2019: https://cuttingedgepr.com/free-articles/core-pr-skills/create-compelling-key-messages/

Theaker, A., & Yaxley, H. (2017). *The public relations strategic toolkit: An essential guide to successful public relations practice*. Routledge.

Budgets

Patel, N. (2019). Social media marketing on a budget: The 4-step approach that works, Neilpatel.com, viewed: https://neilpatel.com/blog/social-media-marketing-on-a-budget-the-4-step-approach-that-works/

Sehl, K. (2019). A social media budget breakdown for every size of business, Hootsuite.com, viewed 29/07/2019: https://blog.hootsuite.com/the-7-components-of-every-social-media-budget/

Helpful Links

Creating Key Messages https://www.youtube.com/watch?v=IEofKLKRP_U

How to Negotiate Price—While Keeping Customers Happy https://www.americanexpress.com/en-us/business/trends-and-insights/articles/negotiate-price-keeping-customers-happy/

How to Set Objectives, KPI's, and Key Supporting Messages https://www.youtube.com/watch?v=jbPr2ChKzcU

Quenseberry's (2019) Social Media Budget Template: http://www.postcontrolmarketing.com/wp-content/uploads/2018/05/SocialMediaBudget-Template.pdf

Social Media Marketing Strategy: Setting Social Media Goals https://www.youtube.com/watch?v=k65ukI5bh4g

Stop Selling, Start Helping: Prescribing Tactics to Win Over Target Audiences

Contents

K. E. Sutherland, *Strategic Social Media Management*, https://doi.org/10.1007/978-981-15-4658-7_6

By the End of This Chapter You Will
- Understand the importance of using tactics that provide value to a target audience.
- Develop skills to identify relevant tactics that connect with target audiences.
- Recognise that quality storytelling is the key to connecting with target audiences and must underpin all social media tactics.
- Understand why incorporating offline tactics and online events into a social media strategy build strong connections with a target audience
- Learn the broad categories of social media tactics and their general benefits and disadvantages.

for target audiences and encourages UGC and CCC.
- Selecting relevant tactics is a process that includes careful consideration of: Goals and SMART Objectives, budget, timeframe, analytics, current platform capabilities, secondary research, content pillars that align with the goals, SMART Objectives and audience personas and alignment to customer personas and journey stages.
- Broad tactic categories are: Paid, Organic and Offline. The pros and cons of each must also be considered during the tactic selection process.
- Content and the tactics must carry each other to victory.

TLDR
- Tactics are the actions that are undertaken to achieve the goals and SMART Objectives of a social media strategy. They are not *the entire* strategy. Each strategic element impacts the others.
- A Goal must be supported by at least two relevant SMART Objectives. At least three appropriate tactics must support each SMART Objective in a social media strategy.
- Social media tactics should focus on giving through problem-solving content rather than blatantly attempting to sell to the target audience at each stage of the customer journey (see ◙ Fig. 6.2).
- Quality storytelling that activates positive emotions creates tactics that connect with target audiences.
- Taking a propinquital approach to social media by including offline tactics and online events in a social media strategy builds deeper relationships with and memorable moments

6.1 Introduction

One chapter is not an ample length to discuss the complexity of social media tactics. In fact, an entire book could be written exploring the advantages, disadvantages and application of each tactic investigated in this chapter. With such a brief scope, it will be of greater benefit to provide guidance on the process of researching, innovating, selecting and implementing relevant tactics that connect with and convert a target audience.

Tactics come and go and can be as dependent on platform capabilities as they are influenced by trends and societal norms. Yet, understanding the fundamentals behind what makes tactics relevant and how quality storytelling must underpin every single one, is knowledge that will set you apart as a Social Media Manager.

One of the most important skills of social media management is the ability to keep moving with its evolution. While the window-dressing will continue to change, the people with whom you are trying to connect walking past the window will not. It is extremely important to stay abreast

6

of current industry trends and platform developments, however, the core strategic components that we have explored so far in ► Chaps. 3, 4 and 5 including a clients' or organisation's audience research, goals, SMART objectives and key messages must shape the lens through which you perceive these tactics, which is exactly what will be detailed in this chapter.

6.2 What Are Tactics?

First, it is important to clearly define what a tactic actually is. In its original meaning and use, the word 'tactic' was coined in the 1620s to describe: "science of arranging military forces for combat," (Etymonline.com, 2019). While literally applying the same meaning today would be taking social media to the extreme, this definition can be used as an analogy. Tactics are the actions that are undertaken to achieve the goals and SMART Objectives of a social media strategy. These activities are also the vehicles that deliver the key messages from a social media strategy to its target audience.

For example, a goal may be to increase online sales. A SMART Objective to support that goal may be to increase online sales by 10% within the next month. The tactics are the relevant social media activities that will help to achieve a 10% increase in online sales and ultimately support the overall goal of the strategy. One of these tactics may be a Facebook ad campaign with a discount offer targeted at people who were previously close to purchasing on the website but abandoned their cart. This book has guided you through the process of developing a social media strategy.

► Chapter 3 explored audience research, always the most important first stage of any strategy. ► Chapter 4 investigated ethics and what to do if events take a negative turn. ► Chapter 5 focused on the importance and development of goals, SMART objectives and key messages. Therefore, the next stage in strategic social media management is the identification, development and implementation of tactics.

When some think of strategy, their thoughts head straight to tactics, yet these actions are not *the* strategy. They are only part of the strategy. If a tactic does not help to support the achievement of goals or objectives, then it is a waste of time and usually money too, which is far from being strategic.

Remember, that the preceding steps of strategy development detailed in ► Chaps. 3 and 5 must inform the tactics that you will ultimately use. Furthermore, the tactics developed and implemented as part of a strategy will also guide the analytics to be monitored and measured to track conversation and performance as we will explore in ► Chap. 7 and the type of content that will need to be curated or created to execute them, detailed in ► Sections 2 and 3.

From the explanation thus far, two key concepts are clear:

1. *Tactics are identified and implemented at a later stage of the strategic process.* It is worth being aware of as many as possible, but generally only a few will be appropriate to support the specific needs of a client, their target audience and the overall social media strategy.

2. *Each strategic component impacts the others.* Therefore, it is essential for the success of the strategy to ensure that all parts of the strategy support the achievement of the others. The alternative will result in each component working in isolation which will erode the strategy's ability to achieve its overall goal.

◘ Figure 6.1. Conveys the structure of a social media strategy as we have explored so far throughout this text. Tactics are placed at the bottom of the pyramid because they are the actions that must support the achievement of all other components. This does not mean that they are the most important part of a strategy.

◻ Fig. 6.1 Model of the Components of a Social Media Strategy

Every component has an integral function. The broad base representing tactics is due to the number of tactics required to adequately support the achievement of the other components.

As detailed in ▶ Chap. 5, for a basic social media strategy it is advised not to identify more than one or two goals. This so that there is a clear focus on what the strategy is aiming for and that all efforts can be concentrated on achieving it. Next, each goal needs 2–3 SMART objectives so that there are specific targets articulated to help support the achievement of each goal. Just as we use a range of methods when researching, approaching a goal using more than one SMART objective helps to support its success by attacking the goal from different angles.

In ▶ Chap. 5 we also discussed the importance of key messages and how three (including at least one call-to-action) are enough to avoid confusion with the target audience and increase the probability that they will be remembered. However, the tactical component needs to be stable, therefore, it is recommended to use at least three relevant tactics to support each SMART Objective.

6.2.1 Tactics: There Is Strength in Numbers

There is strength in numbers and each tactic adds greater support to the achievement of the SMART objectives and in turn, the goal.

A strategy with only one SMART Objective to support its goal and only one tactic to support its SMART Objective is as sturdy as a house of cards in the wind. If the tactic does not work, the entire strategy will fall over resulting in the goal not being achieved. As you will soon discover in your role as a Social Media Manager, not every tactic will work for a client or organisation every time, therefore it is essential to have a range of tactics to support any that fail.

As explored in ▶ Chap. 5 sound planning can help to identify and minimise risks before issues turn into crises and this proactive approach also applies to the development of tactics. Never place the entire success of a campaign on the performance of one tactic. Spread that risk. As a Social Media Manager, you will fail at times, that is the nature of the profession, but how much and how damaging these failures will depend on how well you preempt and prepare for them.

The audience journey is one of the most important considerations when devising tactics to support a social media strategy (as detailed in ▶ Chap. 3). Remember, social media is a tool to cultivate and manage long-term relationships. By focusing on relationship-building rather than selling, trust will grow between a client's brand or organisation and its customers.

6.2.2 Without Trust There Is No Relationship

Trust is required before any meaningful transaction can ever take place. As public relations scholars Heath and Coombs (2006, p. 237) explain, "Trust is earned, it is not granted. It is earned by what organizations do and say."

Every attempt to communicate and connect with current and prospective customers should be approached as an opportunity to build trust, including the development and implementation of social media tactics.

Achieving this can occur by simply placing the needs of a client or organisation's target audience ahead of your own by focusing on giving rather than receiving.

6.3 Social Media Tactics: Focus on Giving Instead of Receiving

> **Social Media:**
> Stop Selling. **Start Helping**
>
> Dr Karen Sutherland

6

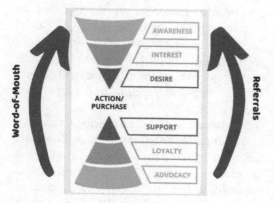

Fig. 6.2 The AIDASLA Model (Balinas, 2019)

Gary Vaynerchuk (2013) best describes this approach to social media tactics and content with the phrase: "Jab, jab, jab, right hook." By this Vaynerchuk is not trying to incite violence. Instead he is suggesting that social media tactics should be aimed at trying to engage with a target audience to build an emotional connection (signified by a jab), and that blatant selling and self-promotion should be kept to a minimum. This makes perfect sense when revisiting the customer journey explored in ▶ Chap. 3 (see ▣ Fig. 6.2 The AIDASLA Model (Balinas, 2019)).

The *Awareness, Interest and Desire* stages of the customer journey must be treated

with absolute care and respect if a prospective customer is going to progress through to the Action/Purchase stage.

The most strategic (and logical) way to do this is to focus on the needs of the customer rather than aggressively pushing a client or an organisation's products and services in an attempt to propel the prospective customer to the Action/Purchase stage before they are ready.

6.3.1 IBM Increase Sales by 400% Using Social Media Content and Employee Advocacy

IBM used social media to increase their sales by 400%, but this significant rise was not a result of aggressive marketing tactics (Vangala, 2012).

The company focused on LinkedIn as its main platform throughout the campaign as it had greater relevance as a professional networking community.

The company empowered staff from across the organisation to become brand advocates.

This coordinated effort involved participants sourcing and sharing content of relevance with the target audience and using it to attract leads and enquiries (rather than resorting to push marketing).

Facilitating employees from across the company to be brand advocates was highly successful for IBM because it allowed people outside of the marketing and sales departments to leverage their existing professional networks to provide value to new groups of people that may not have been reached using traditional marketing and advertising techniques.

Remember, the target audience is the hero/ine of their story and your role is as their guide, to help them through the different stages on their journey. The tactics that you develop, and implement must provide value to the target audience to position a client or organisation as a credible and trustworthy problem-solver.

This is what Vaynerchuk (2013) means with his phrase: "jab, jab, jab, right hook." Vaynerchuk recommends giving to an audience at least three times before asking them to do anything in return.

Providing problem solving information for free will not stop people from paying for services. It tends to have the opposite effect. **Sharing knowledge to help a target audience demonstrates:**
- *Expertise*
- *An understanding of the challenges faced by the target audience*
- *A focus on customer service*
- *Generosity*

Using problem-solving content to support specific tactics is an effective way to build trust and credibility with a target audience. It indicates commitment to a long-term professional relationship where the prospective (or current) customer feels valued, not just a stranger to whom you are trying to persuade to buy your products.

Yet, what is problem-solving content? This is social media content of any form that demonstrates an understanding of the challenges faced by a target audience and provides practical and relevant advice to assist them in overcoming that challenge.

For example, social media managers with real estate agents as clients have a wealth of problem-solving content that they can produce. Customer challenges generally become apparent after going through the audience research stage of strategy development (see ▶ Chap. 3).

Customer personas for a real estate agency may include first-home buyers, expanding families, property investors and downsizers. These are all prospective customers of a real estate agency, but each will face their own distinct set of challenges through the customer journey that can be addressed and supported through the development and implementation of tactics that deliver helpful content.

Identifying helpful information can be as simple as creating content that answers the questions most commonly asked by customers as well as plotting the customer's journey and researching the information that they will need at each stage.

For example, first home buyers may need to know the following information:
- How much deposit is required?
- How to select the best mortgage.
- The process involved with buying a home.
- What to look for in their first home.
- What is conveyancing and how to find a quality conveyancer.

Creating content that provides valuable information around these topics without shamelessly selling to this target audience positions the real estate agent as knowledgeable and helpful. It helps to keep the real estate agent top-of-mind until the time when the first home buyer begins looking at property.

Top-of-mind is a marketing term that means a business or brand is the first one that a current or prospective customer considers when they are heading into the Desire phase (see ◘ Fig. 6.2) (Wilson, 2019). Your aim as a Social Media Manager is to ensure that a client or organisation is in pole position at the time when a target audience is ready to complete the action that you are aiming for, a purchase, donation, registration etc.).

In the case of a first home buyer, reading content from a real estate agent that has helped to inform them about the process may result in the first home buyer viewing the real estate agent's listings first, because some level of trust and positive association with the agency has been established through this content.

6.3.2 What Is 'Pull Marketing'?

Focusing tactics on giving to a target audience rather than receiving does not mean that helpful information to be given freely in all situations or that above-the-line marketing such as advertising should never be used. On the contrary, helpful content is a tactic to attract customers, also known as "pull marketing" (Schultz, 2017).

Once a member from the target audience contacts a client or organisation they are also known as a "lead" or a person worth following up with because they have shown enough of an interest in a brand's products or services to initiate contact (Hill et al., 2017).

This interaction must also be treated with care and sensitivity. Every prospective customer is different. Again, it is important for customer service staff to ascertain the person's needs before blatantly trying to sell to them. Some prospective customers may be ready to buy, but others may want to speak to someone to ask further questions.

Some leads may be in the Purchase/Action stage of the customer journey, but others may still be in the Interest or Desire stages. It is important for customer service staff to gauge where each lead is in their customer journey to avoid ruining your good work as a Social Media Manager in attracting the target audience to initiate contact with the business or organisation.

6.3.3 Client Confusion with Problem-Solving Content

The concept of creating problem solving content can be met with confusion and fear from some clients. They are generally worried that by giving advice away for free that people will then refuse to pay for it. If you experience resistance from clients in this respect, reassure them that your content provides general advice.

While each target audience (and customer persona) will have their own set of challenges, each individual will also require customised advice tailored to address their own unique situations. It is this customised advice that customers must pay for. Problem solving social media content is used to encourage the target audience to trust a client or organisation enough to pay for their knowledge or expertise to solve their specific personal problem.

This is how focusing on giving rather than receiving generally results in reciprocation from a target audience over the longer term. The key is to be patient and commitment to the relationship and the long game by consistently providing value to a target audience through the use of "pull" marketing tactics and content (Schultz, 2017).

6.3.4 What Is 'Push Marketing'?

Advertising is often described as "push marketing" because it utilises tactics that blatantly push a product or service to its current and prospective customers (Schultz, 2017). While it is strongly encouraged to avoid blatantly trying to sell, particularly throughout the early stages of the customer journey, advertising has a valuable place as a tactic in a social media strategy.

However, just as Vaynerchuk (2013) included only one right hook in his sequence, signifying that selling or advertising or asking for some form of action from the target audience should only be used as a tactic around 25% of the time.

That means that 75% of tactics and content should focus on giving with that final right hook being the push to inspire the target audience to convert into being a customer (or repeat customer). This could be in the form of an advertisement for a special offer such as free postage or a 10% discount on a purchase adding a little extra incentive and to convince the target audience to move from the Desire stage to the Action/Purchase stage.

6.3.5 Too Much Too Soon

Imagine targeting the audience with tactics such as these at the Awareness stage. This would be too soon. The target audience would not know or trust a client or organisation's brand, product or service and this could result in losing their attention from the outset. As a Social Media Manager, you have only one opportunity to make a first impression. Therefore, it is important to treat it with the care and respect that it deserves by building trust and relationships by focusing on giving rather than receiving and only using push tactics once that trust has been established.

6.3.6 Customer Focus Continues Even After a Purchase

The focus on giving should not end once the target audience makes a purchase. In fact, this is a crucial time where as a Social Media Manager you can use tactics and content to help a customer feel really positive about their purchase so that when they are ready, demonstrate their loyalty with a repeat purchase and even share their positive experiences with a client or organisation's brand and/or products with others within their network.

Navigating customers through these stages of Support, Loyalty and Advocacy also takes time and care. Often charities damage donor relationships by asking for a further donation too quickly after the last one instead of taking the time to communicate with the donor about the positive impact their donation has made without requesting anything else.

One cannot assume that just because someone from the target audience has performed the action the social media strategy was developed to achieve, such as purchasing a product, that they will automatically do it again. Any long-term relationship takes ongoing attention, effort and care. It is also risky to assume that a repeat customer is going to purchase any new product or service launched by a client or organisation without first taking them through the steps of *Awareness, Interest, Desire and Action.*

> 66 Ongoing loyalty should never be assumed and repeat customers should never be taken for granted. 99
>
> Dr Karen Sutherland

6

It can cost five times more to attract new customers than retain existing ones and increasing customer retention rates by 5% can increase the profits of a business by 25–95% (Reichheld, 2001; Saleh, 2019).

It literally pays to develop and implement tactics and content that continue to foster a long-term relationship with existing customers as well as attracting new clientele.

Now that the importance of giving to target audiences through problem-solving tactics and content has been established, we must delve even deeper to explore the core of developing and implementing tactics and content that truly connect with target audiences.

While the focus is on giving more than receiving, quality storytelling is the vehicle that will break down any barriers between a client or organisation and the target audience to allow relationship building to begin or continue.

6.4 Quality Storytelling Creates Tactics that Connect

Humans make sense of the world through stories. We construct our own and we feel a sense of connection when we listen to the stories of others (Widrich, 2012). The connective power of stories is so strong that scientists have discovered when we are being told a story not only do the language processing parts of our brain become activated any other area in our brain that we would use when experiencing the events of the story are activated too (Widrich, 2012).

This means that if I shared with you a personal story of being heartbroken, the part of the brain where you would normally feel the emotions associated with those feelings would be activated.

Or, if I described in detail a delicious meal that I cooked and ate, the part of the brain associated with food would also be activated.

This is evidence that quality storytelling is a powerful connector and truly the most effective way to build a relationship with target audiences through social media tactics and content.

Sometimes Social Media Managers place less emphasis on the storytelling aspect of their tactics and content than on the technical aspects of their client's or organisation's strategy development and implementation.

All factors are important. As a Social Media Manager, you may have developed the most technically sound strategy, but if the tactics and content do not connect with the people that you are trying to reach, the goals of the strategy will not be achieved. This is why quality storytelling is an essential skill of not only social media management, but for anyone attempting to communicate effectively.

Storytelling does not mean fabricating information to manipulate a target audience. To do so is highly unethical and against the core principles and practices that we explored in ▶ Chap. 4. The process of storytelling involves the construction of information in a particular order and using language, verbal and visual cues to convey a sequence of events and/or knowledge in ways that are both meaningful and understandable to the people with whom you are attempting to connect.

Stories themselves can be simple or extremely complex. Consider an epic tale such as Harry Potter which had an overarching story that tied together the multiple episodes and adventures contained within each novel.

Effective stories have eight different components that help to convey their meaning to audiences. If any of these elements are missing, the result can be a story that is challenging to understand or that does not resonate positively with the audience that it is attempting to connect with. ◘ Table 6.1 explains the necessary components of a story.

Story component	Description
Setting	The location where the story takes place.
Character	The main person, animal or personalised objective (think Toy Story) who drives the action of the story. When it comes to social media content, a target audience should be positioned as the hero/ine of their own story and a client or organisation is the helpful guide to lead them to success.
Plot	The events and actions that take place throughout the story.
Conflict	The challenge and/or tension that the main character/s must overcome. A story cannot exist without conflict.
Theme	The overall purpose of the story. What overarching statement is the story trying to make? This is the moral of the story; the most important point that the storyteller is trying to convey to the audience.
Point-of-view	From whose perspective is the story being told? Is it the main character, a narrator or someone else? Does the point-of-view shift throughout the story?
Tone	This is the lens through which the story is being conveyed. It could be light-hearted or sad. It could be humorous or serious and melodramatic.
Style	Style relates to the way in which a story is told. For example, the types of language used, word choice and the voice of the storyteller.

◻ **Table 6.1** Necessary story components

When considering these story elements, it is evident how each adds a layer of meaning to help the audience to understand exactly what is trying to be conveyed. Imagine a story without a main character or conflict. It would be far from compelling and would not provide the audience with any reason to pay attention.

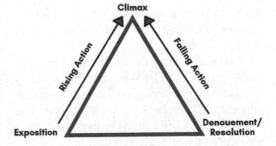

◻ **Fig. 6.3** Freytag's Pyramid Story Structure

6.4.1 The Importance of Story Structure

Quality storytelling involves these eight components and a solid structure. A basic story structure, called Freytag's Pyramid (see ◻ Fig. 6.3) is commonly used to guide the plot of books, movies, plays, social media content and even campaigns and has been proven to be a highly effective form of storytelling.

This story structure was first published by Gustav Freytag in 1863 and has stood the test of time. In fact, a recent content analysis of 155 viral advertising videos found that average shares and views were higher for videos with full story development using four of five points from the Freytag's Pyramid dramatic structure 1872 (Quesenberry & Coolsen, 2019).

Table 6.2   Description of Freytag's Pyramid plot points

Freytag's Pyramid plot points	Description
Exposition	This is the beginning of the story where the storytelling must establish the setting, introduce the characters and provide some information about the upcoming conflict or challenge to be overcome
Rising action	Next, the tension experienced by the main character/s must build with force. Generally, the main protagonist must overcome a series of obstacles that help the tension and conflict to build to a crescendo
Climax	The climax is where the conflict, tension and action come to a head and the main character/s are forced to fight or address everything and everyone that they have been trying to avoid This is the turning point of the story (for better or for worse) and is where the most significant moment of action takes place
Falling action	Falling action is where the conflict from the climax begins to resolve, but there remains some tension or smaller challenge that still needs to be overcome
Denouement/ resolution	The final act where the loose ends of the story are generally all resolved

Figure 6.3 demonstrates that at its very basic level, Freytag's Pyramid has five different points at which the story action needs to progress in order to reach its conclusion. Table 6.2 explains what each story point means.

Pullman (2008) deconstructed the well-known story of 'The Wizard of Oz' to demonstrate how Freytag's Pyramid works in actuality. Table 6.3 explains how 'The Wizard of Oz' fits within the five-point story structure of Freytag's Pyramid.

While there were many other events that occurred in the Wizard of Oz, the ones included in Table 6.3 explain the main plot points that drive the action through the structure of Freytag's Pyramid to the conclusion.

While this structure may seem predictable, it is the basis for countless stories conveyed on a wide range of mediums. As the eight elements of stories are rarely the same, each story can be unique despite it having the same underlying structure.

Table 6.3   The Wizard of Oz's dramatic structure according to Freytag's Pyramid

Freytag's Pyramid plot point	Story action from the Wizard of Oz
Exposition	Dorothy and main characters and conflict are introduced.
Rising action	Dorothy arrives in Oz, kills one witch, angers the other one, receives the ruby slippers and travels to the Emerald City with the Lion, Scarecrow, and Tinman.
Climax	Dorothy melts the witch and seizes her broomstick.
Falling action	The Lion, Scarecrow and Tinman all receive the gifts they were hoping for, but Dorothy cannot return home.
Denouement/ resolution	Dorothy eventually makes it home.

6.4.2 Effective Stories Activate Emotions

Truly effective stories touch our emotions. They make us feel a connection with the main characters and their experiences. This connection occurs because we identify with their story in some way.

Narrative structures used in advertisements have also been found to induce positive emotions in target audiences that lead to action (Chang, 2012; Escalas, 2004). Berger (2016) recommends shifting the focus from relaying features facts and figures to focusing on feelings, because it is emotion that can be more effective in inspiring people to act.

6.4.3 Document, Don't Create

For example, imagine that a client is a caravan mechanic. Developing tactics and content around caravan repairs may not be the most engaging approach to connect with the target audience.

Instead, focusing on what it means to an owner to have a fully functioning caravan will have a much greater emotional impact. Sharing stories about fun family holidays, travel, adventure and making memories as a result of a functioning caravan are more effective ways to activate emotions with the target audience.

Vaynerchuk (2018, p.79) suggests: "Document. Don't Create." By this Vaynerchuk means that it is a more effective strategy to tell the stories of real people than to share fictional ones. In the case of the caravan mechanic, sharing the story of a customer who had a great experience with your client's company and later with their family holidaying in their caravan would evoke more of an emotional response than using paid actors or having a client telling their customer's story.

An emotional centre can be identified within any product and service, although some are easier to find than others. The trick is to dig deep and aim to perceive the product or service from a range of different perspectives and motivations for why customers choose it.

Focus on the problem that the product or service can solve but delve even deeper to identify what having this problem eradicated this will mean to the life of a client's or organisation's customers and to their friends and family members. It is important to include factual information where relevant, but this must be communicated using a story that activates emotion.

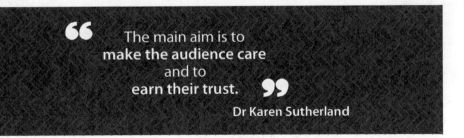

> ❝ The main aim is to make the audience care and to earn their trust. ❞
>
> Dr Karen Sutherland

6.4.4 Not All Emotions Should Be Activated

Storytelling can be an extremely powerful tactic if it connects the target audience's emotions to a client's brand, product or service, but it can also backfire if not utilised in a sensitive way. A major finding from my PhD research exploring social media and charities was that the use of guilt-provoking tactics repelled people from the content and the organisation rather than encouraging them to give (Sutherland, 2015).

Similarly, using stories that aim to generate fear or anger in order to sell a product or service generally only work in the short term if they ever work at all. Remember, that someone's social media feed is a sacred space to them. It's a place where people like to catch up with friends and family and have a positive experience.

6.4.5 Use Less of the Before and More of the After

Using emotional manipulation through storytelling is an extremely risky move and may also be construed as being unethical. For example, in my research, donors and volunteers said that they wanted: "*less of the before and more of the after*" (Sutherland, 2015). What they meant was they wanted charities to stop trying to make them feel guilty about people in need. Instead, they wanted to hear the stories of the lives that charities had transformed as part of their work.

These stories of positive transformation inspired them to act. It was not that they were insensitive to people in need, but they wanted evidence from the charities about the people that they had already assisted. It is a similar case with fear.

Trying to scare a target audience into buying a product because of what may happen if they do not make the purchase can be a recipe for disaster. Instead, focus on how their life will be changed for the better by buying the product. Share the stories of real people who have genuinely experienced these improvements. Again, the aim is to connect with an audience on a deep emotional level to build trust and leave them feeling positive about a client's brand, product or service.

This does not mean that only happy stories are worth sharing. Target audiences respond in a much more positive way when a personal story of sadness or trauma can be transformed into a tale of inspiration. A great example is the story behind an Australian product called 'Bakslap,' a sunscreen lotion applicator that helps people to protect themselves from the sun.

Creator, Raph McGowan (See ◪ Fig. 6.4) was inspired to create the product after the tragic loss of his sister, Tess, to melanoma. Only focusing on the tragedy that Raph and his family experienced would activate the emotions of his target audience. Yet, shifting the focus from personal tragedy to Raph's mission to "...help reduce skin cancer rates globally" leaves the audience in a positive space, ready to be inspired to engage with him, his brand and his product (Bakslap, 2019).

Stories of positive transformation (overcoming adversity, shifting from darkness to light) can be the keys that unlock inspiration, and action from a target audience. In ▶ Section 3 we will explore the different production elements that work together within social media content to communicate powerful stories that evoke the emotions of the target audience.

6.5 Create Deeper Audience Connection with Offline Tactics and Online Events

Clearly, stories can be extremely effective in connecting with a target audience on an emotional level to inspire action. However,

Fig. 6.4 Image of Raph McGowan and Bakslap

offline events can be powerful tactics to deepen relationships and create long-lasting memories between people and a brand, product or organisation. Communicating face-to-face has traditionally been heralded as the most effective form of communication (Esposito et al., 2007).

When people attend an event in person, they use their senses to experience their surroundings, the sights, sounds, smells and objects. They can interact with the people there face-to-face and communicate in real-time with body language and other non-verbal cues all adding to their sense-making. It is these offline experiences that help people to construct their own stories in relation to their feelings, thoughts and attitudes about the situation.

While social media content and online interaction can be a highly effective way to connect with a client's or organisation's target audience, including some form of offline tactic in a social media strategy can deepen that connection by adding another relationship dimension through memory-making via in-person experiences.

Marketing literature often refers to the use of offline tactics as "experiential marketing". This is where a brand message is combined with live interactive moments for a target audience in real time. Smith and Hanover (2016, p. 2) describe offline tactics

as "…nothing more than a highly evolved form of corporate storytelling," and they are correct.

Yet, instead of the target audience consuming the story as they would generally with social media content, they are also participating in the story first-hand. An offline experience also provides the opportunity for the target audience to share their own experience of the event via social media.

However, in a post COVID-19 world, offline events have been required to be re-engineered to accommodate social distancing requirements or completely reimagined into online environments using video conferencing tools such as Zoom, Facebook Rooms, Google Meet, Skype, Facebook and Instagram Live. While online events may not generate the same sensorial impacts as offline experiences, they can still provide a form of face-to-face interaction that helps to develop positive memories and associations between a brand and a target audience. As such, online events should definitely be considered as part of a social media strategy if offline events cannot be organised. Please see ▶ Chap. 16 for more information regarding video conferencing tools.

A great example of this is from Theatre Unleashed, a Los Angeles-based theatre company who performed a play via Zoom when their opening night was postponed due to the COVID-19 lockdown (Melendez, 2020). This event allowed people from all over the world to attend, creating a positive experience for fans and those newly acquainted with the company.

6.5.1 Justifying Online and Offline Events as Tactics to Clients

It can be challenging for a Social Media Manager to justify to their clients the need for online and offline events as a tactic in a social media strategy. The best way to position it in a social media context is the event is a tactic to spark user-generated-content (UGC) within a relatively controlled brand experience such an event. Positive UGC is extremely valuable to a brand or organisation, because it is an endorsement from somebody independent, and this holds much greater weight than any social media content originating from the business. This is why online customer reviewers have such a strong influence on consumer purchasing decisions (Filieri, Alguezaui, & McLeay, 2015; Matute, Polo-Redondo, & Utrillas, 2016). That makes perfect sense. Hearing someone else's experiences who has used a product or service seems to possess much greater legitimacy than the brand itself trying to convince me how good it is.

UGC can be also categorised as a practical example of co-creation theory, an approach that is being used successfully by some of the world's leading brands including: Pepsi, Dell and Contiki (Noonan, 2018; Ouschan, Turkington, & Napoli, 2019). Co-creation theory in action can be described as the instance when, "…brand meaning and value(s) emerge from stakeholder engagement with a company," (Hatch & Schultz, 2010, p. 591). In addition to UGC, content created and shared by users on their own channels, Co-Created Content (CCC) is content created by users but shared by the

brand on its official channels (Fujita, Harrigan, & Soutar, 2019). However, some degree of overlap can exist on the UGC and CCC continuum. For example, if a brand creates a story filter for an event and it is posted by a user on their personal profile. While user has posted the content on their own channels, the brand has created part of it. Nevertheless, the most important aspect is that a member of the target audience is creating positive content and posting it about a brand, which is a key aim and benefit from including events in a social media strategy. Both approaches to co-creation (UGC and CCC) can be extremely effective in increasing the target audience's connection with the overall brand story, the brand itself and the community of existing brand fans through collaboration and relationship building (Kozinets et al., 2010).

6.5.2 Blending Social Media and Offline Events

Creating opportunities for positive UGC and CCC is a bi-product of including online and offline events as a tactic in a social media strategy. The most important focus in terms of event tactics is on the building and further strengthening of relationships with target audiences.

A theoretical approach to the blending of social media and offline spaces is called a propinquital loop (Sutherland, 2016; Sutherland et al., 2018). This approach to social media recommends using social media as a bridge to strengthen relationships with current and prospective customers in-between face-to-face interactions.

The theory was developed from a component of Dialogic and Relationship Management theories from public relations literature (Kent & Taylor, 2002; Taylor & Kent, 2014). ◘ Figure 6.5 demonstrates a model of the propinquital loop.

6.5 · Create Deeper Audience Connection with Offline Tactics and Online...

119

6

◘ Fig. 6.5 Propinquital Loop

What is important to note is that a propinquital loop occurs when social media interactions between brands and current and prospective customers are encouraged (and supported) in moving back and forth between social media and offline spaces on a regular basis.

This movement creates a loop of activity that can have several benefits. Firstly, it means that the target audience remains in close proximity to the brand on a regular basis, the brand, its products and services have a greater chance of remaining top-of-mind and the regular positive face-to-face interaction will continue to deepen the relationship between target audience, the brand and the people behind it.

The key to the success of a propinquital loop is to ensure that there are drivers in each space to propel activity back to the other. Drivers refer to calls-to-action. In marketing and public relations, a call-to-action is a direct request to the target audience to perform a specific behaviour such as "register now for our event" or "share a one-minute video about your experience and don't forget to tag us" (Tuten & Solomon, 2017).

There will be greater exploration of calls-to-action in ► Chap. 7. It is essential to guide people through the propinquital loop and to give them great incentives and rewards for doing so. It is of paramount importance to show the target audience how much you value and appreciate their engagement with a brand. This could be achieved through competitions, special offers or even simple shout outs to say thank you. The target audience will not care about you unless it is clear

that you care about them. That is relationship management at its most basic level.

The frequency of the propinquital cycle will depend on the budget, time and geographic location of a client or organisation, but it is recommended to have at least one major offline event every year with some smaller events at regular intervals.

Having regular events will only increase UGC and CCC and add greater depth to relationships. Offline tactics should follow the same principles already explored in this chapter and include drivers that move audience activity back to social media channels in a meaningful way.

Ensure that offline tactics:

— *Are Problem-Solving:* Have a specific purpose that aligns with the goals of the strategy. For example, a menswear fashion store that holds nights to teach men how to coordinate outfits and tie a Windsor knot.

— *Include the Necessary Story Elements:* Setting, Character, Plot, Conflict, Theme, Point-of-view, Tone, and Style all help to provide a target audience with a richer sensory and ultimately memorable experience. Remember, the event attendees must be the central characters of the story.

— *Follow Freytag's Pyramid:* Have clear stages of the event: Beginning, Rising Action to the Event Climax and then wind down to the Event Close. It is essential to build positive tension, suspense in the lead up to the Event Climax so that those attending feel like a main character in the event story.

6

- *Encourage the Target Audience to Share their Story:* Provide incentives for the target audience to document and share their experience at the event through their social channels.

Have scenes set up that look great in photos and are selfie and "Insta-worthy", ensure that a client's social handles and hashtags are highly visible, provide calls-to-action as part of the event, give prizes to the highly engaged.

- *Are Documented to Share on a Client's Channels:* It is important to share the event on a client's official social media channels. Have a photographer present and ask people to tag themselves when you post the images.

Have someone sharing live content from the event. For example, sharing Stories, Live Video (if appropriate), Live Tweeting etc. so that target audience members who could not attend can still be there virtually.

Adopting a propinquital approach to social media tactics is highly recommended as detailed in this chapter, but time and careful planning is required to make sure that target audiences have only positive experiences to share about a client or organisation's brand on social media and offline.

6.5.3 Social Media Amplifies

Social media is an amplifier, so clearly the aim is to provide the best experience possible to a target audience (Addyson-Zhang, 2018). The Twitter post featuring the sad cheese sandwich from the Fyre Festival not only went viral but has been lodged in the memory banks of millions despite the image actually being of a staff member's lunch not that of an event attendee (Rose, 2017).

If you are new to event management, start small, stay relevant and keep it simple. Seek assistance from people with more expe-

rience and please read the Further Reading section at the end of this chapter for helpful information on event management.

With the fundamental components of tactics understood, it is important to explore the process involved with selecting the most relevant tactics to suit a target audience that also align with client or organisational needs.

6.6 How to Select Relevant Tactics for a Target Audience

Tactics bear the greatest weight of a social media strategy in achieving its goals and objectives, so careful consideration must be used in their selection. ◘ Table 6.4 suggests a series of steps and information that should be considered when selecting relevant tactics to connect with a target audience.

Tactics for each audience persona should support each:
- Content Pillar
- Customer Journey Stage
- Goal, and
- SMART Objective

Furthermore, each stage of the customer journey should have three tactics to support it to increase the probability that people will be inspired to move through these stages.

It is also helpful to you and a client or organisation to include your rationale for selecting each tactic and to provide evidence for doing so.

This adds further credibility to your decisions as a Social Media Manager, keeps you accountable and provides justification for the tactics that you have chosen.

6.7 Test, Monitor and Refine

Selecting and implementing tactics is never a case of 'set and forget'. As a Social Media Manager, the implementation of any social media tactic should be approached as an

Table 6.4 Areas of consideration when selecting relevant tactics for a social media strategy

Area of consideration	Description
Goals and SMART objectives	It is essential to revisit the goals and SMART objectives of the strategy (see ▶ Chap. 5) to ensure that all tactics selected support their achievement
Budget	A client's or organisation's budget will dictate the level and scope of the tactics that can be selected and implemented as part of the strategy The budget (or lack of) will determine the level of paid advertising that can be implemented and whether professional photographers and videographers can be used to create content
Timeframe	The time-frame available to implement the strategy will influence the types of tactics that you will have the time necessary to include. Some tactics require a longer time period to prepare for and execute than others It is important to be realistic about what you can deliver within the time frame expected by a client *It is important to always under-promise and over-deliver*
Analytics	As explored in ▶ Chaps. 3 and 7, social media listening, monitoring and performance measurement data must inform every decision made as part of a social media strategy, especially in relation to tactics Even a simple analysis of what has worked (and failed) in the past will help in tactic selection. Select tactics that have proven to work well with existing followers if that is who you are attempting to connect with and avoid tactics that have not worked so well before. Also, understanding the conversations of a target audience and the problems and challenges they experience will also help guide relevant tactic selection
Current platform capabilities	▶ Chapter 3 explored selecting social media platforms relevant to the target audience. When choosing tactics, it is vital to have an in-depth understanding of the current features and capabilities of these platforms. Social media platforms change constantly so it is important to know what a platform can and cannot do as this knowledge will guide how you will use it to reach the target audience.
Secondary research	Desktop research can also be extremely helpful in identifying (or inspiring) the most effective tactics for a social media strategy In your investigation it is beneficial to include: 　Expert commentary (blogs, podcasts, videos etc.) 　Competitors' social media activities 　Tactics used by similar businesses 　Current trends It is not advisable to apply another brand's tactics directly to a client's target audience Every target audience is different. However, use this research to gain a greater insight into what is out there and use it as the spark to generate your own innovations
Content pillars that align with the goals, SMART objectives and audience personas.	Content pillars can best be described as the key themes that help to communicate a client's or organisation's key messages but will be of value to the target audience Using the previous example of a first home buyer, the content pillars may be: Pre-Purchase, Purchase and Post-Purchase with a number of relevant sub-topics within each pillar that provide valuable information and incentive to engage with the Real Estate Agent providing the information It is helpful to create these in the tactic development stage for a more streamlined transition into the content creation phase (see ▶ Section 3)

(continued)

Table 6.4 (continued)

Area of consideration	Description
Alignment to customer personas and journey stages	Revisit the Customer Personas developed in ▶ Chap. 3 and ensure that the tactics being selected align with each persona. For example, developing a long-form YouTube video for a busy working mother would not align well with someone who is time-poor It is also important to devise and implement tactics that inspire the target audience to move through to the next stage of their journey. Please see ☐ Table 6.5 which is an example template of how to plot out the tactics in this way A copy of this template is also available in the Appendices The distribution of tactics aligned with audience stages, content pillars and audience personas may seem complicated, but it ensures a solid and well-supported strategy

6

Table 6.5 Social media tactic alignment

Customer Persona: Customer Journey Stage: e.g. Awareness			
Goal supported:			
Tactic description	SMART objective supported:	Content Pillar	Rationale
1.			
2.			
3.			

experiment that must be closely monitored and refined when required.

A great example of this is with Facebook advertising where AB testing can determine the creative and text out for two different advertisements that attracts the greatest amount of engagement from the target audience.

The best performing ad is then selected and implemented on a larger scale (see ▶ Section 3). ▶ Chapter 7 will explain the process of social media monitoring and measurement.

The beauty of social media is that underperforming tactics can be easily identified if monitored closely, then tweaked and refined before they veer too far off track. Simple tactical adjustments can make a huge differ-

ence to the overall performance of the strategy, saving precious time and money and increasing their support to achieve the goals and SMART objectives.

Therefore, Social Media Managers must be attentive and vigilant throughout all stages of strategy development and implementation to be in a position to guide its success.

6.8 Tactic Categories

As mentioned previously in this chapter, specific tactics change over time along with the evolution of social media platforms and societal norms. It will be of greater benefit to understand the broader categories of social media tactics available and the pros and cons of the generic tactics that fall within each.

☐ Table 6.6 contains this information. Please note that this is not an exhaustive list and there will be omissions. The purpose of

Table 6.6 Social media tactic categories and their pros and cons

Organic tactics

Definition
Organic tactics are those that do not require payment to a social media platform or influencer to increase their reach to a target audience.
However, it is inaccurate to assume that organic tactics are completely free from cost when considering the time and resources required to deliver them.

Pros:
Less expensive than paid tactics.
Less intrusive than advertisements.
Places strong focus on producing quality content to attract engagement.

Cons:
Organic reach is extremely limited.
The content must be of an extremely high standard to achieve even a decent level of reach.
Engagement tactics to improve reach can take considerable time and effort

Tactic type	Pros	Cons
Posts with images	Perform better than posts using only text.	A basic level of photography and graphic design skills and required to produce content that cuts through on newsfeeds.
Video posts	Achieves excellent reach and engagement on most platforms. Helps the audience connect with the brand and characters in the video.	Either a healthy budget or video production skills and equipment/software are required.
Stories	Facebook, Instagram, and Snapchat Stories are easy to create using a smartphone and can achieve excellent levels of reach. Can be shared from Instagram to Facebook.	Can be confusing at first and time consuming when trying to juggle multiple tasks.
Hashtags	Can increase the reach of content on Instagram, Twitter, LinkedIn, Facebook and YouTube without cost. Can be created specifically for a client's brand, product or service. Can be used to increase exposure in local areas.	Can be overused and considered spammy.
Engagement	Using social media platforms to genuinely engage with a target audience through comments and messages can increase reach and build strong relationships.	Genuine engagement is time consuming and can take considerable effort. However, the benefits are worth it.
Blogging	An effective channel to share longer pieces on topics to a niche audience. Free to create if writing them yourself. A free way to drive traffic to a client's website. Helps with SEO.	Can be time consuming to research, write and/or edit.

(continued)

6

Table 6.6 (continued)		
Content curation	A cost-free way to share content that is created by someone else. (Please see ▶ Section 2).	Can raise issues with plagiarism and copyright if not approached correctly. (Please see ▶ Section 2). Can be time-consuming to curate relevant content. Can be viewed as lazy if overused.
Groups	Creating and facilitating a community of enthusiasts around a client's brand. Builds relationships with and between members of the target audience through group interactions. Can be an inexpensive way to interact with supportive and loyal members of the target audience and encourage regular advocacy. Build positive brand associations for the target audience through your efforts in managing a relevant and supportive online community.	Group moderation and community management can take time and effort. Group specific content should be created that is different to what is posted on public profiles. This can increase workload considerably.
Social media optimisation	A simple and cost-effective way to drive people to social channels. An effective way to encourage people to share your content on their social channels.	Can cost to set up a website with social media functionality if not included in the site already. However, this is standard for most websites now.

Paid tactics

Definition
Paid tactics require payment to a social media platform or influencer to increase their reach to a target audience.

Pros:
Greater reach to wider networks of people and the ability to target audiences with specific characteristics. Also, paid ads facilitate retargeting particularly on Facebook and Instagram when Facebook's pixel code is embedded into a client's website if the target audience has not used Facebook's 'Clear History' feature which disables the pixel function (Hern, 2019).
According to the Marketing Rule of Seven, it can take up to 7 times for a target audience member to encounter a client's brand before they decide to act (Thomas, 2019). The benefits of repetition (but not to achieve wear-out) has also been explored in the advertising literature (Batra & Ray, 1986; Faber, Duff, & Nan, 2012; Nan & Faber, 2004).
Retargeting allows you to show relevant content to people who have already shown an interest by engaging with content, visiting the website etc. This can be highly effective in inspiring people to move through the stages of the customer journey. Retargeting can be even further enhanced Facebook's pixel code works together with Google tags also placed within a client's website, again only if members of the target audience have not opted to clear their Facebook history (Hern, 2019).

Cons:
The cost. While Facebook allows ads for a little more than $1 per day, you will need to pay considerable amounts to reach larger audiences. Also, it can take time to learn the interfaces to place and track paid ads. However, please read the Helpful Links section at the end of this chapter and ▶ Chap. 7 for further training resources. Also, collaborating with influencers can be costly and ineffective is not approached carefully. Further resources are available at the end of this chapter to assist this process too.

Tactic type	Pros	Cons
Advertisements	Greater reach and specific audience targeting. Retargeting. A wide range of advertising types to reach specific goals. Trackable performance.	Cost. Knowledge and training required. The ability to create high quality content is still required.
Boosted posts	Easier to implement than other paid ads.	Cost Reach reported not to be as much as placing ads in Facebook's Ads Manager.
Influencer marketing (Revisit ▶ Chap. 4 for more on Influencer marketing).	Positive endorsement of a client's brand, products or services from someone with a large following of people from a relevant target audience.	Cost can be prohibitive depending on the profile and following of the influencer with whom a client wants to collaborate. Inflated follower numbers and engagement. Some influencers overestimate (or buy likes and followers) to increase their earning power. Not following the agreement and posting the content that they were paid for. A legally binding agreement signed before any collaboration is recommended. Please see ▶ Chap. 4. The influencer behaves in opposition to a client's brand values resulting in reputational damage to a client.
Competitions	A great way to generate interest from a target audience including existing followers and people from new networks.	Knowledge of the required terms and conditions of each platform is required in addition to understanding of the legal requirements in your region. The cost of a valuable prize relevant and helpful to the target audience.
Discount offers	An effective way to inspire people to enter the action stage of the customer journey.	Can be costly if too many people from the target audience redeem the offer. It is important to ensure that the offer is attractive for both the target audience and a client.

(continued)

Table 6.6 (continued)

Offline tactics

Definition
These are tactics that are social media related but occur offline usually involving some form of experience, action or face-to-face activity.
Pros:
Encourage relationship-building, memory-making and UGC.
Cons:
Can take considerable time, cost and effort to organise and can be unpredictable.

Tactic type	Pros	Cons
Organised events	Great to strengthen relationships and build memories through positive in-person experiences. Can be extremely effective in the generation of UCG.	Cost, time, effort, and the ability for things to go wrong in a very public way. Expertise required to deliver a successful event.
UGC games and competitions	Inspires direct interaction with a client's brand and other participants, building relationships and memories in the process. Encourages UGC around a specific brand topic. Helps to reach new networks when participants post their entries and tag brand.	Again, the cost of a valuable prize relevant and helpful to the target audience. Instructions that are confusing to the target audience will result in minimal participation. Vetting the UGC to find quality pieces of content to win the prize. Finally, knowledge of the required terms and conditions of each platform is required in addition to understanding of the legal requirements in your region.

Table 6.6 is to provide a general overview and further research using the sources listed previously in Table 6.4 is strongly encouraged.

Table 6.6 is a condensed list of general tactics. Further information is embedded throughout other chapters in this text.

Conclusion
This chapter explored the importance of developing and implementing tactics that assist and provide value to a target audience. The power of storytelling to connect with target audiences on an emotional level was also emphasised as was the necessity of including offline tactics as a fundamental component of a social media strategy to build positive relationships, memories and generate UGC. Finally, the broad categories of social media tactics were presented. Remember, selecting relevant tactics to connect with a target audience is only half of the task of social media strategy implementation.

As a Social Media Manager, you may have developed the specifications for a highly effective Facebook advertising campaign, but if the content is low quality, the tactic will not work. Furthermore, if the content is impeccable and the tactic is misguided, the tactic will also fail. The content and the tactic must carry each other to victory.

This is why ▶ Section 3 is devoted to content creation to set you up for success.

First, we must explore the importance of social media analytics in the development, implementation and evaluation of strategic social media management, which is presented in our next chapter: ▶ Chap. 7.

Case Study: Starbucks' #WhiteCupContest Proves to Be a UCG Winner

As a tactic to generate audience engagement, User Generated Content and a new short-term design for their cups, Starbucks delivered a competition called the #WhiteCupContest (Starbucks, 2014).

The competition required social media users in the United States and Canada to purchase a Starbucks white cup, decorate it with their original design, photograph it and share the image on social media using the hashtag #WhiteCupContest.

The winner of the competition would have their design printed on a limited edition reusable Starbucks cup. The competition was a success, attracting nearly 4000 entries within three weeks of the competition being announced (Starbucks, 2014).

Throughout the competition, Starbucks reposted entries on a range of platforms including Facebook, Twitter, Instagram and Pinterest.

This case was successful for Starbucks on several levels. Firstly, it encouraged buy in with its target audience with a highly exclusive prize. Having your personal design on a limited edition Starbucks cup is an honour that is not easily achieved.

Next, the competition generated almost 4000 pieces of content that did not have to be created by Starbucks. This alone would have reduced the strain that content curation can have on resources and it provided almost 4000 opportunities for the Starbucks brand to be promoted through the networks of the

competition entrants (people who they may not have been able to reach before) (Starbucks, 2014).

The competition generated engagement through the use of the competition hashtag and with social media users liking and commenting on the photographs of the design. Finally, the competition also encouraged in-store purchases of the white cup throughout the competition on which people drew their designs and of the winning entry after it was announced and available.

The Starbucks #WhiteCupContest is an excellent example of how a simple concept can encourage interaction with a target audience and help to build positive associations and brand relationships as a result. The competition also allowed the target audience to share their creativity and love for the Starbucks brand with others within the coffee community. The only risk with User Generated Content is not being able to have any quality control measures in place in relation to the hashtag. Starbuck could select the best posts to share on their official channels, yet, anything could be posted using the #WhiteCupContent. Yet, not having the brand name Starbucks within that hashtag helped to separate the brand and the post to some degree.

1. How did this competition generate engagement with Starbucks' customers?
2. What are the benefits and challenges with using UGC?

6.9 Interview: Hemalata Moolrajani, Account Manager, Everymedia, Mumbai, India

1. **Please tell me about your current role.**
   I'm designated as an Account Manager at Everymedia. My key responsibilities are client servicing, planning and strategising, and making sure that we have a result. Like seeing how your campaign or brand is working. And I have a team under me. I'm handling almost like four to five clients, ranging from movies, from high intensity to a mid-level, to a lower intensity.

2. **What do you enjoy most about working with social media?**
   Every movie is different and using social media to promote movies must be approached differently for each movie. All sorts of genres that are available, like thriller, drama, family drama, emotional content, comedy means that you must develop social media strategies that align with those genres.
   Also, with new actors it's challenging to promote them to consumers and audiences and help them understand how to create their own fan base. And then the movie release, helping them with the entire marketing.

3. **What are the greatest challenges?**
   Even an A-list star in your movie comes with its own set of challenges. They're already familiar within the market, they already have their own audience. However, at times, these stars aren't available when you want to utilise them to the fullest, to be available for their audience, have a meet and greet. You must run your campaign without them.

4. **How did you come to work in social media? Please tell me your career story.**
   I was doing my Bachelor of Mass Media, BMM from MMK College, and I was always attracted to this glamour world. I really wanted to know how these movies are marketed. I completed an additional diploma degree specialising in advertising and social media. On the completion of my course, I had my campus placement with CNBC and Times of India. Times of India is the leading newspaper in India, where they publish information from entertainment, Bollywood, finance, etc. That's how I began my career.

   I joined Everymedia two years ago with the thought of exploring movie marketing. I heard that these guys were experts in digital movie marketing, celebrities, and brands. That enticed me to be a part of this company too.

5. **This chapter is about selecting, developing and implementing social media tactics, what do you think are the three most important things for Social Media Managers to consider about selecting, developing and implementing social media tactics?**
   Get your brief right. You need to know what the product is or what the campaign is all about. You need to have a brief understanding in two ways. A, what does your client want from you? They have a particular goal in mind and want to market their product in a particular way. Next, you need to know how you are going to promote this particular baby of your client to the audience. How will you create noise in the market?

   Second is your plan of action, and third is how are you implementing it? Since you know that your primary target audience is already set, you're now tapping their friends of friends, and their families. If someone is not a part of your target audience or not following this genre and actor, your challenge is to convert them into your audiences.

6. **What do you think are the benefits of selecting, developing and implementing relevant social media tactics?**

The benefits are that you know who you are supposed to target. You know what language they are following, or you know like either they're tier one, are they digitally savvy or are they not? Are they following you or are they not? What are their likes, dislikes, what do they prefer, what's their geographical locations? All these social media implementations or these other tactics that you need to follow to understand how the holistic approach is going to be.

7. **What are the challenges of selecting, developing and implementing social media tactics?**

At times when you're selecting the tactics for social media, you are restricted by budgets, and not having talent available to you or the actors are fresh faces and they're not yet being accepted in the media.

You must create a strategy which is more user friendly, where with the help of all the algorithms that we have, like your Facebook, Twitter, Instagram, all the data analytics that we get, holding them together and creating another strategy.

At times during campaigns it happens. You've planned for a tactic and it backfires. It's not working out. That's the time that we must pull up our socks and be more attentive, more alert, and imminently come up with a backup plan. The artist, the actor is a public figure out there. You must make sure that their image is not at stake. Your campaigns need to be precisely implemented so that everything falls into place.

8. **What do you think of the current landscape of social media management as a profession?**

It all began when people started realising that apart from the traditional media, everyone is on digital and everyone wants to be everywhere, digitally.

I want to see my product on all platforms, all channels. That's what a client is demanding. And with the need of everything going digital, there are new agencies that are coming up every day. We really need many professionals looking at this as their career opportunity. It's a booming industry and there's looking back. It's a very beautiful industry to be in.

9. **Where do you think the profession and social media is heading in the future?**

It's an industry that has captured the minds and hearts of people and it's something that is not going to stop or end soon. It's just going to grow.

10. **What has been the best piece of advice that you have been given?**

Be proactive and not reactive. That's how you're going to keep up with your clients and with your consumers.

11. **What advice would you give to someone wanting to work in social media?**

It's an emotional rollercoaster. It's going to be fun and there's no looking back.

❓ Questions for Critical Reflection

1. Why shouldn't tactics be considered as the entire social media strategy? Please explain your answer.
2. Why is quality storytelling a powerful way to connect with target audiences? Please provide an example.
3. What are the benefits of focusing on helping a target audience instead of constantly trying to sell to them? Please explain your answer.
4. What is a propinquital loop and how can it assist your client? Please provide examples.
5. What should be considered when devising tactics for a social media strategy and why is each important?
6. Why should a Social Media Manager test, monitor and refine social

media tactics once they have been implemented? Please provide an example to support your answer.

❯ Practical Exercises

1. Think of an important turning point in your life. Plot the events of that story onto Freytag's Pyramid. Consider the social media tactics that you could use to share your story with a target audience.

2. You are the Social Media Manager for a local surfing school. Suggest a piece of problem-solving content for each stage of the AIDASLA Model targeted at people who are completely new to surfing.

3. Provide suggestions regarding how the propinquital loop could be used as a social media tactic to engage with existing customers of an online kitchenware store.

References

Addyson-Zhang, A. (2018). Your go-to guide for Facebook Ads: Five Lessons from BlitzMetrics & Dennis Yu. Medium.com, viewed: 19/07/2019: https://medium.com/@aiaddysonzhang/your-go-to-guide-for-facebook-ads-five-lessons-from-blitzmetrics-dennis-yu-dccf6759710d

Bakslap. (2019). Our story. Bakslap.com, viewed: 16/07/2019: https://bakslap.com/our-story/

Balinas, T. (2019). How to automate your marketing and generate referral business. *OutboundEngine,* viewed 28.05.2019: https://www.outboundengine.com/blog/automate-marketing-generate-referral-business/

Batra, R., & Ray, M. L. (1986). Situational effects of advertising repetition: The moderating influence of motivation, ability, and opportunity to respond. *Journal of Consumer Research, 12*(4), 432–445.

Berger, J. (2016). *Contagious: Why things catch on.* New York: Simon and Schuster.

Chang, C. (2012). Narrative advertisements and narrative processing. In S. Rodgers & E. Thorson (Eds.), *Advertising theory* (pp. 241–254). New York, NY: Routledge.

Escalas, J. E. (2004). Imagine yourself in the product: Mental simulation, narrative transportation, and persuasion. *Journal of Advertising, 33*(2), 37–48.

Esposito, A., Faundez-Zanuy, M., Keller, E., & Marinaro, M. (Eds.). (2007). *Verbal and nonverbal communication behaviours: COST Action 2102 International Workshop, Vietri Sul Mare, Italy, March 29–31, 2007, revised selected and invited papers* (Vol. 4775). Springer.

Faber, R. J., Duff, R. L., & Nan, X. (2012). Coloring outside the lines – suggestions for making advertising theory more meaningful. In S. Rodgers & E. Thorson (Eds.), *Advertising theory* (pp. 18–32). New York, NY: Routledge.

Filieri, R., Alguezaui, S., & McLeay, F. (2015). Why do travelers trust TripAdvisor? Antecedents of trust towards consumer-generated media and its influence on recommendation adoption and word of mouth. *Tourism Management, 51,* 174–185.

Freytag, G. (1872). *Die technik des dramas.* Hirzel.

Fujita, M., Harrigan, P., & Soutar, G. N. (2019). The strategic co-creation of content and student experiences in social media. *Qualitative Market Research: An International Journal, 22*(1), 50–69.

Harper, D. (2019). *Tactics,* viewed 14/07/2019: https://www.etymonline.com/word/tactics

Hatch, M. J., & Schultz, M. (2010). Toward a theory of brand co-creation with implications for brand governance. *Journal of Brand Management, 17*(8), 590–604.

Heath, R. L., & Coombs, W. T. (2006). *Today's public relations: An introduction.* Sage.

Hern, A. (2019). Facebook launches 'clear history' tool – But it won't delete anything, *The Guardian,* viewed: 25.08.2019: https://www.theguardian.com/technology/2019/aug/20/facebook-launches-clear-history-tool-but-it-wont-delete-anything

Hill, C., Hult, T., Wickramasekera, R., Liesch, P., & MacKenzie, K. (2017). *Global business today Asia-Pacific perspective.* McGraw-Hill Education.

Kent, M. L., & Taylor, M. (2002). Toward a dialogic theory of public relations. *Public Relations Review, 28*(1), 21–37.

Kozinets, R. V., De Valck, K., Wojnicki, A. C., & Wilner, S. J. (2010). Networked narratives: Understanding word-of-mouth marketing in online communities. *Journal of Marketing, 74*(2), 71–89.

Matute, J., Polo-Redondo, Y., & Utrillas, A. (2016). The influence of EWOM characteristics on online repurchase intention: Mediating roles of trust and perceived usefulness. *Online Information Review, 40*(7), 1090–1110.

Melendez, S. (2020). For artists, the show must go on—and Zoom is their venue, viewed 09/05/2020: https://www.fastcompany.com/90478442/for-artists-the-show-must-go-on-and-zoom-is-their-venue

Nan, X., & Faber, R. J. (2004). Advertising theory: Reconceptualizing the building blocks. *Marketing Theory, 4*(1–2), 7–30.

Noonan, J. (2018). *Co-Creation Theory and How Companies Are Using It to Their Advantage*, viewed 09/05/2020: https://www.klcommunications.com/co-creation-theory/

Ouschan, R., Turkington, J., & Napoli, J. (2019). Leveraging user-generated content: A visual case analysis of Contiki's brand co-creation campaign. In *Handbook of research on customer engagement*. Edward Elgar Publishing.

Pullman, G.L. (2008). The Protagonist's Emotional Arc, viewed 14.11.2020: http://writinghorrorfiction.blogspot.com/2008/10/protagonists-emotional-arc.html

Quesenberry, K. A., & Coolsen, M. K. (2019). Drama goes viral: Effects of story development on shares and views of online advertising videos. Journal of Interactive Marketing, 48, 1–16.

Reichheld, F. (2001). Prescription for cutting costs. *Bain & Company*, viewed 14.07.2019: http://www2.bain.com/Images/BB_Prescription_cutting_costs.pdf

Rose, N.(2017).The truth behind that now-iconic photo of the Fyre festival 'Sandwich', Vice.com, viewed 19/07/2019: https://www.vice.com/en_us/article/nza8yq/that-photo-of-the-fyre-festival-sandwich-is-fake

Saleh, K. (2019). Customer acquisition vs.Retention costs – Statistics and trends. *Invesp*, viewed 17.07.2019: https://www.invespcro.com/blog/customer-acquisition-retention/

Schultz, D. E. (2017). International marketing communication as the global marketing change agent. In T. C. Melewar & S. Gupta (Eds.), *Strategic international marketing: An advanced perspective*. Hampshire: Palgrave Macmillan.

Smith, K., & Hanover, D. (2016). *Experiential marketing: Secrets, strategies, and success stories from the World's greatest brands*. Wiley.

Starbucks. (2014). Starbucks Invites You to Decorate its Iconic White Cup, *Starbucks*, viewed: 23/11/2019: https://stories.starbucks.com/stories/2014/starbucks-invites-you-to-decorate-its-iconic-white-cup

Sutherland, K. (2016). Using propinquital loops to blend social media and offline spaces: A case study of the ALS ice-bucket challenge. *Media International Australia, 160*(1), 78–88.

Sutherland, K., Davis, C., Terton, U., & Visser, I. (2018). University student social media use and its influence on offline engagement in higher educational communities. *Student Success, 9*(2), 13–24.

Sutherland, K. E. (2015). Towards an integrated social media communication model for the not-for-profit sector: A case study of youth homelessness charities (Doctoral dissertation, Monash University).

Taylor, M., & Kent, M. L. (2014). Dialogic engagement: Clarifying foundational concepts. *Journal of Public Relations Research, 26*(5), 384–398.

Thomas, D. D. (2019). *Chillpreneur: The new rules for creating success, freedom, and abundance on your terms*. Hay House, Inc.

Tuten, T. L., & Solomon, M. R. (2017). *Social media marketing*. Sage.

Vangala, A. (2012). Generate more leads with B2B social media. *IBM Community*, viewed: 23/11/2019: https://www.ibm.com/developerworks/community/blogs/9758d8e8-e9c0-4382-ab1e-a19fc7c1bb52/entry/generate_more_leads_with_b2b_social_media2?lang=en

Vaynerchuk, G. (2013). *Jab, jab, jab, right hook: How to tell your story in a noisy social world*. Harper Business.

Vaynerchuk, G. (2018). Crushing it. New York: Harper Collins.

Widrich, L., 2012. The science of storytelling: Why telling a story is the most powerful way to activate our brains. *Life Hacker*, viewed 14.07.2019: http://lifehacker.com/5965703/the-science-of-storytelling-why-telling-a-storyis-the-most-powerful-way-to-activate-ourbrains

Wilson, B. J. (2019). Top of mind: Use content to unleash your influence and engage those who matter to you. John Hall.

Further Reading

Storytelling

Alexander, B. (2017). *The new digital storytelling: Creating narratives with new media--revised and updated edition*. Abc-clio.

Caporale, B. (2015). *Creative strategy generation: Using passion and creativity to compose business strategies that inspire action and growth*. McGraw Hill Professional.

Events

Sutherland, A., & Khattab. (2019). Chapter 7 Community events and promotions: When locals rise. In *Public relations and strategic communication: Contemporary perspectives* (pp. 201–222). Oxford University Press.

6

Paid Tactics

AdEspresso by Hootsuite. (2019). The Beginner's Guide to Facebook Advertising 2019 By AdEspresso. Adespresso.com, viewed 21/07/2019: https://adespresso.com/guides/facebook-ads-beginner/

Chen, J. (2019). An expert's guide to influencer marketing. *Sprout Social*, viewed 21/07/2019: https://sproutsocial.com/insights/influencer-marketing/

Daniel. (2019). Twitter advertising in 2019: How to create Twitter Ads [Guide]. *Pyramid Digital Marketing*, viewed 21/07/2019 https://prymadigitalmarketing.com/twitter-advertising-guide-how-to-create-twitter-ads/

Dykstra, M.(2019). How to set up a YouTube ads campaign. *Social Media Examiner,* viewed 21/07/2019: https://www.socialmediaexaminer.com/how-to-set-up-youtube-ads-campaign/

Tran, T. (2019). How to advertise on Instagram: A 6-step guide to using Instagram ads. *Hootsuite*, viewed 21/07/2019: https://blog.hootsuite.com/instagram-ads-guide/

Helpful Links

An Online Resource Guide to Freytag's Pyramid: https://www.quickbase.com/articles/an-online-resource-guide-to-freytags-pyramid

Australian Event Management & Planning Resources: https://eventtrainingaustralia.com.au/event-management-planning-resources/

BlitzMetrics Digital Marketing Courses: https://blitzmetrics.com/menu/

Facebook Blueprint (free online courses): https://www.facebook.com/business/learn

HubSpot Free Social Media Certification: https://academy.hubspot.com/courses/social-media

Pixar in a Box (Storytelling Tutorials): https://www.khanacademy.org/partner-content/pixar

Social Media Monitoring, Measurement, Analysis and Big Data

Contents

© The Author(s), under exclusive license to Springer Nature Singapore Pte Ltd. 2021
K. E. Sutherland, *Strategic Social Media Management*, https://doi.org/10.1007/978-981-15-4658-7_7

What You Will

...dia analyt-
...and mea-
...they are

...social
...mea-
...strate-

...ial media moni-

...to Social

...the social media
...nent process as
...1: gather data,
...ort data, use data

...these steps in the
...listening, monitor-
...ivities.

...bring involves the
...of user engagement
...tforms. The terms
...ing and social listen-
...sed interchangeably.
...ish between the two
...defines social media
...al listening in the fol-

...nitoring focuses on the
...of social media users on
...anisation's social media
...e form of comments,
...messages, shared posts

...involves the monitoring
...nversations relating to a
...ct, issue or service taking

- activities and must take place in all phases of a social media strategy (development, implementation and evaluation).
- Vanity Metrics are the results of social media that are not linked to tangible business or organisational goals (likes, follower numbers etc.).
- Conversion Metrics measure how social media activity has been directly responsible for a tangible outcome (purchase, event attendance, store visit).
- The most important items to measure the performance of a social media strategy are: Goal/s and SMART Objectives (Conversion Metrics), Strategy Costs/Revenue and Return on Investment (ROI) and Content performance (Vanity Metrics).
- 'Big data' refers to the analysis of extremely large data sets to gain audience insights, identify relationships, trends, patterns of behaviour and to make predictions.
- The most important functions of a social media report are to demonstrate whether the strategy is achieving (or has achieved) its goals and SMART Objectives and to communicate actionable recommendations to support continuous improvement.

...duction

...7 focuses on a further funda-
...onent of the social media strat-
...listening, monitoring and
...As this chapter will demon-
...tivities take place in all stages
...management: strategy devel-
...nentation and evaluation.
...ing wrote: "Without data,
...r person with an opinion,"

and this is definitely the case when it comes to social media management.

Social media provides rich and detailed data about target audiences, their preferences, activities and conversations that can be analysed and used to inform decisions relating to social media practice. Making decisions purely by instinct can be highly risky, particularly when it involves a client's reputation and their money. While social media can be a rich source of data, the many different metrics and pure volume of data that it generates can be overwhelming.

The aim of this chapter is to simplify and demystify the activities of social media listening, monitoring and measurement so that their use as part of the social media management process can be leveraged to support the achievement of strategic goals and facilitate continual improvement in terms of social media performance.

In a nutshell, this chapter provides advice on how to gather, report and analyse data to formulate and implement actionable recommendations using a range of quantitative and qualitative tools, techniques and methods including sentiment analysis, netnography and the use of big data to glean audience insights.

While this chapter delves into some level of specifics, this chapter is predominantly focused on providing guiding principles that can then be customised to suit the individual needs and goals of customers and organisations.

Every business and organisation is different, but processes and approaches can remain consistent when they are effective. Again, one chapter does not allow enough scope to cover the topics of social media monitoring, listening and measurement in great depth; multiple volumes could be written on each topic.

Therefore, this chapter provides an overview of the benefits, recommended approaches and most important areas of consideration when undertaking these important strategic activities.

Step
Gather I

Step 4.
Use Report Findings to
Improve Performance

Step 3.
Report Data ◀

◘ **Fig. 7.1** The key steps in the so[...] toring and measurement process

7.2 The Four Key Steps [...] Media Monitoring and Measurement

There are four key steps in [...] monitoring and measurem[...] demonstrated in ◘ Fig. [...] analyse/interpret data, rep[...] to improve performance.

This chapter explores [...] context of social media l[...] ing and measurement act[...]

7.3 Monitoring

Social media monit[...] real-time surveillance[...] on social media pl[...] social media monitor[...] ing can often be u[...] However, to disting[...] activities, this text [...] monitoring and soc[...] lowing ways:

- **Social media m[...]** direct activities [...] a client's or or[...] profiles in th[...] reviews, direct[...] etc.
- **Social listenin[...]** of public co[...] brand, produ[...]

place on social media not specifically on a client or organisation's social media profiles.

This section will focus on the importance of profile-specific social media monitoring, its process, helpful tools, data analysis and strategies to use monitoring insights to support continuous improvement and to build positive relationships with target audiences.

7.3.1 The Importance of Social Media Monitoring

▶ Chapter 4 explained in detail what can happen when customer complaints are completely ignored or not responded to within a timely fashion. What may have started as a small issue can soon become a crisis on social media particularly when someone's negative experience with a client or organisation is not addressed. Sometimes the complaint becomes viral when other social media users share their own negative experiences.

7.3.1.1 Lack of Monitoring Results in ASOS Bot Debacle

Online clothing retailer ASOS did not monitor its social media profiles when a customer left a complaint on the official ASOS Facebook profile regarding not receiving a refund for poor quality items.

What other Facebook users soon discovered was that the use of the words "refund" or "response" triggered an automated response from a bot (Watson, 2019). This resulted in thousands of people leaving comments (mainly humourous) containing these trigger words to generate the automated response.

As Chambers (2019) reports, one Facebook user wrote:

» I've never ordered from ASOS but I also want a refund for an order I never received or ordered!

To which the ASOS bot responded:

» Hi Lee, thanks for getting in touch sorry to hear you have I can definitely help - I just need some more information from you.

Facebook users turned the situation into a game for their own entertainment and ASOS became a news headline for all of the wrong reasons.

There were previous news reports a few years before questioning whether ASOS used bots for customer service on Facebook, which ASOS, but this debacle removed all speculation on the issue (Lieu, 2016).

Careful monitoring and a genuine response to the original post could have helped to avoid reputational damage.

7.3.2 Planning

A Social Media Manager must be vigilant in terms of monitoring clients' social platforms, not purely surveilling for negative interactions from customers, but also to identify positive engagement as an opportunity to converse with target audiences and deepen their connection with a client's or organisational brand.

Monitoring should be conducted every few hours, and it is also highly recommended to have push notifications activated to receive alerts from each platform when engagement from users occurs. ❏ Table 7.1 recommends engagement types to regularly monitor. Broader mentions will be covered in the Social Listening section.

7.3.3 Method

Each platform provides notifications to alert Social Media Managers when the engagement types listed in ❏ Table 7.1 occur. It is best not to rely solely on notifications.

Table 7.1 Social media engagement types requiring frequent monitoring

Engagement type	Description
Comments	Counting the number of comments a post generates can give some indication of engagement levels but reading each comment to understand their true content is vital. A post that generates 100 comments may seem like an achievement, but not so if most of the comments are negative. It is also important to respond to every comment in a genuine way while staying true to the brand voice (please revisit ▶ Chap. 4).
Reviews	The content of reviews should also be closely monitored, and every review responded to in a timely manner. As mentioned in ▶ Chap. 4, negative reviews should be perceived as an opportunity to improve the customer experience and turn a negative into a positive. Ignoring negative reviews can have a detrimental effect on a business (Baer, 2016).
Check Ins	Platforms such as Facebook and Instagram allow users to check in to specific locations, also known as geo-tagging. If a client's business location is on their profiles (as it should be) profile owners and admins will receive a notification if someone checks in. This is another great opportunity to interact with that person by welcoming them and liking the post.
Direct Messages	It is essential to monitor direct messages on all platforms and respond to queries within an hour. Chatbots have become hugely popular in automating the fielding of initial requests, but the conversation should always be taken over by a real person soon after (Elliot, 2018).
Shares/ Retweets/ Regram	People share content to endorse it or provide some negative commentary about it. Privacy settings can limit the monitoring of shared posts on some platforms. It is important to track shares wherever possible and thank the person sharing when it is performed positively or apply the issues management steps explored in ▶ Chap. 4 if it is shared negatively.
Likes/ Reactions	Monitoring likes and reactions provides an insight into how favourably content is being received by a target audience or if a post is generating any response at all. This insight can assist in tweaking content if it is not generating the intended response. On some platforms, likes can encourage other people to also respond in the same way. However, this occurrence has been reduced with Instagram and Facebook hiding likes from users. Page and profile owners still have access to this metric.

Instead, proactively check each profile 5–6 times per day to ensure that engagement is not overlooked by mistake.

There are other tools available that offer dashboard functionality so that the activity on multiple social media profiles (and platforms) can be monitored simultaneously.

Three examples of dashboard monitoring tools are listed in ▢ Table 7.2.

7.3.4 Social Media Monitoring for Improved Customer Relationships and Continuous Improvement

Responding to every engagement from the target audience, positive or negative, may seem excessive, but it is the essence upon which strong brand/customer relationships are made.

⬚ Table 7.2 Social media monitoring dashboard tools

Dashboard tool	Description
Hootsuite	Hootsuite allows users to monitor activity on Facebook, Twitter, Instagram, YouTube, LinkedIn and WordPress accounts on one dashboard. This is extremely helpful for social media managers and saves time moving between different platforms. The scheduling functionality of Hootsuite is further explored in ▶ Chap. 8.
Tweetdeck	Tweetdeck is a Twitter monitoring tool that allows multiple feeds and accounts on the same dashboard. This tool is extremely helpful when managing multiple Twitter accounts or facilitating Twitter chats as streams using specific hashtags can be added to the dashboard.
Reputology	Reputology facilitates the monitoring of reviews from more than 100 review sites including Facebook and Google My Business in a single dashboard. This tool also allows Social Media Managers to respond to reviews directly through the dashboard to save time jumping between review sites.
BlitzMetrics Dashboard	BlitzMetrics Dashboard facilitates monitoring and measurement and provides recommendations to help support the achievement of specified goals.

Algorithms on many social media platforms reward engagement and interactions on content with greater reach (Barnhart, 2019). Always be genuine in your interactions and do so out of the desire to build positive relationships with the target audience not to increase reach. This is an added bonus.

People want to feel listened to and acknowledged and it does not matter whether their feedback is positive or negative. Responding can improve brand relationships with the person engaging and with other social media users who witness the exchange. A study by Bazaarvoice (2019) found that 71% of consumers in the survey changed their perception of a brand after seeing a brand response to a review.

Analyse social media engagement for clues on how to improve a brand, its products and the customer experience. Bazaarvoice (2019) suggest that recommendations often contain valuable insights and calls-to-action from customers seeking specific improvements to products or services.

For example, if a review contains language Bazaarvoice (2019) refers to as "pivot language" (terms such as "if only," "I wish," or "one change") this is where enhancements are often suggested.

Furthermore, if a review uses pronouns such as "you," "yours," and "you're" the reviewer may be speaking directly to the brand and these sentences can also contain helpful information to improve (Bazaarvoice, 2019).

> 66 Avoid copy and paste responses. Craft genuine responses on a human-to-human level. 99
>
> **Dr Karen Sutherland**

With social media monitoring understood. It is also necessary to learn how to conduct social listening to monitor the wider conversation occurring online.

7.4 Social Listening

Social Listening falls within the category of social media monitoring, because it involves monitoring the conversations taking place on social media about brand, topics, issues, and topics etc.

However, what differentiates social listening from social media monitoring as defined previously in this chapter is that it involves listening to the public conversations on social media by people who are not necessarily followers of a client's or organisation's social media profiles.

7.4.1 Benefits of Social Listening

Social listening is an integral part of social media management and should be employed throughout all stages of the social media strategy process. Think of social listening as having an "ear to the ground" of what social media users are saying about a client or an organisation. It helps to provide a gauge of public sentiment overall and it can be extremely accurate in predicting outcomes.

For example, Griffith University's Big Data and Smart Analytics Lab in Australia correctly predicted political events such as Donald Trump being elected as U.S. president, the Brexit result and Scott Morrison being elected as Australia's Prime Minister in the 2019 Federal Election through the analysis of social media conversations taking place around these events (Koslowski, 2019).

7.4.1.1 Identifying Reputation Gaps

The main purpose for undertaking social listening is to have an accurate representation of how people within a target audience truly think and feel about a topic, also known as sentiment. Measuring and analysing sentiment (the opinions, thoughts and feelings of social media users) is a form of quantitative research and will be explored in greater detail further in the chapter.

It is important to consider that just because a brand attempts to represent itself in a particular way, it does not mean that this is how people outside of the organisation perceive it. This discrepancy is known in public relations and marketing literature as a reputation gap or a reputation-reality gap (Ndlela, 2019; Lundholt, Maagaard & Piekut, 2018; Aula, 2010) and it can quickly erode organisational reputation if left unchecked, particularly during a crisis situation as discussed in ▶ Chap. 4.

7.4.1.2 When a Hashtag Becomes a Bashtag: #McDStories

A classic example is #McDStories where McDonald's encouraged people on Twitter to share their favourite stories relating to the brand before gauging public sentiment. Instead of generating positive stories, Twitter users tweeted a torrent of negative experiences using the #McDStories hashtag (Jain, Agarwal & Pruthi, 2015; Saleh, Chefor & Babin, 2019).

Not conducting social listening before launching this campaign resulted in McDonald's creating a branded hashtag that turned into a bashtag (Hill, 2012). Listening to what social media users were posting about the McDonald's brand when unprompted may have provided a deeper insight into the sentiment being expressed (positive, negative or neutral). Clearly, the online conversation about McDonald's was not largely positive, so when social media users were asked to provide their feedback, they did so resulting in reputational damage.

Remember, hashtags cannot be deleted, so #McDStories will exist forever containing negative associations. While #McDStories was first tweeted in 2012, people are still using the hashtag for negative tweets about McDonald's 7 years later. This is the perfect example of what can occur when a reputation gap remains unidentified by not conducting social listening.

Social listening usually uncovers one of four following scenarios in relation to assessing online reputation and sentiment. The conversation around a brand or product is generally found to be:

1. *More positive* than predicted.
2. *Neutral* (neither positive nor negative)
3. *As expected,* (whether that is positive or negative)
4. *More negative* than expected.

Social listening can provide vital knowledge to Social Media Managers to address reputation gaps or to further leverage and build on positive sentiment and conversations happening online.

7.4.1.3 Understanding the Conversation to Avoid Tone Deaf Posts

Social listening can help Social Media Managers to gauge the temperature and context of online conversations before jumping in and being perceived as tone deaf or insensitive. There have been a number of brands who have clearly not understood the context of an online discussion before injecting themselves into the conversation and posting something using a completely different context purely for shameless self-promotion.

These instances are often met with comments such as "read the room" meaning the person posting clearly does not understand the context of the conversation and others have perceived their contribution to be insensitive.

For example, when musical artist Prince passed away in 2016 @Homebase_help on Twitter inappropriately used the trending hashtag #RIPPRINCE to gain wider exposure for their brand which generated considerable backlash (Mediafirst, 2017). They wrote:

» Good morning everyone, happy Friday. If you need our assistance we're here until 8 pm today, get tweeting. Have a good day! #RIPPRINCE

Another classic example is the negative backlash DiGiorno Pizza received after inappropriately contributing to a Twitter conversation about domestic violence. The hashtag was #WhyIStayed where survivors of domestic abuse shared their personal stories on an extremely sensitive topic.

The Social Media Manager of DiGiorno Pizza later admitted that they did not read what the hashtag or conversation was about before posting the following:

» #WhyIStayed You had pizza. (Moulder, 2016).

Social listening helps to identify appropriate conversations where brands or organisations can make a relevant and valuable contribution. Ignorantly injecting a brand into a conversation purely for the sake of blatant promotion can result in the creation of issues and reputational damage.

7.4.1.4 Identifying Opportunities to Make a Valuable Contribution

Social listening can help to identify opportunities to contribute something of value to a conversation in real-time and assist people who may be seeking help. For example, monitoring particular hashtags and handles of competitors may identify opportunities to assist their disgruntled customers.

Additionally, not all online conversations have to be serious. In fact, there have been some fun and highly entertaining conversations that have resulted between customers and brands as a result of social listening.

A great example of this was a conversation on Twitter between a customer, Tesco Mobile, Yorkshire Tea and Jaffa Cakes where each brand used their distinctive brand voice to debate whether Jaffa Cakes were really a biscuit or a cake (CampaignLive, 2019). The conversation sounds trivial, but it was a highly engaging exchange that presented an opportunity for each brand to show its personality.

7.4.1.5 Gauging Response to Campaigns and Product Launches

The beauty of social listening is that it allows Social Media Managers to gauge the immediate response to the launch of a campaign or product so that they know if it has been received positively, negatively or indifferently.

Similarly, to identifying a reputation gap, social listening during a campaign or launch period can provide the knowledge to influence the conversation to build positive momentum for and sentiment in relation to the brand.

7.4.2 Planning

Careful planning is required when approaching social listening activities. Social listening is an integral inclusion to a social media strategy and should also be approached in a strategic way. The key challenge with social listening is returning relevant data from which to glean meaningful insights. The barriers that can be presented in relation to gathering relevant social listening data are:

1. **Data Volume**
   The sheer volume of data on the internet can hamper the location of specific information about a client, organisation, brand, product and/or service.

2. **Ethical Barriers**
   Ethical practices are paramount when employing social listening. However, doing the right thing also limits access to data. For example, conversations in closed Facebook groups may be rich sources of data around relevant topics, yet analysing those conversations without permission of the group's administrator and members is highly unethical. This is known as "walled garden" data where access must be granted through a registration process or request to join (Ampofo, 2015).

3. **The Deep Web, the Dark Web and Dark Social**
   These are areas and activities online that cannot be accessed or traced and therefore render social listening activities highly problematic.
   - *The Deep Web:* This is any content on the internet that cannot be accessed using a search engine (Hernández, Rivero & Ruiz, 2019; Ranakot et al., 2017; Hardy & Norgaard, 2016). The only way to access content on the deep web is if you have the exact URL and/or the permission of the content owner to access it. The majority of information on the internet is on the Deep Web.

- For example, private Facebook accounts, any form of password protected cloud storage, even unlisted YouTube videos are also part of the Deep Web. As such, the majority of content on the internet cannot be included in social listening activities which limits understanding of public sentiment, but it completely understandable from an ethical perspective.
- **The Dark Web:** Also known as the 'internet black market', the Dark Web describes the highly encrypted and anonymised use of the internet usually for criminal activity (Lee et al., 2019; Pelton & Singh, 2019). Clearly data of this nature cannot be accessed through regular social listening methods.
- **Dark Social:** A term that describes online conversations that are not trackable through the use of social listening tools such as interactions that take place on Facebook Messenger and WeChat (Tiltman, 2019).
- The term can also refer to the sharing of website links through untraceable sources such as through emails and SMS whereby marketers are unable to track the source of traffic to their websites.
- If you consider that more than 1 billion people use WeChat daily and more than 20 billion messages are sent between users and businesses on Facebook Messenger every month, social listening can only capture a small percentage of the conversations that are truly taking place online (Lee, 2019; Hutchinson, 2019).

4. Listening **Tools that are Restricted to Particular Platforms**
   - A further challenge experience by Social Media Managers can be in finding a social listening tool that can analyse conversations on a wide range of platforms. There are many powerful tools available, but their price can

increase along with the number of social media platforms they can monitor. Sometimes a combination of tools is required to meet the specific requirements of a client or organisation. Recommended tools will be explored in greater detail further in this section.

7.4.3 Developing a Social Listening Plan

As with the development of a social media strategy, it is essential to also identify a goal for any social listening activities undertaken to ensure that they are being approached in a results focused way. Limited time and large volumes of data can present challenges for Social Media Managers.

Developing a plan can avoid returning loads of irrelevant data to wade through to find something meaningful to a specific client or organisation. It achieves this by defining the purpose of the activity to ensure any social listening activities are aligned with overall strategic goals.

The components of a social listening plan are explained below, and a template is provided in the Appendices (■ Table 7.3).

7.4.4 Method

Social listening can be conducted using two broad approaches, manual or automated.

7.4.4.1 Manual Approaches to Social Listening

Manual approaches can employ research methods such as *content analysis* and *netnography*.

- **Content analysis** involves the analysis of social media content to identify specific codes, patterns and relationships (Riff, 2019). It can be a useful method in analysing both quantitative and qualitative data on a much deeper level but can be very labor-intensive.

Table 7.3   Social media listening plan components

Component	Description
Goal	What is this social listening activity trying to achieve? For example, this social listening activity is being undertaken to gauge the response to the launch of our new product x. Not specifying the purpose of the social listening activity before embarking on it will be counterproductive.

Method	This is a succinct description detailing the way in the listening activity will be undertaken. Articulating the method at the beginning of the exercise supports a considered and proactive approach rather than a haphazard one. The method should contain details of:
	   The platforms to be included.
	   The tools to be used.
	   How the analysis will be conducted.
	   How the key findings from the analysis will be used.
	   Why this social listening activity will be useful.
	The method can always be refined once it is implemented, but it is always useful to begin with a map as a starting point.

Topic Area	These are broad categories relating to a client, an organisation, or issue that help to focus the search on particular topics.
	For example, a social media listening exercise for a new McDonald's thick shake might include the following Topic Areas:
	   1. Food and Beverage
	   2. Retail
	These categories will keep the search targeted to returning data that supports the goal of the listening activity.

Key Words	Specific, singular words that relate to the goal. For example:
	   McDonald's
	   Thick shake
	   Flavour
	Many listening platforms and search engines use a method called Boolean Search to help refine search topics (Gross & Horn, 2017).
	For Key Words where a search of online conversations involves identifying singular words the following Boolean Search String could be used:
	   McDonald's **OR** Thick shake **OR** Flavour

Key Phrases	A Key Phrase is a group of relevant words that must be identified in a specific order. For example:
	   Sunshine Coast
	   United Kingdom
	   Hong Kong
	Taking a Boolean Search approach to Key Phrases would take the following form:
	   "United Kingdom"

Qualifiers	Sometimes a keyword will not make sense (or be relevant) unless it is paired with another word. This word is called a Qualifier, because this word qualifies the term as valid to include in your social media content data set. The order of these words is irrelevant; however, they must appear together. Again, using the Boolean Search method to return specific qualifiers should be written as: McDonald's **AND** New **AND** Thick shake These terms could appear in any order, but they are highly relevant to the goal of the listening activity being undertaken.

Table 7.3	(continued)
Component	**Description**
Exclusions	These are words to avoid being returned in a search. They could be words with similar spelling or be related in some way but are irrelevant to the listening activity being undertaken. When using Boolean Search to identify exclusions this is how the search string is constructed: McDonald's **AND** Thick shake **AND NOT** Burger These are simple Boolean Search commands, but some are much more complex to return data of even greater specificity. A link to more complex commands is in the Helpful Links section at the end of the chapter.
Sentiment	Sentiment captures the feelings and opinions of social media users and is usually segmented by social listening tools into the following categories: Positive Negative Neutral It can be helpful to identify words that might fall into these categories. However, sentiment results returned by automated social listening tools must be carefully checked because they can incorrectly categorise content. For example, mention of research the author conducted into the most unprofessional social media behaviours according to employers returns a result of negative sentiment because the author's name and the word "unprofessional" are returned together.

— *Netnography* involves conducting ethnographic research in an online environment. Ethnography involves the in-depth study of humans in terms of their interactions with each other, with technology, their habits and customs etc. and lends itself well to social listening (Kozinets, 2015). However, it can also be extremely labour-intensive and is often limited in its scope because of this.

7.4.4.2 Automated Approaches to Social Listening

There is a wide (and ever-growing) range of automated social listening tools on the market that vary in price, breadth, in terms of platforms monitored and features offered, and reporting mechanisms. Yet, in comparison to manual methods of social listening, there are some key pros and cons.

Pros of Automated Social Listening Tools

— Takes less effort and time than manual methods. Most social listening tools are reasonably intuitive and easy to use.

— Social listening searches can analyse significantly more data than manual methods returning a larger sample that can be more indicative of the target audience's conversation.
— Clear reporting functionality of social listening data.

Cons of Automated Social Listening Tools

— Costs can be prohibitive.
— Do not analyse as deeply as manual methods.
— Often contain errors when classifying sentiment.
— Require some knowledge of Boolean Search to return highly relevant results.
— Reports generated from automated social listening tools still require a human to analyse results and employ sense-making to develop and implement actionable results.

While automated social listening tools have some disadvantages, they can also be extremely helpful and speedy in crawling the

□ Table 7.4   Automated social listening tools

Tool name	Platforms/sources	Features
Talkwalker: Quick Search	Twitter, Facebook, Instagram, Forums, YouTube, Pinterest, Flickr, VKontakte, Newspaper, Magazine, Online News, TV/Radio, News Agency, Press Release, Blogs, Foursquare, Mixcloud, Ekşi Sözlük, Twitch Google Play.	Mention, keyword and hashtag tracking, competitor, trend and sentiment analysis.
Meltwater: Media Intelligence	Blogs, Comments, Facebook, Forums, Product Reviews, Twitter, YouTube, various news sources.	Mention, keyword and hashtag analysis. Share of Voice Analysis (Benchmark) Monitor and sentiment analysis functionality.
Agorapulse	Instagram, Twitter, YouTube, LinkedIn, Facebook.	Hashtag listening.
Awario	Twitter, Facebook, Instagram, Reddit, web, news. Blogs, YouTube.	Mentions, competitor analysis, influencer and lead identification.
Keyhole	Facebook, Instagram, Twitter, YouTube, online media.	Hashtag analytics.
Iconosquare	Facebook, Instagram	Mentions, keyword and hashtag analysis, Industry Benchmarks, Competitor Analysis.
Brandwatch	Twitter, Reddit, forums, blogs and customisable to specific platforms.	Mentions, keywords, hashtags, viral and trending content analysis, competitor analysis, sentiment.

web to find relevant information specific to a client, organisation or issue. Automated tools are not 100% accurate, therefore, the results that they return still need to be scrutinised and closely analysed. However, they can definitely cut down the process of sourcing relative online conversations.

While the tools are constantly changing, □ Table 7.4 contains some recommended social listening tools currently at the time of writing.

7.4.5 Metrics

It is easy to become overwhelmed and lost in the large array of metrics offered by social listening platforms to measure and articulate what is happening within online conversations in relation to a client, brand or issue.

Yet, there are some fundamental measurements that will be most helpful in your analysis.

Essentially, social listening activities are used to gain insights into what social media users think, feel and/or understand about a specific topic and then to use that knowledge to inform the next right action in response.

With that in mind, □ Table 7.5 recommends some key metrics to consider when undertaking social listening activities.

7.4.5.1 Data Analysis

All of the social listening tools mentioned in □ Table 7.4 generate reports of some description. While the representation of social listening data within eye-catching graphs may seem like the end of the process in terms of reporting outcomes to clients or

Table 7.5 Key social listening metrics

Social listening metric	Description
Mentions	The number of times a brand name or keyword has been mentioned in the time period specified (Gonçalves, 2017).
Mentions Over Time	A graph demonstrating the spread of mentions over specified time period.
Engagement	The number of people who have interacted with a post mentioning the brand or keyword in the specified time period (Lipschultz, 2019).
Estimated Reach	The estimated number of people content reached containing mention to a specific brand or keyword.
Demographics (Gender, Age, Geographic Region)	The average age, gender and geographic region of the people mentioning the brand or key word on social media during a specified time period (Sponder, 2011).
Sentiment	The percentage of posts categorised to be position, negative and neutral. Remember, it is always important to check these results manually (Tuten & Solomon, 2017).
Share of Voice	As mentioned in ▶ Chap. 3, Share of Voice is a competitor analysis comparing which brand has received more brand mentions online during a specified time period (Kim, 2016).
Media Types	The online communication channels that mentioned the brand or key word during a specific time period. This is good to know in terms of which platforms are more likely to mention a brand or specific keyword.
Results	The list of sources (articles, tweets, Facebook posts, etc.) that mentioned the brand or keyword.

organisational decision makers, this is far from the case.

The reports generated from social listening tools only provide information as to what is occurring. They do not provide answers as to why and how this information can be leveraged to keep improving. That is the job of a Social Media Manager.

■■ **When reviewing social listening reports answer the following questions:**

1. What does this data show in relation to the strategic goal/s?
2. What does this data show in relation to the SMART Objectives?
3. How much conversation is happening in relation to the client or organisation?
4. Is the conversation mainly positive, negative or neutral?
5. What are the key themes in the positive mentions?
6. What are the key themes in the negative mentions?
7. What are the key themes in the neutral mentions?
8. What are the audience demographics (age, gender, location) of the people talking about the client or organisation?
9. What tactics were being implemented on the days that generated more positive mentions?
10. What tactics were being implemented on the days that generated more negative mentions?

7

11. What tactics were being implemented on the days that generated
more neutral mentions?
12. How have the negative and positive
mentions been addressed?

Answering these questions will assist in
delving much deeper into the results of the
social listening activities to glean more
meaningful insights.

7.4.6 Developing Actionable Recommendations

The next stage of social listening data analysis is to use the insights gained to develop
actionable recommendations for continual
improvement. Actionable means that the
recommendation is able to be implemented.

Sometimes Social Media Managers
make the mistake of recommending particular actions that cannot be implemented due
to lack of resources or organisational con-
straints. These are not useful to anyone.
Ensure that any recommendations made can
be implemented.

When developing recommendations, it is
important to draw from the answers formu-
lated in the first stage of the data analysis and
delve even more deeply to articulate actions
that will assist the client or organisation.

■ ■ Using the reports from the social
listening tool and from the data analysis
as evidence, please answer the following
questions:
1. What actions must be undertaken to
improve the likelihood that strategic

goals and SMART Objectives will be
achieved?
2. How can we increase positive mentions, decrease negative mentions and
convert neutral mentions into positive?
3. How can we increase positive mentions and interactions with our target
audience?
4. How can we better respond to negative mentions?

These questions will prompt the development of actionable recommendations both
before, during or after the implementation
of a social media strategy to help to support
a client or organisation's strategic goals.

The final stage of social listening is to
implement the recommendations made
from the data analysis. It is essential to
revisit the social media strategy to see how
these actions can be best aligned with the
tactics to ensure that all activities work
together to achieve the goal/s and SMART
Objectives.

Next, this chapter will explore one of the
most important parts of strategic social
media management: measurement.

7.5 Social Media Measurement

For a social media strategy to be considered
successful, its tactics must achieve its goal/s
and SMART Objectives (Tuten & Solomon,
2017).

Measurement is the only way to truly
ascertain if a strategy has hit the mark.
Remember the W. Edwards Deming quote at
the beginning of the chapter.

> 66 Data proves that goals and SMART
> objectives have been achieved,
> anything else is guesswork. 99
>
> Dr Karen Sutherland

There are so many aspects to social media measurement that cannot be covered within the scope of this chapter. However, the main components are explored and there is a list of great resources at the end of the chapter to further your knowledge.

Social media measurement involves the active tracking of an organisation's (client's or individual's) social media activities. It differs from social media listening and monitoring because instead of assessing other people's responses and conversations it tracks the performance of the implemented tactics from a social media strategy.

In short, listening and *monitoring is about others' activities, measurement tracks the performance of your actions* related to the implementation of a social media strategy.

7.5.1 **When to Measure**

There are three critical times to measure social media activities as a Social Media Manager:

1. *During the Strategy Development Phase:* As detailed in ▶ Chaps. 3 and 5, thorough research is the foundation of any successful social media strategy. Measurement must take place as part of a thorough social media audit during the strategy development phase to identify the benchmark from where the strategy must begin.

2. *During the Strategy Implementation Phase:* Tracking the performance of a strategy in real-time allows a Social Media Manager to check that the tactics are working to support the achievement of the goal/s and SMART Objectives. This insight can inform when and what changes may be necessary to bring the strategy back on course if it is not working.

3. *At the Conclusion of a Strategy:* Evaluating the success of the campaign once it has concluded is essential because it will determine:
   — If the goal/s and SMART Objectives were achieved.
   — What worked.
   — What did not work.
   — Return on Investment (ROI) (what a client is usually most interested in)
   — Social media's impact on conversion rates (sales, registrations, donations etc.).

Measurement is required at every stage of the social media management process, because data is knowledge and knowledge is power.

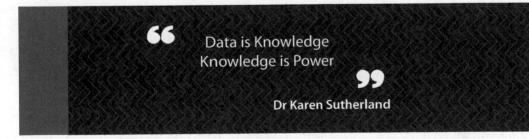

> " Data is Knowledge
> Knowledge is Power "
>
> Dr Karen Sutherland

Not using data to guide decisions is like trying to shoot an arrow in the dark. It is guesswork and guesswork is the opposite of strategy.

7.5.2 What to Measure

There are thousands of different metrics (items of measurement) that can be included in social media measurement activities and these keep increasing due to platform changes and new tools becoming available. It is easy to be overwhelmed by all of the different metrics on offer.

▪▪ Most Important: Goal/s and SMART Objectives

With a social media strategy, its success is measured against whether it achieved the goal/s and SMART Objectives identified at the beginning of the strategy development phase. Any other measurements may provide extra insight, but essentially, these are the core measurements that must be addressed before any others.

▪▪ The Two Main Metric Categories

Social media measurement has two main categories of metrics:

Vanity Metrics and Conversion Metrics and both must be measured as part of a social media strategy.

However, while vanity metrics can contain some insights, conversion metrics are usually what determine whether a social media strategy has been successful in meeting its goal/s and SMART Objectives.

Vanity and Conversion metrics are defined as follows:

Vanity Metrics   Also known as "top-level" or "superficial" metrics (Lipschultz, 2019). Vanity Metrics are the results of social media that are not linked to tangible business or organisational goals. These are generally engagement or performance metrics (likes, followers, shares, reach etc.) that indicate how well a piece of content or a profile is being received by the target audience, but this performance does not equate to a tangible outcome such as a purchase or registration etc.

In short, Vanity Metrics can show what types of content people are responding to, but nothing at a deeper level.

Conversion Metrics   Measure how social media activity has been directly responsible for a tangible outcome (Gonçalves, 2017). Conversion means that a social media user has been converted from one status to another e.g.

- Social media follower to customer
- Social media follower to donor
- Social media follower to volunteer

Or that a social media follower has performed a desired behaviour in response to a call-to-action e.g.

- Called your business number
- Completed an online registration form
- Visited your store

While Vanity Metrics are helpful to show how content is performing, Conversion Metrics indicate the true impact of a social media strategy (Sponder, 2011; Sponder & Khan, 2017).

It is this conversion that should be directly tied to the goals of the strategy plus aligned with overall business or organisational goals. For example, for an online store, sales are directly linked to success. If the goal of the social media strategy is:

» To increase online sales

Then, tracking the number of online sales that were the direct result of the social media strategy is paramount to measuring its success.

While it is helpful to measure how many people visited the online store as a result of the social media strategy, it is conversion in terms of sales that is the true measure of strategy performance.

7.5.2.1 Measuring Offline Conversion

Offline conversion can be more challenging to track than online conversion, but it is definitely possible and necessary.

Building in mechanisms to capture the impact of social media tactics on offline activities takes careful planning in the strategy development phase and often requires assistance from frontline staff to measure it effectively. Again, the aim is to accurately track how a specific social media activity has directly influenced an offline action.

For example, if using Facebook and Instagram to promote a product launch at a bricks-and-mortar store it is important to track how many people attend the event as a result of the Facebook and Instagram promotion.

Without this measurement, the effectiveness of the social media event promotion cannot be ascertained. It is simple to track online ticket sales using platforms such as Eventbrite, Google Analytics and/or the Facebook Pixel if users allow access to this data (Hern, 2019) but tracking how many people end up attending as a result of the social media tactics used can pose a greater challenge.

This is where some other mechanism needs to be implemented such as asking attendees at the event or surveying attendees afterwards (although return rates can be low without some form of incentive).

One of the key responsibilities of a Social Media Manager is to demonstrate the impact of their work to their client or to an organisational decision maker. This data must be captured and reported in an ethical way regardless if the strategic goal relates to an online or offline conversion.

It is also important to understand the different social media metrics so only the most relevant are included in the measurement process.

◘ Table 7.6 presents a range of social media metrics (vanity and conversion metrics) and their definitions. Some helpful advertising metrics are also included.

Table 7.6 Social media metrics

| Vanity metrics | |
Social media metric	Definition
Likes	A measurement of favourability for a piece of content or a profile.
Reactions	A Facebook sentiment metric that denotes love, laughing, surprise, crying and anger.
Share, Retweet, Regram	A measurement capturing when a social media user disseminates content to their own network that was created by someone else. Can signify endorsement.
Comment	When someone writes something on a piece of content in response to it. Can be positive, negative or neutral in sentiment.
Follower Numbers	The number of people who have chosen to stay abreast of content being posted on a social media profile by connecting with it on a permanent basis.
Reach	The number of people who see a piece of content. Often used when trying to raise awareness (Lipschultz, 2019).
Impressions	The number of times a piece of content is displayed on someone's feed (Gonçalves, 2017).
Views	The number of times a video is viewed. Views can vary in duration from 3 to 30 seconds.
CTR (Click Through Rate)	The number of link clicks on a piece of content divided by the number of impressions (Kim, 2016).

(continued)

Table 7.6 (continued)

Vanity metrics Social media metric	Definition
Advertising Metrics	
Social Media Metric	Definition
Cost Per Result	This is one of the most important advertising metrics. It indicates how much each advertising goal costs in advertising spend. For example, if the goal is a landing page view, the Cost Per Result will indicate how much each landing view is costing a client. The aim is to make the Cost Per Result as low as possible (Sponder & Khan, 2017).
Frequency	The number of times the same person sees an advertisement. Frequency is calculated as impressions divided by reach. As explained in ▶ Chap. 6, repetition can help the target audience move through the customer journey stages. However, using different ads at each stage is a better option (Tuten & Solomon, 2017).
Quality Ranking Engagement Ranking Conversion Ranking	A Facebook advertisement's perceived quality or engagement or conversion in comparison with similar ads completing for the same audience. Above Average and Average are the best rankings. These rankings replaced the Relevance Score (Facebook, 2019).
Conversion Metrics (Conversion metrics can vary largely depending on the goal of each strategy)	
Social Media Metric	Definition
Purchase/Sales/Revenue	Number of transactions or monetary figure in sales/revenue as a result of the social media strategy or a specific tactic.
Lead	A lead is a prospective customer who provides their contact details or who is proactive in contacting a business for more information. Some strategic goals are centred on generating leads as a conversion metric. For other strategies a conversion is not counted until a lead becomes a customer. Leads as a direct result of social media activities could be: Direct Messages, Online Registrations, or phone calls (with the person receiving the call asking what prompted them to reach out) (Gonçalves, 2017; Lipschultz, 2019).
LTV	Lifetime Value calculates the average value that a customer will generate for a business throughout their time as a customer (Sponder & Khan, 2017).

■ ■ Further suggestions for tracking conversion metrics:
  ▬ *Social media follower to customer*
    – **Online sales:** Google Analytics tracking purchase journey, Facebook pixel
    – **In-person:** Question during the sales process and recording answer
  ▬ *Social media follower to donor*
    – Tracking from Donate Now button on social media profile to online donation
    – Question on donation form
    – Asking in person and recording answer
  ▬ *Social media follower to volunteer*
    – Question on registration form

- Asking in person and recording answer
- *Called business number*
  - Asking during phone call and recording answer
- *Completed an online registration form*
  - Measuring source of click through on a Bitly link (link tracking)
  - Question on registration form
- *Visited store in-person*
  - Asking in person and recording answer

◘ Table 7.6 represents only a small percentage of the social media metrics currently available.

It is important to prioritise measurement in the following way during and at the end of the campaign to firstly establish the overall performance of the campaign, then the costs or revenue and finally, how well the tactics and content resonated with the target audience

■ ■ What to measure first:

1. Goal/s and SMART Objectives (Conversion Metrics)
2. Strategy Costs/Revenue and Return on Investment (ROI)
3. Content performance (Vanity Metrics)

It is essential to select the metrics of greatest relevance to a specific strategy and the first step to achieving this is to know as much as possible about the wide range of metrics available within each social media platform.

The next stage is to create a measurement framework to map the metrics and measurement activities to be undertaken during and after the strategy.

7.5.3 Planning

The International Association for the Measurement and Evaluation of Communication (AMEC) has developed the Social Media Measurement Framework to guide Social Media Managers to select the most relevant and useful metrics for a strategy (AMEC, 2014). However, it must be noted that AMEC has more recently developed an Integrated Evaluation Framework that takes an integrated marketing communications approach to the measurement of all marketing communication activities (Bagnall, 2020). As this text is social media specific, it will continue to use AMEC's original Social Media Measurement Framework. The Integrated Evaluation Framework can be accessed in the Helpful Links section at the end of this chapter.

◘ Table 7.7 is the paid, owned and earned framework and ◘ Table 7.8 is the programme, channel and business metrics framework with an explanation below each.

Each framework has the following categories of measurement:

- *Exposure:* These are metrics that measure how many people will see a client's brand on social media such as Reach, Impressions, Views etc.
- *Engagement:* This category measures audience interaction. For example, the % increase in likes, comments and shares on a client's Facebook business page compared with the previous month.
- *Preference:* This category requires metrics that quantify when a social media user chooses a client's brand over another. For example, sharing a Facebook post about a client's product or service is a positive way.
- *Impact:* Impact is another word for Conversion. For example, event attendance after promoting it on social media. However, you would need to identify a way to show that it was definitely social media that influenced this metric.
- *Advocacy:* This requires a metric to accurately measure when a social media user shares positive information about a client's brand.

Table 7.7 The paid, owned and earned framework

Paid, Owned and Earned Social Media Measurement Framework

	EXPOSURE	ENGAGEMENT	PREFERENCE	IMPACT	ADVOCACY
PAID					
OWNED					
EARNED					

www.amecorg.com

amec

AMEC (2014)

Table 7.8 Programme, channel and business metrics framework

Program, Business and Channel Social Media Measurement Framework

	EXPOSURE	ENGAGEMENT	PREFERENCE	IMPACT	ADVOCACY
PROGRAM METRICS					
CHANNEL METRICS					
BUSINESS METRICS					

www.amecorg.com

amec

AMEC (2014)

For example, the % increase in recommendations on the Facebook business page over the past 6 months compared with the previous 6 months.

The rows in ◘ Table 7.7 Paid, Owned and Earned Framework represent the following activities:

- *Paid:* Social media activity that a client pays for. For example, Facebook ads or boosted posts.
- *Owned:* Non-paid social media content posted directly on a client's own social media business profiles. E.g. posts on the business' Instagram profile.
- *Earned:* Social media activity mentioning a client's business that is generated by other social media users. E.g. someone sharing a post from a client's LinkedIn business page.

The Paid, Owned and Earned Framework is best for long-term social media strategies because it captures day-to-day social media performance.

The Programme, Channel and Business Metrics Framework is most effective in measuring social media performance around short-term social media strategies.

In fact, using the term 'Campaign' in place of the word 'Programme' adds even greater context to the true function of this framework.

The rows representing the activities in the Programme, Channel and Business Metrics Framework differ from the Paid, Owned and Earned Framework in the following ways:

- *Programme:* Programme is another term for Campaign. These are the activities to measure around a specific short-term social media campaign. For example, the Facebook campaign to promote an upcoming event or a charity's annual Christmas donation drive.
- *Business:* These are the social media activities that are undertaken from a brand or organisational level. For exam-

ple, posts promoting organisational news or communicating brand values.
- *Channel:* Social media activities relating to the specific social media channels used in a client's short-term campaign. For example, measuring activity on Facebook, LinkedIn and Twitter used in a Valentine's Day promotion.

When using these frameworks, quality is always more important than quality. Only include relevant metrics that align specifically the strategic goal/s, SMART Objectives, conversion and content performance that relates specifically to the strategy.

Doing so ensures that only relevant metrics are included, reducing time and effort in the data analysis and reporting stages outlined later in this chapter. Less superfluous data means greater time to develop and implement actionable recommendations for continuous improvement.

7.5.4 Measurement Tools

While there are many social media tools on the market, it can be challenging to find one tool that can measure a wide range of social media platforms while simultaneously being able to measure the varied metrics of each one.

Many of the scheduling and social media management platforms explored in ► Chap. 8 also offer social media listening, monitoring and measurement functionality and can be a good option if searching for an all-in-one solution.

However, the measurement offered by these platforms can be uniform, making it difficult for Social Media Managers to closely analyse the specifics of each social platform.

Using one tool to measure multiple platforms usually results in having to view the metrics of each platform individually anyway, because the analysis does not offer

7

enough specificity. While checking the analytics of multiple social media platforms may seem time-consuming, it can be an extremely effective way of conducting social media measurement.

7.5.4.1 Use Native Measurement Tools First

The measurement tools native to Facebook, Twitter, LinkedIn, YouTube and Instagram have been specifically designed for the characteristics of those platforms and therefore, will generate the most relevant metrics for analysis, leading to more meaningful insights.

Dennis Yu, CEO of BlitzMetrics also confirms this in his interview at the end of this chapter. Therefore, it is recommended to use native measurement tools first, before paying for other tools. ◘ Table 7.9 lists the measurement tools native to each platform.

Google Analytics Is Essential

It is also recommended that a client or organisation uses Google Analytics, also a free tool that tracks website activities including traffic coming from social media profiles, a metric that can also demonstrate the impact of a social media strategy (Sponder & Khan, 2017; Lipschultz, 2019).

Next, the exploration of measurement will continue to include big data and how it can assist in gaining in-depth audience insights.

7.6 Big Data

The term 'big data' refers to the analysis of extremely large data sets to gain audience insights, identify relationships, trends, patterns of behaviour and to make predictions (Gandomi & Haider, 2015; Gudivada, Baeza-Yates & Raghavan, 2015; Panda, Abraham & Hassanien, 2018).

With the analysis often performed by Artificial Intelligence (AI) technologies, big data is used to recommend products on Amazon and programs to watch on Netflix

◘ **Table 7.9** Native social media measurement tools

Social media platform	Native measurement tool
Facebook	Insights (Business Page) **Business Manager:** Ads Manager **Business Manager:** Measure & Report
Instagram	Insights (Business Profile)
Twitter	Analytics
LinkedIn	**Articles:** View Stats **Posts:** No. of views of posts in feed **Advertising:** Campaign Manager
YouTube	Analytics
WordPress	Stats
Snapchat	Snapchat Insights
TikTok	TikTok Insights (with Pro Account)
Pinterest	Pinterest Analytics (Business Account)
WeChat	WeChat Web Analytics

by analysing the data from millions of people who use these platforms (Panda, Abraham & Hassanien, 2018).

Furthermore, it was the analysis of big data that was used by Cambridge Analytica to attempt to sway voters during the 2016 United States Presidential election (Isaak & Hanna, 2018).

In the scope of strategic social media management, big data is now used to gain in-depth audience insights about products, consumer behaviour, competitors, and influencers and this knowledge is being used to customise audience experiences, content and advertising (Melder, 2019).

Big Data is characterised in the literature as having six key characteristics, also known as the 'Six Vs' (Gandomi & Haider, 2015; Gudivada, Baeza-Yates & Raghavan, 2015;

Table 7.10 The 6 Vs of big data	
The V's	**Description**
1. Volume	Big Data set sizes are in multiple terabytes and petabytes which are extremely large. For example, 1 terabyte is the equivalent to 16 million Facebook photos (Gandomi & Haider, 2015).
2. Variety	Big Data can be collected and analysed from structured and unstructured sources and in a wide range of formats including text, images, video, audio and programming languages.
3. Velocity	The speed at which big data can be delivered via mobile devices and other platforms within the internet of things is at unprecedented levels providing large volumes of data within rapid timeframes.
4. Veracity	Big Data can often be unreliable, particularly within its automated analysis such as in the incorrect classification of sentiment, a phenomenon already explored within this chapter.
5. Variability (and complexity)	The wide range of formats and sources from which big data is derived results in data flow rates being sporadic and analysis being challenging because of this inconsistency.
6. Value	In its original form, Big Data cannot be considered very useful. However, the analysis of extremely large data sets can be extremely valuable in uncovering important insights, particularly in relation to target audiences.

Panda, Abraham & Hassanien, 2018). ▪ Table 7.10 explains these characteristics.

7.6.1 Gathering Big Data from Social Media Platforms

Gathering big data from social media platforms can be referred to as 'scraping'. While there are tools that social media platforms permit to scrape data from owned profiles, the API (Application Programming Interface) can limit third party tools from accessing data from other platform users (Lipschultz, 2019).

Permission to scrape data can be platform specific, constantly changes and in some cases, can only be obtained with permission. Facebook in particular has become extremely wary in relation to data scraping after the Cambridge Analytica scandal and subsequent data breaches (Isaak & Hanna, 2018).

To date, Twitter seems to be the most openly accessible platform from which to scrape big data, particularly with software called Python, but this should be investigated at the beginning of any proposed big data activity (Python, 2019).

7.6.2 Big Data Analysis of Social Media

According to (Gandomi & Haider, 2015, pp. 142–143), the analysis of big data generated by social media generally falls into the following categories:

1. *Content-Based:* Data posted by users (images, text, video etc.)
2. *Structure-Based:* Overall structural attributes of a social network.
3. *Community Detection:* Groups of users within a network who frequently interact.
4. *Influence Analysis:* How the behaviour of a user affects other users.
5. *Link Prediction:* Prediction future connections made between users.

▪ Figure 7.2 demonstrates the general process involved with the collection and analy-

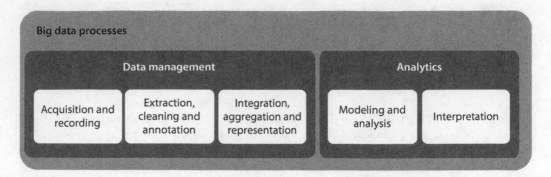

Fig. 7.2 Processes for extracting insights from big data (Gandomi & Haider, 2015)

sis of big data sets. Notice that after the data has been gathered, cleaned and aggregated that it must undergo a two-step analysis process in line with what has already been demonstrated in this chapter.

First the data is presented in a visual form in the modelling and analysis stage (the what) and then it is interpreted to uncover key insights (the why).

7.6.3 Visualisation of Big Data

Data visualization involves the presentation of big data sets in a graphical or pictorial format. The visualization of data is to assist in its interpretation so that trends, associations, structures and patterns can be easily identifiable.

Visualizations of big data can also be interactive and in 3-D formats to facilitate even deeper analyses. There are many data visualization tools available. Three useful tools are presented in Table 7.11.

It is important for Social Media Managers to understand the possibilities in terms of the audience insights that can be gained through big data analysis, as this level of data analysis continues to become more widespread as social media evolves and user numbers increase.

Reporting social media data, in general, is also a vital skill in the process of social media management as explored in the next section of this chapter.

Table 7.11 Data visualization tools

Visualization tool	Description
Gephi	Open Source tool that can generate large scale 3D data visualizations within speedy timeframes.
Tableau	A data management tool that can generate a wide range of visualizations.
Chart Studio by Plotly	Generates 3D interactive visualizations without requiring any coding knowledge.

7.6.3.1 Predicting the Mood of a Nation Using Big Data from Social Media

In a TedX Talk, Chris Hansen from Janys Analytics discussed how he and his team used big data scraped from Twitter to attempt to predict the mood of Twitter users living in the United States over the course of an average year (TedX Talks, 2015).

Hansen found that the sample of Twitter users was close to being accurately representative of the demographic makeup of the general U.S. population, rendering it a useful data set to analyse.

The team spent considerable time creating a sentiment map to identify positive, negative and neutral terms used by Twitter users that could provide an insight into their current moods. Furthermore, emoticons were also used as a measure of mood. Tests were conducted using machine raters compared with human raters to develop an algorithm and machine approach to automate the sentiment analysis process.

Twitter data from U.S. users was analysed to help identify the overall mood of the country at particular times of the year. For example, the data accurately predicted that the mood of people in New Orleans was positive during Mardi Gras celebrations. The data generated from this study was developed into a report called: *Pulse of the Nation: U.S. Mood Throughout the Day inferred from Twitter* (Mislove, et al., 2010).

This example demonstrates how big data can be used to analyse populations and inform prediction in relation to their mood and/or activities.

7.7 Reporting Social Media Activities and Performance

Data collection and analyses are clearly integral phases of social media listening, monitoring and measurement. Yet, just as important is the communication of that information to clients and organisational decision makers.

Knowledge is power and data provides evidence to demonstrate ROI, support proposed changes, and requests for resources.

Some clients and organisational decision makers still do not understand the value of social media and clear and accurate reporting provides evidence for your case (Sutherland, 2015).

Organisational decision makers can be accustomed to receiving the results of traditional media performance in reports. A well-crafted social media report is an opportunity to communicate in a familiar medium, but in a way that inspires change through the use of data as evidence.

Often social media managers must educate decision makers about social media in order to attract support, reporting and communication of data can be highly effective ways to increase knowledge and resources (Sutherland, 2015).

As a Social Media Manager reporting can play a hugely influential role by demonstrating the impact of a social media strategy.

■ ■ The key functions of reporting social media data are:
- ━ *To communicate social media performance*
- ━ *To communicate social conversation* involving a brand, product, campaign, issue and/or competitor
- ━ *To lobby for support* (e.g. resources)
- ━ *To guide continuous Improvement*

> ❝ In the context of strategic social media management, the most important function of a social media report is to demonstrate if a strategy is achieving (or has achieved) its goals and SMART Objectives. ❞
>
> **Dr Karen Sutherland**

■■ If the data demonstrates that the strategy is not working:

— Reporting on these items during the strategy implementation phase allows Social Media Managers to tweak the tactics to guide the strategy back on course if it is not performing.

— Reporting on these items at the end of a social media strategy provides valuable insights into what went wrong and what should be changed for the next strategy.

As explored in this chapter, *social media performance and listening data requires in-depth analysis to be able to communicate the why in addition to the what.*

■■ For example:

— What social media activities are working (or not working) to support strategic goals

— Trends (time of day, types of content receiving the greatest engagement)

— Audience habits and demographics

— How well a client or organisation compares with competitors

— How to enhance performance

— The health of brand reputation

— How positively a product/campaign is being received by its target audience

— How people are responding to an issue or crisis

Yet, there is a wide range of social media reporting styles, each supporting a different function, including: Time-Based, Campaign-Based and Issue/Crisis-Based. The reporting needs to be aligned with the social media activities taking place.

For example, ▶ Chap. 5 discussed how long-term social media strategies are often interspersed with short-term strategies. Therefore, reporting will need to capture data from each of those types of activities.

Furthermore, as part of issues and/or crisis management, additional reports are required to keep relevant stakeholders up-to-date with developments that may damage brand reputation. Each of the three reporting styles is explained below:

■■ **Time-Based Reports**

Time-based reports can provide a brief snapshot of day-to-day performance or a detailed longitudinal analysis. These are usually aligned to long-term or ongoing social media strategies. Reports can be generated:

— Daily

— Weekly

— Monthly

— Quarterly

— Annually

— At the end of a long-term strategy

■■ **Campaign-Based Reports**

Campaign-Based reports communicate the performance of the activities associated with a specific campaign such as a new product launch or offline event. Reporting on a campaign includes the data aligned to the specific short-term campaign strategy goals and SMART Objectives from the launch of the campaign to its conclusion. These types of reports can also be time-based to track the performance of a campaign while it is underway and make any necessary tweaks.

■■ **Issues/Crisis Based Reporting**

Issue/Crisis-Based are usually generated at least daily (sometimes several times per day) depending on the severity of the issue or crisis. These types of reports show the social media response to the crisis so that organisational decision makers can respond appropriately. Issue/Crisis-Based reports are predominantly social listening data, but also show the response to organisational posts that address the issue or crisis. See ▶ Chap. 4 for more information on issues and crisis management.

7.7.1 Developing a Social Media Report

Just as you need an objective or purpose before you undertake any social media monitoring and measurement, you also need to set clear objectives when reporting activities. The first stage of compiling a social media analytics report is to articulate what the report is attempting to achieve for example, what to include, what to exclude and how to present the data.

For example, if the objective of a report is to analyse the social media performance and response of a product launch on Facebook and Instagram, then it would be unnecessary to include data from other social media platforms generated during the same time period.

In most cases it is important to align the reporting objectives with:

– *Strategy/Campaign goals and SMART objectives* (that are already aligned with strategic goals. See ▶ Chap. 5). Did the strategy or campaign achieve these items?
– *The goals from the social listening plan or monitoring and measurement frameworks* (although these will already be aligned with strategic goals and SMART Objectives). Everything must align consistently throughout the social media management process.

Essentially, reporting provides the evidence of whether a specific social media activity achieved its intended goals and objectives.

7.7.2 Audience

Audience is also the most important factor when developing a social media performance report. The report must be customised to suit the person who will be reading it. Therefore, it is essential to understand who will be receiving the report and what their preferences are at the beginning of the social media strategy development phase as this will provide guidance on the most valuable metrics to gather and analyse from the start.

Inaccurately targeting a report can result in it not being read which means there is less opportunity to demonstrate your impact as a Social Media Manager.

Social media performance reports are often left unread if they do not make any sense to the person reading them or contain useless information rendering it difficult for the reader to locate the key findings.

■■ Important audience-related questions to ask when planning a social media report:
 ▬ Who will be reading this report?
 ▬ What does the reader need to know?
 ▬ What doesn't the reader need to know?
 ▬ How knowledgeable is the reader about social media?
 ▬ How much time does the audience have to read this report?
 ▬ Does the reader prefer numbers or graphical representation of data?
 ▬ Is the reader likely to show this report to other people?
 ▬ What sort of file format does the reader prefer?

A report (or any form of communication) must be designed with the audience in mind so that it increases its chances of being understood. For example, a monthly social media performance report developed for a Digital Marketing Manager would be very different to the report compiled for a CEO with a limited grasp on the value of social media. You need to tell the story of social media data in a language a specific audience understands.

■■ Report Sections
There are many different ways to structure a social media report. Again, audience needs will dictate the level of detail that must be included. However, of greatest importance is to get to the point, clearly and quickly. It

Table 7.12 Sections to include in a social media report

Section	Description	Necessary/ optional
Cover Page	Include the name of the report, date, client's logo (if permitted), your logo (if relevant), and your contact details to provide context for the rest of the report.	Necessary
Executive Summary	A brief summary of the entire report including the key findings and recommendations. This may be the only section of the report that is read by a busy client or organisational decision maker.	Necessary
Table of Contents	Helps to navigate the rest of the report but will depend on the length and detail of the information included.	Optional
Background	Sets the scene regarding the organisation and provides an explanation regarding why the listening, monitoring and/or measurement activities were required and why report was generated.	Optional
Goals	Clearly states the strategic goals and SMART Objectives.	Necessary
Method	Briefly explains the platforms analysed, the tools used and the timeframe in which the listening, monitoring and measurement activities were implemented. May not be necessary for a client with a greater interest in the results.	Optional
Results	The visual representation of data (graphs, charts, infographics etc.), description of data and key findings from deeper analysis.	Necessary
Recommendations	Actionable recommendations to enhance social media performance using data and key findings from within the report as evidence.	Necessary
Conclusion	Summarising paragraph to complete the report.	Optional

is important to provide some context for people who are unfamiliar with the activities being undertaken, so including some brief background and methodology information can be helpful, but do not include too much.

Put the most important data up front. Think of your audience.

Table 7.12 suggests various generic sections to include in a social media report and an explanation of each. These sections can be customised (or omitted) depending on the purpose and audience of the report.

Table 7.12 clearly indicates the importance of the Results and Recommendations sections of a social media report as its core components. It makes perfect sense when considering, at the most basic level, the report aims to convey what happened, why it happened and what to do next. The Results and Recommendation sections have been explored in greater detail below.

7.7.3 Results Section

The Results section should contain the visual representation of data, a description of that visual data representation (the what) and then an explanation of the key findings from a deeper analysis of that data (the why).

▪▪ Data Presentation

Most listening, monitoring and measurement tools generate a multitude of clear reports that are simple to read. However, it is essential to select only the most appropriate options to present data in a way that address goals and SMART objectives as well as being meaningful to a client.

■■ **Visual**

Using graphs to represent data can be an effective technique for it to be visually communicated in a meaningful way. There are many types of graphs (pie, bar, column, line, scatter etc.) and it is best to try a number of variations to see which one represents specific data in the clearest way for the reader.

Static and animated infographics should also be considered along with more traditional forms of data presentation as they can be an extremely visually appealing way for audiences to consume statistical data. Many measurement tools generate their own graphs, but their range is often limited. There are also a number of helpful tools available that can develop amazing and effective graphs for reports and presentations.

A brief list of tools is located in the Helpful Links section at the end of this chapter.

■■ **Textual**

Every visual representation of data must include two textual elements:

1. **A description of visual data representation (the what)**
2. **Communication of data analysis (the why)**

Graphs are only a small component of the report and will not be meaningful to a client or organisational decision maker without providing an explanation of what the graph is displaying and why this result has occurred.

For example, if there is a peak in engagement on a particular day, only describing it is unhelpful.

The client can already see this. As a Social Media Manager, it is your responsibility to investigate what happened on that particular day that could have resulted in increased engagement (a particular post

Graph 5 When Your Fans are Online

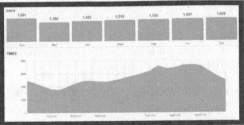

Graph 5 indicates that Sunday is the day (and 8pm is the time) when the greatest number of your Facebook page followers are online.

■ **Fig. 7.3** How to present data visually and textually within a Social Media Performance Report

etc.) and communicate that to a client so that it can be replicated.

With the result described and their key findings explained, the next step is to develop actionable and evidence-based recommendations to include in the social media report.

■ Figure 7.3 provides an example of how data can be presented with recommended visual and textual components.

7.7.4 Articulating Actionable, Evidence-Based Recommendations

The Recommendations section of the report is arguably the most important component and the fundamental reason social media listening, monitoring and measurement activities are undertaken at all. Most businesses and organisations strive for continuous improvement and to meet goals and SMART Objectives. Recommendations provide the key information for this to occur.

However, for the Recommendations section of a social media report to inspire change, the recommendations included must be actionable (as previously explained) and evidence-based (supported by data and key findings already presented within the report). Furthermore, the recommendations must be linked to strategic goals and SMART Objectives.

This is a powerful part of the process because data is used as evidence to create positive change for a client, an organisation and for target audiences.

■■ Overall, recommendations fall into the following categories:
- *Continue* (It is working)
- *Fine tune* (It is okay, but could be better)
- *Stop* (It is not working)
- *New direction required* (A fresh approach is required)

There is always something that can be enhanced in social media management.

The aim is to stop any social media activity that is not being received in a positive way by the target audience, to avoid damage to organisational reputation and negatively affecting stakeholders (See ▶ Chap. 4).

If a social media activity is resonating in a positive way with a target audience but is not directly supporting goals and/or objectives, it is recommended to keep it but tweak it so that it aligns better strategically.

The target audience should always come first. If something is working, keep doing more of that.

If something is performing at an average standard, tweak it, test it and monitor and measure what happens over and over until it works (◘ Fig. 7.4).

Recommendations must use data from the report as evidence to inform and support any proposed change.

Use the following questions as a guide when analysing each visual representation of data in the Result section and in the development of actionable, evidence-based recommendations to include in a social media report.

■■ Questions to ask when analysing social media data:
- What is this data telling me about my client's social media performance? What is apparent?
- What are three key points that this data is making about a client's social media performance?
- Can you see any trends? Any peaks or dips in followers or engagement? If so, what occurred on this particular day to cause this? Investigate the why.
- What is this data telling you about the target audience, when they are posting, how people are engaging with the content, whether or not they are converting? It is up to you to interpret this data for your client.
- What does this data say in relation to the strategic goals and SMART Objectives? Does it support their achievement? Why/Why not?

An example of an evidence-based recommendation is:

Recommendation 1   *Posting on Wednesdays at 8 pm provides the greatest opportunity for engagement with Facebook followers as 80% of followers are online at this time (see ◘ Figure 7.3)*

Notice how the recommendation being made uses data from the report to support it AND refers the reader to the location of that data within the report.

It is essential for any recommendations made within a report to be supported in this way and presented to the reader in a way that makes it clear where the rationale originates.

» Remember, without data as evidence, everything else is guesswork.

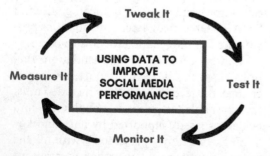

◘ **Fig. 7.4** Tweak it, test it and monitor and measure

Conclusion

This chapter provided a comprehensive examination of social media listening, monitoring and measurement activities and their importance to strategic social media management.

The careful planning social media listening, monitoring and measurement activities that align with strategic goals and SMART Objectives was also investigated and recommendations made in relation to specific tools, methods and processes involved with data collection.

The vital process of in-depth data analysis and the development and implementation of actionable recommendations that support continual improvement also featured predominantly.

The topic of big data as a rich source of audience insights was also presented. The analysis and reporting of social media data as essential social media management skills were explained.

The chapter concluded imparting how powerful data can be in influencing and inspiring positive change when it is communicated with relevance to a specific audience.

Case Study: Chilli's Bar & Grill Hit a Nerve Through Social Listening

U.S.-based restaurant chain, Chilli's Bar and Grill now understands the valuable insights that social listening data can provide about its customers and the ways in which they use Chilli's products.

An example of the hidden gems that social listening can uncover happened when the social media team for Chilli's Bar and Grill discovered that their customers often visit the restaurant to buy take-away just before going to see a movie at a nearby local cinema.

Rather than buying traditional popcorn, ice-creams and other movie-related treats from the cinema snack bar, customers opted to sneak in treats such as burgers and tacos from Chilli's extensive menu (Chilli's Bar & Grill, 2019).

This type of consumer behaviour was identified through social listening activities where social media users posted about their habits of taking Chilli's food into movie theatres with them.

With this knowledge, the Chilli's Bar and Grill Social Media Team decided to play an April Fool's prank on their customers by announcing that they had developed a "… Chicken Crisper Hoodie, complete with thermal insulated pocket…" to assist with the transportation and smuggling of their food into cinemas (Baglietto, 2019).

The response was overwhelmingly positive. Within an hour of the prank being posted, more than 1500 people offered to purchase the fictional piece of clothing at any price (Baglietto, 2019).

This case study demonstrates how social listening can provide previously unknown insights about an audience and their habits in using a specific product. This knowledge was then leveraged by Chilli's Bar and Grill to connect with their customers, demonstrating how well the brand understands their habits and needs, strengthening the customer/brand relationship in the process.

While social listening can be used to identify issues before they turn into crises, it can also be leveraged in a proactive way to build connections with an audience of current and prospective customers. This case study is an example of how powerful social listening can be as a relationship management tool.

1. How can social listening be used for more than only issues and crisis management?
2. How can leveraging social listening data help to strengthen customer relationships?

7.8 Interview: Dennis Yu, CEO, BlitzMetrics, USA

1. **Please tell me about your current role.**
   I'm the Chief Executive Officer at BlitzMetrics, and that means I oversee the company's operations in terms of education training programmes, our agency, and the software platform that we're building. Our job is to create jobs for young adults so they can take their digital marketing skills and start their own company, go work at another company or maybe start or work in their family-run business. All these skills that you need to operate in a modern digital landscape.

2. **What do you enjoy most about your current role?**
   I love seeing the light bulb go off where you see a student that's struggling. Maybe they're struggling with implementing Google Tag Manager, which is difficult and the pixels and the tracking codes, and they're frustrated. But then after a few tries, maybe with a little bit of mentoring from other people they get it, and then they do it over and over again, and you see them start to make money because they're doing it in the real world with clients that are paying for this execution, making money for these clients. Then the thing that really warms my heart when I see these young adults train up other people and help them turn that light bulb on, that means everything to me.

3. **What are the greatest challenges that you experience in your role?**
   I sit between two different generations. There are the young adults that have grown up on Tai Lopez and Gary Vaynerchuk, and they think that they can be a CEO tomorrow and drive Lamborghinis by next month and be making $100,000 a year, and the expectations are, "I just want to be an entre-

preneur. I want right away. I don't believe in college. This is what old people used to do."
   Then there are the business owners who have been around a long time and believe in tradition. They hate on the Millennials, and they're there saying, "Hey, it's about loyalty." This is the way school works. The challenge is bridging those two because the business owners have the money, but they don't understand the technology, especially social media. The young adults, they have that vibrant youth. They're able to succeed by grasping new technology, but they don't understand the process of working with businesses. I sit in between the business owners and the young adults finding ways to be able to bridge that. We bridge that through our training and through our processes.

4. **Please tell me your career story.**
   When I was in high school, I was one of those Asians that always wanted to get a 4.0 GPA. One professor pulled me aside and said, "You might be barking up the wrong tree, because while you might be getting the As, you're missing the bigger picture, which is about building relationships. If you want to be an entrepreneur, you need to understand how to do things that are not measured on a paper or measured in your GPA." I learned this the hard way because I wanted to go to work for Nike, and I applied. I couldn't get an interview because I didn't have the relationships.
   It wasn't until I had a mentor, Al Casey who was the CEO of American Airlines, and he also pulled me aside and said, "Dennis, it's about who you know, not what you know, and about who knows you," and that made such an impact on me of mentors that were opening doors for me that could see around my own blind spots. No matter how hard I worked, no matter how smart I was, it's

still critical to have a mentor that can tell you about these things.

I thought, "How do I replicate that experience so that thousands or hundreds of thousands of other young adults could also benefit from mentorship in the way that I did?"

Every bit of success I have ever had is not because I'm smart or anything like that. It's because a mentor has opened doors for me.

5. **What do you think are the three most important things for Social Media Managers to consider regarding the processes of social media listening, monitoring and measurement?**

One is getting familiar with the data, tools, systems, operations, being able to see what people are saying, interpret, respond back, low-level community management. That's where social media monitoring has come in where you're looking at signals. You're looking at how many people like something. You're looking at sentiment on how many people were saying this positively versus negatively. That's the base level. Tools will do most of that.

The second level above that is building relationships. If you're a real community manager, if you're a real social media person, you're not just responding. You're actually proactive.

Proactive means you have to greet customers and ask them for feedback, collect their one-minute videos, not just only when they come to you and they complain.

Then the third level is you have to be consultative. When you're consultative, you're thinking about, "How do I add value? How do I help these customers do a better job and have more success? How do I motivate other employees? How do I become a figurehead for the company?" Now, I'm not just some low-level person using tools to do community response or

someone who's more like a customer success inside sales manager, but I'm moving up into the executive role.

6. **What do you think are the benefits of social media listening, monitoring and measurement?**

If you look at the real value of monitoring, listening, and analytics, it's taking that data and being able to turn it into analysis. An analysis is, "Okay, fine. I can use Google Analytics. I can use Hootsuite. I can use Crimson Hexagon. I can use all these different tools that all spit out different kinds of reports in different sorts of ways. I have the free tools that Facebook and Google and YouTube and Instagram and all these other guys produce," but it's going from that raw data. Think of that as raw or coming out of the ground and then converting it into gold or whatever the analogy is.

I want to convert that into gold, and that requires this tool that you can't license. This tool that sits between your ears to be able to interpret that data and be able to build relationships, build processes, and figure out how do you identify an unhappy customer and turn them into a happy customer based on certain situations.

No tool does that. How do you figure out customers that are in certain scenarios where they're already happy? How do I collect that data from them or their feedback? Because in a modern society, your marketing is not what you say about yourself. It's what the customers say about you, carries more cred.

So, how do you actively build processes to collect what people are saying about you? That's certainly part of social media monitoring and measurement, right? But most people, they don't get beyond that reports tools. They're so caught up in learning all these different tools they forget they're two levels above that.

7. **What are the challenges of social media listening, monitoring and measurement?**
    The challenge is the misunderstanding of what it's about. The biggest challenge is getting away from the idea that social media monitoring and measurement is about tools and data and charts. All these tools, they deliver different charts. We were in this space. Nike has paid us over a million dollars to build social analytics for them. That's how I know. It was stuff that Adobe or Omniture, whatever you want to call them, they didn't have. We would produce these different charts that they wanted to show how their different properties are doing. So, how is Nike Basketball tying in with Nike when we launched a new shoe with LeBron James, and how does that flow across Twitter and Instagram and YouTube? What's the value of that? We did the same thing for Red Bull, for example.

    We had 70 charts. Then another competitor would come in and say, "Oh, well, we have 80 charts," and then someone else would come in and say, "Oh, yeah? We have 100 charts."

    It's not about the charts and the data. It's about what you are going to do to extract business value.

    As long as people are stuck in the tools and the data and the witchcraft because the whole thing with big data and algorithms lends itself to people selling witchcraft. The tools won't solve your problems for you. It's people like us.

8. **What are your favourite tools for social media listening, monitoring and measurement and why?**
    The best tools are the ones that are made natively. Facebook has made a dozen different tools, not just Insights, but everything within Business Manager. I can look at audiences. I can look at Audience Insights. I can look at Custom Audiences. There are other tools such as the Video Manager, the Asset Library that will show you how your different assets are per-

forming. There's all the tools within paid where I can get different kinds of counts. I can get negative feedback. So, there are a dozen different tools within Facebook.

Google has a dozen different tools as well. Search Console that tells you where all the traffic is coming from and where you rank whether or not people are coming to your website or not. That's tied in with Google Analytics. Google Analytics is tied in with Google Tag Manager. Google Tag Manager allows you to determine triggers of when people have done or not done things.

One of the main problems with the social media monitoring tools is that they only look at social media. If you're only looking at Twitter. They're only looking at public data. If you're looking only at public data, only on the social profiles, you're missing the spillover impact.

This spread across other channels, across relationships is the thing that social media monitoring tools miss because they're not focusing on the ROI. As a business owner, and business owners that employ social media marketers, they're always asking the ROI question. Oh, okay. Great. You got 10,000 likes on your tweet. What's the ROI? How much more did you sell? That's the question to answer.

9. **What do you think of the current landscape of social media management as a profession?**
    Social media is now infused into every part of business operations, because there's two-and-a-half-billion people that are using Facebook, YouTube or Twitter or whatever daily. It has become so big that it includes AI. It includes operations. It includes general marketing. It includes SEO. I would argue social media and PR are now the same thing. I would argue that inbound marketing and all these different marketing strategies, they're all.

A senior social media manager is actually a marketing strategist, because they are driving the business, and they have to prove the ROI, meaning that even if their role is they're in charge of Instagram and Twitter and Facebook, they still have to see it all the way through to the sale. So, they have to be able to talk to the CFO about the ROI.

10. **What has been the best piece of advice that you have been given?**

If you don't quit, you win. The digital marketing business changes so fast. You feel like once you learn this one thing, now another 10 things have popped up. It's like a game of Whack-A-Mole. You can't hit every one down, but if you don't quit, you win. It really is that simple.

❓ Questions for Critical Reflection

1. Why is social media monitoring, listening and measurement an essential part of strategic social media management? Please explain your answer.

2. What is the difference between social media monitoring and listening? How can both assist in the success of a business or organisation?

3. Explain when it is important to measure social media performance and why.

4. What is the difference between vanity and conversion metrics? Please provide an example of each to demonstrate your answer.

5. What is the analysis of big data useful for in relation to social media management and why?

6. Why is the reporting of social media data to a client or organisational decision maker a powerful tool for a Social Media Manager?

7. What is the overall purpose of social media monitoring, listening and measurement? Please explain your answer.

❯ Practical Exercises

1. Pick one of your favourite brands and visit their social media profile on each channel. Examine the comments on their latest post. How quickly did the brand respond? Did they respond at all? Based on your understanding of this chapter, what recommendations can you make to the brand's Social Media Manager in relation to their social media monitoring practices?

2. Pretend that you are an entrepreneur conducting research about the viability of opening a new vegan ice-cream parlour in Hong Kong. Complete the Social Listening Plan in Appendix 2 with the necessary information to undertake a listening activity to assess the online conversation relating to veganism in Hong Kong.

3. Imagine that you are the Social Media Manager for a local charity that helps disadvantaged children. Every year you are responsible using social media to promote the *Annual Gala Fundraising Ball*. The goal is to use social media to attract as many people as possible to buy tickets to the event and make donations on the night. The charity has a presence on Facebook, Twitter and Instagram. Please make a list of the Vanity and Conversion Metrics for this event from the preparation phase through to its evaluation. Also, please explain how you will measure how social media directly influenced any offline conversion.

References

Ampofo, L., Collister, S., O'Loughlin, B., Chadwick, A., Halfpenny, P. J., & Procter, P. J. (2015). Text mining and social media: When quantitative meets qualitative and software meets people. In *Innovations in digital research methods* (pp. 161–192). Thousand Oaks, CA: SAGE Publications Inc.

Aula, P. (2010). Social media, reputation risk and ambient publicity management. *Strategy & Leadership, 38*(6), 43–49.

Baer, J. (2016). *Hug your haters: How to embrace complaints and keep your customers.* New York: Portfolio/Penguin.

Baglietto, M. (2019). 9 social media listening success stories. *Netbase*, viewed 19/11/2019. https://www.netbase.com/blog/9-social-media-listening-success-stories/

Bagnall, R. (2020). *AMEC's integrated evaluation framework*, viewed 5/09/2020. https://amecorg.com/amecframework/

Barnhart, B. (2019). How the Facebook algorithm works and ways to outsmart it. *Sprout Social*, viewed 06/8/2019. https://sproutsocial.com/insights/facebook-algorithm/

Bazaarvoice. (2019). *The conversation index volume 6*, viewed 06/8/2019. http://media2.bazaarvoice.com/documents/Bazaarvoice_Conversation_Index_Volume6.pdf

CampaignLive. (2019). *Tesco Mobile enters hilarious debate with Jaffa Cakes, Yorkshire Tea on Twitter*, viewed 1/8/2019. https://www.campaignlive.co.uk/article/tesco-mobile-enters-hilarious-debate-jaffa-cakes-yorkshire-tea-twitter/1221163

Chambers, J. (2019). People have discovered an ASOS bot responding to Facebook comments and the results are hilarious. *Mama* Mia.com, viewed 19/9/2019. https://www.mamamia.com.au/asos-customer-service-bot/

Chilli's Bar & Grill. (2019). Chilli's menu. Chillis.com, viewed 19/11/2019. https://www.chilis.com/menu

Elliott, C. (2018). Chatbots are killing customer service. Here's why. *Forbes*, viewed 05/8/2019. https://www.forbes.com/sites/christopherelliott/2018/08/27/chatbots-are-killing-customer-service-heres-why/#12f9a74413c5

Facebook. (2019). About quality ranking. Facebook.com, viewed 08/8/2019. https://www.facebook.com/business/help/303639570334185

Gandomi, A., & Haider, M. (2015). Beyond the hype: Big data concepts, methods, and analytics. *International Journal of Information Management, 35*(2), 137–144.

Gonçalves, A. (2017). *Social media analytics strategy: Using data to optimize business performance.* Berkeley, CA: Apress.

Gross, L., & Horn, M. (2017). Opportunities for social listening in higher education. Journal of Education Advancement & Marketing, 2(3), 256–271.

Gudivada, V. N., Baeza-Yates, R., & Raghavan, V. V. (2015). Big data: Promises and problems. *Computer, 48*(3), 20–23.

Hardy, R. A., & Norgaard, J. R. (2016). Reputation in the internet black market: An empirical and theoretical analysis of the deep web. *Journal of Institutional Economics, 12*(3), 515–539.

Hern, A. (2019). Facebook launches 'clear history' tool – but it won't delete anything. *The Guardian*, viewed 25/8/2019. https://www.theguardian.com/technology/2019/aug/20/facebook-launches-clear-history-tool-but-it-wont-delete-anything

Hernández, I., Rivero, C. R., & Ruiz, D. (2019). Deep web crawling: A survey. *World Wide Web, 22*(4), 1577–1610.

Hill, K. (2012). #McDStories: When a hashtag becomes a bashtag. Forbes.com, viewed 19/11/2019. https://www.forbes.com/sites/kashmirhill/2012/01/24/mcdstories-when-a-hashtag-becomes-a-bashtag/#730381f7ed25

Hutchinson, A. (2019). Facebook messenger by the numbers 2019 [infographic]. *Social Media Today*, viewed 2/08/2019. https://www.socialmediatoday.com/news/facebook-messenger-by-the-numbers-2019-infographic/553809/

International Association for the Measurement and Evaluation of Communication (AMEC). (2014). Social media measurement framework documents. AMEC.org, viewed 08/8/2019. https://amecorg.com/social-media-measurement/framework/

Isaak, J., & Hanna, M. J. (2018). User data privacy: Facebook, Cambridge analytica, and privacy protection. *Computer, 51*(8), 56–59.

Jain, N., Agarwal, P., & Pruthi, J. (2015). HashJacker-detection and analysis of hashtag hijacking on Twitter. *International Journal of Computer Applications, 114*(19), 17.

Kim, C. M. (2016). *Social media campaigns: Strategies for public relations and marketing.* New York: Routledge.

Koslowski, M. (2019). The expert who predicted Trump, Brexit - and Scott Morrison. *The Sydney Morning Herald*, viewed 31/7/2019. https://www.smh.com.au/federal-election-2019/the-expert-who-predicted-trump-brexit-and-scott-morrison-20190519-p51owf.html

Kozinets, R.V. (2015). Netnography. In The International Encyclopedia of Digital Communication and Society (eds P.H. Ang and R. Mansell). https://doi.org/10.1002/9781118767771.wbiedcs067

Lee, C. (2019). Daily active users for WeChat exceeds 1 billion. *ZDNet*, viewed 02/8/2019. https://www.zdnet.com/article/daily-active-user-of-messaging-app-wechat-exceeds-1-billion/

Lee, S., Yoon, C., Kang, H., Kim, Y., Kim, Y., Han, D., et al. (2019, February). Cybercriminal minds: An investigative study of cryptocurrency abuses in the dark web. In *Network and distributed system security symposium* (pp. 1–15). Internet Society.

Lieu, J. (2016). Everyone's convinced ASOS' Facebook page is run by robots. *Mashable*, viewed

05/08/2019. https://mashable.com/2016/05/25/auto-respond-facebook-asos/

Lipschultz, J. H. (2019). *Social media measurement and management: Entrepreneurial digital analytics*. New York: Routledge.

Lundholt, M. W., Maagaard, C. A., & Piekut, A. (2018). Counternarratives. In *The international encyclopedia of strategic communication* (pp. 1–11). Hoboken, NJ: Wiley.

Mediafirst. (2017). A tone-deaf tweet and three other self-inflicted social media disasters. Mediafirst.co.uk, viewed 1/08/2019. https://www.mediafirst.co.uk/our-thinking/a-tone-deaf-tweet-and-three-other-self-inflicted-social-media-disasters/

Melder, B. (2019). Understand, predict, and react: How big data social media marketing transforms your campaigns. SocialBakers.com, viewed 04/08/2019. https://www.socialbakers.com/blog/big-data-social-media-marketing

Mislove, A, Lehmann, S., Ahn, Y. Y., Onnela, J. P., & Rosenquist, N. (2010). *Pulse of the nation: U.S. mood throughout the day inferred from Twitter*, viewed 19/11/2019. https://mislove.org/twittermood/

Moulder, H. (2016). *DiGiorno Tweet*, viewed 1/08/2019. https://preparis.com/blog/social-media-can-affect-reputation/digiorno-tweet/

Ndlela, M. N. (2019). A stakeholder approach in managing reputation. In *Crisis communication* (pp. 77–109). Cham, Switzerland: Palgrave Pivot.

Panda, M., Abraham, A., & Hassanien, A. E. (Eds.). (2018). *Big data analytics: A social network approach*. Boca Raton, FL: CRC Press.

Pelton, J. N., & Singh, I. B. (2019). Coping with the dark web, cyber-criminals and techno-terrorists in a smart city. In *Smart cities of today and tomorrow* (pp. 171–183). Cham, Switzerland: Copernicus.

Python. (2019). What is python? Executive summary. Python.org, viewed 05/08/2019. https://www.python.org/doc/essays/blurb/

Ranakoti, P., Yadav, S., Apurva, A., Tomer, S., & Roy, N. R. (2017, October). Deep web & online anonymity. In *2017 International conference on computing and communication technologies for smart nation (IC3TSN)* (pp. 215–219). IEEE.

Riff, D., Lacy, S., Fico, F., & Watson, B. (2019). *Analyzing media messages: Using quantitative content analysis in research*. New York: Routledge.

Saleh, A., Chefor, E., & Babin, B. (2019). An action-based approach to retail brand engagement. In *Predicting trends and building strategies for consumer engagement in retail environments* (pp. 27–43). Hershey, PA: IGI Global.

Sponder, M. (2011). *Social media analytics: Effective tools for building, interpreting, and using metrics*. New York: McGraw Hill Professional.

Sponder, M., & Khan, G. F. (2017). *Digital analytics for marketing*. New York: Routledge.

Sutherland, K. E. (2015). *Towards an integrated social media communication model for the not-for-profit sector: A case study of youth homelessness charities* (Doctoral dissertation, Monash University).

TedX Talks. (2015). New tools to measure our mood and predict the future|Chris Hansen|TEDxMileHigh. YouTube.com, viewed 19/11/2019. https://www.youtube.com/watch?v=Py-1o4sX1hk&list=PLysIctcC2hW1UWlVATLqrUcibQDB4l75x&index=2

Tiltman, D. (2019). Five things marketers need to know about dark social. *Mumbrella*, viewed 2/08/2019. https://mumbrella.com.au/five-things-marketers-need-to-know-about-dark-social-423503

Tuten, T. L., & Solomon, M. R. (2017). *Social media marketing*. Thousand Oaks, CA: Sage.

Watson. (2019). People are trolling an ASOS Facebook bot that keeps offering refunds and it's hilarious. *Punkee*, viewed 05/08/2019. https://punkee.com.au/people-trolling-asos-facebook-bot/63727

Further Reading

Bali, R., Sarkar, D., & Sharma, T. (2017). *Learning social media analytics with R*. Birmingham, UK: Packt Publishing Ltd.

Gonçalves, A. (2017). *Social media analytics strategy: Using data to optimize business performance*. Berkeley, CA: Apress.

Khan, G. F. (2015). *Seven layers of social media analytics: Mining business insights from social media text, actions, networks, hyperlinks, apps, search engines, and location data*. Middletown, DE: CreateSpace.

Lipschultz, J. H. (2019). *Social media measurement and management: Entrepreneurial digital analytics*. New York: Routledge.

Sponder, M., & Khan, G. F. (2017). *Digital analytics for marketing*. New York: Routledge.

Helpful Links

Social Media Monitoring Dashboard Tools

BlitzMetrics Dashboard: https://dashboard.blitzmetrics.com/

Hootsuite: https://hootsuite.com/

Reputology: https://www.reputology.com/

Tweetdeck: https://tweetdeck.twitter.com/

Automated Listening Tools

Agorapulse: https://app.agorapulse.com/auth/login

Awario: https://awario.com

Brandwatch: https://www.brandwatch.com/products/analytics/

Iconosquare: https://iconosquare.com/
Keyhole: https://keyhole.co
Meltwater: Media Intelligence: https://www.meltwater.com
Talkwalker: Quick Search: https://www.talkwalker.com/quick-search

AMEC Social Media Measurement Framework

AMEC's Social Media Measurement Framework User Guide: http://www.social-media-measurement-framework.org/wp-content/uploads/2014/06/Social-Media-Measurement-Framework.pdf

AMEC's Integrated Evaluation Framework: https://amecorg.com/amecframework/

Native Measurement Tools

Bitly.com (URL tracking): https://bitly.com/
Facebook Insights: https://www.facebook.com/business/insights/tools/audience-insights
Facebook Pixel: https://www.facebook.com/business/learn/facebook-ads-pixel
Google Analytics: https://analytics.google.com
Instagram Insights: https://help.instagram.com/788388387972460
LinkedIn Analytics: https://business.linkedin.com/marketing-solutions/reporting-analytics
Pinterest Analytics: https://analytics.pinterest.com/

Snapchat Insights: https://support.snapchat.com/en-GB/a/insights
TikTok Analytics: https://www.tiktok.com/analytics
Twitter Analytics: https://analytics.twitter.com/
WordPress Stats: https://en.support.wordpress.com/stats/
WeChat Web Analytics: https://www.nanjingmarketinggroup.com/blog/wechat-analytics
YouTube Analytics: https://www.youtube.com/analytics?o=U

Data Visualization Tools

Chart Studio by Plotly: https://plot.ly/online-chart-maker/
Gephi: https://gephi.org/
Python: https://www.python.org/
Tableau: https://www.tableau.com/

Visual Data Presentation

Adobe Spark: https://spark.adobe.com
Biteable Animated infographics tool: https://biteable.com
Canva Create visually compelling graphs and infographics: https://www.canva.com/
Excel: https://www.excel-easy.com/data-analysis/charts.html
Plotly Online chart and graph maker: https://plot.ly/create/#/

Social Media Scheduling and Account Management Platforms

Contents

© The Author(s), under exclusive license to Springer Nature Singapore Pte Ltd. 2021
K. E. Sutherland, *Strategic Social Media Management*, https://doi.org/10.1007/978-981-15-4658-7_8

By the End of this Chapter You Will

- Understand what social media scheduling is.
- Learn about the benefits and disadvantages associated with scheduling social media content.
- Learn to identify the best times to schedule social media content for greatest exposure to a client's or organisation's target audience.
- Gain an understanding about the functionality of social media management platforms and how they can support the management of multiple clients, platforms and profiles.
- Know what to consider when selecting a social media management platform.
- Learn about the complexities involved with scheduling content across multiple time zones and geographic regions.
- Gain an insight of some current social media management platforms and their available features.

- At their most basic level, a social media management tool should facilitate a range of social media platforms and clients, content posting and scheduling, direct moderation, listening, monitoring, measurement and the generation of reports.
- Agencies and larger organisations may require additional features in a social media management platform such as workflow processes for teams, integration with other functions such as SEO, CRM, Customer Service, Marketing and Sales, and deeper analytic insights such as visualisation.
- The 10 areas to consider when selecting a social media management platform are: Cost, Compatibility, Number of Feeds Allowed, Workflow, Scheduling, Social Media Analytics, Reporting, Moderation, Ease of Use and Customer Support.

TLDR

- Scheduling social media content to be uploaded when the greatest number of target audience members are using each specific social media channel can increase the probability that they will see it and engage with it.
- Using a combination of analytics, audience research and experimentation can assist in identifying the most optimal time to schedule content according to the specific behaviours of the target audience.
- Scheduling social media content to reach audiences in different time zones can take careful planning and a thorough understanding of each.

8.1 Introduction

The previous five chapters have been devoted to social media strategy development. They have guided you through audience research, the ethical and legal requirements, defining goals, objectives and key messages, devising effective tactics and social media analytics. With these fundamental components of social media strategy locked in, this chapter focuses on understanding and selecting the tools that can support the implementation of a clients' or organisation's social media strategy.

The actual implementation of a social media strategy can have many moving parts in terms of logistics. Understanding what tools are available can assist with this process is worthwhile knowledge to have as a Social Media Manager.

> **"** Different social media management tools have different features and are better suited to specific situations. **"**
>
> Dr Karen Sutherland

8

What is important to note is that different social media management tools have different features and are better suited to specific situations. Some tools are better suited to sole operators where others have increased functionality for large agencies. There are many options available and what is relevant to your current situation will most definitely change over time as your business grows.

For example, some tools are extremely useful to Social Media Managers working across different time zones and geographic regions, yet this extra functionality may not be necessary for someone just beginning as a freelancer taking on their first few clients.

In addition to exploring the features of social media management platforms and what to consider when selecting one, this chapter also explores the topic of social media content scheduling.

The two topics are inherently linked because one of the core functions of a social media management platform is to facilitate the scheduling of content. However, it is important to completely understand the benefits and disadvantages of scheduling content from the outset.

It is always important to question various practices in social media management to completely understand why they exist, what they achieve and whether they are relevant to you and a client's and/or organisation.

In addition to gaining an understanding about social media scheduling, it is also essential to learn how to determine the most optimal times to schedule content according to clients' or organisations' social media analytics.

This text is called '*Strategic Social Media Management*' with the strongest emphasis on strategic social media practice. Even scheduling content must be approached in a strategic way to support the achievement of a client's or organisation's business goals.

8.2   What Is Social Media Scheduling?

Social media scheduling refers to the practice of proactively creating and posting social media content then selecting and setting a future date and time for it to be published on a social media platform.

8.2.1   What Is a Content Calendar?

It is extremely useful for Social Media Managers to have a content calendar as part of their social media strategy so that the content that actions its tactics can be laid out into a plan.

Developing a social media content calendar can act as a map for Social Media Managers during the implementation of a strategy and campaign and provides a tangible outline that a client and/or organisation can provide their approval for before you get started. (See Appendix 3 for a Content Calendar Template).

A content calendar can be a spreadsheet that explains the details of that content to

Table 8.1 Example of a social media content calendar

Week No.			Day:		
Platform	Content Type	Image Link	Copy	Time

be posted on each day and generally has the following information (□ Table 8.1):

The content calendar is an effective way to strategically plan content to help to ensure that it is supporting the goals and SMART Objectives of a client's social media strategy.

8.3 The Difference Between a Content Calendar and Content Scheduling

There is a distinct difference between a content calendar and scheduling social media content.

> ❝ A content calendar is a **plan.**
>
> **Content scheduling** is the **implementation of that plan.** ❞
>
> Dr Karen Sutherland

The content has been created and is waiting to be launched at its specified date and time.

While a content calendar can be hugely beneficial in helping a Social Media Manager to keep themselves organised, there are clear benefits and disadvantages associated with scheduling the content in the calendar ahead of time.

8.4 Benefits to Scheduling Social Media Content

The key benefits to scheduling social media content are:
- *Being proactive rather than reactive.* Scheduling social media content ahead of time allows Social Media Managers to devote enough time to crafting high quality pieces instead of slapping

together posts at the very last minute. As we will explore in ► Sect. 3, developing social media content takes time and care. Scheduling ahead of time can support Social Media Managers in creating pieces of value to the target audience because they are not rushing to meet a deadline.
- *Reaching a target audience when they are most likely to be online.* As explored in ► Chap. 3 and again later in this chapter, examining audience data on a client's or organisation's social media platforms can identify the days and times that existing followers are most likely online (Minguez, 2014).

This knowledge supports Social Media Managers to achieve the greatest exposure and reach for content if they schedule it to go live on social channels at the times when their audience size is the largest. This practice can also be highly convenient for Social Media Managers if these optimal audience times are out of office hours or in completely different time zones. For example, evenings after 8 pm can be a peak time for many businesses, yet generally business hours end at 5 pm.

Without scheduling content ahead to target optimal audience times, a client/s and/or organisation would miss the opportunity to connect with the greatest number of audience members at the same time.

— *Allowing ample time to work through approval processes*. In some organisations there can be many layers of approval before social media content is given the green light to be posted. Scheduling content ahead can give organisational decision makers ample time to review and approve the content (for a Social Media Manager to make any requested amendments) resulting in posts going out when they are relevant.

Trying to force through the layers of social media content approvals at the last minute can result in some content finally being posted when it is already outdated because the permission process took too long.

— *Knowing what content is going to be posted ahead of time*. Scheduling social media content ahead of time avoids surprises for you or a client. Everyone knows what is coming in terms of content. Taking this approach can help clients to develop trust in your abilities because you are approaching social media management in a strategic and organised way instead of running around like in a panic by leaving content creation to the last minute.

8.5 Disadvantages

Along with the advantages, there are also a number of disadvantages that can be associated with scheduling social media content.

— *Missing out on current news, developments and events*. One of the biggest errors that Social Media Managers can make is to set and forget their client's social media content. While scheduling is a great way to organise your time, failing to conduct social listening activities and monitoring what is happening in terms of current events in a client's industry or local area can result in missing out on leveraging current news and trends that can build credibility for a client as an expert.

Scheduling content can be a reassuring practice in that it means that content is guaranteed to be posted on the selected days and platforms. Yet, it is important not to be too rigid with the schedule particularly if a major industry happening or trending topic spontaneously arises.

> **66** It is important to maintain a balance between scheduled content and responding to relevant news and trends. **99**
>
> Dr Karen Sutherland

It is important that Social Media Managers maintain a workable balance between scheduled content and responding to the important things happening around them.

8.6 Oreo Leverages Blackout to Achieve Social Media Success

An excellent example of this is Leo Morejon who is interviewed at the end of this chapter.

Leo and his team were responsible for the legendary Oreo tweet during the 2013 Super Bowl in the U.S. where there was a major power outage at the Mercedes-Benz Superdome in New Orleans where the event was being held (Staff Writer, 2013).

Instead of sitting idly by until the power was restored, Leo and his team capitalised on the situation by tweeting:

Power out? No problem. You can still dunk in the dark. (See ▣ Fig. 8.1). Consider if Leo and his team were not nimble in that moment and instead were fixed rigidly on scheduled content, the opportunity for such worldwide exposure of the Oreo brand would have been lost.

Again, scheduled content is convenient, but the best Social Media Managers continually have their content eyes on to strategically leverage opportunities when they arise.

▣ **Fig. 8.1**   Oreo super bowl tweet

▬ *Forgetting to stop scheduled content during times of issues and crisis.* Even though pausing scheduled social media content is recommended to be part of every organisations' issues and crisis management plan, there have been many organisations that have further exacerbated an already potentially damaging situation by neglecting to do so.

During times of crisis, it can be extremely inappropriate to let scheduled content continue and even more so when that content can be misinterpreted because the current context has changed. It is essential that Social Media Managers are clear on the potential issues that can arise from allowing scheduled content to be posted when a client or organisation is publicly working through an issue or crisis to avoid making the situation even worse.

▬ *Errors can occur when scheduling content for multiple clients and accounts.* While scheduling can greatly assist in the organisation of content for multiple clients and profiles, human error can still occur as the process of juggling becomes more complex and complicated.

Sometimes the wrong content can be posted on a different client's profile or posts can be scheduled on incorrect days and times. It is essential for Social Media Managers to be careful and methodical when scheduling content for their clients and/or organisation.

Most importantly, ensuring that they are within the correct client profile or account and that the content being posted is for the correct client and at the day and time for their target audience.

Another issue that has occurred for Social Media Managers is when they confuse their personal social media profiles for their clients'.

8

8.7 American Red Cross Profile Confusion Results in Embarrassing Tweet

A classic example of the embarrassment caused as a result of confusing personal and organisational profiles occurred when someone on the social media team at the American Red Cross tweeted from the organisation's official Twitter account via Hootsuite (Wasserman, 2011):

» *Ryan found two more 4 bottle packs of Dogfish Head's Midas Touch beer....when we drink we do it right #gettngslitherd*

Clearly this occurred because person from the American Red Cross who posted it thought that they were posting to their friends on their own personal account. This can be a risk in general for Social Media Manager but must also be highlighted as a scheduling risk too.

It is essential for Social Media Manager to ensure that their personal social media activities are always completely separate from their professional responsibilities to avoid the risk of reputational damage to the organisation or business that they are representing.

Scheduling can definitely be a convenient way to manage social media for clients and organisations, but it must be used strategically, and it is important to understand what can go wrong if not used cautiously as the previous examples have highlighted.

8.8 Identifying the Best Times to Schedule Social Media Content

Now that we have explored the benefits and risks associated with scheduling social media content, the next important step is to learn how to identify the most optimal time to schedule content so that it has the greatest chance of connecting with a target audience.

There are two main schools of thought in relation to the scheduling of social media content. The first is to post at times when an audience is not online and the other is to post when the majority of a target audience *is* using social media.

8.9 School of Thought 1. Posting at Times When the Majority of a Target Audience Is Not Using Social Media

The rationale behind this is that content will not be competing with that from other brands who are also posting at times of maximise traffic from people within the same target audience. Therefore, rather than a client's or organisation's content becoming lost, it will stand out to the few who are online.

8.9.1 This Approach Is Not a Popular One and Is Not Recommended for the Following Reasons

- It minimises the number of people who can see the content.
- In turn, it minimises the number of people who can engage with the content.
- Engagement can increase reach on many social media platforms, particularly in the first hour that the content is posted (Patel, 2019). Minimising the opportunity for engagement will result in barely anyone seeing a client's social media content.

8.10 School of Thought 2. Posting at Times When the Majority of a Target Audience Is Not Using Social Media

It is logical to post content when there is the greatest probability that the largest number of people from a client's target audience are going to see it and engage with it. The aim of a Social Media Manager is to create content that resonates with the audience that you are targeting on behalf of a client or organisation.

Content will always be competing with that from other brands but posting at times in a bid to avoid this competition is delusional and minimises the opportunity to reach and build relationships with the greatest number of people.

8.10.1 The Best Time to Schedule Content Is

The topic of the best time to post is a hugely popular one within social media circles. Every year a series of blog posts and infographics are released by social media and digital marketing experts proclaiming that they know the best time to post on the mainstream social media platforms (Gollin, 2019; Sameh, 2018; Arens, 2019).

While guides like these are convenient, they are also extremely general and usually apply to audiences based in the United States.

In ► Chap. 7 we explored the power of social media analytics and again this power also comes into play when making the decision of the most optimal times to post content. The most effective way to identify the best time to post for a target audience is to review the analytics of each of a client's social media platforms.

Avoid basing decisions on blog posts and infographics that may not be accurate and/or relate specifically to a client's business and their current followers. Remember that every organisation and business is different. So too are the behaviours of target audiences and people from a range of demographics.

It is easier to identify the peak traffic times for a target audience on some social media platforms compared with others. For example, using Facebook Insights and viewing the 'Posts' page provides data displaying 'When Your Fans Are Online' in terms of the days of the week and times of the day.

Similarly, by selecting 'Audience' in the Insights of a business Instagram account the days and times when the majority of the profile's audience is online can be clearly identified. Other platforms such as Twitter, YouTube and LinkedIn currently do not provide similar analytic information within the platforms, however, some third-party tools may be able to provide this data.

> Identify the optimal times to post by analysing audience page/profile data.
>
> Dr Karen Sutherland

8.10.2 Leverage Audience Research

Another method to identify the most optimal time to post is to draw on the audience research that gathered by implementing the processes explored in ▶ Chap. 3. By thoroughly understanding the demographic, psychographic and social media habits of a target audience you can use this information like a detective to piece together the time when this group will most likely be using social media.

Remember, that you are aiming to reach individual people not some faceless mass. Therefore, it is extremely helpful when trying to identify the best time to reach a target audience on social media by considering the overall cycle of what an average day looks for them.

Think about the Customer Personas that you created in ▶ Chap. 3 and consider, what times of the day would a person most likely look at social media on their phone, tablet and/or laptop? Using the audience data that you have collected, trying to get into the mind and the lives of the people with whom you are trying to reach with social media content.

For example, if a client wants to connect with the mothers of school aged children, scheduling social media content around school pick up and drop off times would not be advisable because their focus would most likely be elsewhere. However, from conducting thorough audience research you would know the cycle of a target audience's day. You would know that when the kids are put to bed there may be a small window of time left to check social media, and this is when you need to schedule content.

As mentioned in ▶ Chap. 3, research is the foundation of any social media strategy and it should also inform any strategic decisions relating to that strategy.

8.10.3 Experiment Strategically

Analysing audience research and data can help you to better understand the most optimal timeframes to schedule content so that it reaches the newsfeeds of target audiences at the times that they are scrolling through it. However, it is important to keep experimenting and reviewing performance analytics to refine a strategy in terms of the best times to post.

> **❝** It is important to keep experimenting and reviewing performance analytics to refine the best times to post. **❞**
>
> Dr Karen Sutherland

While not every social media platform has native audience insight data like Facebook and Instagram, the majority have performance data of some kind to demonstrate the performance of data when it is posted at certain times of the data. Leverage this knowledge to keep deepening your understanding of a client's or organisation's target audiences so that you can keep returning exceptional results.

As we have covered so far in text, a Social Media Manager's role includes so much more than the creation and scheduling of content. There are complete social media

8.10 · School of Thought 2. Posting at Times When the Majority of a Target...

183

8

management platforms available that help Social Media Managers to perform a range of tasks as we will explore in the following section.

8.10.4 Scheduling Across Multiple Countries and Time Zones

Larger organisations and agencies are required to schedule social media content to be posted in multiple time zone as part of their core business practices. However, sole operators can support clients who are in different time zones or who are aiming to connect with target audiences in different geographical regions.

For a Social Media Manager, scheduling content for multiple clients across a range of social media platforms to reach different target audiences may already seem complicated, yet this level of complexity can be increased by also throwing in the requirement of scheduling content across multiple time zones.

Posting content at incorrect times can reflect negatively on a client's brand. While it may not be the optimal time to reach the target audience, posts can be perceived as unprofessional or missing the mark if the content is time specific and appears on people's news feeds when it should not.

For example, a post that makes a reference about the evening would seem completely irrelevant being posted mid-morning. Sometimes clients use the same content, but the time zones are slightly different, and it is essential to be accurate.

According to Annelise (2017), there are several key actions that Social Media Managers can implement to assist in accurately posting content across several different time zones.

1. *Thoroughly understand each time zone*. Learn the times in the regions in which you are scheduling in comparison to where you are. Find out when there are changes in daylight savings times and public holidays and set up alerts to ensure that you are across these.

2. *Have a visual representation of the multiple times zones that you are scheduling across in your workspace*. A set of world clocks will not only be handy as a reference point, but they will also help you to learn the time differences if they are a constant feature in your view.

3. *Understand how the scheduling functionality works on each social media platform or social media management tool that you are using*. Explore whether these functions and tools allow you to change time zones. The author of this text discovered recently that changing the time zone on a Facebook Ad account means having to delete the existing account to create a new one.

   This means having to add new pixel code to the website, losing all previously created ads and being required to enter in all payment information again. In short, understand what each platform can and cannot do in relation to scheduling across different time zones to avoid making painful mistakes. Annelise (2017) suggests changing the computer's clock function to make the process easier.

4. *Post-Gating or Geo-Targeting Facebook Posts*. In the Settings of a Facebook Page under *General > Country Restrictions*, Social Media Managers can restrict the countries where posts can be seen. Also, when posting Facebook posts, selecting *News Feed Targeting* also allows Social Media Managers to post content to specific Facebook users from a range of demographics such as location, interests, language etc.

   Using this functionality can also provide some control and organisation in terms of scheduling content across different time zone because specific countries and regions can be targeted that fall within that time zone.

   This is a handy feature because it can facilitate more accurate posting of content aimed at specific audiences without always having to use advertising spend. It is a good way to also test content with a target audience before amplifying it with paid advertising.

8.11 Social Media Account Management Platforms

While their specific features may vary, fundamentally, a social media management platform supports social media professionals to fulfil many of the tasks and responsibilities necessary when managing client's or an organisation's social media presence.

Essentially, one of the key benefits of a social media management platform is that it can assist Social Media Managers to successfully look after multiple social media profiles for multiple social media clients. Yet, some social media management platforms offer so much more than that.

What is required from such a tool can greatly differ depending on the size of the business and number and types of clients that you may have. What a sole operator needs may be completely different to an agency or a multinational corporation.

8.11.1 Sole Operators

A Social Media Manager who works independently without employing staff, may only need a social media management platform with basic features. Not to say that the tasks and responsibilities of a sole operator are less than that of an agency, but there are less people involved in managing clients, therefore, this removes an entire level of complexity.

Fundamentally, a sole operator may need the following features to be available in a social media management platform to provide the ability to:

- Conduct social listening relating to a client's and their competitors.
- Monitor, post and schedule across multiple social media platforms.
- Engage with people interacting with a client's content.
- Manage multiple clients within the same management system.
- Measure social media performance and generate client reports

These are the core tasks of social media management and there are some tools that can provide this functionality as will be explored later in the chapter.

For sole operators, the most important feature of a social media management platform is easy organisation and navigation so that they can manage multiple clients without making errors by confusing the platforms and scheduling of different clients.

> 66 Building trust with clients is paramount and this can be eroded by an unreliable or unworkable social media management platform. 99
>
> Dr Karen Sutherland

Remember, building trust with clients is paramount and this can be eroded by an unreliable or unworkable social media management platform. Furthermore, blaming a tool for something going wrong (even if it was the cause) can be perceived as highly unprofessional by the client.

When there is possibly only you and a client as part of the workflow process (you create, client approves, you post and schedule), then opt for a platform that facilitates this in a clear and workable way.

8.11.2 Agencies and In-House Social Media Teams

Using a social media management platform in an agency environment or within an organisational social media team may require advanced features to better support the more complex organisational structure and generally larger client base.

Categorising agencies and in-house social media teams under one banner is highly problematic because organisations and agencies come in all shapes and sizes.

At one end of the spectrum there can be two-person social media agencies or teams and at the other there are multinational entities with offices in most capital cities around the world, operating across a range of time zones.

Clearly the size, structure and client base of an agency or organisation will have a direct influence on what it will need from a social media management platform.

While an agency or social media team will need the same core features as a Sole Operator, it may also require some further functionality such as:

- *Workflow processes* that allow staff to create posts ready to be approved by those more senior.
- *The ability to oversee the work from different teams* from a range of geographical locations
- *Alignment of customer service, marketing and sales within the same platform.*
- *The ability to manage SEO, Customer Relationship Management (CRM) tools, Electronic Direct Mail (EDM) and landing webpage development within the same interface.*
- *The facilitation and management of content scheduling in multiple time zones.*
- *Deeper analytics* such as real-time data visualisation.

While some of these features may also be helpful to sole operators, large enterprises can rely heavily on these features to support not only social media, but the integral business functions.

The greater the number of staff, clients and geographical locations all add layers of complexity and necessity for agencies and organisations with an in-house social media team.

CASE STUDY: Orange Leverages Social Media Management Tool, Socialbaker, to Coordinate Team Activities Across 29 Markets

Fench telecommunications company, Orange, uses the social media management system, Socialbakers to coordinate day-today activities with multiple in-house teams working across 29 different markets (Socialbakers, 2019).

With more than 8 million Facebook fans spanning multiple countries, the team at Orange requires an accurate and dependable social media management tool that can provide real-time insights across a large geographical area (Socialbakers, 2019).

As a social media management tool, Socialbakers provides a range of functionality to support Orange's complex needs, including a Social Media Command Centre that allows the team on the Head Office in Paris, to track the social media activities, performance data and online brand conversations occurring across the company's multiple markets.

Socialbakers also facilitates the scheduling of data across time zones as well as the ability to respond quickly to social listening data customised content. These practices have helped to enhance social customer service for the company greatly improving the online customer experience.

Using a social media management tool in this way has led to increased online interactions with customers and significant follower growth. For example, in the region of Jordan, Twitter followers grew from 1 k to 8 k and Facebook interactions increased from 16 k to 46 k both within 1 year of using Socialbakers (Socialbakers, 2019).

This case highlights what can be achieved when a social media management platform is used to coordinate the social media activities of a company. Orange is a complex example because it is such a large organisation with multiple teams functioning across geographically diverse regions.

However, having the ability to monitor audience interactions and conversations in real time across these regions has provided Orange with valuable insights to enhance their social media performance and greatly improve the customer experience. A social media management platform has also facilitated the creation and scheduling of content across regions helping to streamline a complex task for many large organisations.

1. What have been the benefits for Orange in using the Socialbakers social media management platform?

2. What would be some of the risks for a multinational company when using a social media management platform to schedule posts across time zones?

8.12 Key Considerations When Selecting a Social Media Management Platform

It quickly becomes apparent when searching online for the best social media management platform that there is a wide range of options available.

The plethora of tools available are constantly changing in terms of the sheer number of platforms on offer and their ever-evolving features. It can become extremely confusing as to the option of greatest relevance to best support a business, organisation or clients.

Making a commitment and purchasing a subscription should not be taken lightly. Making an incorrect selection can result in the loss of funds and clients if the tool does not support professional social media management and help you to achieve positive results for clients.

Furthermore, linking clients' social media platforms can take time and effort and these will be resources lost if selection of social media management platforms becomes a series of hit and miss affairs.

Selecting the incorrect social media management platform may not always be avoidable. However, conducting thorough research is crucial to minimise this risk. This research can involve reading reviews and industry news, speaking to other social media managers, even interviewing representatives from the platforms themselves and arranging demonstrations of a range of tools.

Remember, that while consulting with other social media managers and reading reviews may be helpful, you must base your decision on the specific needs of your business and your clients. Using the areas of consideration explored in ❏ Table 8.2 will assist in identifying the most appropriate social media management platform to best

Table 8.2 Areas of consideration when selecting a social media management platform

Area of consideration	Reason
Cost	Clearly how much that you have to spend on a social media management tool will dictate the range of tools that you can consider for your business or organisation. It is important to factor tool subscriptions into the costs charged to clients, as these are necessary to facilitate the social media management for their business. If cost is an issue, begin small and use what accessible tools to build your client base and gradually use better ones as profits increase. Do not pay more than you can afford. Buying high end tools before building a client base large enough to support them can put a business at risk if a client suddenly decides to go elsewhere.
Compatibility	The social media management tool must be compatible with all social media platforms that you manage for clients. Using multiple tools to manage clients' social media can be challenging, complicated and inefficient. Therefore, it is highly beneficial to find a social media management platform that is compatible with the social media sites that you need to use in your role as a Social Media Manager. Another aspect to consider in terms of compatibility is whether paid ad campaigns can be integrated within the social media management tool. Such functionality within the one platform can be extremely helpful.
Number of feeds allowed	It is essential to select a social media management tool that allows you to work on all clients' feeds within its interface with the capacity to add more to cope with a growing client base. Again, it can be problematic using a tool that does not align with the function of your business therefore it is important to select based on the current and projected needs of your business.
Workflow	The need for workflow functionality will be dependent on organisational size and structure. Sole Operators may not need this functionality. Workflow will definitely be a necessity for small, medium and large agencies and organisations. In terms of workflow, important features include ease of use, the ability to see work progress, ensuring that the required approval process can be supported, and that content cannot be altered and posted without approval being sought. The larger the organisation, the more complex workflow processes can become. A social media management tool should help to simplify these processes not complicate them further.
Scheduling	As mentioned previously in this chapter, scheduling functionality is an extremely important factor to consider when selecting a social media management platform. Reflect on the needs of clients. Do you need to schedule across different social media platforms at a range of different times and across different time zones? Be certain that a social media management tool can definitely do everything that you need in terms of scheduling before subscribing.

(continued)

8

Table 8.2 (continued)

Area of consideration	Reason
Social media analytics	It is much easier to have all of the listening, monitoring and measurement functionality that you require within the same platform. Often the social media management platforms with extensive analytics tools are the most expensive. Yet, if you are already paying for another tool of this type, the costs of buying a one-stop-shop may work out to be very similar. It can be helpful to review the listening, monitoring, measurement and analytics activities that you currently undertake to compare them with those available on the social media management that you are considering. A social media management platform should support current analytics practices or further enhance them.
Reporting	As explored in ▶ Chap. 8, reporting is an essential task to keep clients informed and to support continuous improvement. A social media management platform should make this task simple by generating customisable reports to suit the specific needs of clients.
Moderation	Having the ability to respond to comments on a range of different social media platforms within the same interface makes social media management a more convenient activity than having to exit the tool to jump between platforms. It is important to check that there is not a time lag between when people leave comments on a client's social media platforms and when they appear on the feed of the management platform. Time is crucial in addressing issues before they become crises. A social media management tool should support proactive rather than reactive measures.
Ease of use	A social media management tool should be intuitive and logical to use. Of course, there is always an initial adjustment period when learning to use any new technology, however, it should not take a week-long training course to learn how to use it. When reviewing a management platform, attempt the tasks that you will need to complete for clients to see how simple they seem. Then, review the quality of online tutorials and help information to see if they will support your learning.
Customer support	It is essential to assess the level and quality of customer support is available should you need it. Check the communication channels available and whether it is possible to speak one-on-one to a person to work through any issues quickly if they arise. Find out whether the customer service hours align with your working hours. It can be a definite risk to begin using a social media management platform on behalf of clients when there is not any support available. Imagine a feature suddenly not working and the only customer support available are customer forums where nobody can assist. Great customer support is a necessity when using a tool on which your professional reputation can depend.

8.14 · Interview: Leo Morejon - VP of Content, Strategy & Enablement ...

189

8

support your business or organisational needs.

According to Scott (2017), there are several important factors to consider when selecting a social media management platform.

> **Conclusion**
>
> After reading this chapter, you should now have a working understanding about scheduling social media content and social media management platforms. In this chapter we explored the practice of scheduling social media content, what it is and its advantages and disadvantages.
>
> We also examined different methods to identify the most optimal time to schedule social media content, so that it has the greatest probability of reaching a client's or organisation's target audience/s and important considerations when scheduling content across a range of time zones and geographic regions.
>
> The second half of the chapter focused on the benefits of using a social media management platform and how to select a tool to best suit the needs of your business/organisation and clients. The chapter concluded with a comparison of eight leading social media management tools currently available to provide you with a snapshot of the range of platforms on offer.

8.13 Types of Platforms and their Features

The range of available social media management platforms is constantly evolving, therefore, the list of tools available at the time of writing may be different by the time you are reading this. To avoid such disparity, ◼ Table 8.2 only contains eight of the current leading social media management plat-

forms with a brief description of what they can do at this point in time.

Prices have not been included as these will fluctuate, however, links to each platform have been provided in the helpful links section at the end of this chapter. These platforms are worth investigating, but exploration should not end with this table. Continue researching what other tools are on offer that may better suit your specific needs (◼ Table 8.3).

Remember that it is important to assess each tool against what you are hoping to achieve for clients and how well it fits within your budget.

8.14 Interview: Leo Morejon - VP of Content, Strategy & Enablement, Build and Inspire, USA

1. **Please tell us about your current role.**
   My full name is Leo Morejon. I'm a social media marketing, digital marketing expert, and right now, I do a bunch of different things. I work at a company called Build and Inspire, I also run their blog. Basically, Build and Inspire is a brand consultancy, and I focus on execution as far as strategy and also making sure things happen. I'm also a professor at two universities, so I do quite a bit.

2. **What do you enjoy most about working with social media.**
   This is something that I've said many times, but I really just can't get tired of saying it.
   Social media is just human interaction happening online, and I love talking, I love connecting with people. Actually, there was a time back in the day when I used to call myself, I'm too social for social media. I just want to be with the people and talk with them and just be connected. That's what I love

8

Table 8.3   Eight Social Media Management Platforms to Consider

Social media management platform	Compatible social media platforms	Suitable for	Description
Facebook (Creator Studio) Business Suite	Facebook Instagram	Creating and scheduling content.	Facebook Creator Studio and Facebook Business Suite are free tools that facilitates content creation and scheduling across Facebook and Instagram. Please see the Helpful Links section for further information on this process.
Buffer	Facebook, Twitter, LinkedIn, Instagram and Pinterest.	Businesses focused more on scheduling	Buffer is more of a scheduling tool. While it can schedule on a large scale across five different social media platforms, users cannot moderate comments directly, it is not set up for workflow processes, it does not offer in-depth analytics or reporting functionality.
CoSchedule	Facebook Instagram LinkedIn Pinterest Twitter WordPress (and email marketing)	Sole operators up to large enterprises	CoSchedule is a comprehensive organisational tool that supports Social Media Managers to create content, schedule posts (except Instagram), monitor and measure performance, and generate reports. CoSchedule can also automate project workflows for teams of any size.
Hootsuite	Facebook, Twitter LinkedIn, Instagram	Sole operators up to large enterprises	Hootsuite is one of the first social media management platforms available. It displays social feeds in streams in a dashboard interface and facilitates social listening for some platforms, analytics functionality, scheduling across platforms, direct moderation, workflow processes, and reporting. Hootsuite also offers ambassador programs and certifications.
HubSpot	LinkedIn, Facebook, Instagram, Twitter	Sole operators to large enterprises	HubSpot offers a range of tools to support a range of business functions. However, its social media management platform facilitates direct posting and scheduling, monitoring, measurement, workflow processes, direct moderation also, marketing automation, landing pages, email marketing, blogging and lead management. HubSpot also provides a large range of free online training courses and certifications.

8.14 · Interview: Leo Morejon - VP of Content, Strategy & Enablement ...

191

8

Table 8.3 (continued)

Social media management platform	Compatible social media platforms	Suitable for	Description
Later	Instagram	Sole operators Small agencies	Later provides post creation and scheduling functionality for Instagram. This tool facilitates direct posting and moderation, listening, analytics and suggests relevant hashtags. Later can also find the optimal times to schedule posts based on specific audiences and reposting of user generated content.
Loomly	Facebook Twitter Instagram LinkedIn Pinterest	Small agencies to large enterprises	Loomly offers a range of useful features to support teams responsible for social media management. Apart from being able to create posts within the platform, Loomly generates post previews for team review. This platform also organises content, has advanced audience targeting functionality, and analytics and report generation. Loomly also provides content ideas to its users.
Social Report	Blogger Facebook Foursquare Instagram LinkedIn Pinterest Reddit Twitter Tumblr Vimeo YouTube WordPress Xing	Sole operators to large enterprises	Social report is more than a content scheduling tool. It uses analytics to help to target audience characteristics and geographic locations. This tool also supports bulk scheduling of posts, workflow processes and generates performance reports.
SproutSocial	Facebook Facebook messenger Instagram LinkedIn Pinterest Twitter	Sole operators to large enterprises	SproutSocial facilitates a range of functions including content creation and scheduling, asset management, workflow processes, identifying optimal posting times, social listening, in-depth analytics and reporting suite.

about social media. Whatever form it happens, it's about connecting.

3. **What do you find most challenging about working with social media?**

Right now, really it's just keeping up always. I love everything that I do, but you could always be at a party, and there could be some 17-year-old. They're like, "Hey, what are doing? Have you ever heard of this social network?" I'm like, oh no. Tell me about it, you know? Or someone else is like, "Hey, have you ever heard of this cool new thing that just happened with a brand?" I'm like, no, I didn't hear about this. Tell me. Or even when I teach classes, I'm always like, wait, are the kids teaching me? Because I'm like, tell me more about that thing that you're doing. I've never heard of that.

4. **How did you come to work in social media?**

I started running Myspace pages back in the day. Myspace pages for a local coffee shop. Then believe it or not, I went on Craigslist, and I said, "I'm going to get a job," and ended up getting an internship at a company called Iced Media, and my job was pretty much to click on views on videos so I could make sure that I'm refreshing the views and getting view counts, like, click click click. Back then, I didn't know, I was an intern. I'm like, "Whatever. I guess this is what we do." This would be for YouTube, really, and anything, Facebook. Really, Myspace was the place to be. I was like, "Forget this. There's something else to this. Let me go get another job."

From Iced Media, which I was only there for about 3 months or so, that was my internship. It was unpaid. I was like, "I need to make money." I was going into New York City, I'm from New Jersey, and I'm like, "I can't afford to do this. I need a job." So I ended up going to a company called JWT. For those

that don't know, it was Jay Walter Thompson. It's the oldest ad agency in the United States and one of the biggest in the world. I walked in not knowing what it was, but I remember looking up and thinking, "wow. This is an incredible place. How magical is this place?" Just the scenery, the people walking around, it seemed just like the coolest thing, like Mad Men in the future, right?

Social media was a brand-new thing, so I got hired and pretty much became an expert, but in no way was I an expert. I would be in rooms with CEOs and CMOs from everyone from Cadbury to Trident. I had no idea what I was doing. I could tell you horror stories too of losing like $20 thousand for a certain brand's ... I didn't know what I was doing. But I was able to pioneer a lot of cool things with tools. We used to use Radeon 6, and it was just a really fun, exciting time. I still remember I'm the one that actually wrote ... got the novelty URLs for Stride gum and Trident gum. I was the one that registered those.

That was in 2008 or 2009. It was incredible. Then after that, I got hired at a company called 360i I, and they're a digital ad agency owned by a bigger company called Dentsu out of Japan. From there, I was able to work on a little cookie called Oreo, and it was able to gain the first Guinness World Record for the most likes on a Facebook post. Then I really was able to go ahead and do a famous campaign called the Daily Twist, which we did 100 days of culture jacking. Then the big, big one which I'm known for, and my team and everyone around me, and the most fortunate, most blessed thing that I could have been a part of in my career with the Oreo Blackout Tweet. 2013 came, the Super Bowl lights went out, and we tweeted in real time. We were fortunate enough to win a Cannes Lion, Cleo, and countless other awards for that.

I have this philosophy that at an agency, I was always looking for the gold, but I wanted to help people sell with the shovel as well. So, I wanted to do both, and I loved what I was able to do, and I wanted to be able to share that with other people. So, I actually spent some time at Accenture, the big consulting group. I was only there for a little bit before getting an offer from the company that I used to actually work on Oreo called Expion, which is a social media management tool. If it wasn't for those tools and all the tools that have been around my whole life and the beginning of my career, I would never have been able to do anything that I did in my career. Operationalized Oreos so that we could go ahead and post around the world, everywhere from Australia to Indonesia, it was all because of these tools.

I started working for them, and I ended up starting their consulting practice, so basically the agency within the technology services side, and also did sales, did change management. I was there for about 3 years before getting bought at a company called Sysomos, which is a social media listening platform. I was fortunate enough to rise to the ranks to VP of Client Strategy. It was such a great experience. I got to train people on social media, make sure they were using the right tools when they were implementing their strategies. Everybody from Estee Lauder to Mondelez to Coca Cola. I was there for a total of about 4 years, and then left, and then started Build and Inspire.

5. **What do you think are the three most important things for Social Media Managers to consider about social media scheduling and management Tools?**

People always ask me what the best tool is, and it's always based on your needs, so it's based on what you need, really. If you're going to be using the platform for something internationally, like let's say you're working with different countries that speak different languages, then your social media management tool, your scheduling tool needs to fit those needs. You need to work backwards from there. So, I can never say what's a good tool or a bad tool, it's only based on your needs. I guess that's the first thing.

The other thing is, be careful when you're buying tools just because features are cool. I always like to say buy cool features but buy cool features that people will use. That brings me to the third part. You want a provider that's also going to provide services when it comes to implementation and specifically change management. Everyone will offer implementation services, but will they offer change management? Will they be there with you as you deploy across the world, as you train everyone, as you sell into the different local markets? I think that's really important. Features are features. We can get into features all day. Sprinkler has certain features versus Sprout Social versus Sales Force, but look for a partner, and look for something people will use. Because if you don't think your team will use it or people around the world will use it, you spent a lot of money for nothing.

I've seen a lot of clients come to me, saying, "Well, we bought this particular tool," which I won't name, "And it's not working out." Or "It was super cool, but just the implementation is not working out. And now, we need something people will actually use." If no one's using your tool, again. It sounds so simple, but it's not. People get too focused on this or that and the shiny object than like, will people use this, or is the implementation going to be there.

If I did have to answer it from a feature perspective, the ones that excite me now are the ones that use machine learning, AI in other tools to support and recommend things to the marketer. I don't think AI, I don't think machine learning and other tools are so far enough where I want it to be automatic, but I want it to say, "Listen, what do you think about adding this? Or add this image." Or, "This will do better if you use these words versus these other words." That's really what excites me. I want a trusted advisor when it comes to a tool with analytics.

6. **What do you think are the benefits of using Social Media Scheduling and Account Management Platforms?**

You get to sleep. Even when I was at Expion, that was actually one of the selling features when social media tools were not something that were used by everyone. I would say, "Don't you want to be able to go home?" Because a community manager has one of the hardest jobs out there when it comes to marketing. You do every single thing, and it's hard to do every single thing correctly. These tools allow you to do that.

When I first worked on Oreo, if Australia wanted a post, or really any local market outside of North America, outside of the United States, wanted to post, you'd have to send your content to me a month in advance. I'd review it, and then I'd only post on Tuesdays or Thursdays. So, content that you sent me would take at least a month for me to review in my team, and then we'd post it on a Tuesday or Thursday between 9:00 and 12:00 Eastern time. People are going to sleep or just waking up, and it hurt the brand. It helps with making sure the brand can do what it needs to do on social media. I do not understand how any company of almost any size can operate without it.

7. **Do you think it is important for Social Media Managers not to set-it-and-forget-it when it comes to the scheduling of social media content to avoid missing out on opportunities that spontaneously arise, such as the Oreo Super Bowl tweet?**

We would've missed lots of opportunities because one of the things that make the Oreo Blackout tweet really good was the PR behind it, too, like other marketers picking it up, us being able to share with other marketers. If we didn't know that particular post was doing so well, obviously that was real time, but if it wasn't a real time thing that we scheduled, we would've missed a lot of opportunities. That's why specifically for Expion we actually built a tool that even if it was automatically posted, you could get a notification before or after it is posted. I always wanted my community managers to do that, and I always recommended them. So right before it goes up, take a look. Then after, take another look to see if this is doing particularly well. Even from a tactical perspective, if it's doing really well, maybe it's not going to be anything like the blackout tweet, but it's worth putting paid media behind, right? There are so many missed opportunities if you're not paying attention. You can't get those back.

8. **What advice would you give to social media managers who have a scheduling across time zones?**

Across time zones, it's really important to have good collaboration with your team. You want to trust if someone's going to posting in the time zone when you're going to be asleep ... or obviously, even when you're asleep, you can't be manned behind the computer all the time, you can't always be looking at what's going on.

You want to build good collaboration and trust within the rest of the local markets so that when they're posting, you know that they're posting correctly and they're using the tools that they need to use correctly. Sometimes,

8.14 · Interview: Leo Morejon - VP of Content, Strategy & Enablement ...

195

8

that local market person who didn't necessarily know what to do, I can provide support, and it's all being tracked in the tool.

Then when it's posted, we're both accountable, and we know that was the very best thing that could go out. Then there are learnings from being able to look at the tracked meetings.

9. **Which social media management platforms currently use AI and machine learning?**
One that's been doing it for a while from a bigger perspective is Adobe Social or Adobe Social Cloud. For the longest time, they had a lot of machine learning or a lot of analytical tools. I remember as you type something, it would actually tell you, maybe use this word and not that word. I thought that was fantastic. Social Code, more from a social media paid perspective, is fantastic at looking to see what you should be promoting, what you shouldn't be promoting.

I think they're doing fantastic work. Meltwater buying Sysomos and obviously being part of Expion, I think there's a lot of really fantastic tools that are in there that are tried and true and tested from a listening perspective all the way to a visual listening perspective to a management perspective. I think they're doing fantastic things.

Hootsuite, I love the partnerships that they're building out and the module perspective that they have, where you can actually add certain things that aren't necessarily originally built for Hootsuite. I think that's revolutionary. That's really who excites me.

10. **What advice would you give to people when they are selecting a platform? You've said based on your needs, what components of those needs would you consider to be important when selecting? What should they assess for themselves and see if it's a match?**

Budget obviously. We can skip that. That's an obvious one kind of right now. It's really looking at the feature needs. I want to get tactical for a second. Do they have the platforms that you need, do they have the collaboration tools that you need? It's feature, feature, feature. Where other added value things, like I mentioned change management, implementation, customer support, you need and want all that. But nowadays, where it's become a bit of a commodity, you're really looking at the features. I'd say start with platform and then what you need from the individual platforms and put that into a hierarchy. What's going to be more important to you? Facebook, Pinterest, so on and so on. I think you definitely need to start seeing if there's a paid media collaboration aspect to it. If there's a tool out there that doesn't have a paid media, or you're not considering paid media, I think that's something to reconsider. So, start from the overall platform needs, then your resource needs, then go from there.

11. **What do you think of the current landscape of social media management as a profession?**
I think it's even as exciting as it ever was before. We have all these amazing new platforms and abilities to connect with everyone. The bigger problem I guess is that sometimes people think of social media and Social Media Managers as people that just work on Facebook or just work on Twitter, but that's not true. There are discussion boards, there's Reddit, there's Telegram, there's Slack channels.

There are forums, there's VR, there are so many amazing opportunities nowadays for a community manager to still do amazing work and connect with people. I think it's so exciting, and it's only getting more exciting. There's still

8

that aspect of being able and having to know a lot of different things and do a lot of things. It's such an incredible time to be in social media.

12. **Where do you think the profession and social media is heading in the future?**
I think really, it's evolving into a more sophisticated, bigger seat at the table. I think now it has a major seat at the table, but social media has taken, especially from a paid perspective ... it's business. It's not just considered this little thing over here on the side that people focus on and maybe will put in ... But now, it's like you have a seat at the table when it comes to marketing. Not just digital marketing, but marketing. It's only going to evolve from there.

13. **What has been the best piece of advice that you've ever been given?**
Bryan Wiener from 360i I, he was the CEO. He had many different jobs at 360i I, but he would give out a book called the Trusted Advisor, and everything and anything I did, I worked for him for many years, he would always tell me to focus on being a trusted advisor. Which ultimately, I focused on someone who gives versus takes and is always out for my clients' or my friends' best interests.

That's never hurt me once. That's the best thing I can do, whether it's sales, whether it's social media, is be honest, tell them what's going to work and what I think is going to be the best case scenario, and that's the best thing I could ever do. You'll see a lot of the ways I talk about myself and on my website is that I am a trusted advisor, and I will do that before anything else in my career.

❓ Questions for Critical Reflection

1. Why is it important to stop scheduled content when there is an issue or crisis? Please explain your answer.
2. How can audience research assist in identifying the most optimal time to schedule social media content? Explain the process that you would use.
3. Why is relying only on scheduled content a limited way to approach social media management? What can happen as a result?
4. What are some of the benefits of using a social media management platform? How do you feel about using one in your role as a Social Media Manager?
5. Why is it important for there not to be a lag in comments being posted on a client's social media channels and when the same comments appear in the social media management platform interface? What could possibly occur as a result?

❯ Practical Exercises

1. You are managing the social media for a client who has a target audience in Melbourne, Australia and another in Mumbai, India. Research the different time zones and develop a method of how you would post a Flashback Friday post for this coming Friday.
2. You are currently freelancing as a Social Media Manager. You have five regular clients who use Pinterest, Facebook, Instagram and LinkedIn. Using the knowledge gained in this chapter, research the most appropriate social media management platform to suit your needs. Which platform would you recommend and why?

References

Annelise. (2017). Posting to social media in other time zones. Annelise.Ca.com, viewed: 8.06.2019, http://annelise.ca/2017/11/posting-social-media-time-zones/.

Gollin, M. (2019). What are the best times to post on social media in 2019?, *Falcon.IO*, viewed 10.06.2019, https://www.falcon.io/insights-hub/topics/social-media-management/best-time-to-post-on-social-media-2018/.

Minguez, K. (2014). The pros and cons of scheduling your social media posts, *Social Media Today*, viewed: 2.06.2019, https://www.socialmediatoday.com/content/pros-and-cons-scheduling-your-social-media-posts.

Patel, N. (2019). How I gain 1,260 Instagram followers per week, *Neil Patel*, viewed: 10.06.2019, https://neilpatel.com/blog/instagram-followers/.

Sameh, F. (2018). Best time to post on social media In 2019 – An ecommerce guide, *Personalization*, viewed: 10.06.2019, https://www.perzonalization.com/blog/best-time-to-post-on-social-media-in-2019/.

Scott, R. (2017). *Top 10 things to consider when choosing a social media management tool*, SocioSquares, viewed: 10.06.2019, https://www.sociosquares.com/blog/top-10-things-to-consider-when-choosing-a-social-media-management-tool/.

Socialbakers. (2019). Orange: Perfecting internal and external communication with Socialbakers, *Socialbakers*, viewed: 23/11/2019, https://www.socialbakers.com/social-media-content/client-success/orange.

Staff Writer. (2013). 2013: Oreo wins the Super Bowl with 'dunk in the dark' tweet, *The Drum,* viewed: 1.06.2019, https://www.thedrum.com/news/2016/07/10/marketing-moment-101-oreo-wins-super-bowl-dunk-dark-tweet.

Wasserman, T. (2011). Red cross does PR disaster recovery on rogue tweet. *Mashable*, viewed: 2.06.2019, https://mashable.com/2011/02/16/red-cross-tweet/.

Further Reading

Arens, E. (2019). Best times to post on social media for 2019, *SproutSocial*, viewed: 10.06.2019, https://sproutsocial.com/insights/best-times-to-post-on-social-media/.

Barnhart, B. (2019). 9 top social media scheduling tools to save time in 2019, *SproutSocial*, viewed: 10.06.2019, https://sproutsocial.com/insights/social-media-scheduling-tools/.

Gilbert, N. (2019). 20 best social media management software tools of 2019, *Finances Online*, viewed: 10.06.2019, https://financesonline.com/top-20-social-media-management-software-tools/.

Lua, A. (2019). The 25 top social media management tools for businesses of all sizes, *Buffer,* viewed: 10/06/2019, https://buffer.com/library/social-media-management-tools.

Sims, S. (2017). How to choose a social media management tool, *Social Media Today,* viewed: 10.06.2019, https://www.socialmediatoday.com/technology-data/how-choose-social-media-management-tool.

Thorne, B. (2018). 20 vetted tools and tips for managing time zone differences, *I Done This Blog*, viewed: 10.06.2019, http://blog.idonethis.com/tools-for-managing-time-zone-differences/.

Helpful Links

How to Schedule Instagram Posts on a Desktop Without Third-Party Tools: https://www.socialmediaexaminer.com/how-to-schedule-instagram-posts-on-desktop-without-third-party-tools/

Buffer: https://buffer.com/

CoSchedule: https://coschedule.com/

Facebook Creator Studio: https://business.facebook.com/creatorstudio

Hootsuite: https://hootsuite.com/

HubSpot: https://www.hubspot.com/

Later: https://later.com/

Loomly: https://www.loomly.com/

Social Report.: https://www.socialreport.com/

SproutSocial: https://sproutsocial.com/

Sked Social (Instagram Tool): https://skedsocial.com/

Strategic Content Curation

Contents

Strategic Content Curation

Contents

9

With a solid social media strategy in place, a business or nonprofit has a much greater chance of achieving its goals. After developing the social media strategy, it must be implemented. This is where the next two sections of this book will prove to be extremely helpful to guide you through the process of curation and creation of strategic content to support the goals and objectives of the social media strategy.

This section will explain how to strategically (legally and ethically) curate content that will appeal to target audiences and achieve organisational goals. Did you know that you are already a Content Curator? Every time you share a Facebook post or retweet a piece of information, you are curating content. Let's explore the definition of content curation in greater depth.

> **Content:** *Anything created and uploaded to a website.*
>
> **Curation:** *The process of selecting, organising and presenting a collection of items to an audience.*

Handley and Chapman (2010, p. 6) define content as, "...Anything created and uploaded to a website: the words, images, tools or other things that reside there." This list also includes videos and links to online articles. Therefore, social media content is any item that is produced and/or uploaded to a social media networking site.

In the true sense of the word, curation involves the process of selecting, organising and presenting a collection of items to an audience. The Oxford Dictionary (2019) also states that this practice is usually based on a professional or expert knowledge of the items being selected and the audience to which they will be presented. A well-known example is an art curator, who draws on their expert knowledge to carefully select a collection of work to arrange in a specific order to exhibit to the public.

> **Content Curation:** The grouping of digital content to maintain, preserve, and add value.

Therefore, in a social media context, content curation is the grouping of digital content to maintain, preserve, and add value. Pache (2011, p. 20) describes content curation as, "... editing on steroids." A fashion blogger is a great example of a content curator. They use their knowledge of fashion to search for and select the content that they deem to be of most interest to the community they have attracted as blog subscribers. In their blog, they order the curated content in the most logical way and provide their personal commentary to tell their readers a compelling story.

This is why Pache (2011, p. 19) refers to content curators as "...the DJs of the web," because similarly to when a DJ mixes a set of music, a Content Curator must also consider the journey on which they take their audience with the content they select and the way in which they present it and the theories that underpin it. For example, framing theory can be applied to present curated content in a specific context so that the audience is encouraged to construct meaning from it in a particular way. The elements used to present curated content (e.g. written commentary, blog headlines etc.) work together to present curated content in a frame of meaning that align with strategic goals and objectives (Balaban, 2008). This theoretical functionality will be explored further in this section.

Additionally, a content curator never presents others' content as their own. Instead they always ensure that they are permitted to use it and attribute the original creator when they do. These ethical and legal practices relating to content curation are the topics of the first chapter in this section: ▶ Chap. 10, another step in understanding the cycle of strategic social media management.

References

Balaban, D. C. (2008). The framing or the interpretation frames theory. *Journal of Media Research-Revista de Studii Media, 1*(02), 9–13.

Handley, A., & Chapman, C. C. (2010). *Content rules: How to create killer blogs, podcasts, videos, ebooks, webinars (and more) that engage customers and ignite your business* (Vol. 5). Wiley.

Oxford Dictionary. (2019). Curation, *Oxford Dictionary.com*, viewed: 03/02/2019: https://en.oxforddictionaries.com/definition/curation

Pache, C. (2011). Content curators: The DJs of the web. *Journal of Digital Research and Publishing*, 19–25.

Ethical Content Curation

Contents

© The Author(s), under exclusive license to Springer Nature Singapore Pte Ltd. 2021
K. E. Sutherland, *Strategic Social Media Management*, https://doi.org/10.1007/978-981-15-4658-7_10

By the End of this Chapter You Will

- Understand the benefits and disadvantages of content curation.
- Be aware of the theoretical, ethical and legal implications for Social Media Managers when curating content.
- Recognise the importance and the process of checking the accuracy of curated content before posting it.
- Be familiar with best-practices to support the ethical and legal curation of content.

10

TLDR

- Content curation involves the presentation of articles, text, images and video etc. that has been created by someone else.
- Curating content can be an effective way to demonstrate your breadth of knowledge on a topic, but the content must be curated in a legal and ethical way.
- Social Media Managers must ensure that the content that they have curated is accurate and does not breach copyright before it is presented on social media.
- The action of content curation can be explained using Activity Theory to demonstrate how a Social Media Manager uses the internet to work within the rules (norms and laws) to present interesting content to a specific community for a desired outcome.
- Deshpande's (2013) 11 best practices of content curation support Social Media Managers in the ethical curation of content.
- Do not use content if you are unsure of its copyright status or do not have permission for its use. Instead find something else that you are authorised to use or create your own content.

10.1   Introduction

Before we focus on the process of curating content for social media in ▶ Chap. 11, it is essential that we spend some time exploring the ethical issues inherent in its practice. At its very essence, social media content curation involves an author presenting content that they did not create.

Just as in an academic environment, it is essential for an author (or student) to clearly reference the original author's work to ensure that the reader can see from where it originated. This is also the case on social media. It can be a huge mistake to believe that the same rules do not apply in an online environment.

On the contrary, while it is unethical to pass off others' work as your own, there are laws that exist to prevent it from happening. ▶ Chapter 10 will guide you on how to leverage the benefits of content curation, but in a legal and ethical way.

Yet, the benefits of curating others' content may seem unclear at this point, particularly when it seems that a Social Media Manager must walk a tightrope between curation and plagiarism. However, once the ethics and rules are understood, the benefits of incorporating curated content into your social media strategy will far outweigh the effort. Indeed, it will reduce some of that effort over time.

10.2   Benefits of Content Curation

There are four key benefits to using curated content as part of your social media strategy.

10.2.1 Curated Content Can Reduce Time, Resources and Workload

As a Social Media Manager you will be required to keep up a steady flow of fresh content that is interesting and helpful to your target audience, as well as supporting strategic goals. Consider that even with one client, with a profile on Facebook and Instagram, generating a post every 1–2 days for each platform (up to 14 per week) is not uncommon in addition to engaging with followers, developing advertising campaigns, monitoring, social listening and measuring performance.

Unless you are part of a larger team, producing original content every day may be challenging. This is where content curation can assist. Original content should definitely constitute the majority of what is posted, but curated content can supplement it. Using curated content can reduce the costs, time and labour associated with creating original content.

10.2.2 Curating Content Can Position You as an Expert

Presenting a selection of thoughtfully curated content to your audience can increase your credibility as an expert of that particular niche topic. Curating content can suggest to audiences that you have extensive knowledge of what is being written, said and produced on a particular subject and have used this expertise to compile and discuss the most useful content available.

> 66 Presenting a selection of thoughtfully curated content to your audience can increase your credibility as an expert of that particular niche topic. 99
>
> **Dr Karen Sutherland**

10.2.3 Communicating Nutrition Facts Using Curated Content

The Nutrition Guru and the Chef (2019) are focused on curbing the spread of dietary and nutritional misinformation online by sharing facts via social media, in-person presentations and webinars.

They create a steady stream of original content for their social media channels, yet complete this with articles promoting the latest scientific research relating to food, diet and nutrition.

Curating and sharing credible content in this way further strengthens the Nutrition Guru and the Chef's brand as a knowledgeable and reputable source relating to food and nutrition.

Often, the Nutrition Guru and the Chef are one of the first to share industry reports and scientific research on social media, which also positions them as being across the latest developments in their

field and a trusted authority on this specific topic area (◻ Fig. 10.1).

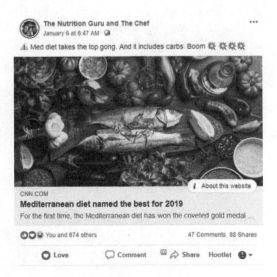

◻ **Fig. 10.1** Curated content from the Nutrition Guru and the Chef (2018)

10.2.4 **Audiences Appreciate Your Efforts**

Audiences will be appreciative of you going to the effort of curating and presenting interesting and useful content of a particular topic. In 2016, it was estimated that 44 billion gigabytes of data are uploaded to the internet every day and this figure is expected to reach 463 billion gigabytes per day by 2025 (Schultz, 2017).

In short, it is impossible for people to trawl through that volume of information to find what is worthwhile. Therefore, by curating content about a particular topic, you are actually providing a service to your audience by saving them from the arduous task of searching through it. However, as we will cover in this chapter and the next, it is essential to curate accurate content in an ethical way and using this approach will help to position you as a trusted authority resulting in people interested in the topic being attracted to your social media posts.

> 66 By curating content about a particular topic, you are providing a service to your audience, saving them from the arduous task of searching for it themselves. 99
>
> Dr Karen Sutherland

10

10.2.5 **Ethical Content Curation Can Foster Professional Relationships and Collaborations**

If you are endorsing someone else's content by sharing it on your social media channels, as we will explore, it is essential to link through and/or tag the original author in the post. If the original author closely monitors their mentions (see ▶ Chap. 7), they may see this and contact you to thank you, follow your profiles or reciprocate by curating some of your content. However, please be aware that if your commentary on a piece of curated content is negative, there is a strong probability that its owner will also be alerted.

This could result in damage to an existing relationship or reputational damage to you, your client or the organisation that you're representing if it garners negative backlash in response. By all means, it is important to be genuine when curating and creating content. However, it is also important to consider the consequences if displaying others' content in a negative way. Some content curators may only ignore your commentary, but their followers may not.

Being negative when curating someone else's content will usually result in reach and exposure, but sometimes this can work against you. Remember that a positive reputation can take years to build, but can be ruined by one careless post.

However, as just highlighted, there can also be some disadvantages to using curated content depending on the approach taken. It is essential to provide a balanced view of the practice. This chapter will also assist in providing guidance and advice to navigate these possible disadvantages.

10.3 Disadvantages of Content Curation

There are three main disadvantages to incorporating content curation into a social media strategy.

10.3.1 It Can Be Overused

If approaching content curation as an easy option to fulfil the ever content-hungry social media environment, it may become a more attractive option than creating content. As advised, the proportion of curated content should not exceed that of created content.

While curated content can take less time to source and post (depending on the technique used to present it), it is a missed opportunity for social media managers to tell their organisation's brand story directly from its source. Only sharing curated content can result in the dilution of brand voice if not approached in a particular way (see ▶ Chap. 12), so ensure that it is only a small percentage of the content posted.

10.3.2 Too Much Can Be Perceived as Laziness

Only sharing other creators' content can be perceived by social media followers as lazy. People follow brands on social media because they feel some degree of connection with them and want to deepen that relationship by keeping abreast of the latest news and content posted. As a Social Media Manager, you owe it to existing (and prospective) followers to create interesting, entertaining and helpful content for your audience. Curated content should supplement that, but it must be thoughtfully selected with the audience in mind and it must support the organisation's strategic goals. For example, posting curated content 2 days out of seven is a reasonable balance.

> 66 Only sharing other creators' content can be perceived by social media followers as lazy. 99
>
> Dr Karen Sutherland

10.3.3 If Unchecked, Curated Content May Be Inaccurate

Sharing others' posts and articles without checking their validity can have extremely negative consequences. In this era of "Fake News" and misinformation the speed and breadth at which misinformation can spread via social media is a phenomenon that many organisations are still trying to grapple with (Compton, 2018).

Sharing a post that is inaccurate reflects extremely poorly on the brand that shared it once the true facts come to light. Furthermore, by sharing a piece of curated content, a brand is essentially endorsing that content as credible and true to their followers. This endorsement then encourages the brand's social media followers to share the content too, increasing the spread of misinformation. This chapter will provide steps on how to check content as part of the content curation process.

10.4 Legal Issues to Avoid when Curating Social Media Content

It would be illegal to go to an art gallery, put your name on a random painting and present it as your own work. While the exact laws in every country are different, such a blatant act would be classed as both fraud, plagiarism and a breach of copyright in most legal jurisdictions. In addition to being illegal, it is clearly unethical behaviour. These laws also apply on the internet.

There really is not any difference if you go to Google Images, find a nice-looking photo that someone else has captured, saving it to your computer and using it in a Facebook post for a client. If you have not sought and received permission from the photographer to use the image, and have not credited them in the post, then you have completed the same act only online.

Let's explore these three areas in greater depth:

10.4.1 Plagiarism

According to the Oxford Dictionary (2019), plagiarism is "The practice of taking someone else's work or ideas and passing them off as one's own." In the context of social media content, using content (text, articles, images, videos, memes etc.) that you did not create without clearly showing their source is plagiarism. While you may not blatantly write in your content that you created a piece of work that is not your own, by not transparently crediting others' work, you are inferring to the audience that the work is yours. It could be described as plagiarism by omission.

Failing to include the content creator's details is the same as suggesting that you are the creator of content that you have sourced from elsewhere. The Instagram account @ thefatjew has been criticised for building a substantial social media following through the use of other creators' content without citing them or obtaining their permission, seemingly a clear-cut case of plagiarism (Abad-Santos, 2015). A further case involved social media influencer, Jay Shetty, who was criticised for using other people's quotes in his content without attributing them (Arbour, 2019).

10.4.2 Copyright

The laws surrounding Copyright, in relation to social media content, will differ between countries. However, in Australia, Copyright is defined as: "...the expression of ideas or information in an original artistic, literary, dramatic or musical work, a cinematographic film, a radio or television broadcast or a sound recording," (Latrobe University, 2019). Therefore, a breach of copyright occurs if "...the use, reproduction or dissemination of copyrighted material by someone who is not authorised to do so..." (Bruce Legal, 2019). In short, using any content without the permission of its owner can be classed as a breach of copyright.

The penalties for copyright breaches are not light. Penalties can result in hefty fines and even jail time (IP Australia, 2019). This may seem excessive for using a photo from Google Images without permission, but it is definitely not worth the risk. If you consider it from the content creator's perspective, it makes perfect sense.

> **66** Using any content
> without the permission of its owner can be classed as
> a breach of copyright. **99**
>
> **Dr Karen Sutherland**

Imagine if you were a professional photographer who makes a living from charging people to use your photos and you noticed that someone was using your work without paying (undermining your livelihood) and, plagiarising your work, blatantly or by omission (potentially damaging your professional reputation), you would expect to be compensated. That is why there are laws there to protect their work.

10.4.3 Fraud

Fraud involves intentionally deceiving others for your own benefit. The Law Dictionary defines fraud as: "...some deceitful practice or willful device, resorted to with intent to deprive another of his right, or in some manner to do him an injury,"(The Law Dictionary, 2019). In the context of social media content curation, if you use content that does not belong to you without permission in a way that deceives others for your benefit (or the benefit of your client) this could be classed as an act of fraud.

For example, if your client sold dreamcatchers online and instead of taking your own photos of the product, you used an image of a dreamcatcher from the internet in a series of Facebook ads, this could be classed as fraudulent. It would not be a true representation of the product being sold.

Furthermore, if you did not have permission to use the image it would also be classed as plagiarism and a breach of copyright. When promoting products on social media it is essential to use actual images of the products or services being sold to provide prospective customers with a true and accurate representation of what they can expect if choosing to make a purchase.

10.5 Curating Accurate Content in a Misinformation and Fake News Era

There are many ethical considerations when curating social media content, but topping the list is the absolute necessity to curate accurate content. Accuracy should be the very first measure of quality when deciding whether to use a piece of curated content on social media. Social media is an amazing tool for connecting people from all around the globe, but it also facilitates the spread of misinformation faster and further than ever before.

Your aim as an ethical Social Media Manager is to do your best not to participate in the proliferation of inaccurate information online. Inaccurate information on social media can be categorised in a range of different ways of which Social Media Managers must be aware:

10.5.1 Fake News

Fake news also known as disinformation, is the "fabricated information that mimics news media content in form but not in organizational process or intent,"(Lazer et al., 2018). This is content that is created to look as though it comes from a credible news outlet but is developed to intentionally mislead social media users.

> 66 **Fake News:** content created to look as though it comes from a credible news outlet, but is developed to intentionally mislead social media users. 99
>
> **Dr Karen Sutherland**

Fake news has become an increasingly important issue since the 2016 presidential election in the United States where it was confirmed that Russian fake news outlets had posted divisive fictional news articles on Facebook, and paid for advertising to deliberately target them at specific demographics to in a bid to influence the outcome of the election (BBC News, 2018).

Some of the most shared fake news articles during this period were articles such as *"Pope Francis shocks world, endorses Donald Trump for president"* which received 960,000 engagements (Richie, 2016). This particular article had a huge impact on prospective voters despite its contents being completely untrue.

Other research also suggests that social media users in the Baby Boomer 65+ age range are more likely to share fake news (Guess, Nagler & Tucker, 2019) than those in the millennial age group. It is important to consider that misinformation can become viral if it remains unchecked and undeleted.

10.5.1.1 Christmas Light Decision Generates Viral Fake News Causing Anti-Muslim Sentiment

In 2016, Sweden's National Road Authority made a decision to ban Christmas lights on street poles for technical and legal reasons (European Council of Skeptical Organisations, 2016).

The story was then hijacked by far-right organisations who completely changed the story, stating that the ban on Christmas

lights was due to avoid offending people of Muslim faith living in Sweden, which was not the case at all.

One Facebook post sharing this fake news story generated more than 43 k reactions, demonstrating the power that disinformation can have in manipulating opinion and stirring up online hatred against specific groups of people (MetroSverige, 2016).

This example highlights the importance of checking the validity of information before sharing it. As a Social Media Manager, it is essential to only curate content that is accurate. Always check the facts of content before posting it.

10.5.2 Hoaxes

Social media hoaxes have been defined as, "…misinformation that aims to deliberatelydeceive the reader," (Volkova & Jang, 2018, p. 576). These are generally social media posts or messages that aim to spark alarm, fear and/or anger.

Some hoaxes also aim to prompt social media users to perform a desired action such as sharing the post with others in their networks. Please read the case study at the end of the chapter that explores a social media hoax that preyed on social media users' fears around security breaches on Facebook around the time of the Cambridge Analytica scandal.

Other hoaxes have included completely fictional posts stating that Facebook is only showing posts to 24 friends or a post claiming publicly that you do not give permission to Facebook to use your content. There was the 'Turn on Notifications' chaos in 2016 when Instagram was changing the order in which people saw posts in their feed. It is essential to check the validity of these posts before sharing them. While it may seem that you are helping others by sharing this information, if it is false and causes unnecessary panic, the opposite will be achieved.

10.5.3 Incorrect Memes

These are memes that depict inaccurate information such as false statistics, photoshopped images that aim to create controversy by intentionally deceiving and misleading the public. Before sharing any memes, it is essential to check the source and that the information being conveyed is factual and accurate.

10.5.4 Satirical News Sites

Be very careful if curating content from satirical news such as *The Onion*. These types of sites are not intending to mislead the public. Instead, they often write outlandish articles based on current news items in a humorous way to entertain readers. However, not everyone understands the joke, and this can backfire if members of your target audience believe the news item to be true.

For example, the article: 'Parenting Experts Warn Screen Time Greatly Increases Risk Of Child Becoming An Influencer, 'The Onion (2019), is purely fictional with humorous intent. However, at first glance, this article may alarm some people if they are not aware that this piece is from a satirical news site.

Sharing entertaining content is highly recommended, but it is also important to make it clear to your audience that your curated content is funny because it is fictional.

10.6 How to Check the Accuracy of Curated Content

Despite social media platforms such as Twitter and Facebook attempting to prevent the spread of misinformation their processes should not be relied upon (Business Day, 2018). Ethical content curation begins with the curator. It is essential to complete the following three steps to assess the validity of a news article before sharing it (Nagler, 2018).

1. **Check the source.** Does the article come from a credible media outlet? Who is the author? Where is the article sourcing its information? Are the images accurate? (Use Google reverse image search to check). Has this information been correctly referenced? Is the source supporting a specific agenda or political viewpoint? Is it a satirical website?
2. **Check for quality and timeliness.** How old is the article? Is it well written without errors in spelling and punctuation?
3. **Use a professional fact-checking website** such as ▶ FactCheck.org, International Fact-Checking Network (IFCN), ▶ PolitiFact.com, or ▶ Snopes.com to assess the validity of the content.

Once accuracy is verified, then it is essential to check that you have permission to use the content. These two steps are not either or. Both must be undertaken and successfully completed before any curated content is ever posted.

10.7 Content Curation Vs Content Aggregation

The process of content curation is often confused with the practice of content aggregation. Before exploring the stages and ethical considerations involved with undertaking content curation, it is essential that the difference between these two concepts are defined.

The greatest difference between the two is that the human element is a fundamental part of content curation, which is lacking in content aggregation. This is why content curators such as bloggers are appreciated by those following them. Please let me explain.

10.8 Content Aggregation and Automation

To put it simply, the best example of content aggregation is conducting a search using Google. Using the key terms of whatever it is that you are searching for, Google returns results in a particular order.

The order is determined by the number of times your selected search terms appear on the webpage, how long the webpage has existed (pages with an established history receive preference) and how many other sites link to that page (this suggests that it is valued by other internet users). However, even with the Google algorithm ranking pages in this particular way, it still requires the person conducting the search to go through and read each site to determine its value.

Therefore, content aggregation is an automated process of finding and organising online information based on key search terms, whereas content curation strongly involves a human element in the process.

10.9 Content Curation and the Human Element

As we will explore, even when automated content curation tools such as ScoopIt are used to source online information about a particular topic, it is necessary for a human being to sort through the content the tool returns.

This is why content curation is such a valuable skill to have, because it contains that human element. Rather than a machine, an algorithm or artificial intelligence selecting and organising content in an automated way according to the types of data that you have previously accessed, the content is thoughtfully selected by an actual person who is usually an expert in a niche area.

This human content curator assesses the value of each piece of content based on their extensive knowledge of the topic, how valuable it will be to their audience and how well it fits within their proposed content structure and commentary. While content aggregation can be effective at sorting through extremely large volumes of information, at this stage in time, it cannot replace that human element.

For example, gamers may be able to use Google to search for the latest releases, but it will take an extremely long time to sort through the thousands of web pages that it returns. Instead, gamers turn to YouTubers such as PewDiePie and Willyrex to hear their reviews of new games, because they value their opinions and experience, plus it saves them from having to sort through thousands of pages of content.

10.10 Theoretical Framework Underpinning Content Curation

The practice of content curation is largely underpinned by what is known as Activity Theory, a theory developed by Engeström, Miettinen and Punamäki (1999), to explain purposeful interaction with the world. Dallas (2007) then applied Activity Theory to the practice of digital curation to provide a theoretical basis and understanding of the practice.

As such, the curation of content must be undertaken from a position of purpose, as with any aspect of social media management that we explore throughout this text. When Activity Theory is applied to content curation

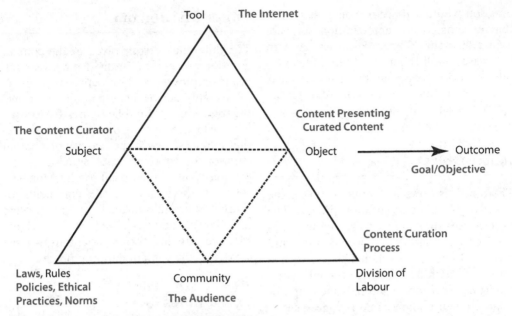

■ **Fig. 10.2**   Activity Theory (Engeström, Miettinen and Punamäki, 1999) with Author Amendments

to explain its process, purpose, participants and proposed outcomes, it helps to remind Social Media Managers that the curation of content for social media is much more involved than simply sharing other people's posts.

As demonstrated in ■ Fig. 10.2 below, there are seven key components of which Activity Theory is comprised: Rules, Subject, Tool, Community, Division of Labour, Object and Outcome. On its own, Activity Theory does not convey much meaning. However, when each component is directly applied to an aspect of the content curation process, it definitely helps to increase understanding of what (and whom) it involves.

Activity Theory's relevance in explaining the process of content curation is clearer when we apply the elements of the task to the different components of the theory.

10.10.1 Tool = The Internet

When breaking down the activity of content curation for social media, the tool refers to

the internet, which is the vehicle that facilitates the entire process. Without the internet a Social Media Manager would be unable to curate digital content (images, articles, videos etc.) and would also be unable to share them online with their audience. This is why the tool is positioned at the very top of the pyramid, as it is the most important aspect of the activity.

10.10.2 Subject = The Content Curator (e.g. The Social Media Manager)

When discussing social media content, the term 'Subject' usually refers to the topic of the content. However, in relation to Activity Theory, 'Subject' relates to the person undertaking the task, in this case, content curation. Therefore, the Subject in the process of content curation is the content curator, or the Social Media Manager.

The Subject is also an essential component of the activity, because without someone to use the tool (the internet), the content curation would not occur. Some may argue that automated content curation software contradicts this theory. However, even in that case it still requires a human being to set up the software in the first instance, therefore, a human subject is vital for the activity of content curation to take place.

10.10.3 Object

The object is a piece of content that is the result of the content curation process. The subject uses the internet to search for valuable content relating to a specific topic and presents that topic to their audience in the form of a blog post, Facebook post, YouTube video or whatever is most appropriate to their audience and key messages.

10.10.4 Community

Logically, the community in this figure represents the niche audience of the curated content. The community (or audience) is located at the base of Activity Theory to demonstrate that a thorough understanding or audience preferences and needs underpin the ultimate success of the activity.

For content curation to be effective, the content being curated must resonate with its intended audience, and it must also be presented in a way that attracts their attention. Furthermore, as highlighted in ▶ Chap. 3, a community is more than an audience.

A community is a collective of like-minded people who help each other for the good of the overall group. Therefore, the development of a community has been carefully facilitated by the Social Media Manager around a particular product, cause or organisation, and it is the knowledge of their needs that must support all decisions and actions in the content curation process.

10.10.5 Division of Labor

The different steps involved in the content curation process can be divided between relevant employees and/or between members of a highly active niche community. Some organisations and public figures have super fans (also known as Top Fans on Facebook) that may assist with the activity of content curation by sourcing valuable content and passing it on to the Social Media Manager, sparking discussion in the comments or sharing a brand's curated content through their own networks. A Social Media Manager can directly ask super fans to assist as part of the content curation process.

10.10.6 Rules

As we will explore further in this chapter, there are many rules (laws, policies and ethical practices) that a Social Media Manager must adhere to particularly as part of the content curation process. For example, it is a breach of copyright law to use someone else's photo without permission and it is unethical to use someone else's inspirational quote without citing them.

Additionally, there are also rules around what others deem to be acceptable or more importantly, unacceptable in particular places on the internet. For example, there are usually guidelines regarding acceptable conduct within Facebook groups that members must adhere to when posting content there. Yet, there are many rules on the internet that are unwritten. These are also known as 'norms'. Widely accepted (and standard) behaviour within a group is known as a norm, and are often inherent within a culture. This is why audience research is so important for a Social Media Manager.

Without understanding the unwritten rules or norms of a target audience, curated and created content is likely to be lackluster at best, not cutting through or resonating because it does not command attention with its understanding of that group.

At the other end of the scale, curated and created content can be highly offensive to a specific audience if it breaks the rules or opposes the norms of that group. Rules regarding the activity of content curation can also relate to the language used in the curated content and its presentation. Acceptable language also relates to norms, for example, whether the use of profanity is acceptable to the audience.

Yet, what is of greatest importance in any communication is to use language that the intended audience can understand, and what is also appropriate for the social media platform on which the curated content is being presented. For example, the language used to engage with a group of senior citizens on Facebook will be very different to what would be used to interact with 18–24-year olds on Instagram.

Again, thorough audience research is the key to accurately understanding what is deemed as accepted behaviour and commonly used language. Rules govern a range of different layers in the content curation process and it is advisable that Social Media Managers have a clear understanding of what the written and unwritten rules are before beginning the content curation process.

10.10.7 Outcome

The outcome of each content curation activity can be defined as the overall result that you are hoping to achieve. Outcomes can be both macro and micro level. At a macro level, a Social Media Manager may be aiming to increase social media followers and influence for their client as a result of posting curated content that is of value to their target audience.

Their overall outcome is likely to be something much more tangible, such as an increase in customers, donations or registrations depending on the organisation and its goals. On a micro level, the outcome of posting curated content may be as simple as attracting a certain level of positive engagement on each specific piece such as likes, shares, views and positive comments.

Generally, when referring to the activity of content curation, the outcome relates directly to the desired behaviour of the target audience that the content curator (or Social Media Manager) is aiming to achieve.

As the Activity Theory model demonstrates, all of the other components, the tool, subject, rules, community and division of labor culminate into the object (the piece of curated content and the way in which it is presented to the audience). It is this object that leads directly to (and directly impacts) the outcome. This relationship between the object and the outcome is extremely important. As Activity Theory suggests, the quality of the object influences the quality of the outcome.

If a Social Media Manager does not understand their intended audience and presents curated content with the objective of inspiring the audience to respond in a particular way, the probability of achieving the desired outcome will be very low. There is much more involved with content curation than sharing other people's content. A deep understanding of the audience is required in addition to selecting the most relevant and helpful way to present the curated content to attract their attention.

Activity Theory is an effective way to explain the most important components relating to the content curation process. With these elements in mind, it is essential to explore best-practice when ethically sourcing, sharing and presenting curated content.

Deshpande (2013) suggests 11 important practices to ensure that content is being curated in an ethical way:

10

10.10.8 Best Practice #1: Never Produce an Article in its Entirety

If you have found an online article that you know your target audience will love, never copy it and paste it into your own blog as this will lead readers to assume that it is your work rather than content that has been curated. Instead, it is better to use only the sections that are relevant, but to mention the author and link to the article to make it clear to your audience from where the content originated.

This is an ethical practice. Sharing helpful and relevant content to your audience is encouraged, but they must know who created it. However, it is perfectly acceptable to share an entire article with your audience if a direct link to the content is included in the post. This is a great opportunity as a Social Media Manager to add some commentary about the article to attract the audience's attention and to position the brand that you're representing as helpful. For example:

By including a link directly to the article, the audience can clearly see the source of the content, and may even be interested enough to further explore other content from the same creator. You were the person who led them to this potentially helpful source, which helps to strengthen the relationship between you and your audience.

10.10.9 Best Practice #2: Try Not to Use All, or Even the Majority, of Articles Available from a Single Source

It can be extremely tempting to keep sharing articles from a content creator whose work positively resonates with an audience. However, it is ethical practice to resist that urge. When the majority of curated content is coming from a single source it can be viewed by the audience as laziness on the part of the Social Media Manager because they are only reading one source. Additionally, the audience can also view the brand as not having a wider knowledge and understanding of their industry. If that single source produces content containing inaccuracies, the Social Media Manager may be unaware due to their narrow focus in terms of the content that they are curating.

Furthermore, while the content creator may seem flattered by the exposure, they may also wonder why the Social Media Manager continually using their content is not producing their own. If you find a highly relevant source of valuable and credible content, try to limit its use by selecting pieces that would be of greatest interest to the audience. Remember, only curating content from a single course can be tiresome for the audience and the content creator.

10.10.10 Best Practice #3: Prominently Identify the Source of the Article

This is ethical practice when curating all types of content: articles, images, videos etc. Just as in an academic essay it is essential to correctly reference any work, ideas, concepts and quotes that are not your own, it is exactly the same when curating content to share on social media.

Tag the content creator in all posts, and if finding them on social media is challenging, at least include their full name and a link to their website. The cornerstone of social media best practice is transparency. It pays to be completely honest and genuine. It does not matter the industry in which you will function, the audience and your customers need to trust you for any relationship to be cultivated.

Dr Karen Sutherland
Published by Karen Sutherland [?] · April 2 at 4:08 PM · ◉

They say that if you can laugh at yourself you will have a lifelong source of amusement. Facebook Live went rogue during the first part of my interview for Real People of the Sunshine Coast this afternoon. Check it out. 😜

699 Views

Real People of the Sunshine Coast was live.
April 2 at 3:30 PM · ◉

Chatting live Karen Sutherland from University of the Sunshine Coast. When things don't go to plan you just keep moving. As you will see the augmented reality gremlins took over at the beginning!

Fig. 10.3 It is important to prominently identify the source of the article

By not prominently identifying the source of curated content, it implies that you created it, which is dishonest and unethical. Your audience will eventually call you out on it, so it is worth following best practices from the outset (☐ Fig. 10.3).

10.10.11 Best Practice #4: Whenever Possible, Link to the Original Source of the Article

As mentioned in Best Practice Number 2, always link to the curated piece wherever possible. This works particularly well when the piece of curated content is an online article or video. However, sharing, retweeting or regramming (re-posting an Instagram post) the original post works just as well if the original author's profile name is prominent.

Sometimes Facebook asks whether you want to include the entire post when sharing someone else's content. Always say yes to ensure that all of the information from their original post is included in yours. You will have the opportunity to add your own commentary at the top of the post. Also use this approach when retweeting. Always include the original tweet in its entirety and add your own content above it to make it clear to the audience that it is curated content that you are presenting.

10.10.12 Best Practice #5: Whenever Possible, Provide Context or Commentary for the Material you Use

The beauty of content curation is that just like as Pache (2011) describes, you have the ability to weave together a range of content in a new way to present to the audience that can help to support an argument about a topic, provide a solution or communicate helpful information that encourages current or prospective customers to use your product or service.

Only sharing others' content without explaining to your audience how it is relevant to their needs will confuse them while implying that the content is not curated. The whole point of using curated content is that you can use it to support organisational goals (and the objectives in your social media strategy).

However, while you may clearly understand the context when curating content, do not assume that the audience does too. Use the presentation of curated content as another opportunity to assist, entertain and inform your audience using your organisation's brand voice. Never share a piece of content without speaking directly to your audience to explain why it is relevant to them (☐ Fig. 10.4).

10

🖼 **Fig. 10.4** It is always better to provide commentary when presenting curated content (see ▶ Chap. 12)

10.10.13 Best Practice #6: When Sharing Images, Unless You Have Explicit Permission to Share a Full-Size Image, Always Share a Thumbnail Image at Most

As Deshpande (2013) advises, it is unethical practice to use images that you find online without seeking permission to do so. While it can be extremely tempting (and easy) to search for the perfect image using Google Images, find it and then use it as the cover image of a blog post, in reality you are stealing someone else's work.

To assume that the owner of the image will never know that you have used it is completely naive, misinformed and unethical. Remember, Google also has a Reverse Image Search tool as well that is used by photographers and artists to track down copyright breaches of their work. In a university class that I taught, we produced a class blog as an assessment task. I forget how many times that I discussed the importance of copyright and seeking permission to use images that were not copyright or royalty free.

The semester ended, and I went on holiday, bushwalking in the middle of Tasmania, Australia. It was there that I received an angry email from a photographer in Japan. One of my students had used one of the photographer's images in our class blog without their permission. The photographer ordered the image to be taken down or legal action would ensue. Copyright infringement is very real and its penalties also extend to the internet. Deshpande (2013) suggests using a thumbnail instead, which may be a way around gaining permission, because only a smaller version is being used.

However, this suggestion is not very practical in our image-laden social media landscape of today. Alternatively, there are some other actions that can be taken to ensure when you are using curated images that you are doing so ethically.

- **Action 1: Check the Copyright Status of the Image, If You Cannot Find It, You Do Not Have It**

There are a range of useful sites now with creative commons and galleries of copyright free images that are free to use (links at the end of this chapter). However, even in these free image libraries it is important to check the usage requirements. Some images may require direct permission from the owner, or a credit when it is used or even just notification of how and when it will be used. It is important to check what the requirements are and adhere to them before using the curated image. This also applies when using Google's image rights filter, because their appearance in a search does not automatically mean that they are fine to use. Always check.

- **Action 2: Without Permission, Find or Create a Similar Image, Using Ethical Practice**

If you do not have permission to use the image that you want, unfortunately, you will have to let it go. Instead, you could find a similar image that you have the rights to use or you could use a tool like Canva, to recreate a similar image. However, the recreation must be approached in an ethical way too. Avoid a direct copy of the image. Instead, try to recreate it by adding your own style. Use different colors, filters and graphics, to represent the image that you originally wanted, but aligning it more with your client's brand. When using a recreated image, it is also ethical practice to credit the owner of the original image in some way. For example, 'Image inspired by…' and tag (or at least mention) the original author. This is ethical behaviour, because although you technically created the image, it was not your original idea or concept, and it is important to make this clear.

- ■ Action 3: Pay for a Subscription to a Stock Photo Website

Sometimes the easiest (and most ethical) way to use curated images in social media content is to pay for play. In other words, paying for a subscription to a stock photo library such as ▶ iStock.com, Getty Images or ▶ Shutterstock.com provides you with the right to use the images on the site. There are many advantages to taking this approach. Firstly, the images are usually of a high quality and have been taken by professional photographers.

There are also usually a range of image sizes that allows greater flexibility to suit your specific content needs. Furthermore, subscribing to an image library saves valuable time and effort in both sourcing an appropriate image (there are usually thousands to choose from) and the permission to use it, because you have already paid for that right. However, there are also some disadvantages. The cost of stock images can be preventative for many. Large organisations with ample budgets will not find this to be the case, but a Social Media Manager just starting out with a few clients may not find this approach very cost effective in the beginning.

Also, using curated stock images for all social media content may not represent a brand as authentically as taking your own photos, particularly for bricks and mortar locations. For example, a coffee shop using a stock image of a couple drinking coffee in a nondescript location may not have the same impact as using a photograph of a couple drinking coffee in a distinctive corner of the coffee shop's interior. Remember, the approach that you take to all curated content, including images, must align with the organisation's strategic goals and objectives.

10.10.14 Best Practice #7: Link Back to the Original Article Prominently, Not Buried All the Way Down at the End of the Post

The reference list, with links to cited content, is usually situated at the end of an academic essay. While this approach may be used with a blog post, it is also important to link through to the original article throughout the piece whenever it is mentioned.

There are three fundamental reasons for doing this:

1. It makes it clear to the reader that the work that you are citing or curating is not your own. The inclusion of a link within a sentence suggests to the reader that the material highlighted by the link has been curated from a different source. However, as mentioned in ▶ Chap. 8, do not link more than 3–4 words within a sentence. Linking an entire sentence can be extremely challenging to read and is far from being aesthetically pleasing.
2. It makes the source of the curated content highly accessible to readers if they are keen to learn more. With all social media practice, audience needs must be first priority. Web designers build entire websites around the user's journey so that their intended tasks can be completed with ease.

Remember, in any form of communication, it is all about the audience. It is not about you. Even social media content and blogs need to be audience-centric. Therefore, when producing any content (whether that is based on curated content or not) as a Social Media Manager, you must plot out the audience's journey through that content (brief or extensive) to ensure that it flows in a logical way and that all of the necessary information is included (and the irrelevant excluded) to suit their needs.

This is why it makes perfect sense to link to the source of curated content throughout the post so that the reader can find out more instantaneously rather than forcing them to scroll to a reference list at the bottom.

3. TLDR will prevent many from reading the entire piece (if it is a blog post) which means that if the reference list is at the very end of the post, the audience will never make it that far. For those unaware of the term TLDR, it stands for Too Long Didn't Read, which suggests that with social media content, less is more.

10.10.15 Best Practice #8: If You Are Reposting an Excerpt from the Original Article, Make Sure Your Excerpt Only Represents a Small Portion of the Original Article

Again, avoid curating too much content the same, and definitely avoid curating too much content from the same article. Just as we explored with Pache (2011), content curation is the art of bringing together a range of different content in different ways that are bound together with your own voice to create a completely new piece of work.

The audience is reading your work because they are generally interested in your perspective on a topic and your views on what other content creators think too. It ruins that expectation of reading a fresh perspective when your content is largely the work of someone else. Remember, copy and paste is not content curation. The process is far more

sophisticated and effective when implemented thoughtfully, skillfully and ethically.

10.10.16 Best Practice #9: If You Are Reposting an Excerpt from an Original Article, Make Your Commentary Longer than the Excerpt You Are Reposting

This best practice reiterates my previous point. If you think about it, this chapter is an example of content curation only in book form. I have curated the 11 best practices of content curation from an article by Deshpande (2013). Instead of posting the entire article, I have critically analysed these practices and provided my own explanation on what they mean and guidance on how they can be practically applied when curating content for social media. It would have been very confusing to the reader if I had only included the Deshpande (2013) article in place of this chapter rather than providing my own commentary.

After all, my name is on the cover as the author, so the expectation is that I am going to be the person actually writing the book. This is the same when curating social media content. You, your client or their brand should be the prominent voice that links the curated pieces together. Leverage this opportunity to place your voice at the forefront rather than replacing it with curated content; instead use it to your advantage.

10.10.17 Best Practice #10: Retitle Any and All Content You Curate

Again Deshpande (2013) makes a valid suggestion that supports all of the advice that we have explored thus far. Even if you curate a piece of content that has a killer headline that would fit your work perfectly, avoid the temptation of using it, because it is an unethical practice. Firstly, you are plagiarising someone else's work by ripping off their ideas instead of developing your own. Furthermore, using someone else's headline demonstrates a distinct lack of creativity on your part. Do your own work.

It helps to develop your own voice rather than using someone else's because it is easier. It is perfectly fine to cite someone else's headline within your work as long as you reference them and link to it to make it clear that it is not your own. There may be some instances where you can quote someone else's title in your title. Yet, to do this ethically and effectively you would also need to reference them in the headline.

This approach is not recommended. It is walking a fine line between what is ethical and what is not and it would be very challenging to do this well, particularly when the ideal blog post length is 60 characters, even less for other platforms such as Facebook (Wainright, 2019; Neidlinger, 2015). That is a lot to achieve in such a limited number of characters. You may be the wordsmith of the century, but in this instance, it may be less laborious (and more ethical) to devise your own title.

10.10.18 Best Practice #11: Don't Use No-Follows on Your Links to the Original Publisher's Content

Search Engine Optimisation (SEO) focuses on how to bring a website up to the highest position on Google (and other search engines) without paying for that position, and links from external sites are one of the techniques used. When an internet user is sent to a webpage from an external link, search engines such as Google, awards it points as a measure of its popularity.

These points help the webpage's position in its search ranking (Marrs, 2017). The greater the number of unique visitors the more prominently the webpage will appear in the search results. Most Content Management Systems such as WordPress have this as a standard setting when creating a link in web content to an external website.

However, some HTML code can be used to prevent external links from getting the boost from search engines to improve their search ranking. This is called a No-Follow link. The No-Follow link has been effective in reducing spammy websites from trying to improve their rankings, so they have their place, but not when it comes to content curation. If you have curated a piece of content, value it enough to include it in your work and have linked to it appropriately, why would you deny the content owner the opportunity to improve their Google ranking? Not doing so is unethical and downright mean. Using a normal follow link is an additional way of thanking the content owner for their work in addition to referencing them correctly. Avoid no-follow links at all costs.

Conclusion

Content Curation can be a highly effective way for Social Media Managers to produce a large volume of interesting and relevant content to their audiences. However, there are many ethical and legal risks inherent with using content created by others. This chapter explored the many benefits and disadvantages involved with content curation.

It used Activity Theory to break down the key components of the action of content curation and provided practical advice to Social Media Managers regarding its ethical and legal implications and how to navigate them using best-practice. Our next chapter will focus on the process of content curation and the various ways to approach it to find the best method to suit your needs and/or the needs of your client/s.

Case Study: Facebook Hacking Hoax

In October 2018, the following message appeared on Facebook Messenger and went viral. This post went viral because rather than checking its validity, people panicked and shared it with everyone on Facebook Messenger friends list.

When looking closely at the message, those with solid experience using social media can clearly identify different elements that indicate that it is a hoax. However, for people with limited social media experience, and those feeling uneasy after Facebook's data breaches (Leskin, 2018) this message confirmed their fears.

Furthermore, because it was sent from someone that they knew, that inferred the message to be credible. This is how the message appeared in my Facebook Messenger Inbox (⬛ Fig. 10.5):

I received this message multiple times. I responded asking if the person had really received another friend request from me, and if so, could they please send me a screenshot. Nobody had received another friend request from me.

Furthermore, why would I assume that everyone received another friend request

> Hi....I actually got another friend request from you which I ignored so you may want to check your account.   Hold your finger on the message until the forward button appears...then hit forward and all the people you want to forward too....I had to do the people individually.   PLEASE DO NOT ACCEPT A NEW friendship FROM ME AT THIS TIME.

⬛ **Fig. 10.5**   Facebook Messenger Hoax

from me and forward it to everyone? It does not seem logical, but when people think their security has been breached, they panic.

Lastly, the message tells me not to accept a new friend request from the sender even though they only mention seeing one from me. When closely analysing this message, it is nonsensical, yet fear causes people not to fact-check. If this message was checked on the fact-checking websites such as Snopes (2018) those receiving it would have been relieved to learn that it was a hoax, and this would have prevented the panic spreading of misinformation.

— *How would you have responded to this message?*

— *What would you advise others to do if they received a message like this?*

10.11 Interview: Ethan Wall - Law Attorney, Author, Marketing Consultant, Keynote Speaker and President of *The Social Media Law Firm* and *Social Media Law and Order*, Miami, USA

1. **Please tell me about your current role and business**

I have a couple different roles that are relevant to what we're talking about. First, I am a social media attorney. I've been practising law for over 12 years. I founded the Social Media Law Firm, which is the first law firm in the world dedicated exclusively to protecting and growing businesses that use social media.

I also founded a company called Social Media Law and Order, which is a social media and digital marketing agency for lawyers and law firms that help attorneys attract more clients using social media and digital marketing. So, I understand both how we can use social media to accomplish our marketing and business development goals, and what are the laws, and legalities, and some of the ethics rules that govern the use of social media to achieve our business objectives.

2. What do you enjoy most about working in the field of social media?

What I enjoy most in this field is that the field is constantly changing. I get bored easily.

Miami Florida and helping to guard them against the legal issues that banks face on social media.

I really love that the landscape is constantly changing. There are always new things to learn, and it allows me to explore my passions which are exploring, travelling, reading, writing, teaching, helping other people all in the area of social media and the law. So, it connects with both my personal passions and with my professional objectives.

3. What legal advice do you give to clients around using other people's content?

Sharing content if it's a blog post, or an image, or something that someone else has done in a way that's legal and ethical. There are a couple big legal issues with using other people's content. So, I'm gonna separate the two issues for the purposes of our conversation.

The first one is taking someone's piece of content and using it as your own. The second might be re sharing, re posting, tagging, repurposing content. Let's just start with the classic example of one that I get all the time. Which is, Ethan I found this photograph on Google, can I use it on my own social media profiles? Alright, so we'll start there.

The general rule is if you don't own the content then you shouldn't use it because you're putting yourself at risk, and you're likely violating the law and someone else's rights. The type of law that governs this is generally copyright law. That means that the moment that I create something whether I write a blog, take a photo, or create a video I own the rights to that work.

If you don't own it then you probably don't have the right to use it, and you're

likely violating the law unless you have permission.

A further aspect relates to using user-generated content. We represent a large international travel-related company. Lots of people who attend this travel company's related events or programming will take their own photos while they're there, and the company itself wants to use their customer's photographs without violating copyright infringement.

That's really the worst thing that someone can do is shoot first, ask questions later because a lot of times we hear from people who innocently use someone else's content because they didn't know that it was a violation of the law. And then get a cease and desist letter, and a demand letter saying you violated my rights.

4. What are the main challenges but also the main mistakes that you see in general from your clients when they come to you?

Clients come to us for, I would say four different types of things.

Some of our clients come to us as social media lawyers because they want to use social media for a business purpose. Some of our largest clients are banks, credit unions, and financial institutions that want to use social media to promote their products and services, and engage with their community, but don't necessarily know how financial laws and regulations apply to promoting a credit card on Twitter.

Second type of client will come to us and say, "We're operating a business online and we want to protect our business and grow so that other people can't steal our concepts." That kind of falls under the realm of intellectual property. Meaning a client will come up with a great name for a product and they want to make sure that as they start rolling out on Instagram, someone doesn't copy their name, and tries to sell knock-off goods or services under their name itself.

I'd say the third area people contact us with is about what I would call social media law. Influencers, where they're hiring influencers, or I am an influencer, and there's a contract presented to me and I want to make sure that it's okay to sign. I'm not waiving my rights. Or maybe I'm doing an online giveaway like, like my post for a chance to win a free gift card or a trip to Australia. There are rules that govern these online giveaways. There are laws that govern them and we will help to protect people who want to use social media as a way to attract more customers or generate their businesses.

The last area and one that we're getting lots of calls about, that's probably the most popular, the most sought after call or email we get is either A, Instagram shut down my account and I can't get it back. Or someone has hacked my social media profile and I can't get them back, can you help me? This is usually because either A, someone violated the rules by violating somebody's copyright, or posting other content that would violate the rules. Or B, someone is harassing somebody, or broke into their account, or phished them and got their email address, or filed false complaints against some profile and theirs was taken down, and Instagram won't reply to them and they can't get it back.

That's happening a lot these days, I mean it's unfortunate because there's very little that we can do about it. But those I would say are the four main areas that we're having people contact us for.

5. **What general advice would you give to a business or a social media manager around adhering to the law?**
I'd probably offer the same advice that carpenters do when they build houses, which is measure twice, cut once.

That's one of the biggest pieces of advice I could say is have the most creative ideas. Figure out what you want to do, but before you execute, all right, just think about what risks might there be, legal or otherwise, before I go ahead and do it.

In terms of what people can do in terms of courses, or online research, there's not a ton out there is an abundance. The caveat is, not everyone's right, and not everyone's an expert, even though the caveat is not everyone's right and not everyone's an expert, even though everybody has an opinion on these things. Doing a little bit of online research and due diligence is helpful but take it with a grain of salt, just like you don't trust everything you hear on TV, can't trust everything you see online.

While as an attorney it sounds disingenuous to say reach out and contact an attorney that's experienced in social media legal issues for your problems, that's really one of the go to thoughts that someone should have because you don't want to get advice about brain surgery from your mechanic.

6. **Where do you think the future of social media law is heading?**
I think one of the futures is dealing with live content. And what I mean by that is a couple years ago my clients would say hey, I'm posting something on Instagram or on Facebook. How does the law apply? And at some point there weren't very concrete answers and now I've got pretty concrete answers for everybody on lots of issues about when you post something on a profile or a platform how could existing laws apply to these new technologies. But now on Instagram you can have Instagram TV. You have stories.

I think that as we move to a generation that's more AI, artificial intelligence, live, plug-in chips into our glasses so that we can see things that are going on, we're going to just experience new technologies that the law never contemplated before. And there's always some catch up time into how the law applies.

In today's day and age, there are things that are utilities. Water, electricity. At some point, I could imagine that access to the internet becomes some kind of utility and how can we go about regulating this in a manner that's both responsible but also allows people to conduct business?

7. **What is the best piece of advice that you've ever been given?**

Best piece of advice I've ever been given was to ask yourself what would you do if money was no object?

For me, spending my time focusing on social media legal issues helps me to pursue my passions, which are exploring, travelling, reading, writing, helping other people, giving back, spending time with my friends, and this niche in social media law.

❓ Questions for Critical Reflection

1. How is content curation different to the way that search engines such as Google gather information?

2. Do you believe the benefits of content curation outweigh its disadvantages and potential risks? Why/why not? Please explain your answer.

3. What is 'fake news' and how can Social Media Managers ensure that curated content is accurate?

4. What is copyright? How can you curate content without breaching copyright laws?

5. What part does the community play in the activity of content curation? How important is their role in this activity? Please explain your answer.

6. What do you consider to be the most important part of ethical content curation? Why?

❯ Practical Exercises

1. You are the Social Media Manager for a local retirement home. Using the best-practice and accuracy checking guidelines in this chapter, find an online article that would interest this prospective retirement home residents and craft a Facebook post ready to share it the public page.

2. Go to one of the fact-checking websites mentioned in this chapter (Snopes, FactCheck etc.) and read the latest social media hoaxes listed there. Have you seen these online? How did you respond to them?

3. As a Social Media Manager, how would you respond to a social media follower who posted a link to a 'fake news' article as a comment in response to one of your client's Facebook posts?

References

Abad-Santos, A. (2015). The Fat Jew's Instagram plagiarism scandal, explained, Vox.com, viewed: 10.04.2019, https://www.vox.com/2015/8/19/9178145/fat-jew-plagiarism-instagram

Arbour, N. (2019). *Jay Shetty Is Full Of SH*T!*, viewed 24.10.2019, https://www.youtube.com/watch?v=Nfu4j7EIGqs

BBC News. (2018). Trump Russia affair: Key questions answered, BBC.com, viewed: 03/02/2019, https://www.bbc.com/news/world-us-canada-42493918

Bruce Legal. (2019). Copyright and social media: A few things businesses should keep in mind, BruceLegal.com, viewed: 03/02/2019, http://www.brucelegal.com.au/copyright-social-media-things-businesses-keep-mind

Business Day. (2018). Google, Facebook and Twitter agree to fight fake news in the EU, *Business* Live.co.za, viewed: 03/02/2019, https://www.businesslive.co.za/bd/world/europe/2018-09-26-google-facebook-and-twitter-agree-to-fight-fake-news-in-the-eu/

Compton, L. (2018). 'Fake news' era of media disinformation will take 50 years to unravel, expert warns, *ABC News*, viewed: 03/02/2019, https://www.abc.net.au/news/2018-09-10/fake-news-era-legacy-hobart-media-literacy-conference/10223510

Dallas, C. (2007). An agency-oriented approach to digital curation theory and practice. In Proceedings:

10

International Symposium on "Information and Communication Technologies in Cultural Heritage (pp. 49–72).

Deshpande, P. (2013). Content curation: Copyright, ethics & fair use, *Content Curation Marketing,* viewed: 03/02/2019, http://www.contentcurationmarketing.com/content-curation-copyright-ethics-fair-use/

Engeström, Y., Miettinen, R., & Punamäki, R. L. (Eds.). (1999). *Perspectives on activity theory.* Cambridge University Press.

European Council of Skeptical Organisations. (2016). Why fact-checking news reports is important, Ecso.org, viewed: 22/11/2019, https://www.ecso.org/news/fact-checking-news-reports-important/

Guess, A., Nagler, J., & Tucker, J. (2019). Less than you think: Prevalence and predictors of fake news dissemination on Facebook. *Science advances,* 5(1). Pp. 1–8. IP Australia (2019) Counterfeiting and piracy, *Australian Government,* viewed: 03/02/2019, https://www.ipaustralia.gov.au/ip-infringement/more-about-ip-infringement/counterfeiting-and-piracy

LaTrobe University. (2019). Copyright in social media, websites and blogs, *LaTrobe University,* viewed: 03/02/2019, https://www.latrobe.edu.au/library/copyright-hub/social-media

Lazer, D. M., Baum, M. A., Benkler, Y., Berinsky, A. J., Greenhill, K. M., Menczer, F., et al. (2018). The science of fake news. *Science, 359*(6380), 1094–1096.

Leskin, P. (2018). The 21 scariest data breaches of 2018, *Business Insider - Tech Insider,* viewed: 03/02/2019, https://www.businessinsider.com.au/data-hacks-breaches-biggest-of-2018-2018-12?r=US&IR=T

Marrs, M. (2017). Follow links vs. no follow links: should you care? *WordStream,* viewed: 03/02/2019, https://www.wordstream.com/blog/ws/2013/07/24/follow-nofollow-links

MetroSverige. (2016). Fact checking online is more important than ever, YouTube.com, viewed: 22/11/2019, https://www.youtube.com/watch?v=Ryjpu-NWYm8

Nagler, C. (2018). 4 tips for spotting a fake news story, *Harvard Summer School - Inside Summer,* viewed: 03/02/2019, https://www.summer.harvard.edu/inside-summer/4-tips-spotting-fake-news-story

Neidlinger, J. (2015). What really is the best headline length? *Co-Schedule Blog,* viewed: 03/02/2019, https://coschedule.com/blog/best-headline-length/

Nutrition Guru & The Chef. (2019). Facebook.com, viewed: 03/02/2019, https://www.facebook.com/thenutritionguruandthechef/

Oxford Dictionary. (2019). Plagiarism, *Oxford* Dictionary.com, viewed: 03/02/2019, https://en.oxforddictionaries.com/definition/us/plagiarism

Pache, C. (2011). Content curators: The DJs of the web. *Journal of Digital Research and Publishing,* 19–25.

Richie, H. (2016). Read all about it: The biggest fake news stories of 2016, CNBC.com, viewed: 03/02/2019, https://www.cnbc.com/2016/12/30/read-all-about-it-the-biggest-fake-news-stories-of-2016.html

Schultz, J. (2017). How much data is created on the internet each day? *Microfocus Blog,* viewed: 03/02/2019, https://blog.microfocus.com/how-much-data-is-created-on-the-internet-each-day/#

Snopes.com. (2018). 'Got another friend request from you' Facebook warning, Snopes - fact check - computers, 03/02/2019, https://www.snopes.com/fact-check/got-another-friend-request-facebook-warning/

The Law Dictionary. (2019). What is fraud? *The law dictionary,* viewed: 03/02/2019, https://thelawdictionary.org/fraud/

The Onion. (2019). Parenting experts warn screen time greatly increases risk of child becoming an influencer, *The* Onion.com, viewed: 03/02/2019, https://www.theonion.com/parenting-experts-warn-screen-time-greatly-increases-ri-1832241704

Volkova, S., & Jang, J. Y. (2018). Misleading or falsification: Inferring deceptive strategies and types in online news and social media. In *Companion of the web conference 2018 on The Web Conference 2018* (pp. 575–583). International World Wide Web Conferences Steering Committee.

Wainright, C. (2019). How to write catchy headlines and blog titles your readers can't resist, HubSpot.com, viewed: 03/02/2019, https://blog.hubspot.com/marketing/a-simple-formula-for-writing-kick-ass-titles-ht

Further Reading

Betts, B., & Anderson, A. (Eds.). (2015). *Ready, set, curate: 8 learning experts tell you how.* Vancouver: Association For Talent Development Press.

Podcast

How to Safely and Legally Curate Content, Convince and Convert with Jay Baer, https://www.convinceandconvert.com/podcasts/episodes/how-to-safely-and-legally-curate-content/

Helpful Links

FactCheck.org: https://www.factcheck.org/

International Fact-Checking Network (IFCN): https://www.poynter.org/ifcn/

PolitiFact.com.: https://www.politifact.com/

Snopes.com: https://www.snopes.com/

Pixabay (free images): https://pixabay.com/

List of Free Stock photo Sites.: https://blog.snappa.com/free-stock-photos/

The Content Curation Process

Contents

© The Author(s), under exclusive license to Springer Nature Singapore Pte Ltd. 2021
K. E. Sutherland, *Strategic Social Media Management*, https://doi.org/10.1007/978-981-15-4658-7_11

🔖 **By the End of This Chapter You Will**

- Identify the importance of sourcing curated content that supports the strategic goals and objectives of your client and/or organisation.
- Understand the steps involved in the content curation process.
- Become aware of the different methods of content curation available.
- Gain an insight into the benefits and disadvantages between manual and automated content curation.
- Be able to determine the best method of content curation to use for the specific needs of your organisation and/or client.

TLDR

- Quality is more important than quantity in the content curation process.
- The process of content curation must also be strategic. Curated content must align with and support the overall social media strategy before it is posted.
- Accuracy of content and adhering to the ethical and legal principles detailed in ▶ Chap. 10 must also underpin the content curation process.
- The key steps of the content curation process are: Goal > Topics > Sources > Sense-Making > Sharing (Kanter, 2017).
- Content can be curated manually or by automated tools, however, a mix of the two approaches is recommended.
- Budget, quality and breadth of sources and time are areas to consider when devising the content curation approach that best suits your organisation's or client's needs.

11.1 Introduction

In ▶ Chap. 10 we explored the ethical and legal implications associated with content curation. We investigated how gaining permission is paramount if you do not own the copyright and clearly referencing authors and linking to their curated article is ethical best-practice. Now that you understand what is considered to be best-practice, you can apply this knowledge to our focus in this chapter: the content curation process.

The focus of this entire book is on strategic social media management and this also applies to content curation. This chapter will provide step-by-step instructions to guide you through the process of content curation and demonstrate how to source and curate content that is interesting and relevant to your target audience as well as supporting your client's or organisational goals and objectives. Content curation is not only focused on sourcing content for the sake of it. Curating content is a strategic tactic and must be approached as such.

Next, this chapter will explore the various methods of content curation: manual and automated and how to find the right balance to suit your needs. As you have gathered, there is much more to content curation than pressing 'share' on a Facebook post. Better understanding of what is involved with the content curation process will increase the probability that your social media posts will engage audiences and build positive brand relationships as a result.

11.2 Curated Content: Quality vs Quantity

The appetite for social media content is ever-hungry and constantly increasing. Domo (2018) predicts that "by 2020, it's estimated that 1.7MB of data will be created every second for every person on earth". However, this constant pressure to produce social media content can lead Social Media Managers to put quantity ahead of quality, particularly in the case of content curation. Instead of carefully selecting content to suit strategic purposes, the pressure to post results in curating any content even remotely relevant in order to get something on their client's newsfeed.

Yet, this haphazard approach could result in damage to organisational reputation and customer relationships. The quantity over quality approach to content curation can be identified easily on Twitter, where it is acceptable to post multiple times per day (Williams, 2019). Some accounts tweet what seems like every hour, curated content that is not always aligned with the profile's brand or audience. Such content includes random quotes and self-promotion that can be tweeted multiple times during the same day.

> **“** By putting the audience first, and providing them with valuable content, curated or created, visibility will be increased and relationships strengthened as a result. **”**
>
> **Dr Karen Sutherland**

This approach seems to have a greater focus on increasing the profile owner's visibility than on providing valuable content and insight to their followers. However, by putting the audience first, and providing them with valuable content, curated or created, visibility will be increased, and relationships strengthened as a result. The difference between the two approaches is that focusing on quantity can be perceived as being self-obsessed. Being committed to quality suggests that you care about providing value to your audience.

With that in mind, Social Media Managers also need to ensure that whatever content that they are curating supports their organisation's or client's social media strategy. As outlined in Section One of this book, any social media activity must support an overarching goal and objective. Content curation can save time when compared to the resources it can take to create social media content, however, it still requires a certain degree of time and consideration to complete the task effectively. Content curation can be a time-saver, but only focusing on that as a key benefit can be an issue.

Revisiting the key concepts from Section 1 of this book, it is essential that any curated content aligns with the following strategic areas before it is included as a social media tactic.

11.3 Goals

How well does the curated content align with the overall strategic goals that your client or organisation is aiming to achieve? If a clear connection cannot be made between the content (or its source) it should not be included.

11.4 SMART Objectives

How does each piece of curated content support the SMART objectives listed in the social media strategy? Again, if a clear connection cannot be identified between the content and at least one of the SMART objectives, the content does not belong as part of the strategy.

11.5 Audience

Based on the extensive audience research that was conducted as part of the social media strategy development, how well does this curated content fit within one of the consumer personas that have been identified within the social media strategy? If relevance to a target audience from the strategy cannot be articulated, then it is better to find alternative content that will clearly resonate with the online community with whom you are trying to engage. Handley and Chapman (2010, p 7) suggest that it is important to assess the quality of curated content from the audience's perspective in the following ways:

- **Interesting:** How interesting will the audience find this content?
- **Relevant:** Does the content align with the audience's day-to-day lives?
- **Valuable**: How helpful will this content be for your audience? Does it help to solve a common problem or challenge?
- **Credible**: Is the content accurate and curated from a credible source?

Remember, that the audience's needs must come first. Assist them with curated content to help strengthen your relationship.

11.6 Key Messages

Key messages are the information that you are trying to communicate with an audience. While curated content does not always convey those messages exactly, it definitely needs to align with the key messages in some way and help to facilitate or at least support what you are trying to impart to the audience.

If you use consistent brand key messages in social media content and then post an article either on a non-related area or that completely contradicts the usual messaging, it may leave the audience confused and feeling disjointed. While sometimes it can be entertaining to play with the audience, there is a fine line between amusement and confusion. The key principles of marketing: parity and difference also relate to social media content, curated or created (Chernev, 2018).

According to Lee and Kotler (2015) when presenting any type of product or service to a target market (in this case it is curated content aimed at a specific audience) it is important to include points of parity and points of difference.

11.7 Points of Parity

Points- of-Parity ensures what you are communicating is recognisable to the audience (Chernev, 2018). It is important that the audience can make sense of your social media posts because they can understand the context or are recognisable to them in some way. Lee and Kotler (2015) defines point of parity as having the necessary components for a brand or product to be considered as a legitimate competitor in a particular industry.

This parity is necessary for prospective customers to consider your client or organisation as a credible choice. Applying this concept to curated social media content means that posts must demonstrate the basic elements that a member of the target audience would consider as important to instill trust in your capability in using the specific platform. It is great to be clever to try to attract an audience's attention while they are scrolling through their newsfeed, however, it is important not to be so unique that the people you are trying to reach cannot draw on any of their existing knowledge or previous experience in the process of sense-making to draw meaning from your content.

Om Indian Cafe   👍 Like Page

This jewellery is so nice.

Junk Jewels
Visit our website

BUY YOUR JEWELS FROM JUNK JEWELS

👍 0   0 Comments   0 Shares

👍 Like   💬 Comment   ↗ Share

Fig. 11.1 Curated content without point of parity

Digital Business Lab
513 followers
5mo   • • •

Here is the Top 10 Instagram Micro-influencers in Hong Kong covered by Marketing Magazine!
Read more on https://bit.ly/2DOrCp3
#DBLHK #TeamDBL #digitalmarketing #influencer #Influencermarketing

Fig. 11.2 Balance between points of parity and points of difference

Firstly, the content needs to look as though it fits logically within the brand curating it. See ◘ Fig. 11.1. This curated post does not seem to fit with what this business is about. The key messages in this post are not aligned with the business objectives. This is from the Facebook page of an Indian restaurant, yet the content has been curated from a jewellery website which does not seem to be a logical fit.

Posts that are not aligned with the brand curating them only confuse audiences into wondering what the organisation is really about. It is essential that any curated content demonstrates a point of parity with your client's brand.

ance between the two. While it is essential that social media content fits within a recognisable context in order to communicate key messages effectively with the audience, the content also needs to be different enough to spark their interest and attention.

We discussed in ▶ Chaps. 3 and 6 about the attention economy in which organisations must compete for social media users' attention. Curated content also needs to achieve this. The theoretical definition of point of difference focuses on establishing differentiation from competitors. This definitely applies to social media activity too, including content curation. See ◘ Fig. 11.2.

This post is clearly branded, includes key messages, and delivers them through the use of curated content. This is an excellent example of a balance between a point of parity and a point of difference. With every piece of content, it is vital to gauge that it is relevant enough to fit within your audience's niche interest area, yet fresh enough to spark their attention.

11.8 Points of Difference

Points-of-Difference may seem contradictory to points of parity and they are. However, a strategic Social Media Manager will ensure that any content maintains a bal-

11.9 Tactics

Tactics "are the specific activities and tasks that must be completed for a strategy to be fulfilled,"(Kim, 2016, pp.74). At their very essence, tactics are the actions that determine the success (or failure) of the strategic goals and objectives. If a tactic does not directly support the goals and objectives stated in a social media strategy, then its inclusion must be justified. Including it may waste time, effort and funds that could be better spent on a tactic that helps to achieve the overall strategic goal.

Content curation can definitely be included as a tactic in a social media strategy. However, it must earn its place. If the content that is being curated does not support the goals and objectives of the overall strategy, then it is incorrect to include it as a tactic. Content curation only names the action taking place, yet it is the content that determines whether this action can be qualified as a tactic.

Remember, to assess every piece of content against the goals, objectives, key messages, content pillars and audience preferences to ensure that it earns its place as a component of the overall social media strategy before deciding to post it. If the content does not clearly align with what the strategy is aiming to achieve, put it aside and keep searching for content that meets your strategic criteria.

11.10 The Content Curation Process

There are many different ways to approach the content curation process. The two key methods are manual and automated. Within these two categories, there are also many different approaches that Social Media Managers can use to source curated content. We will explore many of these methods. As with anything, there are benefits and disadvantages with each approach. It is recommended that Social Media Managers investigate a range of methods to find what works best.

The method employed may also be dependent on the specific needs and indus-

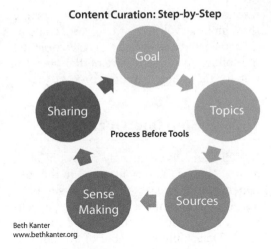

Content Curation: Step-by-Step

Goal

Topics

Process Before Tools

Sources

Sense Making

Sharing

Beth Kanter
www.bethkanter.org

▣ Fig. 11.3 The content curation process – step by step (Kanter, 2017)

try of the client or organisation that is being represented. The key with social media management in general is to be flexible. There are so many options available, that it will always be a manner of testing and experimenting to find what works. However, the tools and platforms also continue to change, which is completely out of our control, so commonly, Social Media Managers are forced to adapt to suit the evolving social media landscape.

Before delving into the intricacies, benefits and disadvantages between manual and automated content curation, it is important to understand the process of content curation from a macro level. Beth Kanter (2017), an expert in social media for the nonprofit sector, has succinctly demonstrated the key components of the process in ▣ Fig. 11.3.

The most important tip that Kanter (2017) expresses in this diagram is that a process must be determined before using content curation tools (which we explore later in this chapter). By this Kanter (2017) suggests that following these steps will help to clearly articulate what it is that you are trying to curate and for what purpose before completing the practice. Approaching content curation in this way will save time, resources and frustration from sorting through large volumes of irrelevant content. Be considered and specific when completing the following steps as part of the preparation for the content curation process.

11.10.1   Step One: Goal

Kanter (2017) is completely correct in placing the goal as the very first step in the content curation process. There should be a purpose underpinning any activity, particularly in the field of social media management. Determining the goal of the content creation about to take place is essential so that it can provide guidance on what it is that you are actually searching for.

Yet, in the case of a Social Media Manager, the goal of the content curation activity must be aligned to the strategic goals of the client or organisation being represented. As mentioned, if curating content as a tactic in a social media strategy, the content being gathered must align directly with the goal or goals identified in that strategy.

11.10.2   Step Two: Topics

The next step is to identify the key topic areas in which you will be curating content. It is important to be specific and ensure that the topics you are searching for align with the content pillars, brand and its purpose. There are so many articles and pieces of content being generated for online niche audiences every minute so working out the specific search terms that will return the most relevant content will help to streamline the content curation process.

Refining search terms will be an ongoing process that must be applied to both manual and automated content curation. If, as a Social Media Manager, you are not extremely familiar with a topic area, it is wise to undertake some initial research to learn the key concepts, theories and terms

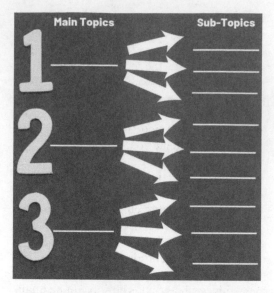

Fig. 11.4   Content curation topic mind map

used. Without this knowledge from the outset, the content curation process will be largely hit-or-miss because it will be based on guesswork.

Begin with three broad topics and add related sub-topics next each one. See Fig. 11.4 this mind-mapping technique will assist you in being able to visualise the breadth (or limitations) of potentially relevant content that could be curated. It also provides a list of topics that can be systematically searched for rather than curating content on topics that are purely top of mind.

11.10.3   Step Three: Sense-Making

Sense-making is another crucial stage of the content curation process. Sense-Making itself is a communication methodology developed by Dervin and Foreman-Wernet (2012) which underpins the "gaining knowledge through the transformation and integration of new information," (Mirbabaie & Zapatka, 2017, p. 2170).

The process of Sense-Making involves not only you as the content curator making sense of the content that you have gathered; it also requires you to present that content in a way that makes sense to you audience. This can be tricky, because what makes sense to you, does not always translate as clearly to your audience.

According to Dervin and Foreman-Wernet (2012) there are a range of variables that impact how people make sense of the world, social media content included. These can relate to personal experience, level of education, language fluency, power structures and access to information.

It seems very complicated, but in any communication process these factors must be taken into consideration. When assessing a piece of curated content, the first step is to ensure that it makes sense to you. You will not be able to present the piece effectively if you do not understand it. Then, you must also consider how your own worldview is shaping that transfer of knowledge. How does your worldview differ from that of your audience? For example, what makes perfect sense to you may be confusing to your parents and grandparents.

Consider the Mannequin Challenge of 2016 (Molloy, 2016) where people would freeze in different settings and situations as someone walked through with the camera. At the time curating a video of the challenge and using it to promote an event for younger people on Instagram would be appropriate, because the likelihood is greater that the target audience is familiar with the Mannequin Challenge.

However, using exactly the same video to promote an event to an older audience of infrequent Facebook users may leave them confused and not allow them to understand what you are trying to communicate because they may be unfamiliar with what the Mannequin Challenge actually is. Therefore, it is essential to assess sense-making from both perspectives, yours and the target audience's.

> 66 The first stage in the Sense-Making process is to ensure that the content that you have curated is clear in its meaning. 99
>
> Dr Karen Sutherland

The first stage in the Sense-Making process is to ensure that the content that you have curated is clear in its meaning. This does not mean that it has to be boring or simple. The beauty of the internet is that is has allowed anyone with a connection to have a voice and create their own content. In the previous stages you have determined the topics that you would be searching for and identified credible sources from which to curate content.

These steps are not foolproof. They have only helped to narrow down the field of the extremely large volume of content that exists online. Sense-Making is really about reviewing what a curation activity has returned. This is one of the most important stages of the process. Think of it as the stage of quality control. If a piece of content is ambiguous or leaves you confused when reading it, the target audience may feel the same way.

This is also the stage when it is vital to employ the legal and ethical considerations that we explored in ▶ Chap. 10. In addition to assessing whether a piece of content makes sense, it is essential to check that it is factually correct and does not contain any potentially offensive information. It is also recommended during this process to show content to others if it seems to be unclear. This can help to determine whether it is worth posting. The knowledge being conveyed in any curated content must help to communicate the key messages of your client or organisation. Key messages do not have to be written word-for-word, but they must be understandable. Assessing any curated (and created) content to ensure that it is Sense-Making and not confusing is the key in communicating your intended message.

11.10.4   Step Four: Sharing

As we have explored, curated content must be extremely high in quality to make it through to the sharing stage. It must be clear and relevant to the audience. It must be factually incorrect and inoffensive, and it must also support and align with the goals, objectives and key messages from the social media strategy. As we will discover in ▶ Chap. 10, there is a wide range of formats and techniques that can be used to share curated content in a social media environment.

The sharing stage required Social Media Managers to consider the best technique to use that suits the type of content being curated and that will achieve the greatest resonance with the target audience. ▶ Chapter 10 will detail the various techniques and processes for selecting the one most relevant. However, be aware that while Kanter (2017) suggests that sharing is the final step in the content curation process, this is not the completion of the task.

> **"** When posting any content on social media, it is essential to be ready to respond to how the audience interacts with the post. **"**
>
> **Dr Karen Sutherland**

When posting any content on social media, it is essential to be ready to respond to how the audience interacts with the post. It is also important to consider tweaking the post if it falls flat and receives very little or absolutely no audience engagement. Sharing content and walking away is a huge error that many organisations make in terms of its social media activity. Social media is named as such because of its two-way functionality. It exists because it facilitates two-way interaction.

The aim in sharing curated content is to instigate two-way interaction. If your target audience begins a conversation with you and each other in the comments of a post, you have the perfect opportunity to build or strengthen your relationship with them and your brand. While sharing technically finishes the content curation process, it kicks off the next stage, the conversation. Never share and walk away. Share and get ready to participate in the discussion that the content generates.

11

SEEK	SENSE	SHARE
Define topics and organize sources	Product: Writing w/links, presentation	Credit sources and answer questions
Scan more than you capture	Annotate, Archive, Apply	Feed your network a steady diet of good stuff
Don't capture unless high quality	Must add value to work or strategy	Comment on other people's stuff
Time: 15 minutes 2x Daily	Time: 30–60 minutes Daily	Time: 15 minutes 2x Daily

Inspired by Harold Jarche: Networked Learning is Working Smarter
Beth Kanter, http://www.bethkanter.org

☑ **Fig. 11.5** The ideal content curation practice, (Kanter, 2017)

11.11 The Ideal Content Curation Practice

In addition to the stages of content curation, Kanter (2017) also developed a helpful guide (see ☑ Fig. 11.5) to assist Social Media Managers with the three key components of content curation: seek, sense and share.

Seek clearly refers to the process of gathering content. Kanter (2017) includes defining specific topics as the very first step and advises that it is better not to capture every piece of content that could be remotely relevant to your audience. Instead, only save high quality content. This will be a huge time-saver. As we have mentioned, high-quality content means that it must tick all of the boxes in terms of it being relevant, meaningful, ethical and legally viable to share with audiences. Kanter (2017) also suggests that spending 15 minutes twice per day searching for content can be valuable for Social Media Managers.

Sense again refers to the sense-making process where a Social Media Manager must assess the clarity of the content, how to convey its meaning to their target audience and how they present the curated content can improve the transfer of knowledge in the final post. Kanter (2017) suggests spending up to an hour per day on this part of the process is advisable. This is an essential part of the process. Only sharing a piece of content without working thoughtfully through this step can greatly impact the effectiveness of the post, therefore, the more time spent on this step will be of greatest benefit in the longer term.

Share as an essential component of the content curation process Kanter (2017) stresses the importance of crediting the content creator for their work and leveraging the two-way functionality of social media by engaging with other people's content. Ensure that responding to engagement on the content that you are posting is a prime focus too. Kanter (2017) also suggests that two 15-minute sessions per day is an ample amount of time to devote to the sharing stage of the content curation process. This, of course, is a rough guide and will ultimately be determined by how much engagement from the audience is being generated by the posts and the analytics that determine when and how often to post on each platform which we covered in ▶ Chap. 7.

Now that the steps involved with the content curation process are clear, it is important to explore the two main approaches to curating content: manual and automated.

11.12 Different Approaches to Content Curation: Manual vs Automated

There are two overarching approaches to the process of content curation: manual and automated. However, within these two categories there are many other related techniques. Content curation is a complex process. While we cannot cover every single technique and tool in this publication, we will explore the key approaches to provide an overview of what is available and give you the knowledge to research further if you would like to learn more.

The overview provided in this section will also assist you in helping to determine the best approach to suit you and client's or organisation's needs.

11.13 Manual Content Curation

Manual content curation is the most traditional approach to sourcing and presenting content online. It requires the content curator to manually search online for relevant pieces that will resonate with their audience. Content can be sourced through search engines, relevant public social media profiles, YouTube, websites, email newsletters etc. (Clarke, 2018). Simply, it involves manually searching within each source for high quality content. There are several benefits and disadvantages when manually curating content.

11.13.1 Benefits

- **The human element is central to the process.**
As mentioned in ▶ Chap. 10, the human element of content curation is what sets it apart from content aggregation the method employed by search engines such as Google. Manually curating content during every step of the process means that the standard of content sources and shared may be higher, because someone has viewed every piece and vetted those that do not fit with the audience and strategic needs of the client and organisation.

- **Gain a greater understanding of the breadth of content and sources available.**
By manually undertaking every part of the content curation process, it allows

Social Media Managers the opportunity to become extremely familiar with the wide range of sources and content that is being produced about specific topics of interest. It also helps to understand the content sources that are not of a great standard, that contain inaccurate or unethical information, in order to avoid them completely.

11.13.2 Disadvantages

- **Increased time and effort in sourcing content.**
Manually curating content can be a huge strain on resources. It takes considerable time and effort to search for particular topics and then assess them for quality. There is so much information available that trawling through such large volumes of content searching for the perfect piece can often seem like a laborious task, particularly if you are searching in the wrong corner of the internet.

- **Potentially missing quality content.**
Another challenge with content curation is potentially missing out on quality sources and content because you are unaware of its existence. The volume of content online is vast, and one person can never be completely across every content creator and their work. While manual content creation can provide a great overview of what is on offer, as only one person navigating the internet, it may also mean that great content is never discovered. While it is important to have a list of credible content creators that you can regularly source content from, it is also important to stay abreast of new sources that become available (Table 11.1).

| Table 11.1 | Sources to manually curate content |

Location	Description
Search engines	Search engines are helpful in two main ways during the process of manual content curation. Firstly, they help to 'cast the net wide' in terms of being able to return a wide range of content on a particular. Secondly, the results from search engines, also help Social Media Managers to learn more about a particular topic that can assist in refining the searching process through an increased knowledge of specific key terms and concepts relating to that topic. However, many search engines such as Google only show the most popular content first. This means that worthwhile and relevant items appear pages down in the search results and may be missed.
News websites	RSS feeds are helpful but taking a truly manual approach means visiting the websites of online news outlets daily to find relevant articles. While it is important to stay across the news developments regarding a particular topic, time constraints can limit manual searches of a wide range of outlets. This can result in reliance on a small selection of sources which are not recommended from an ethical perspective and runs the risk of boring audiences in the longer term.
Blogs	Subscribing to quality blogs written about specific topic areas can be useful for Social Media Managers when manually curating content. There are currently estimated to be 456 million blogs on Tumblr alone (Statista, 2019a, 2019b), which means a wide array to choose from, but it also means that it is essential to assess each blog for quality before becoming a subscriber. Be aware that subscribing to a long list of blogs can result in excessive email notifications and it still requires assessing each blog post to ensure that it is of strategic relevance to your audience and organisation.
Twitter Lists	Again, with 269 million Twitter users worldwide, there are some amazing content curators in every niche topic area that you can think of (Statista, 2019b). A Twitter list helps with manual content curation by compiling a list of Twitter users that share content on a specific topic. It is helpful because each list (and Twitter user on it) can be categorised by topic area and it is possible to have multiple lists. However, this method of manual content curation still requires finding credible Twitter users to add to the list and trawling through their tweets to find quality content. This is another method that casts the net wide, just not as wide as a search engine.
Social Bookmarking	Social Bookmarking can be a huge help to content curators because it helps to save the locations of specific pieces of content on the web and organise this content into categories. The practice gained popularity between 2007 and 2010, but there are still some great tools currently available than are really useful for Social Media Managers such as: Pinterest and Pinboard.
Social Media Profiles	It is essential for Social Media Managers to follow influencers and experts in their organisation's or client's specific topic areas. This is an excellent way of manually curating quality social media content from people who have social proof (e.g. a history of producing valuable content that is endorsed by a large following). However, it can be overwhelming and time-consuming to keep across every piece of content being produced and shared on social media channels. There are some tools that can assist with this process, such as Hootsuite. Besides being a scheduling and analytics tool, Hootsuite has great dashboard functionality that facilitates the monitoring of multiple profiles simultaneously on the same screen. This will not solve the challenges faced with manual content curation in terms of monitoring everything that is happening on social media, but it can help.

11

□ Table 11.2 Tools for Automated Content Curation	
Content curation tool	**Description**
Scoop.it	Scoop.it provides some functionality for free or a paid version which has a wider range of features. It crawls social media, web and user content to find keyword matches and provides it back to the user via an email and a list within the Scoop.it interface. It also acts as a social platform, allowing users to create their own boards around particular topics that other users can follow. Sharing across social networks is also a paid feature allowing users the convenience of posting directly from the Scoop.it interface. It can struggle with very narrow keyword searches and like any content curation tool, it still requires a person to assess the content before posting it on their social channels.
Google Alerts	Google Alerts is an extremely helpful tool that is completely free to use. It automatically searches online news, blogs and websites for the keywords that you specify and sends an email with a list of relevant resources. The email frequency is set by the user; therefore, you can have an email sent as soon as a keyword is featured somewhere online (great for social listening) or opt for a list to be sent at the end of each day, week or month. This is one of my favourite tools because it is free, keep me across the main topics for that day so that I can weigh on the conversation and inspire me to create my own content if a topic is extremely timely. It is also very easy to set up. I have alerts set up on topics related to social media and aspects of digital marketing that help to keep me current and informed.
BuzzSumo	BuzzSumo is also a tool that provides free functionality and the opportunity to pay for a wider range of features. What is distinctive about BuzzSumo is that it searches Facebook, Twitter, Pinterest and Reddit for content based on specific keywords, and ranks the list in terms of the number of times each piece of content has been shared on each platform. It allows users to see the number of times a piece of content has been shared on each social media platform. Paying for the Premium version also allows users to see the influencers that have also shared each piece of content and the websites that have linked to it too, to provide a great overview of the types of audiences most interested in the content. BuzzSumo Premium also facilitates shareability directly to your own social platforms, which is convenient. Other helpful features include monitoring and measurement of Facebook pages, influencer search and trending content. BuzzSumo helps to gain an understanding of the most shared content around a particular topic. This knowledge can help to find content that has a strong probability of resonating with audiences and it can also help when crafting your own content.
Feedly	Feedly is a free and a paid tool that allows users to bring all of their favourite blogs, news sites, podcasts and YouTube channels onto one dashboard using RSS feeds. After sourcing a wide range of credible sources, Feedly lets users see new content as it is uploaded to the web all on one screen. There is also functionality that enables sharing directly to Twitter, Facebook, Google+, Evernote, Pinterest or LinkedIn and scheduling tools such as Buffer. Feedly can also send notifications on iOS, via email and Slack when new articles are available and has team functionality. This is a paid feature that facilitates multiple people on the same team access to the same dashboard and the ability to communicate with each other within the platform too.
Curata	Curata is a paid curation tool that also incorporates creation and scheduling functionality. It is a one-stop shop for Social Media Managers; however, it is limited in its ability to monitor and measure the performance of social media content curated, created and posted via the tool.

11.14 Automated – Benefits and Disadvantages

Automated content curation involves the use of tools that scrape the web for content (social media, blogs, online news articles) on specific topics set by the user and returning them back to the content curator in a list form. Many of the tools available are free, and some allow the user to pay for extra features. Similarly to manual content curation, there are benefits and disadvantages with automated content curation.

11.14.1 Benefits

■ **Time savings.**

Automated content curation saves time because a program is searching the web for you allowing you to concentrate on other pressing tasks related to social media management. Using a content curation tool (see ❑ Table 11.2) can almost be a case of set and forget to save you from manually trawling through countless websites and social media content looking for quality pieces.

■ **Wider Breadth.**

Some content curation tools can search through 35 million web pages per day (DaCunha, 2018). Compare that level of search functionality with how long it can take to curate content manually. Content curation tools far surpass humans in terms of the quantity of sources that they can sort through. That is a fact, yet, as we will discuss, gathering large volumes of content in a specific area may be helpful, but quality is also an essential factor of content curation.

■ **Convenience.**

Curated Content comes to you. Many automated content curation tools compile a list of relevant pieces that are then sent to your email inbox. The frequency of these emails can be set by the user to daily, weekly or whenever a relevant piece of content is located. Having a list of content on the different topic areas of benefit to your client or organisation sent directly to you is definitely much easier than manually compiling lists in Word docs and Excel spreadsheets.

11.14.2 Disadvantages

■ **Removing the human element.**

The key feature that sets content curation apart from content aggregation is the human element. Automated tools rely on algorithmic software to crawl the web to find relevant content. The only human element involved is in their set up when the user specifies the topic areas for the tool to search. Rather than a human being carefully and considerately searching through content, a computer completes the same tasks on a much larger scale.

When you think about it, the concept of content curation being automated seems to defeat the overall purpose and benefits of what the practice is actually known for. As we have explored in this chapter and in ▶ Chap. 10 the main reason why content curation is so popular particularly when it is employed by bloggers and other social media influencers is because it has that Human Element.

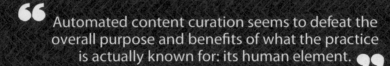

> **"** Automated content curation seems to defeat the overall purpose and benefits of what the practice is actually known for: its human element. **"**
>
> **Dr Karen Sutherland**

While human error is always a risk when gathering content in posting on social media leaving the entire process up to an automated piece of software could actually leave Social Media Managers open to much greater risk (Wohn et al., 2017). In the next section in this chapter will discuss how to create an approach or even a balance between manual and automated content curation that will actually benefit your client or organisation without leaving the task to be so laborious for Social Media Managers.

- **Lack of quality control.**

At least with manual content curation it is possible to assess each piece of content for quality, accuracy, and relevance to your target audience. However, with automated content curation it means that the software is really only bringing back pieces of content relating to particular search terms. Although it is different to Google and a Google search content curation tools crawl the web looking for those particular keywords in social media content and in blogs and online articles.

Some content creation tools contain the capacity to rank pieces of content in terms of quality relating how many times it has been shared so that you know the influence of the person who originally posted the content. Yet content curation tools cannot know your audience as well as you, well not yet anyway. Automation can be attractive, but this again defeats the purpose of what social media is all about.

11.14.3 Automating Quotes on Twitter Does Not Generate High Engagement Rates

Some Twitter users utilise automated tools to tweet multiple times per day so that people are constantly seeing their content. Nimble Quotes allows users to automate quotes to be tweeted via their Twitter account. However this approach does not seem to generate great rates of engagement with the audience, because it looks automated and does not have the same human-element as manually curated content. Automated curated posts can be perceived to be very random particularly when they are not relevant to current trending topics.

Rather than people engaging genuinely in a Twitter conversation around a particular trending hashtag they use a tool to automate their presence on that platform. Twitter users who leverage automated tools are being seen but completely automating this process can also negatively impact their reputation. While content curation tools can be extremely helpful there still needs to be some human element involved.

11.14.4 Automated Content Curation Tools

There is a wide range of content curation tools available online; some free, some paid. There is also a lot of variation in the sources that they curate content from, how they present it and they're shareability across social media and other web-based platforms.

The ◘ Table 11.2 is a list of the mainstream tools available at the time of writing. As with social media, the only constant is change, therefore, it is wise to check regularly about new tools becoming available that have greater efficiency or if specific tools are no longer available (this happens regularly).

Even if you are a manual content curation advocate, it is wise to experiment with a range of tools to see how well they suit your needs.

While these automated curation tools have their differences, they are all the same in one important aspect; they all still require a human to sort through the content before sharing it on social media. There are some scheduling tools that can automate posts using Feedly on platforms such as Twitter, but this is not recommended.

Yes, it can be a case of set and forget, but it is essential to know what is being posted on your organisation's or client's behalf, particularly if people are trying to engage with the content and with your brand. A Social Media Manager needs to be completely across what is being posted and should be ready to engage with their audience. Set and forget functionality undermines what social media management is all about connection.

11.14.5 Developing the Best Content Curation Approach for Your Client or Organisation

So far in this chapter we have explored the steps involved in the process of content curation, what manual content curation involves and the benefits and the benefits

and disadvantages of automated content curation tools. Now you need to decide. Are you going to use a manual approach or an automated approach or a mixture of the two. My recommendation is to use a mixture of the two that is best suited to the needs of your client and your organisation. It may seem very confusing trying to work out the best approach, but this decision does not have to be a challenging one if you consider the following principles when working out the best approach. Here are three important things to consider when devising your content curation approach and processes:

1. **Budget:** A lack of funding for the extra features of an automated content curation tool while logically cut it out of the race when making your decision unless you can lobby for internal funding. If you have a budget for an automated tool, then it is important to revisit the goals, objectives and tactics from your social media strategy and use these to assess which tool will best support their achievement. For example, if there is influencer marketing as part of the strategy in addition to content curation, then a tool like BuzzSumo can help to facilitate both tactics. Be strategic with every decision, particularly when it costs time or money.

2. **Sources**: It is essential to understand the sources of curated content. This applies to both manual and automated content curation. If an automated tool is not including some important industry specific sources this means that you will have to write those manually. It is extremely important to know this from the beginning instead of relying too heavily on an automated tool and realising later that you have missed out on some very timely and important news that could be of benefit to your audience. To position your client or organisation as an industry leader you must

be ahead or at least on top of the latest developments in the field, not miss it completely.

3. **Time:** It is important to honestly estimate the amount of time that you can devote to content curation as part of your average workload. Is up to 2 hours as Kanter (2017) recommends realistic? If not, an automated tool may assist in gathering the content and the limited time that you do have should be spent on assessing the quality of the curated content and crafting it into posts to share.

These three key components will help you to decide how you will undertake the content curation process. Even automated tools require some human curation. The next step after receiving the list of curated pieces returned from your preferred tool or method is to assess the quality of the content using the method detailed previously in this chapter.

Conclusion

This chapter explained the different steps and considerations involved in the content curation process. The benefits and disadvantages of manual and automated content curation process were also explored as well as a range of methods and tools that can be used to facilitate both approaches. The key points to remember are to find an approach that best suits the needs of your client or organisation, to assess all curated content for quality by checking how well it aligns with the components within your social media strategy before sharing it and to ensure that the content adheres to the ethical and legal considerations outlined in ▶ Chap. 10.

In ▶ Chap. 12 we will explore the wide range of ways that curated content can be shared to resonate with your audience and generate engagement.

Case Study: American Apparel's Content Curation Disaster

In 2014, American Apparel created their own public relations nightmare due to a piece of poorly (and unethically) curated content. In the lead up to the 4th of July Independence Day celebrations in the U.S.A. a younger social media coordinator used Google Images to source and curate a relevant image to share on the American Apparel's public Tumblr account.

The social media coordinator selected the image below (Plautz, 2014) (see ◘ Fig. 11.6), assuming that it was a photograph of a smoke trail from the aftermath of a firework, branded it in the colours of American Apparel and posted it on the Tumblr site with the hashtags #Smoke #Clouds.

The image was not related to fireworks. Instead it was the image of the Challenger Space Shuttle explosion that occurred on live television in 1986 where seven people lost their lives.

The backlash was fast and furious. American Apparel's reputation was dam-

◘ **Fig. 11.6**   Content curation error (Plautz, 2014)

aged. Despite the post being deleted quickly, and a company spokesperson making a swift apology, this inconsiderate mistake went viral, and here we are, using it as an example of what not to do years later. This case only highlights that social media mistakes have a global audience and are long remembered well after they occur.

Such an error was not due to malice. It occurred as a result of incompetence and lazy practices. If the social media coordinator followed the best-practice guidelines and processes detailed in ► Chaps. 10 and 11 of this book, such an error could have been avoided.

Consider what we have learned so far and think about the important steps of content curation that the Social Media Coordinator from American Apparel missed when sourcing this image. This staff member's excuse was that they were not yet born when the Challenger disaster occurred and therefore did not know of the tragedy.

This is not a valid excuse. Here are the two key process errors that could have helped to avoid this public relations crisis for American Apparel:

1. The image was sourced using Google images and permission for use of the photo was not obtained.
2. The original webpage hosting the image was clearly not accessed as this would

have provided the true context of the image (and hopefully would have rendered it as inappropriate with the Social Media Coordinator).

Overall, the curated content did not seem to undergo any sort of quality check before it was posted, and it resulted in the American Apparel brand being damaged in the process. It was more than a poorly curated image, the carelessness in which it was selected and posted was perceived as insensitivity to the families of the seven people who died in the tragedy.

This public relations disaster could have been avoided by using an image library, better research and seeking permission to use the image. All of these actions would have prevented this image from being used.

— What steps should have been undertaken to check this image?
— Where would you have curated an image to use for this promotion?

11.15 Interview: Albin Lix – Founder & Managing Director at Digital Business Lab, Hong Kong

1. **Would you please introduce yourself, and talk about your role, and where you work, and what you do first up?**
My name is Albin Lix. I'm the Founder and General Manager of Digital Business Lab. Our agency is a social media specialised agency. We develop strategy. We produce content. We hire engaging influencers, and we also work on data, analytics for B2C and B2B brands all over Asia, the Chinese market, Western markets, Facebook, Instagram, WeChat, so different channels.

2. **What do you enjoy most about working with social media?**

Of course, we have a constant evolution of our job with new features, new content formats, and new opportunities. That's probably one of the most challenging ideas. The other very interesting part of our job on a daily basis is we are constantly mixing data analysis and content creation to make sure that we are basically inspiring the audience of our clients. At the same time we need to pay attention to overall engagement and performance of the audience we are targeting.

3. **How did you come to work in social media?**
Before moving to Hong Kong to set up the company, I was working for different brands as an e-commerce manager. I also worked for a data analytics company mixing different experiences in

those agency settings. Basically when I arrived in Hong Kong, in a very opportunistic way, I started listening to our leads and clients. I realised that right now a traditional communication agency is covering a bit of social media. Event agencies are covering a little bit of social media. Same for PR, and same for traditional digital marketing agencies, but, there is almost not exclusive and highly specialised social media point of contact for brands nowadays. That's why we decided to create Digital Business Lab.

4. **How many clients would you have at Digital Business Lab?**

Just to give you an idea of the company size, we are almost 20 people right now in the company. We have a limited number of clients, I would say probably 12–14 active clients, which is not a lot. But, as mentioned earlier, we provide full package strategy, content production, and video. We consult data. So, we try to reach a critical amount of work to basically be able to reach or show significant resources for our clients. We have a limited number of clients, but we spend a significant amount of time supporting them.

5. **What do you think are three important things that social media managers need to consider when they're actually going through that process of curating content for clients, or the organisations they're working for?**

Our first recommendation is always to try to clarify what is the company's social media strategy, according to the overall strategy of the company. One specific company will try to be the leader, because their price is cheaper than every other competitor. We need to basically align the social media strategy according to the company's strategy. We cannot have the right strategy on social media, if at the very early stages there is no direction at the company level.

Then as soon as we have the social media strategy, and we start identifying channels, social media brand on social media is a media.

Behind every media there is a content strategy and an audience strategy. So, we need to make sure we can create the right amount, and the right quality of content. Of course the biggest challenge for brands, because their first job is not to create content. Their first job sometimes, or most very often, is to do retail, or to provide services. So, we need to think about the content supply chain. We need to think, "Okay, if we decide and if we think five posts a week is the right amount, we need to identify where this content is coming from." And we need to find the right balance between quantity, quality to make it happen.

Curated content is definitely one of the very accurate options to consider, because obviously it's not a content created 100% from scratch, so it's very cost effective. However, this curated content strategy needs to be aligned with the overall plan, mix in different ingredients, curated content, content made from scratch, and sometimes content coming from stakeholders, influencers, and employees.

6. **What do you think are some of the benefits of using curated content?**

The first one is I would say of course the cost. The cost is, and how fast it's possible to basically share existing content, curated content. The top benefit is a little bit of reaction. If you identify a very interesting trend, and if you have to feel more, if you have to write the full article from scratch, or if you have to create a new post from scratch, it's going to take a bit of time, and it is going to take a bit of investment.

7. **What do you think are some of the challenges when using curated content?**

The challenge of curated content is, of course, to make sure you are not just

11.15 · Interview: Albin Lix – Founder & Managing Director at Digital Business...

251

11

reusing 100% of one existing content, but you can provide value behind that. That's basically the first challenge is the curated content needs to be part of a vision and a strategy, where basically you can provide your own opinion on top of the curated content, own opinion, own insight, own reaction, to provide more value, and to give a little bit more than what the user could initially have through the original post. That's the first challenge.

The second challenge is definitely the process behind curated content. It's very important to implement the proper process, where you apply the right identification phase. You already set up in advance some specific tools to identify content. You can also work on the transformation. What is again who is involved in your organisation to adjust the content, and who is in charge to monitor the performance of this content to make it even better the next time.

8. **Do you think curated content can be used to help customers and followers?**
It shows that you are a kind of hub, where you centralise all the top information. So, basically if you do a lot of curated content, you can showcase yourself as an aggregator, as a hub. Where, basically if your audience follows you they will have every key information about one specific topic. So basically your audience saves time. That's something very interesting.

It's an opportunity for the audience sometimes to enjoy some different content, with a different tool. I always remember this example from ASOS, the fashion retailer, when it was a couple of years ago. You probably saw this video, I think probably Australian guy, a surfer, was almost bitten by a shark and he survived. Basically, I was super surprised because ASOS was the ... It's a fashion brand. They talk a lot about products, et cetera. But, because this

video was pretty cool, and at the end actually very positive. He punched the shark hard. This company was one of the first one to reuse this content. Because they did it, they had a very early stage that provided value, because again they act as a media.

9. **What are some of your favourite content curation tools?**
For content identification we are using Google Trends, very popular content. Sometimes a bit limited, but at least you can already have a kind of overview of the coming trends. Scoop.it, This solution is quite interesting to save some research, so you can set up some research in advance. Then every day you can see what kind of fresh content you can quickly reuse. You can quickly share through your social media, or even through your blog. Then you have some operational connection also through ScoopIt. Because, as soon as you already fine tune and basically your blog post, for example, you can quickly distribute this content through social media in one click, and also through email marketing. So, is not only about identification. ScoopIt can also help with amplification.

About the analysis, and if you want to go a little bit deeper, we just recently signed a strong partnership with Meltwater. This solution is extremely powerful to basically listen, identify topics, identify also influencers.

The challenge is not only to identify, but it's also to understand if we are catching a growing trend, or if we are basically catching a dying trend. That's super important to monitor, and Meltwater can definitely help you do it.

10. **What do you think of the current landscape for Social Media Managers? What do you think the industry is like for them at the moment?**
Now it's possible to do very advanced targeting on Facebook and Instagram,

using retargeting, playing with email, that are basic imports. Retargeting website visitors, et cetera. So, we can then basically repeat communication, and it's a kind of customer relationship management, or even fans relationship management journey, where we can apply different impressions, and re-target people smartly. Also, very big news 2 weeks ago, Instagram recently released that they are launching at a beta version, Instagram Checkout, where we can now start purchasing on Instagram. So, it's huge.

If you are interested in working in social media try to work and always try to understand the creative angle, and the data angle at the same time, because it's impossible to be good and to understand properly I think social media, if you only cover one of these two priorities, one of these two angles. That's the first recommendation I have.

The second recommendation I have, and it's probably mostly for brands I try to push it so for our clients is it's always important to make sure you are not like analysing what's other competitor did a few months ago, or even sometimes a few years ago. Because, things are changing very fast. If companies are trying to reproduce exactly what other brands from the same industry did a few months earlier, you will always be late. Social media is also about taking a risk, under control, but taking a risk.

11. **Where do you see social media heading in the future?**

I think is going to also depend on algorithms, to make sure that social media right now, the biggest one is managed by a very huge sphere, Venture and Vista, they are looking for short-term profits. At the very early stage social media was not created to purchase, or to push advertising. It was created to

help people to share content together. So, I feel like if tomorrow we have too much advertising, or and I would say product or any advertising without any inspiration, and if we have less organic content, people will feel bored.

The second direction I wanted to share with you is about the social media life cycle. We are close to China here in Hong Kong. What we see in China is extremely interesting, because it's on this specific case we have a similar effect in China, and also out of China. It means if we analyse different generations, people are using different social media. We see that there are constantly new trends coming. Even if we have the very powerful WeChat, exactly like we have the very powerful Facebook, younger generations start to use different channels, because sometimes they are bored. They want to create their own to enjoy their own social media, more aligned with their generation.

For example, right now in Australia, Snapchat is probably super popular. So, if you have a 16 years old kid, they are using Snapchat. If you are 30 years old, you are using Instagram. If your parents are connected on social media, they are using Facebook a lot. So, in China it's almost the same effect. Now we have TikTok. We have Douyin. We have Red Book. All these new channels are basically for the younger generation, where parents are using the traditional channel like Weibo, and WeChat. So, to answer more specifically to your question, I feel like we need to make sure that the historical social media have to respect their audience to keep promoting, keep pushing interesting content, creative advertising, and also content coming from the community of the users at the first part.

Second part is to make sure that tomorrow the challenge of marketers is also to be aware about the latest trend. Because, there is a constant probably not renewal, but there is constantly new actor, and new social media channels, basically every day. I'm sure in the coming 5, 10, 20 years we're going to have more and more channels for younger, and younger generations, because again people want their own tools to communicate together.

12. **What is the best piece of advice you've ever been given?**

I think one of the best pieces of advice we try to share with the applicants we are receiving here at Digital Business Lab, or even from our network, is if tomorrow someone wants to work in digital marketing and social media you must show that you are able to create things out of the box by yourself.

The beauty of social media is you can basically do things by yourself. You can try to experiment on social media. Especially if someone is looking for this kind of position, Social Media Manager, or a Community Manager, or a Head of Content Production for example. To take initiative, could be through creating a blog, or launching a small test advertising campaign to show that you are basically curious.

Curiosity is super important. So, as soon as you can show to your network to the people you meet, that you are creating differences. As soon as you start to create value, and again because it's all about innovation, if you can mix curiosity and creativity, I think it's something fantastic, and it's a very good start to move forward on a beautiful career on social media.

❓ Questions for Critical Reflection

1. What are the benefits of including curated content to support the overall social media strategy?

2. What is the difference between points-of-parity and points-of-difference in relation to curated content? Why is a balance between both important?

3. Why is sense-making so important when selecting and presenting curated content?

4. What are the benefits and disadvantages of manual and automated content curation? What approach do you think is best and why?

5. How could you avoid a content curation disaster like the one explored in the Case Study section of this chapter?

❯ Practical Exercises

1. Pick a topic of your interest and find five pieces of content using one of the manual content curation techniques explored in this chapter. Use Kanter's (2017) steps of content curation to undertake this task and assess the content according to Handley and Chapman's (2010) four quality principles: Interesting, Relevant, Valuable, Credible. How many pieces of content make it to the final cut? Please share your experience with the rest of the class.

2. Using the same topic from the first exercise, use one of the free automated content curation tools to conduct a search for content about your chosen subject. Remember to use Kanter's (2017) steps and assess the quality of the content according to Handley and Chapman's (2010) four quality principles to curate five pieces of content. How many pieces of content did you have to assess to find five quality pieces using an automated tool? Which approach (completely manual or part automated) did you find most effective? Why? Please share your experience with the class.

References

Chernev, A. (2018). *Strategic marketing management.* Chicago: Cerebellum Press.

Clarke, T. (2018). The complete guide to content curation: Tools, tips, ideas, *Hootsuite Blog*, viewed 23.02.2019: https://blog.hootsuite.com/beginners-guide-to-content-curation/

DaCunha, M. (2018). The 7 best content curation tools in 2017, *The WordStream Blog*, viewed 23.02.2019: https://www.wordstream.com/blog/ws/2017/05/01/content-curation-tools

Dervin, B., & Foreman-Wernet, L. (2012). *Sensemaking methodology as an approach to understanding and designing for campaign audiences* (pp. 147–162). California: Public Communication Campaigns.

DOMO. (2018). Everyone on the same page, all the time – See how data's connecting everyone to everything across the world, every minute, *DOMO*, viewed 23.02.209: https://www.domo.com/solution/data-never-sleeps-6

Handley, A., & Chapman, C. C. (2010). *Content rules: How to create killer blogs, podcasts, videos, eBooks, webinars (and more) that engage customers and ignite your business* (Vol. 5). New Jersey: Wiley.

Kanter, B. (2017). *Content curation primer, Beth's Blog – How connected nonprofits leverage networks and data for social change*, viewed 23/02/2019: http://www.bethkanter.org/content-curation-101/

Kim, C. M. (2016). *Social media campaigns: Strategies for public relations and marketing*. New York: Routledge.

Lee, N. R., & Kotler, P. (2015). *Social marketing: Changing behaviors for good.* Thousand Oaks, CA: Sage Publications.

Mirbabaie, M., & Zapatka, E. (2017). Sensemaking in social media crisis communication – A case study on the Brussels Bombings in 2016. In *Proceedings of the 25th European Conference on Information Systems (ECIS)*, Guimarães, Portugal, June 5–10, 2017 (pp. 2169–2186). ISBN 978-989-20-7655-3 Research Papers. https://aisel.aisnet.org/ecis2017_rp/138

Molloy, M. (2016). What is the mannequin challenge? The best videos so far, *The Telegraph*, viewed 23.02.2019: https://www.telegraph.co.uk/news/2016/11/05/what-is-the-mannequin-challenge-bizarre-freezing-craze-among-tee/

Plautz, J. (2014). American apparel apologizes for using challenger disaster photo instead of fireworks, *Mashable Australia*, viewed: 23.02.2019: https://mashable.com/2014/07/04/american-apparel-challenger/#K2Tj3SHsZZqG

Statista. (2019a). Cumulative total of Tumblr blogs from May 2011 to January 2019 (in millions). *Statista*, viewed 23.02.2019: https://www.statista.com/statistics/256235/total-cumulative-number-of-tumblr-blogs/

Statista. (2019b). Number of twitter users worldwide from 2014 to 2020 (in millions), *Statista*, viewed 23.02.2019: https://www.statista.com/statistics/303681/twitter-users-worldwide/

Williams, H. (2019). How often should you post on social media? *Meltwater*, viewed 23.02.2019: https://www.meltwater.com/uk/blog/how-often-should-you-post-on-social-media/

Wohn, D. Y., Fiesler, C., Hemphill, L., De Choudhury, M., & Matias, J. N. (2017, May). How to handle online risks?: Discussing content curation and moderation in social media. In *Proceedings of the 2017 CHI Conference Extended Abstracts on Human Factors in Computing Systems* (pp. 1271–1276). Denver Colorado USA: ACM.

Further Reading

Berman, R., & Katona, Z. (2016). *The impact of curation algorithms on social network content quality and structure* (No. 16-08). *SSRN Electronic Journal.*

Fotopoulou, A., & Couldry, N. (2015). Telling the story of the stories: Online content curation and digital engagement. *Information, Communication & Society, 18*(2), 235–249.

Kilgour, M., Sasser, S. L., & Larke, R. (2015). The social media transformation process: Curating content into strategy. *Corporate Communications: An International Journal, 20*(3), 326–343.

Hudgens, R. (2016). The 3 Most Effective (And Overlooked) Content Curation Strategies, *Content Marketing Institute*, viewed: https://contentmarketinginstitute.com/2016/04/content-curation-strategies/

Rayson, S (2016). The 23 best content curation articles of 2016, *Anders Pink Blog*, viewed: 21.02.2019: https://blog.anderspink.com/2016/12/the-23-best-content-curation-articles-of-2016/

Helpful Links

Scoop.It.: https://www.scoop.it/
Google Alerts.: https://www.google.com.au/alerts
Pinterest.: https://www.pinterest.com
Pinboard.: https://pinboard.in/
Hootsuite.: https://hootsuite.com/
BuzzSumo.: https://buzzsumo.com/
Feedly.: https://feedly.com/
Curata.: http://www.curata.com/

Techniques to Present Curated Content to Engage with Audiences

Contents

© The Author(s), under exclusive license to Springer Nature Singapore Pte Ltd. 2021
K. E. Sutherland, *Strategic Social Media Management*, https://doi.org/10.1007/978-981-15-4658-7_12

By the End of this Chapter you Will

- Understand the ways that curated content can be used to share brand stories on social media.
- Learn a range of techniques to present curated content to target audiences.
- Develop skills to curate content in ways that aligns with your organisation's or client's brand voice.
- Understand how not to present curated content and why.
- Learn the most appropriate ways to present curated content on the mainstream social media platforms.
- Important considerations when presenting curated content include: structure, flow, revelation, juxtaposition and rhythm.
- The presentation of curated content is a fantastic opportunity to connect with and show appreciation to the content creator.

TLDR

- All curated content must have a purpose, be relevant to the audience and be presented in a way that is appropriate to the platform.
- Every piece of curated content must add value to the audience.
- The presentation of curated content must align with brand voice plus strategic goals, objectives and content pillars.
- Commentary should accompany the presentation of all curated content as it is another opportunity for a brand to connect with its audience.

12.1 Introduction

In ▶ Chap. 12, we build on the knowledge that you have gained so far in relation to content curation. In ▶ Chaps. 10 and 11 explored ethical content curation and best-practice approaches in gathering and selecting content created by others. After you have a collection of great content, the next step is presenting it to your audience in ways that will resonate and help them.

Therefore, in ▶ Chap. 12 you will learn a range of techniques to support you when presenting curated content on a range of social media platforms to communicate key messages that appeal to target audiences. There is so much more to content curation than pressing 'share' on someone else's post. This chapter demonstrates a range of approaches to ensure that posts presenting curated content remain fresh and interesting to audiences.

> ❝ There is so much more to content curation than pressing 'share' on someone else's post. ❞
>
> **Dr Karen Sutherland**

What does "presenting curated content" actually mean? Presenting curated content describes the way in which Social Media Managers share other creators' content with their audiences. The practice of presenting curated content can be approached from a spectrum of ways from the very basic to the highly sophisticated.

There are clearly some techniques that are best to avoid and some methods to openly embrace and these will be explained in this chapter. However, one essential item to remember in relation to sharing curated content is that it must seem like it naturally belongs in the context in which it is being presented. Every piece of curated content must earn its place, and we will delve further into techniques to achieve this throughout the chapter.

However, just as in ▶ Chap. 11 we explored Kanter's (2017) process of content curation, there is also a recommended process to follow when preparing to share the content gathered through the content curation process. These steps are outlined below:

12.2 Step 1. Begin with a Purpose

Just as we have explored throughout this text, it is essential to clearly define your purpose in sharing this curated content. Are you aiming to inform, entertain, educate or assist your audience with this content? Having a clear direction from the outset will increase the probability that your content will achieve greater impact with your target audience.

There are many approaches that can be taken and if you are not clear on which one you plan to take from the beginning, the final post can end up being confusing to your audience. It is also important to revisit your organisation or client's social media strategy during the process of purpose identification to ensure that it is in line with the overall goals and objectives trying to be achieved.

▣ Table 12.1. Explains four communication styles that should be considered when ascertaining the purpose of curated content. These are called the 4 Models of Public Relations Practice but are a very

▣ **Table 12.1** The 4 models of public relations practice in a content curation context	
Model	**Definition**
Press Agentry/ Publicity	This model is used for purely promotional means. In the context of curated content, the Press Agentry or Publicity Models is not recommended for use unless such blatant promotion is of direct value to the audience. Curation of positive articles reviewing a business could fall into this category, but as a Social Media Manager it is important to ask, how is this content helping my audience? Curated content that falls into this category may be helpful during the awareness phase of the customer journey but may not be very useful to existing customer unless the content helps to strengthen their trust, loyalty and confirms their decision to support your organisation or client's brand.
Public information	By its very nature, the Public Information Model describes content that is curated and shared with the intention to inform the audience, but not necessarily generating engagement with them. On social media, the Public Information Model should be used very sparingly because it really does not comply with the two-way functionality of the technology. Social media promotes and facilitates interaction and connection. Curating a piece of content without encouraging any response from the audience is a very outdated way to use social media. It is an approach that was used in its early days by corporate organisations which received considerable backlash from users who wanted a more human interaction on social media with organisations. In terms of curated content, the few appropriate uses of Public Information Model could be in a crisis situation. For example, a local fire station may share the updates of a bushfire from the official emergency services Facebook page and provide some commentary relevant to the local area.

Table 12.1 (continued)

Model	Definition
Two-way asymmetrical	This model is focused on persuading audiences to think or respond to a call-to-action in a particular way. This approach generally uses persuasive tactics such as credible advocates or experts, research findings and statistical evidence to encourage audiences to behave is a way that is of benefit to the business or organisation.
	This approach may be helpful during the consideration phase of the customer journey. However, this approach is often criticised in the public relations literature because it is accused of being manipulative. If using this approach, the content, research and statistics used must be accurate and they must be used in an ethical way.
	For example, a sunscreen company sharing independent peer-reviewed research that provides empirical evidence that wearing 15+ can prevent melanoma is ethical. Sharing a story about one person dying from melanoma who never wore sunscreen is not. This approach to content curation should be adopted with care and caution.
Two-way symmetrical	The two-way symmetrical model of communication is often described as an aspirational approach to public relations. This model encourages the two-way communication between organisations and its stakeholders. In a social media environment, this model most embraces the interactive and conversational nature of the technology. Its objective is to resolve conflicts and develop solutions that are of mutual benefits to businesses and their customers.
	It seems like a great fit, but the power balance between business and customer still needs to be understood in a social media context. Ultimately, the owner of a business' social media profile has the power to delete comments (not recommended) and block a user.
	Yet, a customer has the power to leave negative reviews and share a negative experience quickly and to a wide network of people. That aside, sharing curated content that sparks discussion and engagement with a target audience is definitely recommended.
	Not only does this assist in building and strengthening communities around an organisation or brands, the greater amount of engagement that is generated from a post, the wider the audience that it can reach. Engagement is what many social media platforms use as endorsement for a quality piece of content.
	Therefore sharing content that encourages discussion is a recommended approach to curated content on social media.

useful as theoretical frameworks to guide the proposed outcome of curated content. Each theoretical model is explained and demonstrated with an example of curated content. The 4 Models of Public Relations practice were developed by Grunig (1983) after extensive research of public relations practices. Despite their age, these four models can still be applied to help both explain and underpin the communication of curated content for social media.

12.3 Step 2. Identify Your Audience

Again, it is important to revisit the organisation or client's social media strategy to select the most appropriate audience to share this content with. Remember, if you are aiming at everybody, you will not connect with anybody. There may be more than one audience segment in your social media strategy. Select the audience segment that would most appreciate this curated content so that it has the greatest impact in terms of engagement and response to its call-to-action.

> 66 If you are trying to communicate with everybody, you will not connect with anybody. 99
>
> Dr Karen Sutherland

12.4 Step 3. Select the Most Appropriate Social Media Platform

Social media platform selection will depend greatly on who the target audience is and the platforms that they use; it is important to be where the audience is. Overall, the specific social media platforms should be selected as part of the audience research process in the strategy development phase. However, there is usually more than one platform that will be included as part of that strategy. Step 3 involves narrowing this platform selection down to match the curated content with the most appropriate platform.

For example, if there is a helpful YouTube video that your audience will find useful, it may not receive the level of reach that you are hoping for if you post the link to Facebook as this platform gives greater exposure to native video. In fact, a study conducted by Quintly found that native Facebook videos achieved 86% greater reach than linking to a YouTube video (Ayres, 2018).

Therefore, it is worth choosing a different platform within your selection or searching for the content creator's Facebook page and trying to share the video from there. It is important to remember that just because

you have researched your target audience for the most appropriate platforms on which to reach them, it does not mean that all of these chosen platforms will work with any type of curated content that you are planning to use. Constant assessment of the match between curated content and platform is necessary.

12.5 Step 4. Develop a Plan for the Content that Incorporates the Curated Piece/s

Once the purpose, audience and platform have been identified, the next step is to plan the content around the curated piece. There can be two different ways to approach this. Firstly, during a content curation discovery session, you may find a range of valuable pieces that all follow a particular theme and would be great to arrange together in an article.

Alternatively, you may have an idea to create content around a particular topic and then curate content that will support the overall purpose of the piece. In both cases, you will need a plan to guide the way that the curated content will eventually be presented to the audience. This will be dependent on the platform that is selected to share it in terms of the following components:

- Optimal character length
- The types of post (e.g. longer posts for WordPress blogs or LinkedIn articles or shorter posts for tweets and Facebook posts).
- The number of curated pieces in the post
- The types of curated content to be included in the post (e.g. images, videos, memes, quotes, articles etc.)
- The tone of the piece
- The main points of the piece
- The curated content to support each point
- The most appropriate order for each curated piece to appear throughout the piece.

Many of these items will be explored in greater depth throughout this chapter. Once these preparatory four steps have been addressed, it is also worthwhile to consider the following foundational knowledge before moving to the practical techniques associated with sharing curated content. Below are four key points to underpin this practice.

12.6 Key Points to Remember When Presenting Curated Content

12.6.1 All Curated Content Must Add Value to the Audience and Strengthen the Piece Being Posted

The value of curated content must be continually assessed to ensure that it will be of value to the target audience. It can be tempting to gather a stockpile of curated content ready for a rainy day. It is recommended to find curated content when the time permits and to save it ready for future use. However, when the day arrives to use saved curated content, it must undergo the same level of assessment as mentioned in ▶ Chaps. 10 and 11.

This is because the content may be out of date if not used straight away. It is also worthwhile to check Google Trends to see if the topic of the curated content is one that is still being frequently searched for. The details in the content may be inaccurate or the information being communicated may be tired or considered as "old news".

> **"** Sharing outdated content can damage a brand's reputation, porticularly if it tries to position itself as being ahead of the curve. **"**
>
> **Dr Karen Sutherland**

Sharing outdated content can actually damage a brand's reputation, particularly if it tries to position itself as being ahead of the curve. Before posting any curated content, it is necessary to ask the following:

"Is this content still accurate?"

"Will the audience consider this content to be news?"

"How helpful will the audience find this content?"

"What tasks will this content help my customers to achieve?"

If you cannot provide clear and positive answers to these questions, then it is worth searching for alternative content. If you are not excited about the curated content that you are planning to post, chances are that your audience will not be either.

Every piece of content must earn its place on your followers' news feeds. Social media users are protective of the their news feeds. If they have chosen to include you in their feed by liking or following your profile or page, please respect that by sharing with them a steady stream of curated content of the highest quality to them.

12.6.2 Never Add Curated Content Purely for the Sake of Adding It

The second point carries on from the first. It can be tempting to keep pumping out content to remain present on the feeds of your target audience, but if you are posting curated content just for the sake of it, you will lose the respect of your supporters very quickly and will eventually lose them as your followers if you continue with the practice. If time and care have not been taken in finding valuable and accurate content and then crafting a post around it to suit the audience and the platform, your audience will pick up on this very quickly. Doing so promotes the attitude that you really do not care about your followers or want to make any attempt to understand them, which is the opposite of what social media should be used for.

Every action that you take on social media on behalf of an organisation or client should be aimed at connecting and engaging with your target audience otherwise it is a lost opportunity. Therefore, even if you feel under pressure to post, avoid sharing mediocre, outdated or inaccurate content at any cost. Otherwise it will end up costing you followers and reputation.

12.6.3 You are Providing Readers with Something New to Consider About Each Piece of Curated Content

With the quality of the content evaluated and its value to the audience clear, purely sharing it without providing any commentary is not enough. In fact, as mentioned in ► Chap. 10, it can actually be deemed as unethical. It is rare for a piece of curated content to be completely understood without any context provided by the person sharing it.

Furthermore, it can also be a missed opportunity to connect further with your target audience by using your client's or organisation's brand voice to begin an interesting discussion about it.

Generally, people follow a particular brand, page or profile because they are interested in hearing from it; they are interested in what it has to say.

Therefore, purely sharing other people's content without providing any context or commentary can be quite disappointing and may be considered by the audience as somewhat lazy or lacking effort.

> ❝ When curating content, you are not saying:
> "Look at this"
> "Check this out. Here is what I think about it.
> What do you think about it?" ❞
> Dr Karen Sutherland

When curating content, you are not saying, "Look at this".

You are saying: *"Check this out. Here is what I think about it. What do you think about it?"*

Posts that do not provide any context or commentary regarding curated content, can appear to be automated which completely misses the point of what curation is about: the human element.

12.6.4 Remember, It Is Always About the Audience. It is Not About You

The audience should always be the main priority when posting any social media content including in the presentation of curated content. By posting curated content that is helpful, valuable, informative or entertaining to the target audience, they will begin to trust your brand and will respond positively over time.

Social media is a long game and the presentation of curated content can be as integral as its selection in building trust and a positive relationship with your audience. Being strapped for time is not an excuse to shirk on presentation, particularly when to do so may confuse or disappoint a brand supporter who does not understand the message or purpose being conveyed in the curated content.

> 66 Remember, it is always about the audience; it is not about you. 99
>
> Dr Karen Sutherland

12.7 Ways that Curated Content Can Help to Share Brand Stories

There are countless ways to use curated content to share your brand story. By definition, a brand story is the narrative told to consumers that helps to convey the qualities, attributes, history, values and objectives of the brand, its products, services and people (Lundqvist, Liljander, Gummerus, & Van Riel, 2013; Huang, 2010). As explained in ▶ Chap. 6 a brand's story must be clear to a Social Media Manager and all staff before posting on social media.

It is essential that the brand story is a representation of the lived ideals of the organisation to avoid a reputation gap. The literature defines a reputation gap as "…the difference between internal reputation — specifically how customer-facing employees perceive their company — and external reputation — specifically how customers perceive the company," (Davies, Chun, & Kamins, 2010, p. 532). In short, a reputation gap is the difference between what a brand says about itself compared with customers' true experience.

In a content curation context, it is important to select and present only content that is in line with your organisation's values. Remember the online furore that resulted from organisations such as McDonald's encouraging customers to share their #McDStories. McDonald's was hoping to crowdsource positive stories from Twitter users to curate using this #McDStories hashtag, but it had the opposite effect due to its reputation gap (Jain, Agarwal, & Pruthi, 2015).

A similar incident happened to the New York Police Department with the #MyNYPD hashtag that resulted in images of alleged police brutality being shared by Twitter users (Xanthopoulos, Panagopoulos, Bakamitsos, & Freudmann, 2016) and in Melbourne, Australia with the #YourTaxis campaign to try to encourage positive stories from taxi passengers. Again, the hashtag was used to share sarcastic and negative experiences (Dumay & Guthrie, 2017).

While these incidents specifically relate to the use of a hashtag, the moral of these stories is that if an organisation presents a story about itself to customers and customers' experiences are very different to the narrative being presented, they will respond to try to correct this brand story by sharing their own. Ensure that the content being curated and presented aligns with the customer experience, not the aspirations of the brand or organisation.

The beauty of curating content is that you have the power of selecting the content that best suits the needs of your audience and your brand, as well as how it is presented. Critics who say that curating content is a lazy way to approach social media, clearly are not completing the process correctly (Holland, 2018).

Admittedly, curating content without any thought or commentary from the brand or organisation presenting it can definitely be perceived as indifference or apathy towards social media followers. However, putting in effort to the careful selection of content that is helpful to your audience and further articulating its value when presenting that content, could not be deemed as a lazy approach. It all comes down to caring. If you do not care about your audience, they will not care about you. It is that simple. Furthermore, every piece of content needs to help to tell a brand or organisation's story. When it comes to sto-

rytelling, it is essential to make the audience care (Gladstone & Stasiulis, 2017).

Curated content can be used to further your organisation's or client's brand story, almost in the same way that a plot device is used to progress the action in a fictional story. Below are examples of some of the ways that curated content can be used to tell a brand story.

Sometimes multiple devices can be used in the same piece. For example, a list of the five best tools to track your fitness progress brings together a list approach with providing value for the reader. This can work really well. Be sure not to use too many of the devices in the same piece and this can be confusing to the reader. It is definitely a case of quality over quantity.

A key consideration must be that the curated content supports the communication of the brand story, but it cannot *be* the brand story. It is essential to add commentary (e.g. text, captions etc.) that align the curated content with the brand story and strategic goals, objectives and key messages (as explored in Section 1). Using the devices in ◻ Table 12.2 can assist in achieving this advanced level of content curation.

12.7.1 Different Purposes for Curated Content that Support Brand Storytelling: As Part of a List (the Top Five... Etc.)

A LinkedIn article written by Petrone (2019) provides an excellent example of curating content to be used as part of a list (see ◻ Table 12.2). The article, '*The 10 Things You Should Do In The First 30 Days of a New Job,*' provides valuable advice to new employees while weaving in other helpful sources to further support the points being made. The curated pieces were a mixture of

Table 12.2 Different purposes for curated content that support brand storytelling

Plot device	Description
To further the brand story	If you have been sharing brand history and values through created content, curated content can also assist in progressing this story. For example if your client has a family business and its core consumer base is mothers, curating content relating to family life and motherhood help to continue that brand story around family.
As evidence to support a claim, argument or viewpoint	This device works extremely well in a blog post and LinkedIn article or in a series of posts on Facebook or Twitter. For example, if a brand or organisation is lobbying for change or is trying to raise awareness of an issue, sharing accurate curated content to help provide evidence for a specific cause can be an effective way to present curated content. In fact, any broad claim that you make should be supported by evidence if it is going to be perceived as credible by the audience. Remember, that fact and opinion can be very different things. It is always important to check the validity of your statements before sharing them with others.
To compare different examples relating to the same topic	Again, this is more effective in longer pieces such as blog posts and LinkedIn articles. Comparative pieces using curated content allow the reader to see the similarities and differences in a selection of content that they may have never assembled together on their own. This can be a highly effective use of curated content that is interesting to the reader as long as careful consideration has been used to both source and arrange the content. The juxtaposition on curated content can change the overall flow and meaning of the post. It is important to arrange the pieces in different sequences to find the most engaging one for the audience. For example, a blog post that compares different tweets responding to a celebrity scandal.
As part of a list (the top five… etc.)	Lists of curated content are hugely popular. BuzzFeed thrives on its use of lists such as the 16 Times Whole Foods Offended Society In 2018 (Loewentheil, 2018). Bringing curated content together in a list can be a great way to inform, entertain and amuse your audience. Lists can also be extremely helpful for those in your target audience who do not have the time to trawl the internet for information. The more useful the list is, the greater the appreciation from the audience. Think of items relating to your brand that will not blatantly promote your product. For example, a leather accessory brand may write a blog post called, *5 Top Tips to Look After Leather*. The piece could bring together helpful information that guides people to look after any leather products.
To provide context	Providing context is one of the best uses for curated content, particularly in longer pieces such as blog posts and LinkedIn articles. It helps the audience by linking to further information about a particular topic so that they can understand more about it. When mentioning a particular event, industry term, brand or product, its name should be linked to accurate information about it so that the reader can learn more if they want to. These opportunities are often missed and can lead to frustration on the reader's part because they have to conduct their own Google search to learn more or may not read the rest of the piece because they do not completely understand its context. Make it an easy read for your audience and a learning opportunity for those who want to take it.

(continued)

Table 12.2 (continued)

Plot device	Description
To provide extra value to the reader	Curated content can and should be presented in a way that is of great value to the target audience. However, to do this well, you must understand their needs and try to solve a common problem that they may be experiencing with the content that you curate. For example, a real estate business could bring together all of the resources necessary for first home buyers to educate this audience about what is involved and make the process as simple as possible. First home buyers often don't know what they need to do and by providing them with a one-stop-shop they will be grateful for this resource that makes their lives easier.

those written by the author, other sources and links to the LinkedIn profiles of people relevant to the article. The way that Petrone (2019) has organised the information into a list using bold subheadings helps the reader to easily scroll through the content (particularly on a mobile phone) to gain a sense of what the overall article is about before going back to read the entire piece. Presenting curated content in a list form can be a highly effective method to help the audience consume the content.

12.8 How to Share Curated Content that Aligns with Brand Voice

We have explored ways to share curated content so that it aligns with a brand story. The commentary that aligns a piece of curated content to a brand story plays a vital part in ensuring that it communicates that brand narrative. The most important component that can influence the success of that commentary is brand voice. Pahwah (2018) defines brand voice as: "...is how a brand conveys its brand personality to the external audience."

As explored in ▶ Chap. 6 brand personality, story, voice and tone must be decided (or identified and documented) as part of the research phase of social media strategy development and used in all content,

curated, created and when interacting via social channels. The commentary that is used to present curated content must also align with these brand components so that it is identifiable to the audience and helps to build trust through its consistency.

Taking this approach has some definite benefits. For example, a study by Barcelos, Dantas, and Sénécal (2018) found that using more of a human brand voice rather than an official corporate tone on social media has proven to increase a consumer's purchase intentions.

When writing accompanying commentary for the presentation of curated content on social media channels, Handley and Chapman (2010, p.34) have some valuable advice on how to maintain a consistent brand voice and tone:

Handley and Chapman (2010, p 34) encourage Social Media Managers to:

— **Be you**

Use a consistent and authentic brand voice to represent your client or organisation. Avoid using a cold, stuffy corporate tone. Understand your brand's personality and use it to bring the brand alive in its introductions to curated content. Brands have been criticised in the past for broadcasting information as a faceless organisation on social media rather than as real people communicating on behalf of an organisation (Xu et al., 2016).

— **Relax and write the way you would naturally speak**

As we have learned, social media is a tool for two-way communication. Consider how interesting it is to have a conversation with someone on Facebook whose posts are written using the same language as in an academic essay. Even scholars in academic-related Facebook groups do not communicate in that way.

It is important to loosen up and write commentary for curated content in language that is personable, human and engaging. Focus on writing in the same way that you would naturally speak, so that it sounds as though an approachable human wrote it; someone with whom the audience would like to interact.

However, it is still important to adhere to the strategic brand elements already mentioned and be professional. Avoid swearing. Once the bar is lowered, it is difficult to raise it up again to a higher standard.

> 66 The commentary that presents and weaves together curated content must flow and be easy to read. 99
>
> Dr Karen Sutherland

— **Be conversational**

Similar to the previous point. The commentary that presents and weaves together curated content must flow and be easy to read. When reading it, the audience should almost be able to hear the writer's voice chatting to them about the topic like they are an old friend. Patel (2019) suggests that in blog posts that people write directly to the reader using words such as "I" and "You" as though you are engaging them in direct conversation. This technique can also be applied to the presentation of curated content and it helps to build trust and a relationship to the audience by engaging with them on a one-to-one level.

— **Avoid marketing speak and jargon**

Use casual expressions if your audience will understand them.

Show don't tell (do not say how good or bad something is). Share a story about its impact.

Create content that is entertaining and informative. Ask yourself 'would you read this to the end?'

12.8.1 Aligning Content with Brand Voice: Real Stories of Country Women

Real Stories of Country Women (2019a, 2019b) is a project that shares the stories of women living in regional areas of Australia. Its brand voice embodies a no-nonsense, friendly country hospitality. This voice is clearly conveyed through its created content, but also in the content that it curates and shared across its channels on Facebook (2019a) and Instagram (2019b). Curated content includes articles and videos relating to the bush environment in terms of the drought and stories from other sources (such as ABCTV and online newspapers etc.) of the women who work hard to battle such challenges and how they cope while doing so. Misaligning content with the brand voice of Real Stories of Country Women would involve sharing curated content using a corporate brand voice regarding topics completely unrelated to country women, such as metropolitan public transport. This would only confuse followers and diminish their trust in the project for not staying true to its mission. This is why it is extremely important to ensure that there is strong alignment between brand voice and the types of content being created and curated on its social media channels.

12.9　Planning for Content Curation Success

If you fail to plan, you plan to fail. It is the same with the presentation of curated content. Planning is easy when presenting only one piece of curated content. Consideration really must be around what the commentary will contain and how the overall piece will fit in with the rest of your content strategy.

However, for longer pieces such as blog posts or LinkedIn articles, planning needs to be more extensive to ensure that you are making the most out of the content that you have curated and presenting it in a way that enhances sense-making and impact for the audience.

As mentioned by Pache (2011) a Social Media Manager should approach the presentation of curated content in the same way that a DJ arranges music for a set. To achieve this, the following must be considered:

12.9.1　Structure

A Social Media Manager needs to have an overall vision for the finished piece containing all pieces of curated content. It is easier when this occurs at the beginning of the presentation process. However, the creative process can occur quite organically, so this vision may change once the pieces of curated content are arranged.

However, it is vital for the overall structure of the piece to seem logical and understandable to the audience. For example, it will be confusing to an audience to believe that they are going to read a Top 5 list that has only four items on it.

12.9.2　Flow

In a longer piece, the curated content must be arranged in a way that flows logically for the audience. The pieces must add to the story being told and they must be presented in a way that is not jarring for the reader. For example, reading a well-written paragraph of text and having a long web address at the end can interrupt the flow of the piece for the reader and they may not continue. Always look at the piece from the reader's perspective.

It is important to keep them hooked on the line and engrossed in your content for as long as possible. Avoid breaking that attention with the unsophisticated presentation of curated content.

12.9.3　Revelation

In a blog post or a LinkedIn article, like in any piece of content, it should tell a story. The best stories contain particular plot points that drive the reader through its action. For example, at the beginning of a blog post or article, it is important to provide details of the action to follow, an opening sentence containing the who, what, where, when, how and why of what the reader can expect. Then the rest of the article must live up to that promise and the curated content being presented must support it too.

This is why it is important to plan out the piece at the beginning to ensure that the important points of the article are in a logical order for the reader to understand the meaning of the piece. Knowledge being imparted in the piece should build so that if a reader is unfamiliar with the topic at the beginning, they have learned more about it by the end. The curated content should support the readers' learning journey so that more in-depth information is revealed as the article progresses.

If the main points and curated content are not arranged in this way, the reader may drop out early because they do not understand what is trying to be conveyed. It would be like a university lecturer expecting students to complete the final exam at the beginning of the semester. That would be unfair. Pay the same consideration to your reader and reveal more complex information to them as their knowledge grows throughout the article.

12.9.4 Juxtaposition

The Oxford Dictionary (2019) defines the term juxtaposition as: "The fact of two things being seen or placed close together with contrasting effect." Consider the term 'juxtaposition' in the context of presenting curated content. Just as a curator at an art gallery may arrange paintings in a particular way, certain paintings next to others to convey a particular meaning, content curators also must consider the meanings interpreted by the audience when positioning curated content for social media.

Not considering the order and juxtaposition of content pieces can have a negative impact. This can sometimes be apparent on online news websites where there is a story about a highly sensitive topic and an ad for something related, but highly inappropriate appears on the page. The ad is randomly placed there, but the juxtaposition between the two items can be completely off-putting for the audience and often referred to as being 'tone deaf'. For example, a news story reporting a tragic house fire with an advertisement for matches embedded in the body of the article may seem very insensitive. Similarly with curated content, it is important to look at the overall piece to see the order in which the content is placed and preempt the possible meanings and interpretations that the reader can make in the order and positioning of each content piece.

Each piece should complement the content before it and after it to help move the reader logically through the action, using each curated nugget of information like a stepping stone to the end. If the curated content is not positioned in a logical way that facilitates sense-making for the audience, they may become stuck halfway through a piece and bail out before ever making it to the final paragraph.

12.9.5 Rhythm

The rhythm of the piece is also important in both the writing and arrangement of curated content. In a longer piece such as a blog post or LinkedIn article varying the sentence length and structure helps to provide a varied reading experience for the audience, and a similar approach can be taken to the presentation of curated content.

Rather than only linking through to articles, enhance the rhythm of the piece by using a range of curated content such as images, embedding YouTube videos and social media posts. Ensure that the post is balanced and consistent. For example, if you a blog post or LinkedIn article has an image above one subheading, maintain consistency by placing a relevant image above each subheading.

If there is only text in the first half of the piece and three or four images in the second half, this will seem to be unbalanced from the reader's perspective. It is much more aesthetically pleasing to the reader to be consistent in the way that images, YouTube videos and text are distributed throughout the piece. However, the focus must be on accuracy, relevance and appropriateness. Avoid adding images only to balance out the piece.

Remember, every piece of curated content must earn its place. Ensure that the items added for balance are factual, are relevant to the target audience and the what the piece is communicating and enhance its meaning for the reader.

> Quick Tips for Presenting Curated Content in Longer
> 1. **Plan the structure of the post** (beginning, middle, end and key points for each)
> 2. **Review the credible content** that you have gathered (articles, images, videos etc.)
> 3. **Identify which content will support each point** while maintaining momentum and flow for the reader.
> 4. **Ensure the content chosen builds knowledge** as the piece progresses.
> 5. **Support all statements with examples and evidence.**
> 6. **Any statistical information, images, videos, quotes etc. must be linked to its original source.**
> 7. **Any titles, names of people, brands, products, website names should be linked through to accurate and relevant information regarding them.**

12.10 Ways to Avoid Presenting Curated Content

12.10.1 Including Long Web Addresses

Always delete web addresses from posts if the content can be accessed without the link. Platforms such as Facebook and LinkedIn often generate an image from the content link that users can click to take them directly to the site, therefore the original link can be deleted.

Similarly, never include a long URL in a blog post. It is unattractive and jarring to the reader, interrupting the flow of the piece. Instead link to a few relevant words. However, do not link to an entire sentence. That looks just as messy.

On platforms such as Twitter, where a link may be necessary, it is worth shortening it and customising it using a tool such as ▶ Bitly.com (◘ Fig. 12.1).

12.10.2 Not Including Commentary

When presenting curated content it is essential to add some commentary that aligns with the brand sharing it and provides some context for the reader. Only sharing a piece of content without adding anything can be confusing to the audience and is a missed opportunity to connect with them (◘ Fig. 12.2).

12.10.3 Not Captioning Images with a Link to Their Source

The importance of copyright was explored in depth in ▶ Chap. 10. However, even when using a copyright free image it is important to name and link through to its source (◘ Fig. 12.3):

For example:
Source: Canva

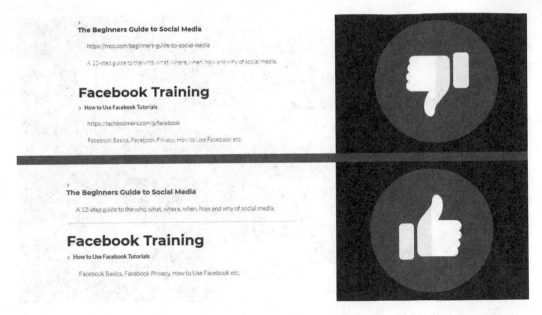

Fig. 12.1 Avoid using long website addresses. Instead link to a few relevant words

Fig. 12.2 Not including commentary is a missed opportunity when presenting curated content

Source: Canva.com

Fig. 12.3   Always caption a curated image and link through to its source

(and link the word Canva through to where the image has been sourced)

12.10.4 Not Linking Through to Content to Save the Reader Googling

Not linking through to information about titles, people's names, product names, places, events, causes etc. the first time they are mentioned can result in a reader abandoning the content because they do not understand its context or leave it to Google for more information and never return.

Making it easy for the reader to click through to specific content that you have selected for them to add context around a topic helps to build their relationship with you because you are assisting them.

Furthermore, in a blog, if you select for the new link to open in a new browser window, you will not drive people away from your webpage (■ Fig. 12.4).

12.10.5 Not Tagging Content Creators in a Curated Post

Not only is this unethical by not crediting the content source (see ▶ Chap. 10), it also presents a missed opportunity to thank the creator (building an association) and potentially leveraging their influence to reach a wider network of people (■ Fig. 12.5).

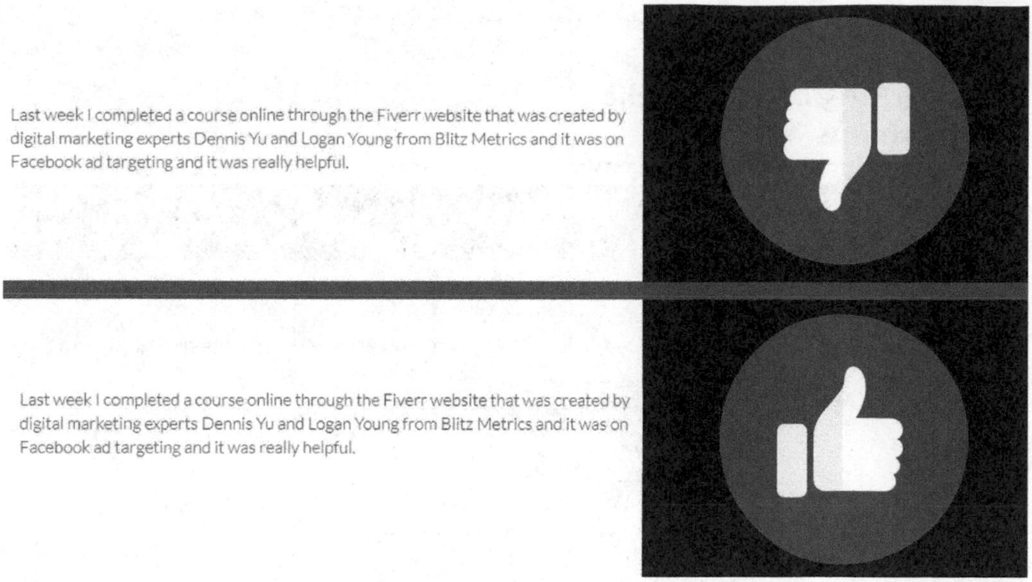

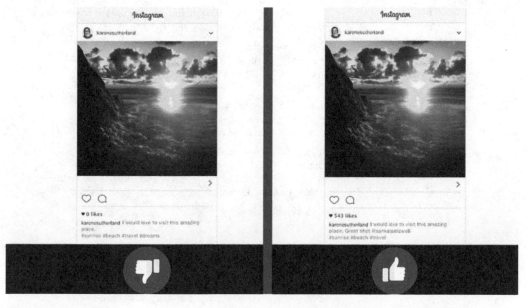

Last week I completed a course online through the Fiverr website that was created by digital marketing experts Dennis Yu and Logan Young from Blitz Metrics and it was on Facebook ad targeting and it was really helpful.
Last week I completed a course online through the Fiverr website that was created by digital marketing experts Dennis Yu and Logan Young from Blitz Metrics and it was on Facebook ad targeting and it was really helpful.

Fig. 12.4 Link through to information when mentioning names, products and websites etc. to help the reader and save them time searching

Instagram
karenesutherland
0 likes
karenesutherland I would love to visit this amazing place.
#sunrise #beach #travel #dreams
Instagram
karenesutherland
543 likes
karenesutherland I would love to visit this amazing place. Great shot @sankalpalizwell
#sunrise #beach #travel

Fig. 12.5 Always tag or mention the content creator when presenting their content in your post

12.11 Appropriate Ways to Present Curated Content on Mainstream Social Media Platforms

Social media platform	Type of content	Presentation technique
Facebook	Video	Share from an existing Facebook post. Write commentary. Do not link to YouTube or another external video source.
	Image	Provide commentary Tag image owner
	Link	Provide commentary Tag author or article Delete link if preview is generated Use copyright free relevant image if image is not generated automatically.
	Text	Include an image and commentary with the curated post. Use relevant hashtags (3 at most)
Twitter	Video	Commentary with retweeted video (tagging creator) or YouTube link with image.
	Image	Commentary with retweeted image (tagging creator) or uploading and tweeting image with commentary and source tagged.
	Link	Share shortened link. Tag creator if possible Provide commentary for context Include image if one is not generated.
	Text	Retweet with commentary Tag original creator and others who may be interested Use relevant hashtags (3 at most)
LinkedIn	Videos	YouTube videos, remove the link once the preview generates and add commentary. LinkedIn posts from other users that feature video. Add commentary and mention content creator.
	Image	Provide commentary Tag image owner
	Links	**In an update** Provide commentary Tag author or article Delete link if preview is generated Use copyright free relevant image if image is not generated automatically. **In an article** Links should be embedded the same as in a blog post. Link to 1–3 relevant words. Mention the author where relevant.
	Text	Include commentary Ensure that the creator is easily identified. Use relevant hashtags (3 at most)

12

Social media platform	Type of content	Presentation technique
Instagram	Image/video	You will need an app such as repost for Instagram to do this. Add your own caption. Tag the creator in the caption and thank them.
	Story mention	Tag creator Thank or compliment the creator in some way Use gifs and fun text. Use relevant hashtags for greater reach.
	IGTV	Can share through to stories Tag creator Thank or compliment the creator in some way Use gifs and fun text. Use relevant hashtags for greater reach.
	Links	Included in bio, but make it clear where they are sourced Can be included in stories if you have 10 k+ followers. Tag the content creator At this point in time, links do not work in captions.
YouTube	In video	Pay homage to another creator's content by mentioning it in your video In superimposed titles show their name and mention their channel If using data etc. mention the source by name and include a link in the video description. Never use other creator's video footage or music in your video without their permission.
	Video description	Always provide the name and link to any curated content that you include in your video. Use this section to provide links to relevant and valuable content created by yourself and curated from others.
Snapchat	Images and video	Similar to Instagram stories Tag creator Thank or compliment the creator in some way
Blogging	Videos	Many blogging interfaces such as WordPress allow YouTube videos to be embedded directly into the post. This clearly shows the content creator. If linking through or using an uploaded video file clearly write the content creator's name and link to their website or other relevant information about them.
	Image	Include a caption with the content Creator's name and link through to exactly where the image was sourced.
	Links	Link to 1–3 relevant words. Mention the author where relevant. The curated content should fit logically and naturally in the piece and should not the flow for the reader.
	Text	Many blogging platforms such as WordPress have features to make direct quotes more prominent. These are useful. Include the author's name and link through to where the quote was sourced.

Conclusion

This chapter followed on from ▶ Chap. 11 to explore the various approaches, techniques, stages and functions involved with the presentation of curated content. A range of theoretical frameworks were investigated to demonstrate different approaches to the communication of curated content to support strategic goals and objectives to a range of audiences. Best-practice techniques in relation to longer pieces and specific platforms were also provided. The key points to remember are to present curated content in a way that is ethical, supportive to strategic goals and objectives, relevant to the audience and appropriate to the social media platform selected.

▶ Chapter 12 concludes this section about Strategic Content Curation. Section Three of this text focuses on Strategic Content Creation and provides the knowledge to develop a range of social media content to support the achievement of strategic goals and objectives.

Case Study: Using Curated Content for Paid Ads on Social Media

Many social media platforms have strict rules around using other people's content in paid advertising. For example, Facebook no longer allows the boosting of posts that have been created on a page that you do not own. These regulations change constantly, so it is important to check what is allowed on each platform. However, for Social Media Managers it is important to consider the ethical implications involved with using someone else's content in a paid ad for your organisation's or client's brand. These considerations must include clearly identifying the goals and objectives of the ad and if the content creator has provided permission for the content to be used in this way.

If the purpose of the ad is to generate leads or sales for a commercial business, it may be considered as unethical if you are using someone else's work to achieve this without compensating them. However, if the content is being used in a paid ad for the benefit of the audience and the content curator first while providing your brand with some extra exposure last, then this is a much more acceptable use of the content. For example, HubSpot (2018) launched a free social media certification. My Facebook page followers are largely small business owners and students who I knew would be extremely interested in educating themselves. I posted a link to the course on my Facebook page explaining what it was and why it would be helpful. I completed the course myself so I could share from experience.

In the presentation of this curated content I did not include a call-to-action (see ◘ Fig. 12.6). I did not try to promote

◘ **Fig. 12.6** Ethically using curated content in a Facebook ad

12.12 · Interview: Shelby McQueen - PPC (Pay-Per-Click) Consultant - Reload....

277

12

my services. My purpose for sharing this content was purely to assist my audience. I had already spoken to a representative from HubSpot and they were supportive of me promoting the course.

The initial post performed well. There was a great level of interest in the form of comments, likes and shares. This positive response indicated to me that my audience found the post valuable, so I decided to promote the post using the Facebook Ads Manager to increase its reach to others who would also find it helpful.

Therefore, in specific instances it is appropriate to use curated content in a paid ad on social media, but the content creator must provide you with their permission and it demonstrates greater integrity to do so for altruistic reasons first.

1. Provide an example of when it may be unethical to use curated content in an ad on social media?
2. What should be the core motivation if using curated content for paid social media advertising?

12.12 Interview: Shelby McQueen - PPC (Pay-Per-Click) Consultant - Reload Digital, London

1. **Please tell me about your current role?**
   My specific title is a PPC Consultant, so pay-per-click. But, being agency life, I help out any which way that I can, which means getting on board with different SEO projects or design projects or helping out the account managers. It's all sort of varied. But my main day-to-day is pay-per-click advertising.

2. **What are your favourite parts about working with social media?**
   I really like the creativity that comes along with it and being able to take on someone else's brand and tell their story in a way that really changes their presence online. I think it's really inspiring to see the transformation that businesses go through when they really enhance the online world and start to really incorporate strong messages and values through their presence online. I think it's just the way of the future, and it's just very exciting to be part of.

3. **What are the greatest challenges?**
   There are many. There are so many variables to the work that you do online that can be really challenging to optimise correctly for these clients. There are circumstances where some clients might not see results overnight, and it's hard to communicate to them the work that we're doing, the importance of the work that we're doing and the importance of the determination to stay long-term to really grow those sort of benefits over a long amount of time. I think there are so many audiences and things online that it's hard to just give a black and white answer on how things are going to go for clients, so sometimes communicating that can be a bit challenging.

4. **How did you come to work in social media? Please tell me your career story.**
   I studied at the University of the Sunshine Coast in Queensland, Australia. I graduated at the end of 2017 after completing a Bachelor of Public Relations. I first started working in the social media space when I was finishing my degree. I was doing some social media courses with you, Karen, at USC, as well as an internship. At my internship, they had a position opening for a social media

contractor, just helping out with organic content at that time with different businesses on the Sunshine Coast. I applied for the job as an intern and they offered it to me and that evolved into me starting my own business and helping other businesses on the Coast to grow their organic presence online as well. I'm now working in London in an agency that helps a lot of e-commerce and lead generation brands all across the world.

5. **What do you think are the three most important things that Social Media Managers need to consider when presenting curated content?**

It needs to be on brand. So whether that's colours, the tone of the voice, the imagery that you're using, anything that sort of makes up your identity, it needs to be very on brand. It needs to be consistent. There's nothing worse than seeing something from a business one week and then not seeing anything for like the next month. You need to show your audience that you're committed to staying up to date with them, you're involved in their life and their happenings and different industry trends and updates. You need to go back on it all the time and refine and report and analyse and keep moving forward with different things that are evolving every single day.

6. **What are the challenges of using curated content?**

Some of the challenges, obviously, come with copyright and ownership of that kind of content online. If a company has put the call out for user-generated content and use those things on their platforms but making sure that you're resharing these things in a legal way can be challenging. Just asking for permission from most people is one of the most important things.

7. **What are your favourite tools for curating content?**

Depends on the client we're working for and how big the scope of the work is, but I prefer mostly manual content curation.

8. **What do you think of the current landscape of social media management as a profession?**

I think it's growing, but there are many people that I talk to who can't believe what it is that I do in my day-to-day job. I think it's growing, but I don't think it's mainstream just yet. I think a lot of people believe it's too good to be true at the moment, but there are definitely brands out there that are really understanding the importance of having a social media manager and how powerful that can have an impact on your business.

9. **Where do you think the profession and social media is heading in the future?**

I think it's going to become very corporate. I think there are a lot of businesses who are taking on a lot of Social Media Managers in-house now, instead of outsourcing to agencies, because they can see how easy it is to fill up one person's week with social media tasks. I think it will start becoming sort of like an integrated part of businesses inside their business, rather than outsourcing.

10. **What has been the best piece of advice that you have been given?**

My dad always used to tell me, "If there's ever an opportunity that you really, really want, just bite off more than you can chew, and chew like hell."

❓ Questions for Critical Reflection

1. How can The 4 Models of Public Relations practice were developed by Grunig (1983) assist when presenting curated content on social media?

2. Why is it important to include commentary when presenting curated content?

3. What is brand voice and why should the presentation of curated content align with it?

4. How can you check that the curated content being presented adds value to the target audience?

5. Why is it important to mention and thank content creators when presenting their content?

> **Practical Exercises**

1. Find an online article and prepare it to be presented on LinkedIn, Facebook and Twitter. What is its purpose? Who is the audience? How will its commentary differ between each platform? How will it generate engagement with the audience?

2. Pick your favourite brand and review their Facebook content. Curate a piece of content that its audience would find valuable. Prepare the post using the same brand voice. What commentary would you include to connect with their audience? Why would their audience find this post valuable?

References

Ayres, S. (2018). Study proves: Facebook native videos have up to 86% higher reach! Agorapulse.com. Viewed 12.04.2019, https://www.agorapulse.com/social-media-lab/facebook-videos-reach.

Barcelos, R. H., Dantas, D. C., & Sénécal, S. (2018). Watch your tone: How a brand's tone of voice on social media influences consumer responses. *Journal of Interactive Marketing, 41*, 60–80.

Davies, G., Chun, R., & Kamins, M. A. (2010). Reputation gaps and the performance of service organizations. *Strategic Management Journal, 31*(5), 530–546.

Dumay, J., & Guthrie, J. (2017). Involuntary disclosure of intellectual capital: Is it relevant? *Journal of Intellectual Capital, 18*(1), 29–44.

Gladstone, B., & Stasiulis, E. (2017). Digital storytelling method. In P. Liamputtong (Ed.), *Handbook of research methods in health social sciences*. Singapore: Springer.

Grunig, J. E. (1983). Organizations, environments, and models of public relations.

Handley, A., & Chapman, C. C. (2010). *Content rules: How to create killer blogs, podcasts, videos, ebooks, webinars (and more) that engage customers and ignite your business* (Vol. 5). John Wiley & Sons.

Holland, T. (2018). Why content curation is lazy at best and unethical at worst. Skyword.com. Viewed 12.04.2019, https://www.skyword.com/contentstandard/creativity/why-content-curation-is-lazy-at-best-and-unethical-at-worst/.

Huang, W. Y. (2010). Brand story and perceived brand image: Evidence from Taiwan. *Journal of Family and Economic Issues, 31*(3), 307–317.

HubSpot. (2018). Social Media - Free Certification Course. Viewed 08.04.2019, https://academy.hubspot.com/courses/social-media.

Jain, N., Agarwal, P., & Pruthi, J. (2015). HashJacker-detection and analysis of hashtag hijacking on Twitter. *International Journal of Computer Applications, 114*(19).

Kanter, B. (2017). *Content curation primer, Beth's blog - How connected nonprofits leverage networks and data for social change,* viewed 23/02/2019, http://www.bethkanter.org/content-curation-101/.

Loewentheil, H. (2018). 16 times whole foods offended society In 2018. BuzzFeed. Viewed 23.03.2019, https://www.buzzfeed.com/hannahloewentheil/ridiculous-whole-foods-products.

Lundqvist, A., Liljander, V., Gummerus, J., & Van Riel, A. (2013). The impact of storytelling on the consumer brand experience: The case of a firm-originated story. *Journal of Brand Management, 20*(4), 283–297.

Oxford Dictionary. (2019). Juxtaposition. Viewed 28.03.2019, https://en.oxforddictionaries.com/definition/juxtaposition.

Pache, C. (2011). Content curators – The DJs of the web. *Journal of Digital Research & Publishing.* pp. 19–25. Viewed: 12/04/2019, http://ses.library.usyd.edu.au/bitstream/2123/8137/1/DRPJournal_5pm_S2_2011.pdf.

Pahwah, A. (2018). What is brand voice? Guidelines to create a right brand voice. Viewed 24.03.2019, https://www.feedough.com/brand-voice-guidelines/.

Patel, N. (2019). If I had to start a blog from scratch, I would. Viewed 24.02.2019, https://neilpatel.com/blog/blogging-principles/.

Petrone, P. (2019). The 10 things you should do in the first 30 days of a new job, *LinkedIn,* viewed 19.11.2019, https://learning.linkedin.com/blog/advancing-your-career/the-10-things-you-should-do-in-the-first-30-days-of-a-new-job.

Real Stories of Country Women (2019a). *Facebook.* Viewed: 19.11.2019, https://www.facebook.com/storiesofcountrywomen/.

Real Stories of Country Women (2019b). *Instagram.* Viewed: 19.11.2019, https://www.instagram.com/storiescountrywomen/.

Xanthopoulos, P., Panagopoulos, O. P., Bakamitsos, G. A., & Freudmann, E. (2016). Hashtag hijacking: What it is, why it happens and how to avoid it. *Journal of Digital & Social Media Marketing, 3*(4), 353–362.

Xu, A., Liu, H., Gou, L., Akkiraju, R., Mahmud, J., Sinha, V., et al. (2016). Predicting perceived brand personality with social media. In *Tenth international AAAI conference on web and social media*.

Further Reading

Moore, P. (2019). *How to curate content like a pro, and build your brand in 2019*. Viewed 08.04.2019, https://www.socialmediatoday.com/news/how-to-curate-content-like-a-pro-and-build-your-brand-in-2019/547462/.

Rosenbaum, S. (2014). *Curate this: The Hands-on, How-to Guide to Content Curation*. Magnify Media.

Rosenbaum, S. C. (2011). *Curation nation: How to win in a world where consumers are creators* (Vol. 1). New York, NY: McGraw-Hill.

Salat, Z. (2018). *The most dangerous content curation mistakes: Learn how to find the best sources for content to curate*. Smartketeer.com.

Wagner, A. (2017). *How to use content curation the right way*. Viewed 08.04.2019, https://www.forbes.com/sites/forbesagencycouncil/2017/09/01/how-to-use-content-curation-the-right-way/#37ee9a12b63e.

Helpful Links

The Ultimate Guide to Content Curation (With Examples!). https://smartblogger.com/content-curation/

Social Media Character Counter: https://sproutsocial.com/insights/social-media-character-counter/

The Ultimate Guide To Social Media Post Lengths In 2020. https://bytraject.com/social/social-media-post-lengths/

32 Ways to Find Great Social Media Content. https://www.youtube.com/watch?v=3mKJQuREIHw&t=14s

Google Trends https://trends.google.com/trends

Report for Instagram http://repostapp.com/

Bitly (link shortener). https://app.bitly.com/bbt2/

Strategic Content Creation

Contents

Strategic Content Creation

Contents

The overarching theme of this text encourages social media management to be approached in a strategic way, and this is also the case with the creation of social media content. In 1996 Bill Gates proclaimed that 'Content is King' and he was definitely accurate with this statement (Evans, 2017). Each piece of content, whether it is text, image or video must support strategic goals, convey key messages and be relevant to the target audience (Dolan, Conduit, Frethey-Bentham, Fahy, & Goodman, 2019; Felix, Rauschnabel, & Hinsch, 2017; Kreiss, Lawrence, & McGregor, 2018). Content must suit each social media platform, cut through the noise to grab the attention of the target audience and fulfil its tactical purpose.

> 66 Content must suit each social media platform, cut through the noise to grab the attention of the target audience and fulfil its tactical purpose. 99
>
> **Dr Karen Sutherland**

Developing social media content can be a thoroughly exciting and creative process, but it can also be challenging and frustrating if graphic design, video production and copywriting are completely new skill areas.

You will not be a professional graphic designer, copywriter or video producer after reading Part III and completing the practical exercises it prescribes. However, Part III will provide a comprehensive understanding of the basic principles of quality social media content creation for specific clients and audiences. This knowledge will support the direct creation of social media content and provide in-depth understanding of the process when briefing a specialist to produce content on behalf of a client.

The first three chapters of Part III will focus on the strategic creation of textual, image-based and video content for social media and will provide direction on when it is feasible to produce content directly and when appointing professional external providers is a better idea.

The final chapter of Part III, and the entire text, is devoted to exploring the future of social media management and focuses on the self-care of Social Media Managers. Research studies have highlighted a link between excessive digital media use (including social media) and lower psychological well-being (Hunt, Marx, Lipson, & Young, 2018; Twenge & Campbell, 2019).

In some cases, Social Media Managers may be required to be connected online for considerable lengths of time, be under pressure to produce large quantities of content within limited time periods, experience stress dealing directly with the public and managing issues and crisis situations.

Therefore, it is necessary for ▶ Chap. 17 to explore and recommend strategies to minimise the potential risks and impacts that can be associated with the profession.

References

Dolan, R., Conduit, J., Frethey-Bentham, C., Fahy, J., & Goodman, S. (2019). Social media engagement behavior: A framework for engaging customers through social media content. *European Journal of Marketing*. https://doi.org/10.1108/EJM-03-2017-0182

Evans, H. (2017). *"Content is King" — Essay by Bill Gates 1996*, Medium, viewed 05.09.2019: https://medium.com/@HeathEvans/content-is-king-essay-by-bill-gates-1996-df74552f80d9

Felix, R., Rauschnabel, P. A., & Hinsch, C. (2017). Elements of strategic social media marketing: A holistic framework. *Journal of Business Research, 70*, 118–126.

Hunt, M. G., Marx, R., Lipson, C., & Young, J. (2018). No more FOMO: Limiting social media decreases loneliness and depression. *Journal of Social and Clinical Psychology, 37*(10), 751–768.

Kreiss, D., Lawrence, R. G., & McGregor, S. C. (2018). In their own words: Political practitioner accounts of candidates, audiences, affordances, genres, and timing in strategic social media use. *Political Communication, 35*(1), 8–31.

Twenge, J. M., & Campbell, W. K. (2019). Media use is linked to lower psychological well-being: Evidence from three datasets. *Psychiatric Quarterly, 90*(2), 311–331.

Writing for Social Media

Contents

© The Author(s), under exclusive license to Springer Nature Singapore Pte Ltd. 2021
K. E. Sutherland, *Strategic Social Media Management*, https://doi.org/10.1007/978-981-15-4658-7_14

By the End of This Chapter You Will
- Learn why text-based content is the foundation of all social media posts.
- Understand the key principles of good writing.
- Gain an insight into the key stages involved in the copywriting process: Prepare, Write, Revise, Edit, and Schedule/Publish.
- Know how to write for mainstream social media platforms including blog posts, dialogue for chatbots, voice assistant compliant copy and responses to customer complaints.

TLDR
- Text-based social media copy is an integral component of content because it provides context, is searchable, reduces misinterpretation and increases accessibility and reach.
- The fundamental principles of good writing for social media are goals, objectives, purpose, accuracy, correct and consistent grammar, spelling and punctuation, style, brevity, clarity, structure, narrative, tone of voice, brand personality, key message/s and call-to action, a strong lead, audience appropriateness and platform suitability.
- The five key stages of the social media copywriting process are: prepare, write, revise, edit, and schedule/publish. However, the revision and editing stages may occur multiple times before the copy reaches the schedule/publish stage.
- Search Engine Optimisation (SEO) involves a range of tactics to increase visibility of content in online searches

which can include incorporating the search terms used by the target audience into written copy.
- Every social media platform has different content requirements. It is important to check these specifications regularly and write copy that is optimised for each platform.
- Writing scripts for chatbots and copy that is optimised to be visible to virtual assistants are skills Social Media Managers should develop.
- When responding in writing to customer complaints on social media: offer corrective action, connect the customer with someone that can offer a solution and thank the complainant

14.1 Introduction

Social media can be perceived as being a predominantly visual platform (as we will explore in ▶ Chaps. 15 and 16), due to the high levels of engagement that images and video can generate across channels (Brubaker & Wilson, 2018; Marshall, 2018). Yet, underestimating the power and necessity of well-written copy can be an error made to the detriment of a social media strategy. Generally, audiences consume text online in snack-sized portions reading an average of 28 words per website visit (Weinreich, Obendorf, Herder, & Mayer, 2008). Therefore, the written word can play a considerable role in cutting through the wide range of content a target audience scrolls past on a daily basis in social media's attention economy (Quesenberry, 2018).

Great copy interrupts and creates a connection with an audience.

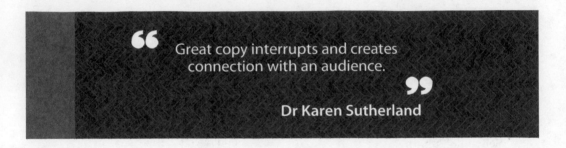

" Great copy interrupts and creates connection with an audience. "

Dr Karen Sutherland

This is why the same degree of care and focus must be placed on the textual and visual elements within social media content (Carroll, 2017). Each must work together to strengthen the other to achieve the strategic goals and objectives as outlined in ▶ Section 1. The aim of this entire section is to provide guidance, tools and processes to create all types of quality content: text, images and video. It is of no coincidence that copywriting for social media is the topic of the first chapter in this section, because it is the foundation of all social media content.

▶ Chapter 14 provides the processes, tools and techniques to write engaging copy for mainstream social media platforms. The chapter begins with an investigation of the importance of text-based content before exploring the fundamental principles of good writing. These principles can be applied to any form of writing but will be analysed within a social media context.

In addition, the key stages of the copywriting process will be clarified before examining the text-based capabilities and recommended approaches to writing content on mainstream social media platforms including Facebook, LinkedIn, Twitter, Instagram, YouTube, TikTok, blogs and chatbots. This chapter also provides advice on how to write responses to complaints on social media profiles before concluding with an interview with social media professional, Umang Malik Aggarwal, Founder/CEO of The Social Mango and The Tender Curve from Mumbai, India who provides her insights into writing effective social media copy.

14.2 Why Text-Based Content Is Important

Written copy plays a vital and strategic role on social media for a range of reasons, but sometimes it is not given the attention it deserves in favour of more visual types of content. While it is important for photos, graphics and videos to be on point, these content types still require quality text-based elements to reinforce and boost their performance.

There are five key reasons why written copy is such an important component of social media content. Written copy:

14.2.1 Provides Context for Visual Elements

An image on its own does not always convey all necessary information to a target audience. Often, text is also required to provide another layer of meaning to the audience. Without accompanying written copy, a target audience may misunderstand the post completely. ◻ Fig. 14.1 demonstrates the differences in the meaning that can be conveyed when an image is posted with and without written copy.

Furthermore, with platforms such as Facebook previously limiting the reach of images with more than 20% text the post, extra text is necessary to communicate important information to the audience including calls-to-action (Facebook, 2019a).

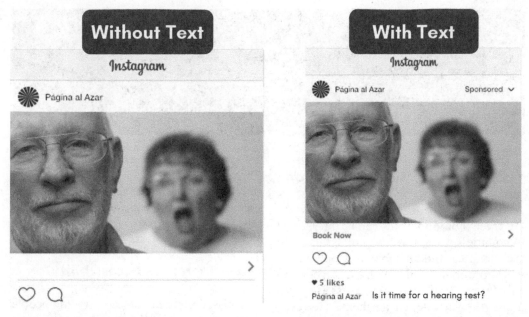

Fig. 14.1 Without text the image could be perceived as an argument. With text sets context for the image

Well-written copy can be the deciding influence that inspires someone to watch a video, take further notice of an image or click on blog post link because it provides some further explanation regarding what they can expect if deciding to delve deeper.

14.2.2 Is Searchable

Text is much easier to search on social media platforms than photographs, graphics and Video (Smith, 2016). While Google offers free reverse image functionality, this is not available on most mainstream social media platforms. Instead, (often paid) third party tools are available. Text-based content is easily searchable on each social media platform, which makes perfect sense considering searches within platforms require users to enter text into the search field, returning a text-based response, such as profile name. Text on a graphic is not searchable. Therefore, it is essential to include written copy and alt-tags on images with all social media posts so that users can find them if using the search engine functionality within a social media platform. Not including written copy will result in a lack of visibility on a social media platform by greatly reducing efforts in Search Engine Optimisation (SEO).

Defined in very simple terms, SEO describes a range of tactics that encourage traffic to a particular website (Smith, 2016). In a social media context this practice is also known as Social Media Optimisation (SMO), this involves increasing the likelihood that a client or organisation's profile or content ranks highly in searches to drive traffic to their profiles and content (Jantsch & Singleton, 2016). The aim is to be easily located if someone is searching using terms relating to a client's brand, organisation, products or services.

Advice regarding SEO will be further in the chapter in relation to audience appropriateness and helpful tools will be listed under Helpful Links at the end of this chapter.

> ❝ A picture may be worth a thousand words, but these thousand words can be interpreted in countless ways ❞
>
> **Dr Karen Sutherland**

14.2.3 Reduces Misinterpretation

A picture may be worth a thousand words, but these thousand words can be interpreted in countless ways. Effective communication is clear, direct and unambiguous. Sometimes it is appropriate to play with the target audience by encouraging them to guess as a technique to generate engagement. However, these techniques should be used only rarely. Instead, it is important to communicate precisely, particular if the goal of the content is to inspire the target audience to perform a desired behaviour or action.

It is important to avoid confusing the target audience at all costs. When people do not understand they often switch off and focus on something else that makes greater sense. The content produced for a client or organisation will be competing directly with content from other businesses etc. Therefore, it needs to grab the audience's attention and be understandable within seconds to avoid them scrolling past and/or losing interest because it takes too much effort and/or takes too long to grasp the key message/s. Written copy is the best way to make it easy for the audience and minimise the risk of misinterpretation.

14.2.4 Increases Accessibility

Text-based content is necessary for people experiencing a visual impairment to access social media platforms. Tools called screen readers are used to communicate written content from websites (including social media sites) via voiceover or braille (Brinkley & Tabrizi, 2017). A screen reader works as its name suggests by reading the text from webpages including the alt text to describe images (explored more in ▶ Chap. 15) and the closed captions from video transcriptions (see ▶ Chap. 16). Not paying close attention to the written components of social media posts, images and video can impact audience size if a proportion cannot access the content.

> ❝ Not paying close attention to the written components of social media posts, images and video can impact audience size if a proportion cannot access the content. ❞
>
> **Dr Karen Sutherland**

14.2.5 Increases Reach

Text-based social media content can increase the reach and exposure of posts in two key ways. Firstly, great copy that engages, entertains and amuses is more likely to be shared than written content that does not resonate with its audience. As explored in ▶ Chap. 7, the sharing of content is one of the most effective ways to reach new audiences. Great copy inspires a target audience to show it to people in their networks to share the feeling and experience that it prompted in them.

Secondly, the strategic use of hashtags can also increase the reach of content to new audiences (Stanton, Hobson-Powell, & Rosenbaum, 2019). For example, a hairdressing salon using Instagram with the goal of attracting new customers should use hashtags with the names of nearby suburbs along with content captions and Instagram stories to ensure that posts are visible to users consuming content via those hashtags (who would most likely be from the local area).

In short, not placing a strong emphasis on developing quality written content can result in confused target audiences plus reduced reach, searchability and accessibility. Writing quality content is a skill that must be perfected over time. However, key principles exist that can greatly assist in guiding the way to a better writer writing more effective social media content.

14.3 Fundamental Principles for Good Writing

Writing for the web (including social media) is very different from writing for other communication channels such as brochures or corporate reports (Smith, 2016). People consume information on a screen very differently than from hard copy materials (Whitaker & Smith, 2009). More specifically, web users prefer to consume information in small bites with ample space between them as opposed to attempting to glean information from large slabs of text (as highlighted in ▶ Chap. 10 with the result of TLDR).

Inspiring an audience to read a piece of content in its entirety is the aim of every post. Strong writing coupled with a compelling and relevant visual component are the keys to making this happen. Yet, for the written component of a social media post, the following principles will directly impact the quality of the finished copy.

14.3.1 Goals, Objectives and Purpose

Clearly define the goal and objective of the copy before beginning the writing process keeping in mind that every piece of content must support the achievement of at least one of the strategic goals and SMART Objectives and its topic must align with a content pillar (see ▶ Chap. 5).

It is also worthwhile revisiting the 4 Models of Public Relations Practice: Press Agentry/Publicity, Public Information, Two-Way Asymmetrical, Two-Way Symmetrical explored in ▶ Chap. 12 because these theoretical approaches can help to solidify the purpose of the written piece in line with strategic goals and objectives (Grunig, 2003).

Is the goal of the copy to inform, engage, promote or persuade and how does this goal align with the overall goals and objectives from the social media strategy? These are key areas to consider before writing.

14.3.2 Accuracy

As explored in ▶ Section 2, all information contained within in any written copy (created or curated) must be factually correct. Honest and truthful content is the most ethical approach to writing.

Statistical Exaggeration	Statistical Reality
75% of people love our product	**We asked 4 existing customers and 3 like our product**

Fig. 14.2 Statistical Exaggeration versus Statistical Reality

This includes avoiding the overstatement and exaggeration of flattering information about a client or organisation, omitting necessary facts that can manipulate a target audience and using statistics to share a false narrative. For example, ■ Fig. 14.2 demonstrates how the same statistics can be communicated in different ways to imply very different things.

14.3.3 Correct and Consistent Grammar, Spelling and Punctuation

Nothing looks more unprofessional and incompetent than published written copy with errors in spelling, grammar and punctuation. The aim of strategic social media management is to build trust between a target audience and a client or organisation. Sharing posts containing errors can be perceived as amateur and unreliable.

Therefore, it is essential that written copy is posted error-free. It is also important to read over published posts carefully soon after they have been posted, just to make sure errors have not slipped through, and can be amended quickly if they have.

Consistency is also a key writing principle. Some words and punctuation approaches can vary, but still technically be correct. For example, words such as "center" and "centre". In these cases, it is important

to select one variation and apply it consistently throughout the piece. Which variation to use will depend on the style adopted.

14.3.4 Style

There are four main style categories commonly attributed to writing: Expository, Descriptive, Persuasive and Narrative (England, 2019).

Expository Writing: Focused on explaining a concept or imparting specific information.

Format include recipes, instructions and How To pieces.

Descriptive Writing: More creative pieces such as poems and fictional pieces.

Persuasive Writing: These are used to encourage or inspire the audience to take some form of action such as changing their opinions or responding to a direct call-to-action.

Narrative Writing: Anecdotes and storytelling as will be explained further in this section.

Styles can sometimes overlap depending on the overall goal of the piece and the platform requirements of where it will be posted.

14.3.5 Brevity

Brevity refers to the concise use of language. In short, less is more. It is better to use fewer words to make the same point wherever possible, and this is definitely the case in a social media context. People can scroll through their feeds at fast speeds and will rarely stop to read a lengthy piece of prose. Instead it is essential to get to the point quickly in a way that cuts through other competing content to attract and hold attention.

Thorough editing is an essential practice to achieve brevity with written social media

14

Verbose Copy

If you would like to learn how to cook this recipe, you will be able to find this one and others on our website. (24 words)

Brevity

Learn to cook this recipe and others on our website. (10 words)

Fig. 14.3 Increasing brevity within social media copy

Complicated Language

The extreme dynamism of social media technology can directly facilitate a two-way communication model.

Clear Language

Social media supports conversations.

Fig. 14.4 Complicated versus Clear Language

copy, as explained in the Copywriting Process further in this chapter. It is fine to be verbose with a first draft, but then it is important to edit ruthlessly. ❑ Figure 14.3 demonstrates how social media copy can be edited to increase brevity.

14.3.6 Clarity

Clear writing removes anything that can be misunderstood, for example, ambiguous language, jargon and acronyms. The best writers can communicate to a wide range of audiences.

Using complicated words may demonstrate a wide vocabulary, but this is ineffective if the target audience does not understand what they mean. Larger organisations can sometimes forget that internal stakeholders have their own language in terms of organisation-centric words and concepts.

These terms must be defined, simplified and translated to an audience if they are unfamiliar.

Clarity also relates to making the subject prominent and removing redundant and unnecessary filler words. Again, ruthless editing is the key.

❑ Figure 14.4 demonstrates the difference between complicated and clear language.

14.3.7 Structure

The structure of social media copy will be influenced by the specific character restrictions of each platform, but that does not mean that it has to curb creativity. For example, a long form piece could not be posted within a single tweet due to Twitter's 280 character limit (Perez, 2018).

Instead, if the entire story could not be communicated in one tweet, it would need to be written so that it could be understood by the target audience through a series of tweets.

Structure also refers to the formation of words to create sentences and the arrangement of sentences to construct the overall piece. Writing should flow and should have a particular rhythm relevant to the message conveyed. Provost (2019, p. 58) demonstrates how sentence length and structure can impact the rhythm and flow of written copy with the following statement:

» This sentence has five words. Here are five more words. Five-word sentences are fine.

» But several together become monotonous. Listen to what is happening. The writing is getting boring. The sound of it drones. It's like a stuck record. The ear demands some variety.

» Now listen. I vary the sentence length, and I create music. Music. The writing sings. It has a pleasant rhythm, a lilt, a harmony. I use short sentences. And I use sentences of medium length. And sometimes when I am certain the reader is rested, I will engage him with a sentence of considerable length, a sentence that burns with energy and builds with all the impetus of a crescendo, the roll of the drums, the crash of the cymbals - sounds that say listen to this. It is important.

» So write with a combination of short, medium and long sentences. Create a sound that pleases the reader's ear. Don't just write words. Write music.

Reading your work aloud is an effective way to test the structure and rhythm of written copy. In most cases, a sentence is too long if you run out of breath before finishing it. Pay close attention to structure. Use it to both command the reader's attention, create an impact and increase sense-making.

14.3.8 Narrative

Narrative is another word for storytelling. In ► Chap. 6 we explored how storytelling can build a deep emotional connection with a brand, a cause or an organisation. As will be explored in greater detail throughout ► Section 3, stories can be communicated on social media through written copy, imagery and video. A story does not need to be lengthy in terms of word count. A story can be communicated in one sentence if written well.

◘ Figure 14.5 demonstrates a one-sentence stories that could work on social media.

◘ **Fig. 14.5**   A One-Sentence Story

— For a story to work it must contain the necessary components as discussed in ► Chap. 6:
— Setting
— Character
— Plot
— Conflict
— Theme
— Point-of-view
— Tone
— Style

Furthermore, a narrative structure is recommended to have a beginning, rising action, climax, falling action and resolution as per Freytag's Pyramid (also explored in ► Chap. 6) as this helps to sustain the audience's attention and is a familiar structure to do so.

It may seem a challenging feat to include in a single tweet but should be considered when writing any social media copy to help it to be structurally sound for the target audience.

Words can be tremendously influential and have the power to evoke a particular mood, scene, emotion and feeling through storytelling. The correct adjectives used when describing a food product can make someone feel hungry. It is essential to approach the creation (and curation) of all content as a storyteller not merely as someone sharing information. It is up to a Social Media Manager to bring that information to life for a client's or organisation's target audience through the strength of their writing.

14.3.9 Tone of Voice and Brand Personality

Writing is the perfect opportunity to capture and communicate a brand's voice and personality. A great example of this is a chatbot. When the script is well-written according to branding guidelines, a chatbot can facilitate a rich conversation between individuals from the target audience and a brand by bringing it to life.

Consistency is the key and it is a helpful practice to create a brand persona (similar to the customer persona developed in ► Chap. 3) to use as a guide. It helps to personify the brand and can provide a list of favourite words and terms relevant to the brand personality that can be used in social media copy.

A brand can be fun, cheeky or more mature and authoritative and this must be consistently demonstrated in all forms of communication including via social media.

14.3.10 Key Message/s and Call-to Action

Also discussed in ► Chap. 5 social media copy must be very clear about the key message/s that it is attempting to convey to the target audience and exactly what each piece of content is asking the audience to do. Less is more in relation to key messages.

In a shorter piece, only include one to avoid confusing the audience with too much information. Always lead with the most important information. It is risky to assume the reader will make it through the entire piece. ◘ Figure 14.6 demonstrates a comparison between a punchy piece of content and a wordier more confusing piece.

Calls-to-Action

E.g. 1. Wordy

If you have nothing to do this weekend and feel like doing something new, why don't you come down and see us at our new store in Buderim, on the Sunshine Coast.

E.g. 2. Punchy

At a loose end this weekend? Visit our new Buderim store on the beautiful Sunshine Coast.

◘ **Fig. 14.6** Wordy versus Punchy Calls-To-Action

14.3.11 Lead Strongly

The first sentence, also known as the lead, is the most important part of social media Copy. A well-written lead will hook the audience to read more. Even if a visual element first attracts the audience's attention; it is the first line of the written copy that can sustain it. Blogs are the only exception.

With blogs, the headline is the key to attracting audience attention, but the lead follows closely in second place. Blog writing will be covered in greater detail further in this chapter.

The most compelling leads are succinct and cut through the noise of competing content. They can make a strong or controversial statement that inspires the target audience to stop scrolling, read further and feel connected to a brand.

Asking a highly relevant (and rarely asked) question can be effective, but it must identify a common challenge experienced by the target audience (◘ Fig. 14.7).

The term 'BREAKING NEWS' can also grab attention, but it must accurately reflect the information being shared (◘ Fig. 14.8).

Humour can also work but test it before posting to ensure it does not offend or fall flat (◘ Fig. 14.9).

An effective lead sentence must not promise something that it does not deliver. The ability to interrupt attention should not be abused. That is the best way to damage trust with the target audience, which is the opposite to strategic social media management.

◘ **Fig. 14.7** Leading with a Question

Fig. 14.8   Breaking News Lead

Fig. 14.9   Humour Lead

14.3.12 ...See More

A lead must be so compelling that it the target audience cannot resist but click on "... See more" to read the entire post. The first few lines of posts on platforms such as Facebook and LinkedIn just before the "... See more" fold are absolutely crucial in hooking the reader into committing to read the rest of the piece.

Copy that can prompt such an action from the target audience is powerful. There may be a number of approaches to achieve this such as:

- Making a controversial statement and promising to list the reasons for it.

- Hinting that a secret will be shared further down the post.
- Asking a question.
- Beginning a personal story that leaves the audience wanting to know more.

As mentioned in ▶ Chap. 5, the key is to make the target audience care enough that they want to know more. If writing a longer post, the lines before the "See more" fold must be approached strategically. Never assume the audience will automatically want to read the entire piece. Work hard in inspiring them to do so.

14.3.13 Audience Appropriateness

Audience appropriateness means writing copy that is both relevant and acceptable to a specific group in relation to its culture, education, religion, geography or age etc. offending an audience is always best avoided for obvious reasons.

While it is essential to use language that the audience is familiar with and can understand simply, written content must delve even deeper to evoke positive emotions, feelings and actions. This is why in-depth audience research is required so that a Social Media Manager can create copy that resonates with the people with whom they are trying to connect.

Language can be powerful. Particular words can hurtle people back to their childhood or remind them of a special day such as their wedding or graduation. However, understanding an audience to this depth requires the level of research detailed in ▶ Chap. 3 of this book. ◻ Figure 14.10 demonstrates the difference between social media copy that is audience-appropriate and copy that is not.

It is always a good idea to test social media copy with a few members of the target audience to ensure that it can be clearly understood and is appropriate for the specific group's demographic and psychographic characteristics.

Social Media Copy for Retirees

Inappropriate for Audience

**Don't make the fam salty these hols.
Ensure your gifts are lit.**

Audience Appropriate

**Don't upset the family these holidays.
How to pick the perfect gift.**

◘ **Fig. 14.10** The Difference Between Audience Appropriate and Inappropriate Copy

14.3.14 SEO

SEO is also aligned to the principle of audience appropriateness. Using relevant language and terms can be of even greater use than purely sense-making. Incorporating the terms that a target audience will use when searching for a client, brand, organisation or related product or service can also generate connections and engagement (Giomelakis & Veglis, 2019). Tools such as Google Search Console and SEM Rush (explore them in the Helpful Links section) are helpful tools to identify popular keywords relating to a client's business or an organisation that can be then incorporated into social media copy. This does not mean stuffing written copy with search terms. It means using relevant words that fit naturally within a sentence. Learning how to write copy that connects with target audiences on a range of levels is a useful skill to develop as a Social Media Manager.

14.3.15 Social Media Platform Suitability

Platform suitability is extremely important in terms of social media copy. Pushing the same content out across different platforms without optimising it for the specific characteristics of each one is strongly discouraged.

Each platform has its own content specifications and unique audience. Written content (or any content) should never be approached as one-size-fits-all, as will be further explored later in this chapter.

Of course, it is fine to begin with a base piece of content, but it must be tweaked to suit each platform in order to give it the best chance of performing well.

◘ Figure 14.11 demonstrates what can happen when posting the same content across different social media platforms.

14.4 The Copywriting Process

Great social media copy rarely happens by chance, particularly for those new to content creation. Some people have a natural writing ability, but generally, strong copywriting skills are the result of considerable training, effort, and practice over a long-term period. Learning to write well is a continuous and challenging journey.

However, there are five common stages that are recommended to support the development of text-based social media content as demonstrated in ◘ Fig. 14.12 and explained in ◘ Table 14.1 With experience, the time it takes to work through these stages may be reduced, but the steps will.

These steps are further explained in ◘ Table 14.1.

14.5 Writing for Specific Social Media Channels

The writing advice and guidelines in this section are social media platform-specific and accurate at the time of writing. As highlighted many times throughout this text, social media changes rapidly, so it is important to stay abreast of any platform changes. Advice on how to approach this is detailed in ▶ Chap. 17.

■ **Fig. 14.11**　Example of a Post Pushed from Instagram to Facebook without Tweaking it to suit the Platform

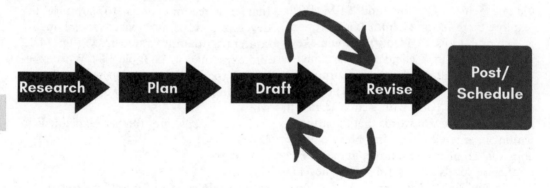

■ **Fig. 14.12**　The Stages of the Social Media Copywriting Process

14

When creating written copy, it is vital to remember the "social" in social media. Cold corporate writing does not belong on a social network. While it is important to be professional, writing for social channels should be focused on being conversational, chatty, and friendly. Clearly, writing must align with the brand voice. However, even serious topics can be presented in an approachable and engaging way to prompt discussion without minimising the message.

Further in this chapter we will explore platform character limits and recommendations. These are only a guide. Sometimes copywriting rules can be broken in certain situations.

Table 14.1 Definitions of the social media copywriting process stages

Copywriting stage	Description

1. Research	Similarly, to the social media strategy development process, the first stage of developing written content must involve research. The piece must be researched to ensure all information is interesting and accurate
	
	The research stage must also involve revisiting the social media strategy (and additional sources) to determine if the content being proposed directly aligns with the:
	  Goals
	  At least one SMART objective
	  Audience
	  Platform, and
	  Key messages
	Additionally, research can be a powerful tool to provide ideas and inspiration for what to write leading into the second stage of copywriting

2. Plan	The planning stage involves drawing on the information gathered in stage one to brainstorm and plan the written piece
	Stage one provided the strategic parameters within which the written content must work. Stage two promotes the further development of ideas and concepts within those parameters
	The planning stage also requires the identification of the:
	  Key point/s to cover.
	  The length (character count) of the post.
	  Structure of the piece
	  Style and tone (see ▶ Chap. 5)
	  Call-to-action
	  Accompanying visual elements
	Having this information and detail ready makes it much less challenging when beginning stage 3

3. Draft	With a solid idea of what to write and its necessary structure, the drafting stage is where this information is used to make it a reality The drafting stage is clearly the most creative, which may also be perceived as the most challenging This stage of the copywriting process will be daunting if trying to write a perfect piece of content on the first attempt. Approaching copywriting in this way usually results in performance anxiety leading to procrastination One of the best pieces of writing advice ever given is: "Make a mess and clean it up," (William G. Perry Jr. in Bolker, 1998, p. 33) With writing, logically, it is easier to work with something rather than nothing. What is most important is to lay down some words as a starting point so that they can be polished and reworked to develop the piece of content required Sometimes the drafting process may result in content of questionable quality initially. However, the action of writing can help to unblock barriers that result in it flowing easily The only writer's block is not beginning in the first place If there is time during the writing phase, it is recommended to draft the same piece of content in several ways. It is rare for the first attempt to be the best one

(continued)

■ Table 14.1 (continued)	
Copywriting stage	Description
4. Revise	This is where the content written in the previous stage is edited or "cleaned up" so that it is fit for purpose. It is recommended that stages 3 and 4 are undertaken more than once when drafting a piece of written content
	Writing is a process of tinkering and polishing before it leaps from the screen with a life of its own. It is also recommended to test content with at least someone from the target audience before posting it publicly to ensure that it is pitched correctly
	When revising content, it should be checked for the following:
	Accuracy
	Grammar, punctuation, spelling and syntax.
	Brevity. Is the copy succinct and punchy.
	Brand voice. Does the copy embody the correct tone? Is it playful or entertaining?
	Suitability for the social media platform
	Audience suitability. Does it use terms and language that the target audience will understand?
	Clarity of call-to-action
	Alignment with the strategic elements identified in the research and planning stage
	Measurement. How will the success of this content be evaluated?
	Suitability with visual elements. Together do they communicate a consistent message?
	Quality of accompanying textual elements: Links, hashtags, alt text and closed captions.
	With these elements addressed (multiple times) and the final draft achieved, the last stage in the process is to post or schedule the content
5. Post/schedule	While this stage involves sending pieces of written content out into the world, the process does not end here
	When posting or scheduling, preview what the post looks like first because further edits may be required to optimise the content for the platform. Social media sites change regularly
	Also, sometimes content can be formatted differently once uploaded to a specific platform
	Once the content has been posted, then it is important to monitor its performance to ensure that it is working as intended (see ▶ Chap. 7). Sometimes further editing can be required when a piece of content has already been posted if it is not resonating with the target audience

14

■ ■ **Please Note**

Sprout Social has created a helpful tool to gauge character length when writing social media copy for mainstream platforms. Please see the Helpful Links section for details.

14.5.1 🅕 **Facebook**

Facebook offers a wide range of formats where written copy can be used to engage with audiences on personal profiles, business pages and within groups.

14.5.1.1 Written Copy Categories

━ Status Updates
━ Comments
━ Image captions
━ Video captions
━ Facebook Stories
━ Instant Articles
━ Facebook Messenger
━ Advertisement

14.5.1.2 Maximum Characters

- **Posts:** 63,205 characters (Social Report, 2018).
- **Ads** (except Carousel ads):
  - Text – 90 characters,
  - Headline – 25 characters,
  - Link Description – 30 characters.
  - Carousel ads: Text – 90 characters, Headline – 40 characters Description – 20 characters (Johnson, 2018).
- Facebook username character limit: 50 characters
- Facebook Page Description: 155 Characters
- Facebook Comments: 8000 Characters
- Messaging (63,206 character limit)

14.5.1.3 Recommended Character Length

- 40–50 characters.

How long is 80 characters? This entire line is exactly 80 characters. Brief huh?

14.5.1.4 Hashtags

Use hashtags scarcely, 1–3 at an absolute maximum. Never push a post to Facebook from Instagram that has scores of hashtags. It is not aesthetically pleasing for the audience. Make sure that hashtags are chosen strategically to reach a target audience.

14.5.1.5 Emojis

The use of emojis on Facebook have been linked to "have positive relations with the number of shares," (Chang & Tseng, 2020, p.159). Therefore, including at least one relevant emoji with text is recommended. Even warnings can include emojis to attract audience attention, for example: ⚠️ ⚠️

14.5.1.6 Links

Facebook's main aim is to keep users within the platform for as long as possible. Therefore, including links in organic posts may reduce reach because they are encour-aging users to go elsewhere. It is worth experimenting by posting links to external web pages in the first comment to assess how it affects post reach (Lozano, 2019). It is different with advertisements and boosted post because they offer the option to include a link.

14.5.2 Rules Can Be Broken with a Large and Highly Engaged Audience

It must also be stated from the outset that some rules can be broken, but only in specific circumstances. Generally, people who do not comply with the platform rules recommended in this chapter already have a large and highly engaged audience, so they do not need to. Social Media Influencers have seemingly earned the right to create the content as they please without it affecting reach or engagement.

For example, when building a brand and following on Instagram, it is recommended to use a range of relevant hashtags (up to 30 are allowed) on posts to increase exposure of content to relevant users from a client's or organisation's target audience (Rosli & Husin, 2019). However, brands with a considerable following tend to use only branded hashtags or none at all. This is due to the brand already having a strong influence, and a large and engaged audience, so that it can rely on these alone for reach. Therefore, building a following such as this can be challenging in the beginning without the strategic use of hashtags.

Additionally, less is more is the recommended approach for Facebook copy. Facebook posts with 80 characters or less have been found to receive 66% more reach than lengthier posts (Bullas, 2018). To further confirm this, Facebook has limited the amount of text allowed in advertisements to three lines only (Facebook, 2019b). Yet, some influencers write amazing copy that breaks this convention. Their posts can be lengthy but contain space between sentences to assist with readability and convey a compelling story. Longer posts work well for them because again, they have developed and facilitated a large and engaged community around their brand and their written content is of an extremely high quality. If the content is exceptional and has a large and engaged audience, recommended character lengths will not apply.

For example, branding expert at BrandedMedia.io, Jeff J Hunter, regularly posts longer-form Facebook content usually conveying a personal story or opinion on a highly contentious topic and still generates significant levels of reach and engagement. ◙ Figure 14.13 is an example of one of Jeff J Hunter's best performing Facebook posts for 2019. This post vastly exceeds the recommended character limit. However, the number of likes and comments indicates that the post clearly resonated with the target audience enough to generate a strong level of engagement.

Jeff J Hunter explains his strategic motivation for this post:

» The reason why I did that "Defriend Me" post was to solidify my audience. It does three things. Firstly, by saying my friends list is full, it raises the awareness of me being popular and increases the value of my friends list. Then by defining my characteristics about who I am or what I am to give people excuses or reasons to unfriend me, what I am actually doing is solidifying and strengthening my base. Finally, it develops my "know, like and trust factor" by being authentic.

Clearly, in some circumstances platform recommendations can be contravened without consequence. When creating content for a new client or organisation, it is advised to work within the platform conventions first to test the performance of content with the target audience. Over time, as a Social Media Manager, you will learn more about what works well with an audience and what falls flat (see ► Chap. 7). Once, an audience is better understood, then it may be possible to

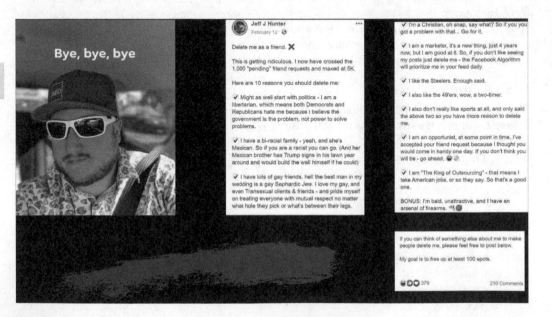

◙ **Fig. 14.13**   Jeff J Hunter Long-Form Facebook Post

experiment gradually to gauge the response, particularly in terms of post length.

Knowing the rules before you break them can be an effective way of approaching copywriting for social media. Now it is time to learn the rules.

14.5.3 Twitter

The textual capabilities on Twitter are much less compared with other platforms, but these limits require content creators to be succinct and punchy with written copy to get to the point without verbose explanations. Every tweet must be written as a lead.

14.5.3.1 Written Copy Categories and Maximum Characters

- Tweets (280 characters)
- Replies (280 characters not including @ names)
- Retweets (280 characters)
- Direct Messages (Up to 10, 000 characters).

14.5.3.2 Recommended Character Length

Tweets between 71 and 100 characters have been reported to generate the greatest engagement and 16% more retweets than longer posts (The Social Report, 2018). *How long is 71 characters you ask me? This line is 71 characters long. This with the one above is 100.*

14.5.3.3 Hashtags

Again, three at most works well. More than three looks spammy. Twitter hashtags are recommended to be a single word or a few letters that are under six characters is length (Shelyner, 2018).

14.5.3.4 Emojis

The use of emojis in tweets have been found to benefit brands by increasing audience engagement therefore it is recommended to use one or two relevant emojis in tweets where appropriate (Mathews & Lee, 2018).

14.5.3.5 Links

Including a link within a tweet can be an effective way to direct a target audience to more information about a brand or organisation. However, studies have indicated that links within tweets reduce the likelihood that it will be liked and/or retweeted (Pancer & Poole, 2016).

While Madalyn Skalr's tweet in ▪ Fig. 14.14 uses more than the recommended character length, the copy contains an effective balance of commentary, hashtags, an emoji and tags of other organisations to generate engagement.

14.5.4 Instagram

Despite Instagram being predominantly an image-based social media platform, text plays an important role in conveying infor-

▪ **Fig. 14.14** Twitter Written Copy Example

mation about a brand, helping content to reach its intended audience and building relationships with them.

14.5.4.1 Written Copy Categories and Maximum Characters

- Image Caption (2200 characters)
- Hashtags (30 hashtags)
- Bio (150 characters)
- Username (30 characters)
- Story Text
- Comments (2200 characters)
- Replies
- IGTV captions

14.5.4.2 Recommended Characters

Similarly, to 'See more…' on Facebook and LinkedIn, Instagram only allows for 125 characters before '…more'. Therefore, it is recommended that captions (or at least the first line) are 125 characters or less so that they can be seen in their entirety in the main feed (The Social Report, 2018).

125 characters allow much greater opportunity to communicate with text compared with recommendations for Twitter and Facebook.

Long form captions are becoming popular, but the lead must be strong, interesting and concise to compel the audience to click '…more'.

14.5.4.3 Hashtags

Speculation abounds in relation to best-practice use of hashtags on Instagram. Some of the key discussions and advice are as follows:

- **How many**

  When building an audience, it is perfectly acceptable to use a range of hashtags relevant to the audience as a tactic to increase exposure. Experiment to see what works for a specific client and their audience. When an audience is over 10 k followers and highly engaged, using a maximum of three hashtags is recommended.

- **The best hashtags to use**

  The best hashtags are those that are relevant to a client, organisation, brand, products, services and target audience. Hashtags should be used strategically. If a strategic goal is to encourage people in a particular town to visit a store, use the hashtags most like to put a client's content in front of people from that town. Using popular hashtags such as #love might result in more likes, but few of those will be from the target audience.

- **Hashtags in Caption or Comments**

  A recent study conducted by Social Insider and Quuu of 649,895 posts from over 6700 accounts found that "…profiles up to 100 k followers have a better Reach Rate when using hashtags in the caption and profiles with more than 100 k followers have a better Reach Rate when posting their hashtags in comments, (Lozan, 2019).

14.5.4.4 Emojis

Using emojis in captions, comments and bios have been found to have a positive impact on consumer perceptions and decision-making (Xavier, 2018). Using emojis on Instagram is highly recommended.

14.5.4.5 Links

The use of functional links on Instagram is limited to:
- Bio
- Advertisements Instagram Stories for profiles with more than 10 k followers

This example from India digital marketing agency, MediaTribe uses relevant text and hashtags and does not use hashtags excessively.

14.5.5  LinkedIn

As a professional social media channel, Linked in offers a wide range of options for written copy.

14.5.5.1 Written Copy Categories and Maximum Characters (Johnson, 2019)

- **Profile**
  - First Name (20 characters)
  - Last Name (40 characters)
  - Professional Headline (120 characters)
  - Vanity URL: 29IM (Instant Message) (25 characters)
  - Address (1000 characters)
  - Website Anchor Text (30 characters)
  - Website URL (256 characters)
  - Phone number (25 characters)
- **Profile Sections**
  - Summary (2000 characters)
  - Experience Section Position Title (100 characters)
  - Experience Section Position Description (2000 characters)
  - Skills (Per Skill) (80 characters)
  - Publication Title (250 characters)
  - Publication Description (2000 characters)
- **Status Updates**
  - Profile (1300 characters)
  - Company (700 characters)
- **Articles**
  - Headline (100 characters)
  - Post Body Text (110,000 characters)
  - Image or Photo Credit (Under Article Image) (250 characters)
- **Groups**
  - Discussion Subject Title (200 characters)
  - Discussion Body (Thread) (2000 characters)
  - Discussion Comments (1000 characters)
  - Discussion Subject (2000 characters)
- **Recommendation** (3000characters)
- **Company Page**
  - Name (100 characters)
  - About Us (2000 characters)
  - Status Update (700 characters)
- **Showcase Page**
  - Name (100 characters)
  - Description (200 characters)
- **Career Page**
  - Page Name (50 characters)
  - Company Leaders Headline (150 characters)
  - Company Leaders Description (150 characters)
  - Employee Testimonial (400 characters)
  - Custom Module Title (150 characters)
  - Custom Module Body (500 characters)
  - Custom Module URL Label (70 characters)

14.5.5.2 Recommended Characters

As discussed, LinkedIn hides any copy over 140 characters on status updates, replacing it with the 'See more...' fold. Therefore, the post lead must inspire the reader to want to read the rest. Shelyner (2018) recommends 25 words or less to keep within these limits.

Have you ever wondered what 140 characters looks like on LinkedIn? It requires content creators to write in a disciplined and concise manner.

Yet, over the past few years, longer form status updates have become more prevalent. These posts have well-spaced copy and incorporate emojis and hashtags and tag other users and organisations that helps to increase reach. Please see ◘ Fig. 14.15 for an example of longer form posts.

LinkedIn articles 1900–2000 words in length have been reported to perform the best in terms of views, likes, comments and shares (Shelyner, 2018).

14.5.5.3 Hashtags

Using relevant hashtags at the bottom of a LinkedIn status update can be an effective way to gain exposure in a specific industry area. Using no more than three industry-specific hashtags allows for people interested in those areas to view content using that tag. Furthermore, sometimes content using a hashtag can 'trend' resulting in everyone connected to the content owner being notified about the content trending. See ◘ Fig. 14.15 as an example.

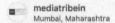
mediatribein
Mumbai, Maharashtra

Liked by **thisismaheshj** and **others**

mediatribein A very happy 73rd Independence Day to everyone. 🇮🇳
Not just today, but it's everyday, we realize that we feel extremely proud and privileged to call ourselves Indians. Jai Hind. 🇮🇳 #happyindependenceday #happyindependenceday2019 #independenceday #independencedayindia

🔲 **Fig. 14.15**   Instagram Post Copy Example

14.5.5.4 How Emojis Can Help with Personal Branding on LinkedIn

On LinkedIn, emojis can be used effectively as a way to communicate a personal brand. LinkedIn influencer, String Nguyen (see her interview at the end of ► Chap. 15) believes that selecting one emoji to signify your personal brand can help people to remember it (O'Brien, 2019).

String uses a fried chicken emoji to denote her personal brand,

» It's like my digital signature. That's the power of personal branding if you get it right, and it's like a visual anchor for me as well. Every time you think of fried chicken, you will think of String, String said in an article on the topic (O'Brien, 2019).

However, caution is recommended. LinkedIn is a professional network and it is better to be perceived as competent rather than cute. Emojis are a great way to demonstrate a brand but use them sparingly or as functional pieces with text. 🔲 Figure 14.16 demonstrates how emojis can be used as bullet points in a post the break up text.

Dr Karen Sutherland
Social Media Educator, Author, Researcher & Consultant at the University of th...
1mo • Edited

Have you ever had a client meeting like this? Today, University of the Sunshine Coast's Social Media Management students delivered a Work In Progress presentation to their clients in our Cave facility.

🔺 Students are halfway through implementing a six week campaign live on their clients' social media channels.

🔺 Results students have achieved for their clients have been positive. Here are some of the stats: bookings through Facebook up from 5 to 70, 3-second video views increased by 112233% (seriously) and a Facebook Ad Cost Per Result (CPR) down to $0.07 all in the last three weeks.

🔺 Congratulations to our hardworking Social Media Management students. You are definitely demonstrating your knowledge, skills and impact.

🔺 Thank you to our amazing clients Zen Chi Natural Therapies, Triple Zero Property, Macneil & Co. , Dolphin Marine, The Sunflower Hotel and musician, Moana, for helping students to learn this semester.

🔺 Also, a big thank you to USC Australia and to Dennis Yu from BlitzMetrics for supporting this initiative.

#socialmedia #highereducation #education

to seventy in the last three weeks and

🔲 **Fig. 14.16**   Long Form LinkedIn Post with Emojis, Hashtags, and Users Tagged

14

Red triangles were used, because they align with the author's branding colours of red, black an white and are noticeable without being intrusive and diverting attention away from the written copy.

14.5.5.5 Links

LinkedIn facilitates links in posts, comments and articles. A study by Lekkas (2019) found that posting a link in the comments rather than in the post generates greater reach and a higher click-through-rate. Therefore, it is recommended to let the reader know that a link is in the comments and to post it there.

14.5.6 ▶ YouTube

Text plays an extremely important role on YouTube in enticing users to watch videos, providing information for the target audience to learn more about a brand, organisation, product or service and with searchability.

14.5.6.1 Written Copy Categories and Maximum Characters

- Channel title (100 characters)
- Channel descriptions (1000 characters)
- Video title (70 characters)
- Video descriptions (5000 characters)
- Tags (500 characters)
- Links

14.5.6.2 Recommended Characters

While YouTube video title character length is only 70 characters, it is recommended to keep it to 60 to avoid it being cut off on search pages (Becker, 2019).

This is a YouTube video title with only 60 characters, brief.

It is important to be clear and concise about what the video title is to help the audience find what they are looking for.

Video descriptions are an excellent opportunity to share further information about a brand, organisation, product or service such as links to social media handles, contact information and links to websites.

However, YouTube also has a 'SHOW MORE" function that only allows 100 characters before placing the rest past the fold. Ensure that the first 100 characters encourage the audience to find out more.

How strong are the first 100 characters in this YouTube description. Would read more or go elsewhere.

14.5.7 Primal Video's Video Descriptions Demonstrate how a Business Can Have Less AND More

Video production company, Primal Video demonstrates how written copy in the video description field on YouTube can be used to its greatest advantage. ◻ Figure 14.17 demonstrates how Primal Video has used a succinct but comprehensive lead to explain the content of the video (YouTube, 201. This video has been produced in a 'How To' format, therefore it is offering helpful advice to the viewer rather than blatantly selling its services and this is reflected in the description. Next, the description offers viewers a, "FREE GUIDE: The ULTIMATE Video Editing Process," again, offering additional helpful advice which is also a great way to gather email addresses to build a database of people interested in the brand.

Primal Video has also optimised the YouTube video description field after the 'SHOW MORE' section as ◻ Figs. 14.17, 14.18 and 14.19 demonstrate.

Primal Video uses the rest of the video description to share additional content that may be of interest to its target audience. As ◻ Fig. 14.18 demonstrates, has provided links to further videos and free trials to video production software that may be useful to its audience.

Fig. 14.17 Primal Video YouTube Video Description Lead

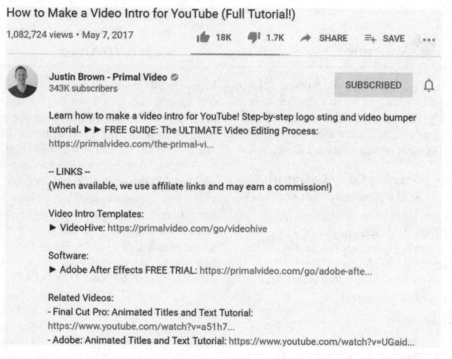

Fig. 14.18 Primal Video YouTube Video Description Part 1

Furthermore, Primal Video provides information about the equipment it uses to produce videos and the opportunity to subscribe to its newsletter while also providing a more detailed description of the original YouTube video (which is effective SEO practice to help search engines find it if people are searching for content on this topic) (■ Fig. 14.20).

Finally, Primal Video ends its description with links to further helpful resources and provides full disclosure regarding that is part of an Affiliates Program. This means that Primal Video may receive some form of

*** GEAR WE USE ***
https://primalvideo.com/gear

🔖 Join the Primal Video Accelerator waitlist: https://primalvideo.com/pvaccelerator 🔖
Learn how to build an audience, generate new leads on autopilot and SCALE your business
with video step-by-step in our fast-track Primal Video Accelerator program!

--

~ Learn the ULTIMATE Process for Editing Videos Faster (FREE DOWNLOAD):
https://primalvideo.com/the-primal-vi... ~

Subscribe to Primal Video weekly updates: https://primalvideo.com/subscribe

-- How to Make a Video Intro for YouTube (Full Tutorial!) --

Animated Video Intros are a great way to brand your videos and create a professional,
consistent image across all of your content. The best part? It's simple to make your own
youtube intro or video bumper, and you can do it all without the need to pay for expensive
software on Mac or PC!

In this video, we'll show you how to make video intros and YouTube intro templates without
the need for a specialised YouTube intro creator - and all using just a free trial of Adobe After
Effects.

▶ **Fig. 14.19** Primal Video YouTube Video Description Part 2

^^^^^^^^^^
GEAR WE USE: https://primalvideo.com/gear
Check out all the gear we use and recommend at Primal Video!
****

--- Related Content ---
- Final Cut Pro: Animated Titles and Text Tutorial: https://www.youtube.com/watch?v=a51h7...
- Adobe: Animated Titles and Text Tutorial: https://www.youtube.com/watch?v=UGaid...
- Best Live Streaming Tools to Increase Facebook Live Viewers:
https://www.youtube.com/watch?v=uwXi5...

DISCLOSURE: We often review or link to products & services we regularly use and think you might
find helpful. Wherever possible we use referral links, which means if you click one of the links in this
video or description and make a purchase we may receive a small commission or other
compensation.

We're big fans of Amazon, and many of our links to products/gear are links to those products on
Amazon. We are a participant in the Amazon Services LLC Associates Program, an affiliate
advertising program designed to provide a means for us to earn fees by linking to Amazon.com and
related sites.

Category   Film & Animation

SHOW LESS

▶ **Fig. 14.20** Primal Video YouTube Video Description Part 3

commission if someone purchases a product after they have referred it. This is highly ethical practice on behalf of Primal Video (see ▶ Chap. 4 for more information about ethical social media practice).

14.5.7.1 Hashtags

When uploading a YouTube video, there is space to provide tags. If you want a client's videos to be found by the target audience, they need relevant tags added into this section. Tags also help to design user preferences within the platform (Tiwari, Jain, Kothari, Upadhyay, & Singh, 2018). Overlooking this step in the process will dramatically reduce the video's reach. It is worth using the SEO tools (please see the Helpful Links section) to identify the key terms that people are using when searching for information relating to a client or organisation (Lockwood, 2018). Use those keywords as tags to assist the audience in finding you sooner.

14.5.7.2 Emojis

At time of writing, emojis are not part of the YouTube platform but a plugin such as Tube Buddy can allow emojis to be added to copy.

14.5.7.3 Links

Live links can be included in the video channel About section and in video descriptions.

14.5.8 ● Snapchat

Snapchat is predominantly a platform for snackable visual content, but there are some textual elements worth exploring.

14.5.8.1 Written Copy Categories and Maximum Characters

- Chat
- Text over snaps (80 characters)

- Advertisements
  - Brand Name (25 characters)
  - Headline: (34 characters)

This line of text is 80 characters. Do you think it's an ample length for a snap.

14.5.8.2 Hashtags

Hashtags on Snapchat are not functional as they are on other platforms in terms of grouping like content together. Instead they are used as more of a statement e.g. #delicious.

14.5.8.3 Emojis

The use of emojis on Snapchat is highly recommended. One study suggested that the use of emojis on Snapchat "...encourages follower engagement, but also helps garner a sense of community..." (Gkoni, Edo, Bollen, & Ecott, 2017).

14.5.8.4 Links

Adding a link to a snap is possible by clicking on the paperclip icon and typing in the URL (◘ Fig. 14.21).

14.5.9 ● TikTok TikTok

Another visual-based platform. Yet, text still plays a role in the facilitation of video descriptions, bio and two-way interaction between creators and audiences.

14.5.9.1 Written Copy Categories and Maximum Characters (Stelzner, 2019)

- Bio (150 characters)
- Video Captions (140 characters)
- Comments
- Direct Messages
- On Videos

14.5.9.2   Recommended Characters

The 150 character limitation on bios encourages Social Media Managers to describe their client or organisation concisely.

Furthermore, the 150 character limit on video captions also includes hashtags so content creators must find a balance between describing their video and including highly relevant hashtags to increase its reach.

145 character limits do not allow for verbose ramblings. Instead, it requires succinct writing. Together these sentences are 150 characters.

14.5.9.3   Hashtags

On TikTok, hashtags can greatly assist in reaching target audiences. Again, using relevant hashtags is most effective. However, the 150 character limit does not allow for many to be used in a video description, therefore, it is important to choose wisely.

14.5.9.4   Emojis

Emojis can be used in all types of TikTok content and are recommended as they align with the fun, highly creative and younger age demographic of the majority of TikTok users.

14.5.9.5   Links

URLs are not functional on TikTok however including a web address may prompt users to leave the platform to search for the site (Stelzner, 2019) (■ Fig. 14.22).

Indian digital marketing leader, Digital Pratik uses the caption on his TikTok video to hook the reader to watch until the end includes a range of personally branded hashtags along with those relating to the video topic. Digital Pratik also uses emojis in his caption. At the time of writing, this specific video had received 1.7 million views.

14.5.10   Weibo

Weibo is a micro-blogging site and one of China's largest social media platforms and has similar functions to other platforms originating in the West including posts, videos and stories.

14.5.11   Written Copy Categories and Maximum Characters

- Posts
- Stories

◻ **Fig. 14.22** Example of Tik Tok Video Caption from Digital Pratik

- Comments
- Text on Stories
- Direct Messages

Weibo does not have character limits on posts anymore. However, only the first 140 characters will be shown before a "full text" fold requires the user to click to read more (Wang, 2018).

14.5.11.1 Hashtags

On Weibo, hashtags have the same function as social media platforms originating in the West, but they are structured differently with a # at the beginning and the end, for example: #weibo# (Wang, 2018). The use of hashtags is highly recommended.

14.5.11.2 Emojis

Emojis feature prominently on Weibo by users as another form of expression. Brands using have also been reported to experience higher performing content than those not using emojis in their posts (Li, Guntuku, Jakhetiya, & Ungar, 2019; Li, Rzepka, & Araki, 2018).

14.5.11.3 Links

Links can be added to most content on Weibo including posts and business functions (Wan, 2019).

14.5.12 Blogs

Regular blog posts can be an effective SEO tactic by keeping content fresh on what may otherwise be a static website (Barbar & Ismail, 2019). Blog writing is a worthwhile skill for a Social Media Manager to have and can be a useful way to repurpose content for a range of platforms.

Approached in a conversational style, in the same may as other social media copy, blogs have specific characteristics that help to engage and inform a target audience.

Blogs are an effective technique to share curated content with audiences as explored in ► Chap. 12. They help to share new knowledge while linking through to existing content as supporting evidence.

14.5.12.1 Recommended Length

Various studies have suggested longer-form blog posts perform better than shorter pieces in terms of views and shares. The best performing blog post length is between 1000–3000 words (Moogan, 2015; Patel, 2019). However, it must be quality content, or it will not perform at all.

14.5.12.2 Topics

Blog posts that are focused on providing helpful information to the target audience work extremely well. Lists of items, How To articles, Explainers, Reviews as great examples of content that may be helpful to a target audience.

Conducting thorough audience research as explained in ► Chap. 3 will provide an in-depth insight into the challenges that a target audience may face and the content that could assist them.

14.5.12.3 Format

The following techniques should be used when writing blog copy:

Brief and Literal Headline: The headline must give the reader a clear indication of what the blog post is about. Six words or less is the recommended length. The headline is usually what grabs an audience's attention and helps them to decide whether to read further.

Strong Lead: The first line in a blog post must sum up the entire post in one sentence. It must include the Who, What, Where, When, How and Why of what is to follow all neatly wrapped up in a sentence.

For example,

» If you're just starting out on social media (or would like to understand what all of the fuss is about), here is a list of free online resources that may help, (Sutherland, 2019).

Bold Subheadings: Make the post easy for the reader to consume by including a bold subheading at the beginning of every main paragraph. This allows the reader to scroll through the post to read the main points instead of forcing the audience to read the entire piece, which is highly unlikely.

Break Up Text: Remember, people consume copy on the web in small bites. Space out the text by grouping 1–3 relevant sentences together and allowing space between each paragraph.

Lists and Bullet Points: Lists and bullet points are another effective way to organise and structure information while breaking up text into more consumable chunks for the audience.

Link from words not URLS: Avoid including URLs in a blog post. They are not aesthetically pleasing to the eye and can interrupt the flow of a piece. Instead link from 2–3 relevant words.

Include Photos and Video: Visual elements also add context for the reader and help to break up the text. However, remember to include alt-text and captions with sources for images and closed captions for video.

TLDR: It can be helpful to the reader to include a brief summary with the key points made in the post at the very beginning or as the conclusion so that time-poor audience members can understand the overall gist without having to read the entire piece.

Invite a Comment or Discussion: The best parts of a blog post can occur in the comments section. Social media is two-way and blog writing should be approached as a way to inspire discussion with and between readers. Ending the post with an invitation to the reader to leave a comment or share their thoughts is a great way to do this.

Categories and Tags: Categorising blog posts helps to organise them in relation to other pieces on a website. Tags help people to find a post when they are searching for it. Use a range of relevant tags and use the SEO keyword tools in the Helpful Links section to identify the best ones to use according to the topic of the blog post.

14.5.12.4 A Strategy to Repurpose Blog Content

Writing blog posts does not have to be a laborious task. One of the simplest ways to create a blog post and repurpose the content is:

— **Step 1:** Record an interview with an expert about a topic that will help the target audience. A video recording can be of greatest use. Even a Zoom video recording is great.

- **Step 2:** Have the interview transcribed.
- **Step 3:** Use the interview transcription to create video closed captions. Share the video on YouTube and slice it into segments for Twitter, LinkedIn, Facebook and Instagram where appropriate (more of this in ▶ Chap. 16).
- **Step 4:** Use the video transcription to create a blog post. Edit the content and add in links through to supporting content.
- **Step 5:** Use the blog post copy to create a LinkedIn article.
- **Step 6:** Use great quotes from the interview to create graphics aligning with your client's brand and citing the expert and share them across platforms according to platform specifications.

The aim of a blog is to inform the audience in a way that is most convenient for them to consume. Blogs should be highly informative and helpful, but easy to read.

An example of an extremely well-written and structured blog post is by social media leader, Peg Fitzpatrick (2019) called, *3 Savvy Ways to Make Shareable Content*.

This post has a concise but clear headline, subtitles and images to break up the text, links to helpful curated content and an invitation to the reader at the end to engage with the author.

Most importantly, it provides helpful and relevant content plus instructions on how to practically apply the information shared in the article.

Further blog writing resources are listed at the end of this chapter.

14.5.13 💬 Chatbots

A chatbot is powered by Artificial Intelligence (AI) software to provide automated and relevant answers in real-time to users asking questions through its interface for example, Facebook Messenger (Følstad, Nordheim, & Bjørkli, 2018).

When created correctly in terms of scriptwriting and function, chatbots provide a positive brand experience for customers and provide a convenient and timely solution in providing answers quickly and without impacting human resources.

When created incorrectly with an illogical script and functionality that causes the conversation to go around in circles, chatbots can cause frustration and negatively impact brand reputation.

Tools to create a chatbot are listed in the Helpful Links section. However, when writing the script for a chatbot it is important to:

- Pre-empt all of the questions that customers may ask. Research this thoroughly.
- Ensure the script sounds chatty, friendly and conversational. Test it.
- Make sure all information is correct.
- Check the logical progression of the conversation so that it makes sense. It can be helpful to create a flow chart of the conversation (Beck, 2019). See ▣ Fig. 14.23.
- Approach a chatbot as only a way to help people to begin engaging. A human customer service person must take over ASAP.

While it is important to focus on writing a natural conversational tone, a study by Følstad and Skjuve (2019, p.1) found that the "...chatbots' ability to efficiently and adequately handle enquiries..." was of greater importance to customers.

▣ Figures 14.23, 14.24, 14.25 and 14.26 demonstrate very basic examples of chatbot dialogue used to respond automatically when people make contact via Facebook messenger and then decide to opt in or out of future communication. This chatbot dialogue was developed and implemented using a tool called MobileMonkey (see the Helpful

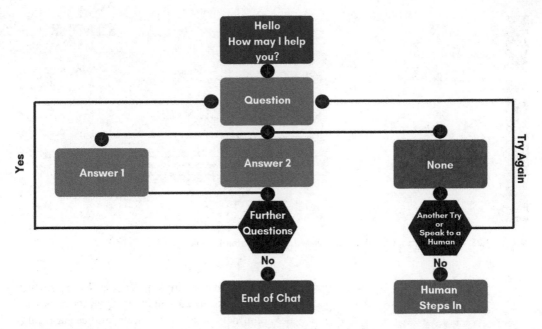

Fig. 14.23   A Flowchart of a Chatbot Conversation

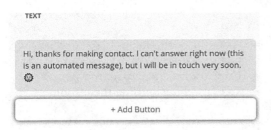

◖ **Fig. 14.24** Chatbot Facebook Page Welcome Message

Links section at the end of the chapter for details) (◖ Fig. 14.27).

14.5.14 Voice Assistants

When exploring how to write for chatbots, it is also essential to consider writing for voice assistants such as Amazon Alexa and Google Home. At the stage of writing, voice assistance search websites for answers to their owner's questions.

Voice Assistance expert, Nick Myers as cited in PR Daily explains that people tend to use long-tail keywords when using a device such as Alexa (Winchel, 2019). Long-tail keywords are very specific search terms usually containing four or more words such as "first class train travel around India" as opposed to a broader search like: "travelling in India" (Hallebeek, 2018). Therefore, to be found by a voice assistant, content creators must incorporate specific terms into written copy to increase the likelihood that their content will be found.

Furthermore, Nick Myers also recommends including a page with questions and answers on a website. Where people type search terms into a search engine, they tend to ask a voice assistant questions in complete sentences like they were speaking to a human (Winchel, 2019). Web copy should be written to reflect this so that it will increase its visibility with voice assistants when they are searching.

For example, the Government of India has a well-written Frequently Asked Questions page for its #StartUpIndia program (Government of India, 2019). It pro-

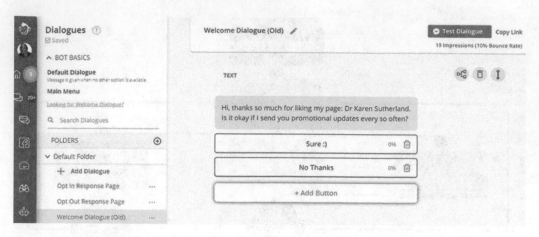

Fig. 14.25   Chatbot Response When Someone Likes a Facebook Page

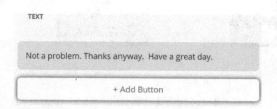

Fig. 14.26   Chatbot Response If Someone Opts Out of Receiving Further Information

Fig. 14.27   Chatbot Response If Someone Opts Into Receiving Further Information

vides clear answers to common questions that can be found easily by voice assistants such as Google Home and Amazon Alexa.

14.6 Crafting Responses to Complaints

As outlined in ▶ Chap. 4, customer complaints on social media must be addressed swiftly to avoid what may seem like a minor issue transforming into a crisis. When crafting responses to customer complaints on social channels various research studies have suggested the following approach: (Bazaarvoice, 2019; Einwiller & Steilen, 2015).

Do Not
— Ask the complainant to discuss the matter offline
— Copy and paste prepared responses
— Take too long crafting the response

Do
— Offer corrective action
— Connect the customer with someone that can offer a solution

Thank the complainant.
For example,

» Hi Jenny, I'm so sorry that your lamp is faulty. Please bring it into our Maroochydore store with your receipt and ask for Tom. He is expecting you. He will offer you a full refund or a new lamp, whatever you prefer. Thank you so much for bringing this to our attention.

Generally, customers with a complaint want to be listened to and a solution to be offered quickly and written responses must reflect this.

Conclusion

This chapter explored why text-based content is the foundation of all social media posts and the key principles required to create quality written copy. The five key stages of the copywriting process were explained, and vital topics examined including how to write a strong leading sentence and Search Engine Optimisation. Finally, essential copywriting components were analysed for the major social media platforms along with advice instructing how to write for chatbots, voice assistants and approaches to crafting responses to customer complaints.

Case Study: BabyCentre UK's Chatbot Increases Engagement Rate by 1428% Compared with Email

BabyCentre, part of the Johnson and Johnson brand family, is the world's number one digital resource for parents (b; BabyCentre, 2019a). The UK version of the website helps 8 in 10 expected mothers and has a monthly reach of 2.5 million people (BabyCentre, 2019a). BabyCentre UK also has a social media presence on Instagram, YouTube, Pinterest, Twitter and Facebook following of approximately 750 k people (Facebook, 2019b).

BabyCentre UK developed a Facebook chat with the goal of providing helpful advice in a simple way to its audience, while creating positive brand associations and strengthening customer relationships in the process.

The chatbot is highly customised to user needs and begins the conversation by asking the age of the user's child or a specific developmental phase the parent is undergoing with their child.

Each answer then moves the conversation to the next stage through the presentation of relevant content based on the user's answers.

The target audience found the chatbot to be extremely helpful, because it made finding information relevant to their own personal situation without having to trawl through websites or search engine results.

Placing the audience's needs first and providing customised, valuable and helpful content relating to parenting significantly increase the rate of traffic to the BabyCentre UK website.

The Facebook chatbot had a "84% "read" rate and a 53% CTR" or Click-Through-Rate (Siu, 2018).

Furthermore, the BabyCentre UK chatbot generated 1428% more engagement than the industry standard associated with email marketing activities (Siu, 2018; Ubisend, 2018).

A key factor in the success of the BabyCentreUK chatbot was the quality of its writing. Chatbot dialogue was clear and concise. Its tone was warm, friendly and helpful. Its automated answers logically followed the conversation without causing users to feel frustrated by not receiving the information that they were seeking.

The BabyCentre UK Facebook chatbot is an excellent example of how effective strong writing can be when coupled with AI technology. The writing was pitched accurately to the target audience and AI technology helped to customise the user experience, bringing the most relevant information to the user saving them time and effort.

1. Why do you think parents responded so positively to the BabyCentreUK chatbot?
2. What principles would you adopt from this case study and apply to the development of a chatbot for a client?

14.7   Interview: Umang Malik Aggarwal, Founder/ CEO – the Social Mango & the Tender Curve, Mumbai, India

1. **Welcome Umung. Can you please introduce yourself and let me know about your current role.**

    My name is Umung. I run two companies. The first company is the Social Mango. The Social Mango is into social media and digital marketing, so we take a client's work on a daily basis and we give them a solution for each of their digital problems. The other company is called The Tender Curve. The Tender Curve is actually an eCommerce gifting platform. The theme of the gifting items that we provide online is happiness and moderation.

2. **What do you enjoy most about working with social media?**

    Nothing is determined. The work is so broad that anything can come up anytime. And the industry is so fast, and it is so creative and innovative. I like all these factors in there.

3. **What are the greatest challenges?**

    The most challenging work will be to take up a client which has a technical background. For someone who's into marketing since a long time it takes us a lot of time to research and come out with a solution that exactly fits their needs.

4. **How do you come to work in social media? Tell me your career story.**

    When I graduated from Bristol, in the UK, I did my Masters there, I found the online world very entertaining, probably because I liked to shop a lot. I started researching the websites, the colours that they used, the platforms on social media, how they started promoting it back then. Because of that I slowly started learning on my own, and as I started progressing towards it, I started taking up tiny little work. However, my interest levelled up when I was in Australia for my MBA There I got to work with an agency, so I was 2000% sure that this is the industry that I wanted to be.

    I came back home. The work was pouring in when I came back to India. Instead of working for someone else, I thought, why not work for myself? And then we got a lot of projects, and currently we are engaging with many good clients. The feedback that we've received is extremely good. We have a success rate of over 90%.

5. **What are the three most important things that social media managers need to know about writing social media content?**

    First thing is research. Research your competitors. So, what happens is that I have a perception that my brand has this particular personality. But then as we start marketing in that way we soon realise that the audience perception of our brand is a bit different. Research plays a very crucial part along with competitor analysis. The second part would be the language. If you are targeting a B2B industry the language needs to be very crisp and precise. You cannot talk gibberish; it has to be spot on.

    The third thing that one needs to know is that the keywords that a person is using for any content they are writing. It has to be spot on again. You can use a keyword planner to make a list that suits your organisation. Be it B2B or B2C.

    Also, the content style needs to be tweaked to suit each social media platform. For Twitter it has to be a limited count and the hashtags need to be around three, maximum four. For LinkedIn as well.

6. **When social media content is written well, what do you think are the benefits?**

14.7 · Interview: Umang Malik Aggarwal, Founder/ CEO – the Social Mango ...

321

14

When content is really written well, you are indirectly telling your target audience that, "Hey, I know what business I'm into. I know how I market my stuff. I know that I'm really good at it." So, a blend of text, a nice usage of colours/creative, and videos. These three, when combined together, they go a long way. So, you have many permutations and combinations with these three elements alone. You can change your strategy on a monthly or weekly basis depending on what your status is presently, and you can come up with many options.

7. **What do you think are the challenges of writing effective social media content?**
The first challenge would be the topic. If someone is not aware of what exactly they want to get out of their blog, I think one should not write it. If you are sure this is the issue that I want to talk about today, just start writing. That is the most important thing, because picking up a topic about which you're not passionate about would not justify the blog or the content you have written. Thoroughly do your research and select the topic that you feel is very important to you, and that it would be beneficial to all the other people out there.

8. **What are your favourite tools for producing social media copy and why?**
There is an online character counter on which we actually type the content, and then we finalise it for all of the social media platforms or even for a website. If we are writing a blog, the first draught is first written on Excel, or Word normally. Then when we have to refine it more and see how much the character counts for each and every paragraph is. I don't believe in using too many tools for content writing. It must come from the mind and heart. It's only after the first draft, maybe you move on to the online tools.

9. **What do you think of the current landscape of social media management as a profession?**
We are here to stay. The Australian market is developed while the Indian market is still developing. We have many interns who come down here who have finished their diploma and they train with us. The only thing that I feel we are lagging in as of now is practical exposure for the students. In the coming five years I see this industry to be booming a lot because as of now it's gaining a lot of traction.

10. **What has been the best piece of advice you've ever been given?**
You always have a choice. If you're not getting something out what you had expected, there's always a plan B. Similarly, for social media marketing, or any client work that you get, just keep on trying. If one thing is not working, the second thing will always work.

11. **What advice would you give to someone who is trying to work in the field of social media?**
I always ask them to research a few things about social first, and then go for a diploma course, or any certification course. The more innovative and more imaginative you are in the field, the better.

❓ Questions for Critical Reflection

1. Why is text an essential component of social media content? Please explain your answer.
2. What is Search Engine Optimisation (SEO) and   does it apply to text-based social media content?
3. What is a lead in relation to copywriting and why is it important on platforms such as Facebook, LinkedIn and Instagram?
4. What are the five stages of the social media copywriting process? Please explain what happens at each stage.

5. When is it okay to break the rules in relation to written copy and social media platform character recommendations? Please provide an example.

6. Why should a blog end with an invitation to the reader to continue the conversation?

7. What points should be included when writing a response to a customer complaint on social media?

> **Practical Exercises**

1. Using the advice on blog writing from this chapter and following the five stages of the copywriting process write the copy for a brief 300 word blog post about one of your favourite topics.

2. Use the SEO/Keyword tools in the Helpful Links section to identify the most popular search terms relating to your chosen topic. Incorporate these keywords into your blog post in a logical manner.

3. With the Sprout Social Character Counter Tool (also in the Helpful Links section) craft posts with each platform's recommended character limit for Twitter, LinkedIn and Facebook promoting your blog post. Share your experiences throughout this process with the rest of the class.

14

References

BabyCentre. (2019a). About Us, *BabyCentre*, viewed: 25/11/2019: https://www.babycentre.co.uk/e1001100/about-us

BabyCentre. (2019b). BabyCentre, *Facebook*, viewed: 25/11/2019: https://www.facebook.com/BabyCentreUK

Barbar, A., & Ismail, A. (2019). Search engine optimization (SEO) for websites. In *Proceedings of the 2019 5th international conference on computer and technology applications* (pp. 51–55). ACM.

Bazaarvoice. (2019). *The Conversation Index VOLUME* 6, viewed: 06/08/2019: http://media2.bazaarvoice.com/documents/Bazaarvoice_Conversation_Index_Volume.pdf

Beck, B. (2019). How to write a script for a chatbot: Key elements for good dialogue flow, *Clear Voice*, viewed 28.09. 2019: https://www.clearvoice.com/blog/how-to-write-a-chatbot/

Becker, B. (2019). YouTube SEO: How to Optimize Videos for YouTube Search, viewed 15.11.20: https://blog.hubspot.com/marketing/youtube-seo

Bolker, J. (1998). *Writing your dissertation in fifteen minutes a day: A guide to starting, revising, and finishing your doctoral thesis*. Holt Paperbacks.

Brinkley, J., & Tabrizi, N. (2017). A Desktop usability evaluation of the Facebook mobile interface using the jaws screen reader with blind users. In Proceedings of the human factors and ergonomics society annual meeting (Vol. 61, No. 1, pp. 828–832). Sage CA: Los Angeles, CA: SAGE Publications.

Brubaker, P. J., & Wilson, C. (2018). Let's give them something to talk about: Global brands' use of visual content to drive engagement and build relationships. *Public Relations Review, 44*(3), 342–352.

Bullas, J. (2018). 10 Powerful tips to increase fan engagement on facebook, *Jeff Bullas*, viewed 27.09.2019: https://www.jeffbullas.com/10-powerful-tips-to-increase-fan-engagement-on-facebook/

Carroll, B. (2017). *Writing and editing for digital media*. Routledge.

Chang, W. L., & Tseng, H. C. (2020). The impact of sentiment on content post popularity through emoji and text on social platforms. In *Cyber influence and cognitive threats* (pp. 159–184). Academic.

Einwiller, S. A., & Steilen, S. (2015). Handling complaints on social network sites–an analysis of complaints and complaint responses on Facebook and twitter pages of large US companies. *Public Relations Review, 41*(2), 195–204.

England, J. (2019). Writing styles: How to find yours with writing style examples, *Self-Publishing School*, viewed 26.09.2019: https://self-publishingschool.com/writing-styles/

Facebook. (2019a). About text in ad images, Facebook.com, viewed 26.09.2019: https://www.facebook.com/business/help/980593475366490

Facebook. (2019b). Changes to text and aspect ratios on mobile news feed, Facebook.com, viewed 27.09.2019: https://www.facebook.com/business/help/313270659381227

Fitzpatrick, P. (2019). 3 Savvy ways to make shareable content, *Peg Fitzpatrick*, viewed: 25/11/2019: https://pegfitzpatrick.com/shareable-content/

Følstad, A., Nordheim, C. B., & Bjørkli, C. A. (2018). What makes users trust a chatbot for customer service? An exploratory interview study. In *International conference on internet science* (pp. 194–208). Cham: Springer.

Følstad, A., & Skjuve, M. (2019). Chatbots for customer service: User experience and motivation. In *Proceedings of the 1st international conference on conversational user interfaces* (p. 1). ACM.

Giomelakis, D., & Veglis, A. A. (2019). Search engine optimization. In *Advanced methodologies and technologies in network architecture, mobile computing, and data analytics* (pp. 1789–1800). IGI Global.

Gkoni, N., Edo, D., Bollen, Y., & Ecott, S. (2017). *Snapchat fams as a subculture: How influencers use emojis for commodifying cross-platform engagement* (Doctoral dissertation, Masters thesis, New Media & Digital Culture, University of Amsterdam).

Government of India. (2019). Frequently asked questions, *#StartUpIndia*, viewed: 25/11/2019: https://www.startupindia.gov.in/content/sih/en/faqs.html

Hallebeek, W. (2018). SEO basics: What are long tail keywords? *Yeost*, viewed 28.09.2019: https://yoast.com/what-are-long-tail-keywords/

Jantsch, J., & Singleton, P. (2016). *SEO for growth: The ultimate guide for marketers, web designers & entrepreneurs. SEO for Growth.* Duct Tape Press.

Johnson, E. Z. (2019). Character limits: LinkedIn 2019 + Free Download, *LinkedIn,* viewed 28.09.2019: https://www.linkedin.com/pulse/maximum-character-limits-counts-linkedin-2018-eric-johnson/

Johnson, T. (2018). Facebook Ad Specs and Image Sizes 2019 | The Easy Guide, *Tinuiti,* viewed 28.09.2019: https://tinuiti.com/blog/social/facebook-ad-specs-and-image-sizes-2018-the-easy-guide/

Lekkas, N. (2019). Linkedin Experiment: Link In Post Vs Link In Comment, *Growth Rocks,* viewed 28.09.2019: https://growthrocks.com/blog/linkedin-abtest-link-in-comment/

Li, D., Rzepka, R., & Araki, K. (2018). Preliminary Analysis of Weibo Emojis for Sentiment Analysis of Chinese Social Media. In 人工知能学会全国大会論文集 第 32 回全国大会 (2018) (pp. 1J304-1J304). 一般社団法人 人工知能学会.

Li, M., Guntuku, S., Jakhetiya, V., & Ungar, L. (2019). Exploring (dis-) similarities in emoji-emotion association on twitter and weibo. In *Companion proceedings of the 2019 world wide web conference* (pp. 461–467). ACM.

Lockwood, D. (2018). Optimise Your YouTube Title, Description, and Tags, *Bold Content Video,* viewed 28.09.2019: https://boldcontentvideo.com/2018/01/24/optimise-youtube-title-description-tags/

Lozan, T. (2019). [Instagram Hashtag Study]: 649,895 brand posts show if it's better to put Instagram hashtags in the post's caption or in the first comment, *Social Insider,* viewed 28.09.2019: https://www.socialinsider.io/blog/instagram-hashtag-study/?fbclid=IwAR3rc0_3chGZj_hngWhQ7o-674bRsGg9ptzkSjduQzDp3dHFGkCTgYfMs-Rys

Lozano, D. (2019). 5 Ways to generate more engagement (and Reach) on Facebook, *Social Media Today,* viewed 28.09.2019: https://www.socialmediatoday.com/news/5-ways-to-generate-more-engagement-and-reach-on-facebook/546515/

Marshall, C. (2018). *Writing for social media.* Swindon, UK: BCS, The Chartered Institute for IT.

Mathews, S., & Lee, S. E. (2018). Use of emoji as a marketing tool: An exploratory content analysis. *Fashion, Industry and Education, 16*(1), 46–55.

Moogan, P. (2015). How to generate content ideas using Buzzsumo (and APIs), *Moz,* viewed 28.09.2019: https://moz.com/blog/generate-content-ideas-using-buzzsumo-and-apis

O'Brien, J. (2019). LinkedIn video guru 'String' Nguyen uses fried chicken as her branding, *The Courier Mail,* 10, June, 2019: viewed: 24/11/2019: https://www.couriermail.com.au/business/linkedin-video-guru-string-nguyen-uses-fried-chicken-as-her-branding/news-story/c45a4244b3a900fa6ee4a507c2bac73d

Pancer, E., & Poole, M. (2016). The popularity and virality of political social media: Hashtags, mentions, and links predict likes and retweets of 2016 US presidential nominees' tweets. *Social Influence, 11*(4), 259–270.

Patel, N. (2019). How long should your Blog articles be? (With word counts for every industry), *Neil Patel,* viewed 28.09.2019: https://neilpatel.com/blog/long-blog-articles/

Perez, S. (2018). Twitter's doubling of character count from 140 to 280 had little impact on length of tweets, *Techcrunch,* viewed 26.09.2019: https://techcrunch.com/2018/10/30/twitters-doubling-of-character-count-from-140-to-280-had-little-impact-on-length-of-tweets/

Provost, G. (2019). This Sentence Has Five Words, viewed 15/11/20: http://www.robmacdougall.org/blog/2010/09/this-sentence-has-five-words/

Quesenberry, K. A. (2018). *Social media strategy: Marketing, advertising, and public relations in the consumer revolution.* Rowman & Littlefield.

Rosli, N. A. A., & Husin, M. H. (2019). Initial exploration on an effective social media analytics method and algorithm for instagram hashtags. *International Journal of E-Business Research (IJEBR), 15*(3), 1–15.

Shelyner, E. (2018). The ideal social media post length: A guide for every platform, *Hootsuite,* viewed 28.09.2019: https://blog.hootsuite.com/ideal-social-media-post-length

Siu, E. (2018). 9 Most innovative chatbot examples in 2019 from top brands [+ How to Build Your Own], *Impact*, viewed: 25/11/2019: https://www.impactbnd.com/blog/marketing-chatbot-examples

Smith, R. D. (2016). *Becoming a public relations writer: Strategic writing for emerging and established media*. Routledge.

Stanton, R., Hobson-Powell, A., & Rosenbaum, S. (2019). Conference hashtags: A case of# RTP18–the 2018 exercise and sports science Australia conference. *Journal of Clinical Exercise Physiology, 8*(1), 26–29.

Stelzner, M. (2019). TikTok: What marketers need to know, *Social Media Examiner,* viewed 28.09.2019: https://www.socialmediaexaminer.com/tiktok-what-marketers-need-to-know-rachel-pedersen/

Sutherland, K. (2019). Free social media resources for beginners, *Dr Karen* Sutherland.com, viewed 28.09.2019: https://drkarensutherland.com/2017/07/29/free-social-media-resources-for-beginners/

The Social Report. (2018). The ultimate guide to social media post lengths in 2019, *The Social Report*, viewed 28.09.2019: https://www.socialreport.com/insights/article/360020940251-The-Ultimate-Guide-to-Social-Media-Post-Lengths-in-2019#h_3957890676751544765094168

Tiwari, S., Jain, A., Kothari, P., Upadhyay, R., & Singh, K. (2018). Learning user preferences for recommender system using youtube videos tags. In *International conference on computational science and its applications* (pp. 464–473). Cham: Springer.

Ubisend. (2018). Online Media Chatbot Hits an 84% Read Rate, *Ubisend*, viewed: 25/11/2019: https://www.ubisend.com/case-studies/media-chatbot-increase-read-rate

Wan, V. (2019). The ultimate guide to Sina Weibo: The largest micro-blogging platform in China, *Dragon Social*, viewed 28.09.2019: https://www.dragonsocial.net/blog/chinese-social-media-weibo-and-twitter-comparison/

Wang, Y. (2018). An introduction to Sina Weibo for journalists, *Interhacktives*, viewed 28.09.2019: https://www.interhacktives.com/2018/02/22/how-to-use-sina-weibo-as-a-journalist/

Weinreich, H., Obendorf, H., Herder, E., & Mayer, M. (2008). Not quite the average: An empirical study of web use. *ACM Transactions on the Web (TWEB), 2*(1), 5.

Whitaker, W. R., & Smith, R. D. (2009). *Mediawriting: Print, broadcast, and public relations*. Routledge.

Winchel, B. (2019). Voice search, AI and beyond: Why marketers must embrace technology, *PR Daily*, viewed 28.09.2019: https://www.prdaily.com/voice-search-ai-and-beyond-why-marketers-must-embrace-technology/

Xavier, S. C. D. C. (2018). *With or without emoji?: Impact of the use of emojis on online service booking on consumer perception* (Doctoral dissertation), viewed 28.09.2019: http://hdl.handle.net/10071/17605.

Further Reading

Handley, A. (2014). *Everybody writes: Your go-to guide to creating ridiculously good content*. Wiley.

Iezzi, T. (2016). *The idea writers: Copywriting in a new media and marketing era*. Macmillan.

Marshall, C. (2018). *Writing for social media*. Swindon, UK: BCS, The Chartered Institute for IT.

Maslen, A. (2019). *Persuasive copywriting: Cut through the noise and communicate with impact*. Kogan Page Publishers.

Helpful Links

Chatbot Builder

Chatfuel: https://chatfuel.com
MobileMonkey: https://mobilemonkey.com/

Copywriting Tools

Sprout Social Media Character Counter: https://sproutsocial.com/insights/social-media-character-counter/

Search Engine Optimisation (SEO)/ Keyword Tools

Keyword Tool: https://keywordtool.io
LSI Keyword Generator: https://lsigraph.com/keyword/
Google Search Console: https://search.google.com/search-console/about
SEMrush Keyword Research: https://www.semrush.com/features/keyword-research

Adding Emojis to YouTube

Tube Buddy: https://www.tubebuddy.com

Creating Compelling Images, Graphics, Memes and Infographics

Contents

© The Author(s), under exclusive license to Springer Nature Singapore Pte Ltd. 2021
K. E. Sutherland, *Strategic Social Media Management*, https://doi.org/10.1007/978-981-15-4658-7_15

📖 By the End of this Chapter You Will

- Understand the theoretical underpinnings and the integral role that visual content plays in storytelling and generating engagement with target audiences on social media.
- Learn basic photography principles to capture and edit quality images for social media.
- Know more about graphical content such as images, infographics, memes and geofilters, tools that can assist in their development.
- Gain an insight into the visual content requirements of the mainstream social media platforms.
- Understand why including Alt text to increase accessibility and searchability
- Learn how to brief a photographer and graphic designer.

TLDR

- When used together, quality visual and written content can have a powerful impact on audience engagement.
- Visual content can enhance storytelling, communication, brand recall and build strong connections with target audiences on social media.
- Semiotics is the science of signs and helps to explain how audiences can attach meanings and form perceptions about a brand based on their consumption of visual social media content.
- Gestalt Principles propose that the position of graphical elements can guide the eye and the mind into seeing visual content in particular ways, namely that when viewing objects, the whole is greater than the sum of its parts.
- All visual content must align with strategic goals and objectives, convey at least one key message and be audience and platform appropriate.

- The three stages of the photography process are: Pre-Production (Planning), Production (Photoshoot), and Post-Production (Editing).
- The 'Rule of Thirds' is a guiding principle to assist in the composition of photographs.
- It is important to accurately brief professional graphic designers and photographers to avoid poor quality outcomes and extra cost.
- Layout, branding and photographic images are all key components to consider when creating graphical content for social media.
- Infographics are a highly effective tactic to communicate statistical data in an interesting and digestible manner to target audiences.
- Memes, GIFs, Filters and Geofilters should all be considered as tactics in a social media strategy but must be audience appropriate and align with strategic goals and objectives.

15.1 Introduction

With the importance clarified of quality copywriting on social media, this chapter will explore the power of visual content. Yet, both types of content do not perform well in isolation. They need to work together to achieve the best results. A study by Brubaker and Wilson (2018) found that while visual content is effective in attracting attention on a newsfeed, it is written copy accompanying the visual element that helps convert the audience's attention to engagement.

While ▶ Chap. 15 focuses on the process and production of visual social media content, please draw on the knowledge gained from ▶ Chap. 14 to consider how written copy and visual content can work together as a complete post.

The aim of this chapter is to provide an in-depth insight into various categories of visual social media content including photographs, graphics, infographics, memes, GIFS and geofilters and the processes, their strategic function in supporting goals and objectives and communicating key messages, plus the tools required to produce them. However, this chapter does not suggest that the expertise of professional photographers and graphic designers is redundant. Instead it guides Social Media Managers on the process of visual content creation as well as providing direction on how to brief professional suppliers if there is a budget to outsource photography and graphic design services. It will never be a case of one or the other. This chapter will prepare readers for both options.

The chapter also delves into a range of theoretical frameworks that underpin the functionality of visual content. Theories including Semiotics, Gestalt Principles and the Rule of Thirds are discussed to explain how and why visual content can positively resonate with target audiences. The visual content specifications of each of the mainstream social media platforms is discussed before the chapter concludes with an interview with a Social Media Manager based in Johannesburg, South Africa, Mongezi Lupindo.

15.2 Why Visual Content Is Important on Social Media

There are countless reasons to support the argument surrounding the importance of visual content on social media. Whether referring to photographs, graphics, GIFs or geofilters, each has a key function in communicating, informing and entertaining target audiences through posts, Stories, profile images and other formats according to the specific characteristics of each social media platform.

> 66 Visual content provides another layer of meaning in addition to written social media copy. 99
>
> Dr Karen Sutherland

Visual content provides another layer of meaning in addition to written social media copy. Reasons why it is integral to provide this opportunity for sense-making to the audience are:

15.3 Visual Content Enhances Storytelling

In ▸ Chap. 5 the power of storytelling was discussed in particular its effectiveness in conveying information and building connections with audiences. Visual content as a component of digital storytelling can be imperative in communicating a narrative with a target audience through the practice of showing rather than telling (see ◘ Figs. 15.1a and 15.1b) (Robin & McNeil, 2019).

Rather than relying on slabs of text to tell an audience the action of a story, sharing a visual representation of a scene from that story can assist the audience in understanding that action, the setting and characters. A single image can also convey the tone and theme of a story depending on the various visual elements used, for example, lighting and colour (Long, 2011).

15.5 · Visual Content Builds Connections Between People behind a Brand ...

329

15

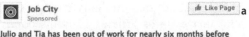

Julio and Tia has been out of work for nearly six months before coming to see us at Job City. Within a few weeks that had found amazing jobs and began new careers in fields that they had never dreamed they would ever be working on. Job City can help you to find direction if you have not had any luck finding work. It is definitely worth taking half an hour to speak to our highly qualified employment professionals who can provide helpful advice and direction.

Julio and Tia has been out of work for nearly six months when they can to see us at Job City. Within weeks they had found amazing jobs.

☐ **Fig. 15.1** (**a**) Text heavy content. (**b**) Visual storytelling with minimal text

15.4 Visual Content Increases Visibility of a Brand, Product and Service Rather than Describing It Using Text

While text can be helpful in describing a person, brand, product or service, it requires the audience to visualise how these items appear. Sharing a visual representation using a graphic or a photograph assists the audience by allowing them to see for themselves. Furthermore, providing accurate imagery helps an audience to gain an insight into a brand and its products or services before deciding to purchase (remember the customer journey) by helping to build trust between the audience and the brand.

For example, a study conducted by Edwards et al. (2015) found that LinkedIn users with a profile photo are perceived as more socially attractive and more competent than users who do not have one on their profile. Therefore, visual content used in combination with written copy can strongly influence audience perception more so than using text on its own.

15.5 Visual Content Builds Connections Between People behind a Brand and Their Target Audience

Similar to the point above, using photographs and video (see ▶ Chap. 16) to raise awareness of and sharing the stories of the people behind a brand, product or service can be a highly effective tactic in building trust, familiarity and connection with a target audience.

People are interested in the lives and stories of other people as explored in ▶ Chap. 5. Helping a target audience to learn why a business or product was created from the person behind it can add a much greater depth of meaning and connection than focusing purely on product features. Visual content can help to share those stories. People are more likely to purchase from a person with whom they feel a connection than from a large faceless corporation (Bleier, De Keyser, & Verleye, 2018).

Furthermore, building connection through visual content is essential for a local bricks-and-mortar store. Prospective and existing customers can feel as though they know the store owner or staff members when they see them regularly on social media. This helps to foster a positive relationship and sense of familiarity. Customers are more likely to return to a store where they feel a positive connection with the people there (Duggal & Verma, 2019; Khamitov, Wang, & Thomson, 2019).

15.6 Visual Content Conveys Information in Small Bites

Visual content lends itself extremely well to the continual scrolling of smartphone users of social media, because it allows small bites of information to be consumed along the Way (Fox, Nakhata, & Deitz, 2019). More than 90% of information transmitted to our brains is visual and 65% of people have been reported to be visual learners (Buşan, 2014; Trafton, 2014). Furthermore, MIT research-ers have found that humans can process entire images in as little as 13 milliseconds (Trafton, 2014). These statistics alone help to support the case for including visual content on social media.

Infographics (as explored later in this chapter) are an excellent example of how complex information such as statistical data can be represented in a visual way, making it more digestible to audiences in a social media environment (see ◘ Figs. 15.2a and 15.2b).

In some cases, key messages conveyed in graphics and photographs can be comprehended faster than stopping to read written copy. The reasons for this will be explained in the following section relating to semiotics.

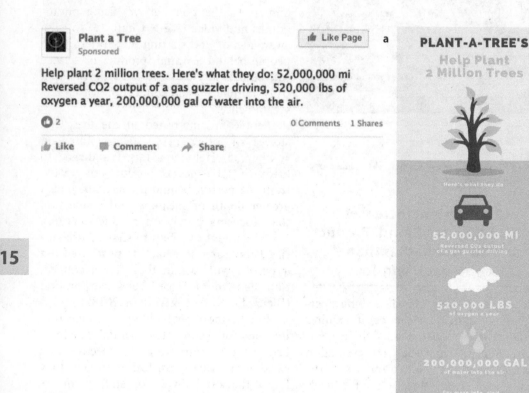

◘ **Fig. 15.2** **a** Conveying data as text. **b** Conveying data as infographic

15.7 Visual Content Attracts Attention and Increases Views

A compelling and vibrant photo, graphic, infographic, GIF or meme can be highly effective at cutting through competing content on a newsfeed to attract the attention of a target audience. Using bold colours can help to attract the eye and interrupt a scrolling social media user.

In addition to attracting attention, posts with a visual element are reported to receive 94% more views on social media (Bullas, 2018a, 2018b). Therefore, every social media post should include some sort of visual element to increase the likelihood that it will be viewed by a target audience.

15.8 Visual Content Can Generate Greater Engagement than Text Alone

Photographs posted on **Facebook** have been reported to generate 37% higher rates of engagement than posts only featuring text (Bullas, 2018a, 2018b) and this is not an uncommon occurrence across other platforms in relation to visual content (Gretzel, 2017). Images, photographs and GIFs resonate on greater levels with audiences than text alone. A study conducted by Manic (2015, p1.) suggested that: "loyal customers are achieved and kept through visual content…" Yet, research has also highlighted that written copy and visual content generate greater engagement when used together (Brubaker & Wilson, 2018; Fox et al., 2019). However, both forms of content (visual and text-based) must be of high quality and audience-focused for any engagement to be generated.

15.9 People Remember Visual Content More than Text

People are reported to remember visual content more than text. For example, when hearing a piece of information, on average, only 10% of it will be recalled. However, communicate the same information with an image and 65% will be remembered (Medina, 2018).

The aim of being top-of-mind was discussed in ▶ Chap. 3. Using visual content is a helpful and effective tactic to embed a brand, organisation, product or service in the mind of current and/or prospective customers. Creating visual content that helps a target audience remember the solution a client or organisation presents is one of the most effective ways for its use in a social media strategy.

There are many theories that aim to deconstruct and explain why visual content such as images and photographs have such a profound impact on human sense-making. However, for this text two of the key theoretical frameworks, Semiotics and Gestalt Principles, are examined to convey why visual content can be effective in communicating with target audiences.

15.9.1 Semiotics

In its simplest definition, semiotics can be described as the science of signs, (Erton, 2018). As a theoretical construct, semiotics is focused on understanding how meaning is attached and generated from particular items, icons or symbols (Poulsen, Kvåle, & van Leeuwen, 2018; Price & Wells, 2009; Triggs, 2017). This directly applies to visual content because semiotics attempts to explain "the mental construction which arises when there is recognition between an expression (signifier) and its content (signified) (Triggs, 2017, p. 427). Target audiences can attach specific meanings to the visual representations of brands, products and services that are posted on social media.

For example, if a local cafe posts a photo of a burger from its menu (see ◘ Fig. 15.3) the target audience knows that the image is not the actual burger. Instead, it is a visual representation of the burger (signifier) and the audience can use that visual representation to form perceptions about the taste and quality of the burger and of the cafe.

An important consideration for Social Media Managers when creating visual content is that audience perception is subjective and cannot be controlled. This is also a key criticism of the early presentations of semiotics as a theory (Price & Wells, 2009). Clearly it is essential to visual content that communicates key messages and supports strategic goals and objectives, but an image can be interpreted in countless ways depending on the demographics and psychographics of the audience. Again, this is another reason why audience research is so important. Audience perception may not be controllable but having an extensive understanding about how a specific group constructs meaning around specific topics and issues can assist in navigating sensemaking.

For example, if trying to raise awareness of a new child's toy to parents, a photo only featuring the toy may not cut through to attract their attention. However, a photograph featuring a child and a parent smiling and enjoying playing with that toy may have a greater impact. This is because on its own, the toy does not have any context. Yet, demonstrating how the toy can be used and its positive impact on people with whom the audience can identify (child and parent) helps to create a connection with them and the product (◘ Fig. 15.4).

15.9.2 Gestalt Principles

Gestalt originated as a movement in German psychology that suggested the perception of images is reliant on how visual elements are structured and organised instead of being contingent on individual sensations (Wright, 2016). The governing premise of Gestalt Principles is that the whole is greater than the sum of its parts, (Cherry, 2019). The principles of Gestalt proposed that the position of graphical elements can guide the eye and the mind into seeing visual content in particular ways. There are six key Gestalt Principles demonstrated in ◘ Fig. 15.5 Good Figure, Proximity, Similarity, Continuation, Closure and Symmetry. These principles aim to advise photographers and designers to create content that is logical for the audience and assists with sense-making.

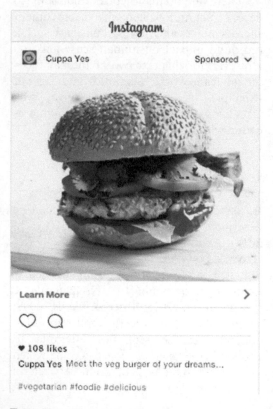

◘ Fig. 15.3   Burger example

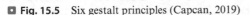 **Fig. 15.4** Child's toy with and without context

Gestalt Principles

 Good Figure

Objects grouped together tend to be perceived as a single figure. Tendency to simplify.

 Proximity

Objects tend to be grouped together if they are close to each other.

 Similarity

Objects tend to be grouped together if they are similar.

 Continuation

When there is an intersection between two or more objects, people tend to perceive each object as a single uninterrupted object.

 Closure

Visual connection or continuity between sets of elements which do not actually touch each other in a composition.

 Symmetry

The object tend to be perceived as symmetrical shapes that form around their center.

Fig. 15.5 Six gestalt principles (Capcan, 2019)

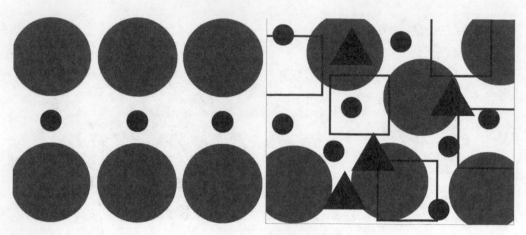

◘ Fig. 15.6 Graphics Applying and Not Applying the Gestalt Principle of Similarity

15.9.3 Applying Gestalt Principles to Social Media Content

When developing visual content for social media following Gestalt Principles can greatly assist in connecting with a target audience in ways that assist them in digesting and comprehending information in user-centred ways.

For example, ◘ Fig. 15.6 demonstrates two graphics where the first applies the Gestalt Principle of Similarity and the second does not.

Which graphic is more aesthetically pleasing and easier to understand?

Applying Gestalt Principles to social media content can encourage sensemaking by the target audience when they scroll through their news feeds, because the message attempting to be conveyed will be easily understood if it is logically organised.

The post in ◘ Fig. 15.7 applies Gestalt Principles. It contains abstract elements such as dots and a squiggle, but these are presented in ways that balance the overall image. The text is clear and is evenly spaced in the centre of the graphic so that it can be easily read. Furthermore, while there are three main colours used in the graphic (red, black and white) they are also evenly placed

◘ Fig. 15.7 Example of Facebook Post applying Gestalt Principles

within the image. The graphical items within this post are coloured and positioned to make the text the main feature, helping to complement and encourage its comprehension by the target audience.

With the case for visual social media content presented and two relevant theoretical frameworks examined the chapter will explore the practical process of visual content creation relating to photography and graphic pieces including: images, infographics, memes, GIFs and filters and geofilters.

15.10 Social Media Photography

Using photographs on social media has proven to be a powerful tactic that can greatly increase engagement. Tweets including photos receive 35% more retweets than those without and Facebook posts with images generate 2.3 times more engagement (Pinantoan, 2015; Rogers, 2014). While there are many paid and free stock image libraries online as explored in ▶ Chap. 10 knowing how to capture and edit quality photographs can be a more genuine way to visually represent a client or organisation's brand on social media.

Understanding the basics of photography can greatly assist a Social Media Manager in creating quality content and in comprehensively briefing a professional photographer if there is a budget to outsource the task. Both aspects of photographic content creation are explored. It must be stated that digital photography is the key focus in this chapter with a further concentration on smartphone photography.

15.10.1 Process

The photographic process has three key stages: Pre-Production Production and Post-Production. These stages are the same as in the video production process that will be explored in ▶ Chap. 16, but the tasks within them vary slightly.

15.10.1.1 Pre-Production Phase

The pre-production phase is all about planning (Wright, 2016). Even when photographs are taken spontaneously, some degree of preparation is required to allow that to occur. The key considerations for a Social Media Manager in the photographic pre-production phase are:

- **Functional smartphone or camera equipment**: Ensure that batteries are charged, lenses are clean, tripods work and there is enough space to store photographs.
- **Location**: Some shooting locations will need to be organised and booked in advance. Arrange and confirm access for the shoot ahead of time.
- **Talent**: Also known as the subject. If the shoot requires other people to be in the photographs, inform them of the required details so that they know when and where they need to be. Advice on what to wear on the day should also be provided. Finally, if taking photographs on behalf of a client, brand or organisation, it is recommended to have each person sign a release form (and a parent to sign on behalf of children under 18 years of age) providing written permission for the images to be used. A link to a photographic release form template is in the Helpful Links section at the end of this chapter.
- **Shot List**: To plan well for an organised photoshoot, write a list of the essential images required and some extras to guide the shoot on the day.

15.10.1.2 Production Phase

The production phase is when photographs are gathered, also known as the photoshoot. There are some key photographic principles to follow during this phase to assist in gathering all required images.

Areas for consideration when shooting photographs for social media are:

- **Check the image file size on camera devices**: If the images are too small they will not work well on social media and will be challenging to edit. See information on file sizes further in this chapter.
- **Revisit the shot list**: Have a clear understanding of the shots that need to be gathered.
- **Ensure the talent signs the release form**: It is better to do this at the beginning of the photoshoot because it can be forgotten if left until afterwards.
- **Lighting**: Ensure that the talent or subject in the photo is well-lit. Natural lighting works well. If inside, a three-point lighting set-up can be effective using whatever lights are available. Please see ◘ Fig. 15.8 and ► Chap. 16 for more information.

Also, if photographing into the sun often a blue or green light will appear in the photo (see ◘ Fig. 15.9). To avoid this place the blue or green dot directly on the sun and it will not appear in the image. Alternatively, this dot can be removed using an editing tool in the post-production process.

- **Composition**: Applying the Rule of Thirds is the most effective way to frame a shot if new to photography. This involves dividing the screen (on a smartphone or camera) into a grid of nine even spaces (see ◘ Fig. 15.10). Most smartphones and cameras have settings

◘ **Fig. 15.9** Sun blue dot

◘ **Fig. 15.10** The Rule of Thirds

to turn apply this grid when taking photographs.

The aim is to put the subject of the image (talent, animal or object) on one of the intersecting lines rather than directly in the middle of the frame (Long, 2011; National Geographic, 2011). This helps to balance the shot and makes it more pleasing to the eye. The grid lines also assist in taking a more stabilized image.

- **Gather more than you need**: It is better to walk away from a photoshoot with more images than not enough. Take many photographs from a range of different angles. Shoot low and high, wide and close. Move around the talent or subject

15

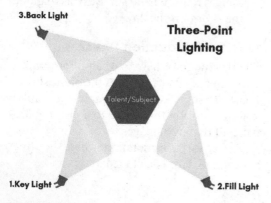

◘ **Fig. 15.8** Three-point lighting

taking a wide range of photos. Ask the talent to pose in different ways without annoying them.

— Often, it is not until the post-production phase that you will get to see all of the images gathered. Although, it is recommended during the photoshoot to keep checking images on the shot list to stay on track but to be ready to take others that may also work if the opportunity arises.

15.10.1.3 Post-Production Phase

The beauty of the post-production process is that it allows the correction of many of the errors that have occurred during the shoot Wright, 2016). However, this does not mean that the editing process should be relied upon to fix everything. There are some results that editing tools cannot achieve.

However, the wide variety of editing tools currently available can greatly assist in improving the quality of photographs. This can include straightening an uneven shot, reworking an image so that it better applies the Rule of Thirds or intensifying the colours to make the image pop from a newsfeed to attract the attention of a target audience.

Every image should undergo some form of editing. It is very rare to capture the perfect image for social media. The key is not to feel daunted about photo editing. Jump right in and experiment, particularly with the manual editing functions to gain an in-depth understanding of what they do.

15.10.2 Filters

The alternative to manual image editing is to use a filter. A filter applies a pre-set look to a photographic image in terms of its lighting, contrast, saturation and hue etc. It can be applied quickly and simply when uploading photographs to most social media platforms which is an easier option than using the manual image editing options. Many of the image editing tools also provide filter options. Filters can also be used in combination with manual editing depending on the look trying to be achieved. For branding purposes it is recommended to select one or two filters and use only those to achieve a consistent look.

15.10.3 A Word of Warning

If creating visual content for a product, the images posted on social media must be an accurate representation of the items sold to customers. For example, highly stylised food photographs can be a disappointment to customers if they are not served up reality in (Sutherland, 2017).

15.10.4 Image Editing Tools

There are a wide range of photo editing tools available. Some are paid, some are free, some take extensive training to use and others can be used by those new to content creation. Experimenting is highly recommended to find a tool that is most suitable. The truth is that photos always need to be edited, but the best tool is highly subjective. ◻ Table 15.1 provides a brief list of the many options available.

While taking images as a Social Media Manager can be a fast and inexpensive way to create photographic content, it is worth encouraging a client or organisational decision-maker to appoint a photographer at least twice a year to take photos that can be used as stock images. In 2 hours, a professional photographer can gather enough content to last a few months.

Therefore, with the basics of photography covered, it is important to know how to effectively brief a professional photographer if a client or organisation has the budget to appoint an external supplier.

Table 15.1	Image editing tools
Image editing tools	**Description**
Snapseed	Snapseed is a free and powerful photo editing smartphone app that provides a wide range of filters and allows an extensive selection of features for customised editing. It can also save images at high resolution so that they can be used for other purposes. A highly recommended tool.
Adobe Photoshop Lightroom	This a paid tool that has different levels of functionality depending on the different subscription plans. It is both a smartphone app and desktop program that offers an excellent range of photo editing features in line with Adobe Photoshop.
PicMonkey	PicMonkey is a paid photo editing tool that also offers templates to create other social media posts and advertisements.
GIMP	A free and open source image editor, GIMP can be downloaded to your desktop. It has many of the same features as Photoshop, but its offerings are not as extensive. A great tool for basic photo editing and it reasonably user-friendly.
Adobe Photoshop	This is an industry standard tool that can take some training to master, but the quality of images it produces is worth the time, effort and cost. Knowledge of photoshop is an invaluable skill to have as a Social Media Manager.

15.10.5 Briefing a Photographer

Accurately briefing a professional photographer is essential to avoid costly errors, frustration and disappointment. This is particularly the case when appointing a photographer to cover an event. If the photographer does not capture the required images, the moment has passed, and the opportunity is lost.

When selecting a professional photographer, it is recommended to view a sample of their previous work to ensure that it is in line with what you are aiming to achieve. A photographic brief does not have to be lengthy, but it must be comprehensive and specific to provide the photographer with an in-depth insight into the images they need to gather and produce.

A photographic brief should include:

— **Budget**: This will inform the photographer of the time that they can allocate to the job. Please have realistic expectations. A limited budget will also return a limited result.

— **Deadline**: By when do the image files need to be ready? Is this turnaround time achievable?

— **Shoot Details**: Inform the photographer of the location, start and finish time and the date of the shoot. Do not forget to include contact details of someone who will be there to liaise with them on the day. Also include a run sheet if the shoot is taking place at an event.

— **Background**: Why is this shoot necessary?

— **Goals and Objectives**: What is the purpose for these images? What do they hope to achieve and how do they support the strategic goals and objectives of the social media strategy and wider organisational or business strategy?

— **Audience**: Who are these photographs intended for? With whom are they hoping to communicate?

- **Key Messages**: What are these photographs trying to communicate?
- **Branding**: Supply a copy of the branding guidelines, particularly information on brand voice and look and feel so the photographer can reflect these in their images.
- **Shot List**: Write a list of the photographs that you need rom the photographer including the names of people that you would like to feature in them.
- **Deliverables**: Include the file types required and the social media platforms where the photographs will be posted. Also, include information about to whom and where the final image files should be sent.

However, this chapter will focus on the broad categories of graphical content including graphics, infographics, memes, GIFs and geofilters to provide a basic understanding of each, their purpose in supporting strategic goals and objectives, an explanation of important terms and concepts relating to each format and recommended tools to support their production.

Advice on how to brief a professional graphic designer is also offered in the case of a client or organisation having the budget to outsource to an external supplier. It is important to clearly articulate what is required when appointing an external supplier to achieve a quality result without incurring extra costs.

15.11 Graphical Social Media Content

There are a number of different forms of graphical social media content that can be facilitated by mainstream social media platforms. ▣ Tables 15.2 and 15.3 provides specific details and recommendations for each platform.

15.11.1 Graphics

A graphic is a visual image that is not a photograph. However, photographs can be used as part of a graphic in combination with typography, patterns, textures and colours. There are as many variations of graphics as possible photographs that can be captured.

Table 15.2 Graphic design tools

Graphic design tool	Description
Canva	Canva is a user-friendly graphic design tool that can help to design everything in terms of social media content, even animated posts. It has a range of templates and design as well as paid options but offers a wide variety of features for free. There is also an app to support content creation on mobile devices.
Adobe Spark	A user-friendly tool that can create a wide range of visual content for most social media platforms. Adobe Spark is not a free tool but is more reasonably priced than industry-standard tools such as Adobe InDesign.
Over	Over is similar to Canva and Adobe Spark in that it provides a range of templates and graphics that can be customised to suit branding guidelines and needs. It offers a free trial, but it is predominantly a paid tool.
Adobe InDesign	An industry-standard graphic design tool that offers the ability to create content at a highly professional standard. It is a paid tool and can require some training to master its features.

□ Table 15.3 **Important graphic-related terms**. Please note that these terms relate to image files in general and are relevant to graphic and photographic content

Term	Definition
Pixel	In photographic and graphic design contexts (not related to Facebook advertising) a pixel is the smallest unit of a digital image that captures its information regarding light and colour. The greater the number of pixels in an image when it is designed or capture, the higher its quality (National Geographic, 2011).
dpi	Dots Per Inch is used to measure the resolution of an image. 72dpi is an acceptable size for social media content, but 300dpi is of much greater quality and is of printable standard.
Resolution	The number of pixels in an image usually measured by the height and width of an image: (e.g. 2048 × 1536) and the total number of pixels in an image: (e.g. 3,145,728 pixels or 3.1 Megapixels) (Microscope, 2019). The higher the resolution the better quality image, however, high resolution images also mean larger file sizes.
JPG & PNG	.jpg and .png are the two supported static image files supported by social media platforms. PNG files can be superior to JPG because the image does not lose quality when compressed.
Thumbnail	A thumbnail is a smaller version of an original image.

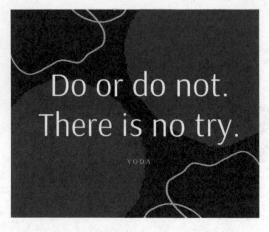

□ Fig. 15.11 A quotation graphic on social media

A completed graphic depends on the person designing it, the platforms they plan to use it on and the tools that they have at their disposal to create it.

Quotations are excellent examples of social media graphics (see □ Fig. 15.11). Notice how the quote is a combination of type, colour and shapes making it different to a photograph.

15.11.2 **Graphical Components**

The following components must be considered when designing graphics for social media:

- **Layout**: Check the recommended image sizes for each platform and use that space so that it communicates key messages and attracts audience attention. Revisit Gestalt Principles explored previously in this chapter. The Rule of Thirds also applies to graphical content.
- **Branding** (logo, colour, font): Ensure that graphical content meets the branding guidelines of the client or the organisation. Use the correct font, high-resolution logo (with permission) and the correct hex or RGB colour codes.
- **Photographs** (if using them): If including a photograph within graphical content ensure that it aligns with the brand voice and guidelines and that you have the necessary permissions for its use.

15

Graphics can be extremely effective in attracting attention on a feed if they are bold in colour and message. In terms of text on graphics, less is more. As mentioned in ▶ Chap. 14, Facebook can limit the reach of posts with graphics that have 20% or more of text (Facebook, 2019). Therefore, graphics should not be another way to communicate written copy. Instead they should be used to captivate the audience through visual imagery.

Furthermore, graphics are the perfect vehicle to share the visual representation of a brand using brand colours, fonts and brand voice. The most important areas of consideration when designing graphics for social media are that they support strategic goals and objectives, convey key at least one key message and are audience and platform appropriate.

15.11.3 Helpful Graphic Design Tools

Visual content creation tools are ever-changing, therefore, including a comprehensive list in this chapter would be counterproductive. Instead, ◻ Table 15.2 includes a few tried and tested tools that have been available for a number of years (links to each in the Helpful Links section at the end of this chapter). Please note that some of the photo editing tools mentioned in ◻ Table 15.1 such as Adobe Photoshop can also be used to design graphical content.

15.11.4 Infographics

Infographics are defined as: "a visualization of data or ideas that tries to convey complex information to an audience in a manner that can be quickly consumed and easily understood," (Byrom, 2014; Siricharoen & Siricharoen, 2018). Generally, infographics are the combination of graphical compo-

◻ **Fig. 15.12**   Infographic example

nents coupled with statistical information that convey data in a much more aesthetically pleasing and digestible format to a target audience.

◻ Figure 15.12 is an excellent example of how what may be dry statistical data in text form can be much easier to comprehend within an infographic.

In a social media context, an infographic is 30 times more likely to be read than a text-based article and the website traffic of companies using infographics has been found to grow 12% more than those who do not (Kolowich, 2017). Infographics can bring data to life and make it much more interesting (and less complicated) for the audience to understand. It is important that the information included in an infographic is

THE AWAKENING

- centre of attention
- updating insta story as we speak
- supportive friend even when you make bad decisions

YOGI BEAR

- wears activewear everywhere (even weddings)
- feels sorry for people with peanut allergies
- your go-to reliable friend

MOTHER EARTH

- brings their own straw
- refuses to miss their weekend Farmer's market trip
- "there's nothing like waking up early to watch the sunrise"
- fantasises about trying a new smoothie but never does

STRAWBERRIES & DREAM

- LOVES disney
- glad 90s fashion is back
- "we should go strawberry picking and take cute pics!!!"

WILD JUJU

- rehearses their order in their head 200 times
- favourite food is berries
- asleep by 8pm sharp
- still thinking about the stranger that smiled at them

CHARLIE BROWN

- pats every dog they see
- immediately regrets making social plans
- knows 'Seinfeld' is better than 'Friends'

SUNSHINE SPROUT

- asks where the recycling bin is at parties
- runs up Mt Coolum
- friends with literally everybody
- secretly binges murder documentaries

HIP WIGGLER

- has signature dance moves
- accidentally kills house plants
- loses wallet constantly
- loveable but infuriating

PASSION POP

- despises Winter & can tell you exactly how many days until Summer
- is glad leopard print is on trend again
- doesn't remember where they parked
- has no inside voice

GREEN GOODNESS

- always has a holiday booked
- does yoga everyday
- knows how to make kale chips
- has a phobia of moths

Fig. 15.13   Example of an alternative approach to an infographic by Janisha Chaudhary

arranged in a logical order to tell the story of the data in a way that can be comprehensible to the audience.

Statistical data does not have to be the only focus of an infographic. Figure 15.13 demonstrates an alternative approach that helps a target audience identify with a brand and its products generating engagement to build a positive connection in the process. The post itself asked the audience, "Which smoothie are you?"

Remember, to revisit the strategic goals, objectives, key messages, audience research and platform specifications to design an infographic that supports the need of a client of organisation. Helpful tools exist to create professional-looking infographics for social media platforms are detailed in Table 15.4

(with links included in the Helpful Links section). Canva can also create infographics but is not included in this list.

15.11.5 Memes

The term "meme" was first written by Richard Dawkins (1976, p. 192) who defined it as "an idea, behaviour or style that spreads from person to person within a culture". In a social media context, a meme refers to pieces of visual content that generally comprise of photographic, graphic and written content to make a specific point. Memes can be amusing and funny, political and discriminatory. This content can also be used to share misinformation on the internet.

◻ Table 15.4	Infographic design tools (Bullas, 2018a, 2018b)
Infographic design tool	**Description**
Visme.co	An online tool with customisable and professional-looking infographic templates. A paid tool with limited free options.
▶ Easel.ly	An online tool that does not require an account to use. Provides a wide range of visually attractive infographic templates for free.
PiktoChart	Offering free and paid options, PiktoChart provides customisable templates for infographics and other forms of visual content such as presentations and posters.

15.11.6 Why Use Memes?

As a Social Media Manager, when used correctly, memes can be an effective way to establish relevance by being part of an existing conversation occurring online. For example, if a humorous meme is shared among a target audience, sharing that meme and somehow relating it back to a client's brand (or applying a further humorous approach) can help to build connections with the audience by fostering a sense of camaraderie and conviviality (Varis & Blommaert, 2015).

15.11.7 How to Create Memes

Creating a new meme can be risky if it is not well-received, but alternatively, it can be a huge hit and be shared extensively also increasing the reach of a client or organisation's brand.

It is important to research correctly to ensure that using a meme will resonate positively with the target audience rather than falling flat, or even worse, causing offence. ◻ Figure 15.14 demonstrates an example of a meme used to connect with an audience.

Memes can be created manually using the tools that we have already explored in this chapter or through the use of online meme generators as listed in ◻ Table 15.5.

15.11.8 GIFs

Graphic Interchange Format (GIF), created in 1987, was unique in that it can play multiple frames on a loop within the same image file without being the size or resolution as a video file (Miltner & Highfield, 2017). In the Internet's early days, GIFs were used to apply small graphic animations to websites that included dancing babies and 'Under Construction' messages.

GIFs waned in popularity until sites such as Myspace, Reddit and Tumblr began featuring the content and advances in technology allowed for snippets of video to be looped with a file (Booth, 2015; Miltner & Highfield, 2017; Thomas, 2013; Ulanoff, 2016) (◻ Fig. 15.15).

15.11.9 Why Use GIFS?

Currently, GIFs have become a hugely popular content type and are used by individuals and brands to entertain and connect with target audiences on social media. GIFs could be considered as animated memes, but it is the animation that distinguishes it from other graphical content and adds a new layer of meaning.

Creating GIFs that align with strategic goals and objectives can effectively communicate key messages to a target audience well

Fig. 15.14   A meme: University of the Sunshine Coast, Australia's version of the Dolly Parton challenge

15

as demonstrating a fun and playful aspect of a brand. Using GIFs helps to convey key messages with a short timeframe (2–5 seconds) on a deeper level than static images because the animation aspect of this content helps to create greater context for a target audience (Lepard, 2017).

The use of GIFs also positions a brand as keeping up with trends by participating in current online conversations taking place on social media. Attracting attention is one of the greatest benefits of using GIFs because they add movement to a newsfeed as the target audience scrolls through.

15.11.10 How to Create GIFs

It is possible to create GIFs to use as social media content and there are countless tools available. Some considerations when creating GIFs are:

- **The Audience:** Ensure that it is a piece of content that will resonate with them and

Table 15.5	Meme creation tools
Meme creation tool	**Description**
Imgur	Imgur's Memgen is a free, user-friendly meme generator that allows users to customise existing memes or create news ones by uploading different backgrounds.
Livememe	Livememe provides access to images of people appearing in the internet's most popular memes. The user can add their own text to the background. This is also a free tool.
Quickmeme	Quickmeme is a free tool that facilitates customisation of text on existing memes.

Table 15.6	GIFs creation tools
GIF creation tool	**Description**
Giphy	A free and user-friendly online tool that makes GIF creation a simple exercise. Supports video links from YouTube and Vimeo (please only use content that you have permission to use). Giphy also has a database to search for existing GIFs.
Ezgif	Provides options to create GIFs from images or video. Less user-friendly than Giphy but still reasonably simple to use. This is a free tool.
Makeagif	Makeagif offers free and paid options to create GIFs via a user-friendly interface from a wide range of content including pictures, YouTube, Facebook, webcams and video sources.

Fig. 15.15 An example of a GIF Made with Canva

that they will want to share. Test a GIF with members from the target audience before posting it publicly. The aim is to inspire the audience to share it, not to cause offence.

- **Branding:** Do not use bold branding. Check that the GIF aligns with branding guidelines and brand voice but approach it as a fun piece of content not an advertisement.
- **Loop the action:** Looping the video helps the target audience see the GIF multiple times if they miss the action upon first seeing it.
- **Use Fewer Colours:** Orsow (2017) also suggests that reducing the number of colours used, because it reduces the file size and helps to create longer and more involved GIFS.

Table 15.6 provides details of some helpful online tools to produce GIFs and links to each are in the Helpful Links section. Canva also has templates to create GIFs.

15.11.11 Filters and Geofilters

Filters and Geofilters are graphical and animated content powered by Augmented Reality technology and generally used on Stories functions such as Snapchat, Instagram and Facebook Stories (Callahan, Church, King, & Elinzano, 2019). Users can apply filters to change their appearance or suggest they are in various locations depending on the filter that they have access to (see ◻ Fig. 15.16).

A filter is available to any platform user, but a geofilter can only be accessed by users in a specific geographical location (Chamberlain, 2016) (◻ Fig. 15.17).

◻ **Fig. 15.17**   Example of a Geofilter

15.11.12 Why Use Filters/ Geofilters?

Filters and Geofilters can be themed around specific events, products or holidays so and can be targeted to reach particular audiences, therefore, can be a worthwhile tactic to support strategic goals and objectives and communicate key messages. However, researching the target audience is key.

◻ **Fig. 15.16**   Example of a filter

15

15.11.13 Australian Liberal Party Slammed for Using Snapchat Filter to Lure Younger Voters

Using filters and geofilters as a way to "speak to the young people" can be fraught with issues particularly when the finished product does not speak their language. Doing so can result in a brand being perceived as out-of-touch. This was definitely the case for the Australian Liberal Party during the 2016 Federal election when they used a poorly devised Snapchat filter in a bid to lure support from younger voters (News.com.au, 2016; Vice, 2016). The filter was described as "cringeworthy" and depicted a "...an animated, white-gloved hand slotting a ballot paper marked "Vote Liberal" into a ballot box while a banner reading "a plan that works" unfurls over the head of the person in the picture," (News.com.au, 2016). Media outlets and Snapchat users criticised the Australian Liberal Party for using the filter suggesting that they were out-of-touch for trying to reach younger voters in such a poorly executed way. Leveraging a platform used by a target audience is only half the tactic. Utilising it in a way that is relevant to that audience is key.

15.11.14 How to Create Filters/Geofilters

Implementing filters and geofilters in a social media campaign used to be a paid tactic on Snapchat or reserved on Facebook and Instagram exclusively for approved brands and content creators. However, Facebook and Instagram have now opened access to its filter creation tool, Spark AR, to all users (Canning, 2019a). Filters still need to be approved before they are allowed on the platform, but this content type is worth exploring as an alternative way to generate audience engagement.

Important considerations when creating a filter or geofilter:

- **The Audience**: Ensure that the design will be something of interest and value to the audience. Use audience research from ▶ Chap. 3 to guide decisions and test the design with members of the target audience. Also, make sure that the filter makes the target audience the star (Canning, 2019a). Remember, it is not about the filter, it is about the target audience.
- **Branding**: Ensure the filter aligns with branding guidelines and brand voice without being too overpowering. The aim of a filter is to provide the target audience with a fun and memorable experience so that they build positive associations with a client's brand or organisation. It is not about blatant advertising.
- **Dynamism**: Include some movement or animation within the filter to add more to the user-experience (Canning, 2019a).

Below is a brief list of tools that can support the creation of filters and geofilters. Please check the Further Reading section for an article by Canning (2019a) that contains detailed instructions on how to create and upload filters to Instagram. Also, please see the Helpful Links section for links to the tools mentioned in ◻ Table 15.7.

15.11.15 Briefing a Graphic Designer

A client or organisational decision-maker may have a budget to appoint a professional graphic designer to create social media content. This is highly advantageous for a Social Media Manager who is not formally trained in graphic design as it will support the creation of quality content while allowing time to be devoted to other tasks.

> 66 Outsourcing to a graphic designer can prove to be a frustrating and costly experience if the important details of the task are not clearly articulated from the outset. 99
>
> Dr Karen Sutherland

◻ **Table 15.7** Filter and geofilter creation tools

Filter/ geofilter creation tool	Description
Spark AR Studio	A free tool created by Facebook to support the design and implementation of filters within Instagram. It can take some practice to use in the beginning, but worth the practice.
Lens Studio	Lens Studio supports the creation of filters for Snapchat. It is extremely user-friendly and free to use.
Snapchat Create	A free tool owned by Snapchat that supports the design and implementation of Community Filters (geofilters), filters and filter advertising. A helpful tool for creating content for target audiences on Snapchat.

15

Outsourcing to a graphic designer can prove to be a frustrating and costly experience if the important details of the task are not clearly articulated from the outset. Graphic Designers generally allow for a few revisions within their initial fee and will charge for any extras. Avoiding an extensive revision can be achieved with a clear brief provided to the designer at the beginning of the appointment. Similarly, to appointing a photographer, it is recommended to view previous work of a graphic designer to ensure that it is of a standard to suit your needs.

Important information to include when briefing a graphic designer (DeFelice, 2019; Snap Marketing, 2015):

— **Budget**: How much budget is there to support this design project? Is it realistic for what is hoped to be achieved?
— **Deadline**: By when must this design be ready? Is it achievable?
— **Background**: What is the background of the organisation or business and why is this graphic design required?
— **Goal and Objectives of the Design**: What is this design aiming to achieve? How will it support strategic goals and objectives on both an organisational and social media context.
— **Audience**: To whom is this design attempting to communicate? Provide the audience persona developed in ▶ Chap. 3.
— **Branding**: Supply the branding guidelines (including colour codes, approved logo and brand voice). Also supplied examples of other branded graphical content.
— **Social Media Platforms**: On what social media platforms will this design feature and as what specific types of content (Facebook post, Instagram Stories ad etc.)?
— **Market Positioning and Competition**: How is the client or organisation position against their competition? Who is the client's or organisation's main competitors? Include links to their social media profiles.

- **Copy and Images**: If the design requires written copy and specific images or photographs ensure that these are supplied when appointing a graphic designer to avoid delays once the work commences.
- **The Approval Process**: Explain who must be involved in the design approval process in relation to a client or organisation so that the graphic designer can leave ample time to accommodate all stakeholders whilst still meeting the deadline.
- **Included Amendments**: It is extremely important to find out from the graphic designer how many amendments are included in their initial fee and the cost of any extras.

With the processes of visual content creation examined, it is important that best practices are followed when uploading it to social media platforms. Including alt text with every image upload is an essential practice for a Social Media Manager.

15.12 Increasing Accessibility of Visual Content with Alt Text

Alt text is short for 'alternative text' which is text that is added to the HTML code that describes what is in the image (Christensen & Pionke, 2019). Many web interfaces, WordPress as an example, provide prompts for alt text when uploading visual content.

Social media sites such as Instagram and Facebook automatically add alt text to images (125 characters) whereas platforms such as LinkedIn now allow users to add up to 120 characters of alt text manually (Elliot, 2019).

Adding alt text is considered to be best practice in web and social media content creation because:

1. It makes the image accessible to visually impaired users allowing screen readers to find and describe the image via audio or braille.
2. It provides context and more accurate descriptions so that the image can be found and indexed by search engines. Being specific and accurate with image file names can also assist with SEO in this way too.
3. The alt text will be displayed if an image is broken so that the audience can still understand what is meant to be there even if the image cannot be loaded.

When writing alt text, keep the description concise (between 120–125 characters depending on the platform) and include only enough information that the person reading it will understand what is in the image. For example (■ Fig. 15.18),
A cat and a kitten enjoy the sunshine (73 characters)

As opposed to
A black cat and a ginger kitten lie on a red welcome mat in the sunshine on a beautiful summer's day on a Sunday in December (124 characters)

Do not skip the step of adding alt text when uploading visual content. Including alt text has many advantages. Strategically, it increases the reach, visibility and accessibility of content to a wider audience and should be included as a routine step in best-practice visual content creation (Bennett, Mott, Cutrell, & Morris, 2018; Morris, Johnson, Bennett, & Cutrell, 2018).

15.13 Visual Content Requirements for Specific Social Media Platforms

As ■ Table 15.8 demonstrates, the types of visual content facilitated on each social media platform and their specific requirements can vary widely and are constantly changing. While the details included in ■ Table 15.8 are accurate at the time of writing, it is recommended to check for any changes when creating content just to be sure.

Using graphic design tools such as Canva can also ensure that content meets all size requirements because templates within the tool are current in terms of accurate dimensions according to each platform.

Again, it is important to check social media platforms when creating content to ensure that specifications relating to visual content have not changed.

◨ **Fig. 15.18**   Adding alt text to LinkedIn images

◨ **Table 15.8**   Visual content supported by mainstream social media platforms with size recommendations (Arens, 2019; Google, 2019; Gotter, 2019; Hughes, 2019; Kolowich, 2019; WordPress, 2019; Yates, 2019)

Social media platform	Visual content types	Recommended size
Facebook	Profile picture	180 × 180 pixels
	Cover photo	820 × 312 pixels
	Post image	1200 × 630 pixels
	Link image	1200 × 628 pixels
	Highlighted image	1200 × 717 pixels
	Event image	1920 × 1080 pixels
	Stories	1080 × 920 pixels
Twitter	Profile photo	400 × 400 pixels
	Header image	1500 × 500 pixels
	Tweet image	440 × 220 pixels

15

Social media platform	Visual content types	Recommended size
Instagram	Profile photo	110 × 110 pixels
	Photo thumbnail	161 × 161 pixels
	Post image	180 × 180 pixels
	Stories	180 × 920 pixels
LinkedIn	Profile photo	400 × 400 pixels
	Background image	1584 × 396 pixels
	Company logo	300 × 300 pixels
	Square logo	60 × 60 pixels
	Company cover image	1536 × 768 pixels
	Company page banner image	646 × 220 pixels
	Company page hero image	1128 × 376 pixels
	Post and link images	1104 × 736 pixels
Pinterest	Profile picture	165 × 165 pixels
	Pins	Scaled at 236 pixels
YouTube	Channel profile image	800 × 800 pixels
	Channel cover photo	2560 × 1440 pixels
	Video thumbnail	1280 × 720 pixels
Snapchat	Advertisement image	1080 × 920 pixels
	Geofilter	1080 × 920 pixels
TikTok	Profile photo	200 × 200 pixels
Weibo	Profile photo	200 × 200 pixels
	Cover image	900 × 300 pixels
	Background image	1600 × 900 pixels
	Banner image	560 × 260 pixels
	Post image	440 × 400 pixels
WordPress (blog)	Profile photo (Gravatar)	512 × 512 pixels
	Thumbnails	150 × 150 pixels
	Featured image	1200 × 600 pixels

Table 15.8 (continued)

Conclusion

This chapter explored the importance of visual social media content and its influence on storytelling, information dissemination and audience engagement. Theoretical frameworks underpinning visual content such as semiotics, Gestalt Principles and the Rule of Thirds were also explored. Basic photography principles were examined to support Social Media Manager capturing quality images on behalf of a client or organisation. Additionally, key components relating to graphic design for social media were analysed including the production of images, infographics, memes and filters, and tools that can assist in their development. Furthermore, the importance of including ALT text as best-practice when posting images on social was discussed.

Guidance was also provided on how to brief professional visual content suppliers, photographers and graphic designers for high quality outcomes. The chapter concluded with an overview of the visual elements supported by mainstream social media platforms and the recommended sizes of each.

Case Study: Canva Generates 11.4 k Social Shares with Image Size Infographic

Graphic design tool, Canva, used social listening to understand the common questions asked by their customers and then used that insight to create a piece of highly shareable social media content (Patel, 2019). After extensively researching their target audience, Canva discovered that their customers frequently asked questions regarding the size specifications of images across mainstream social media platforms including Facebook, Twitter, Instagram, Tumblr, and YouTube (Kliever, 2019).

To address these commonly asked questions, Kliever (2019) wrote a blog post called: *'The complete social media image size guide: With awesome design tips,'* which included a wealth of useful information on the topic to assist current and prospective Canva customers.

However, the added value of this blog post was a colourful and well-designed infographic that contained all of the key image size requirements for the main social media platforms. An infographic such as this is useful because it can be shared easily via social media to other social media users. It can also be printed out and hung on the wall like a poster within a workstation so that it can be referred to as needed to prevent the person requiring the information from having to look it up online every time that they need it.

Kliever (2019) also wrote the article and designed the infographic with Search Engine Optimisation (SEO) principles in mind so that it could be easily located by people looking for the information covered in the blog post. This approach resulted in the infographic being shared online 11.4 k times generating significant exposure for Canva as a brand and providing such useful content assisted in generating positive brand associations with their target audience.

Patel (2019) recommends taking this approach to help encourage widespread sharing of social media content. Firstly, to identify information that a target audience regularly wants to know and create content to provide that information in a way that is of greatest use to them. In this case, the blog post was usefulful, but the infographic presented the information in an aesthetically pleasing way so that it could be easily identified to save trawling through the entire article to find an image size. This is yet another case of the powerful impact a well-designed infographic can have in engaging with a target audience on social media.

1. Why was Canva's infographic so successful?

2. What steps would you take if developing an infographic for a client?

15.14 Interview: Mongezi Lupindo, Social Media Manager, Africa and Middle East at Sage, Johannesburg, South Africa

1. **Welcome. Can you please introduce yourself and tell me about your current role?**

My name is Mongezi Lupindo. I'm South African, and I'm currently a social media and content manager for a global organisation called Sage. It's a software as a service company. It's a tech company.

I'm a Social Media and Content Manager for that. I look after organic social, which is really more around supporting campaigns, employee advocacy, influencer marketing, that kind of stuff.

2. **What do you enjoy most about working with social media?**

You learn something new every single day. Then also you get to interact with everyone, with every function across the organisation. That has been the most exciting thing for me. Whether it is chatting to ops people, operations, customer service, HR, brand, every space. I get to interact with everyone, and then learn quicker about the business than I would have in a normal traditional role.

3. **What do you find most challenging working with social media?**
While organisations are quite comfortable with or understand the impact of social media in the organisation, proving ROI remains a huge challenge. It's seen as a necessary evil. I always say it's like social media is a necessary evil. It has to be in every campaign, but people don't really, it's like it's always sort of put the last. You get called last in any of the planning sessions, which makes it much more ad hoc, and then now it becomes much more difficult to actually show true value.

Social media should start being seen as part of the marketing mix with its own measurements, with its own strategies. Not as a by-the-way. We have to have it, but that's one of those challenges.

4. **How did you come to work in social media? Tell me your career story.**
Quite by chance actually. Fresh from college I worked as a marketing manager/jack of all trades for a small export company. During that time budgets were quite thin and stretched. I remember that at that time I was doing trade shows, and they were quite expensive, and some advertising in trade show magazines as well.

Then I decided, I'm sure clearly there could be a better way of doing things, and digital was starting to become mainstream, especially here in South Africa. I started experimenting with Google Ads, and Facebook Ads, and I did a course, and I'm like, oh geez, I quite like this. So, I decided, okay great, let me experiment more on social media. I enjoyed it. I later did my honours and my dissertation was around social media.

Then I thought, okay great, now I quite like this. I went into advertising, where I've just specialised in social media ever since, across different sectors. From not for profit organisations, financial institutions, national tourism boards, automobile, tech now. I've really just walked across. B2B, B2C.

For about 7 years I've been a specialist in social media.

5. **If you could think of three important things that a social media manager, or social media professional should consider when creating visual content, what would you suggest?**
If you're looking over the past 5 years, since Instagram came in the picture, where visual imagery has just been one of the big things, especially that consumers use. It's primarily, when memes came in, the way people were using that just to communicate a single idea in just a picture. That's how communication has evolved.

You have to think of why people use social media in the first place. From information, seeking information and sharing information, that's one of the big themes of social media. Then also entertainment. Entertainment is one of the primary reasons why we use social media. We want to be entertained, and enjoy ourselves, and laughing, so that we can pass it on.

Those are the three main things that you have to try and get right. Whether it's sharable? From an information perspective. Is it entertaining? Also, how does that fit into that person's life, or values, or being that relevant? Those are the three things that I always look for.

I'll always look at trends. Since I'm in South Africa, for example, Twitter, especially in the urban areas, is so big, and people communicate with memes. We're always trying to incorporate the bigger themes, whether visually around that, those trends, in our campaigns, because that's how we get relevance. It really should be just maybe timely, interesting, something that people would share. Those are the key ingredients to creating compelling images or visuals.

6. **What do you think are the benefits of using visual content?**
Social media is a visual medium. Also, images grab attention. People don't want to be reading a whole bunch of information, so visuals make it easy in that it simplifies complex information into a really cool, easy visual. Whether it's an infographic, or a little short video, or a little meme. Where it's really that attention grabbing, but also just simplifies information into digestible chunks.

7. **What do you think are some of the challenges with using visual content?**
The challenges I find is that there's so much content out there. How do you break through the clutter, and be as relevant, and get the right mix? For example, as I said before, we've experimented a lot.

From high production content, where you've spent so much money on content, and it just does not perform well. Versus the low fly type of cellphone images, which is, what I find, especially with big brands who have their reputation on the line, that they're really afraid of experimenting, especially with sort of lower quality cell phone stuff. Getting that balance right, that whole high valued, high production, high cost content, versus really just low fly, quick let's take this on a phone and publish.

8. **How can visual content assist customers?**
There's so much clutter and there's so much competition out there for people's attention. It's just really just to simplify your message, simplify the solution. Bring forth your message in a few seconds really of looking at your content.

That then helps the customer to make better informed decisions quickly.

9. **What are some of your favourite tools that you use to create some visual content?**
Canva and GIPHY, Those are really cool. Because they're apps, you can use them on their phone, very quickly to use.

10. **What is the current landscape for, say social media management as a profession, or even social media specialists as a profession in South Africa?**
When I started you were expected to know everything. From being a Copy Writer, to a Community Manager. From long to short form copy, to analytical, to strategy. All those functions into one.

Now we're finding that, 5 years later, the roles are much more specialised. Now people understand that social media actually touches every aspect of the organisation. Now you're finding there will be five people in a social media team. I mean, About 2 years ago I was heading up a social media team of six people. A Community Manager, Writers, Strategists. It has become this big ecosystem that supports the rest of the business. People are starting to see it that way.

11. **Where do you see social media heading in the future?**
Social media is reaching its maturity stage and its adoption in most big organisations. People are now more comfortable and are willing to invest in social media. I'm predicting, as we mature, and as we are able to start proving performance marketing, especially for the organisations, we start seeing even greater career progression within the profession.

As soon as we start showing ROI and demonstrating how social media is actually impacting the organisation and this is how we fit into the entire customer journey. As soon as we start

15

proving those key points, we are earning our seat at the table, which we now start seeing more positions of Vice Presidents of social media. That's where it's going.

12. **What has been the best piece of advice that you have been given?**
You should always draw from human truth. Whatever content you're putting, or whatever strategy, whatever idea you have, use the human truth to tell that narrative. For me has been one of the greatest pieces of advice. As we are telling stories, our brand stories on social media, we should always draw to the human truth.

13. **What advice would you give to someone who wants to work in social media as a profession?**
Social media is ever-evolving, so don't be afraid to learn. Surrender yourself to learning and experimenting. That's the best thing that you could ever do for yourself. Learn about the organisation, learn about the people in it, learn about the different formats. Don't be afraid to experiment with different formats when they come. Be the first person to know about social media. You want to be the go-to person. Position yourself that way.

In my experience everybody thinks that they know social media. You go to a room with execs and they come up with these ideas. You're internally rolling your eyes. Be in a position of knowledge and be an advocate for social media.

Understanding measurement is essential. If you really are going to earn a seat at the table, get buy in, and more budget, you have to start speaking the language of ROI, and measurement, and showing value. Those are the most important things.

❓ Questions for Critical Reflection

1. Name five key benefits of using visual content on social media. Please explain your answer.

2. What is semiotics and how does it apply to visual social media content? Please provide an example.

3. What is the key premise in relation to the Gestalt Principles? Why is this important when creating social media content?

4. What is the 'Rule of Thirds' and how does it assist when taking photographs?

5. What are the key components of graphics and why should they be considered during content creation?

6. Why is it important to accurately brief a professional graphic designer or photographer?

7. What is an infographic and what type of information are they helpful to communicate?

8. What are the differences between GIFs, memes, filters and geofilters? Please explain your answer.

❯ Practical Exercises

1. Using the advice from this chapter, follow the three stages of the photography process. During the Production Stage take the following photographs:
   - Human Subjects (1 person, two people, 3–5 people. Portrait and undertaking an activity)
   - Nature (tree, flower, clouds, landscape, waterscape, sunrise/sunset)
   - Animals (cat/dog, bird, any safely accessible animals).
   - Food
   - Objects

   In the Post-Production Phase use these photos to experiment with the free image editing tools featured in ◘ Table 15.1 to find your favourite. Explain your experience with the rest of the class.

2. Select some of the statistics referenced in this chapter to create an infographic to communicate the impact of using visual content on social media. Use one of the tools listed in

❏ Table 15.4. Share your infographic design process with the class.

3. Using the advice and tools suggested in this chapter, identify a currently trending topic and create a GIF or a meme about it. Share your rationale and experience with the rest of the class.

References

Arens, E. (2019). Facebook, Instagram, Linkedin, Pinterest, Twitter - Always Up-to-Date Guide to Social Media Image Sizes, *Sprout Social*, viewed 29.09.2019, https://sproutsocial.com/insights/social-media-image-sizes-guide.

Bennett, C. L., Mott, M. E., Cutrell, E., & Morris, M. R. (2018). How teens with visual impairments take, edit, and share photos on social media. In *Proceedings of the 2018 CHI conference on human factors in computing systems* (p. 76). Montreal: ACM.

Bleier, A., De Keyser, A., & Verleye, K. (2018). Customer engagement through personalization and customization. In *Customer engagement marketing* (pp. 75–94). Cham: Palgrave Macmillan.

Booth, P. (2015). *Playing fans: Negotiating fandom and media in the digital age*. Iowa: University of Iowa Press.

Brubaker, P. J., & Wilson, C. (2018). Let's give them something to talk about: Global brands' use of visual content to drive engagement and build relationships. *Public Relations Review, 44*(3), 342–352.

Bullas, J. (2018a). 6 Powerful Reasons Why you Should include Images in your Marketing – Infographic, *Jeff Bullas*, viewed 30.09.2019, https://www.jeffbullas.com/6-powerful-reasons-why-you-should-include-images-in-your-marketing-infographic/.

Bullas, J. (2018b). 20 Cool Tools for Creating Infographics, *Jeff Bullas*, viewed 30.09.2019, https://www.jeffbullas.com/20-cool-tools-creating-infographics/.

Buşan, A. M. (2014). Learning styles of medical students - implications in education. *Current Health Sciences Journal., 40*(2), 104–110. https://doi.org/10.12865/CHSJ.40.02.04

Byrom M (2014) The power of visual communication infographic, *Business2Community*, viewed 30.09.2019, http://www.business2community.com/infographics/power-visual-communication-infographic-0797752#rLdrC6ZhKpq4JAwU.97.

Callahan, C., Church, S. H., King, J., & Elinzano, M. (2019). Snapchat usage among minority populations. *Journal of Media and Religion, 18*(1), 1–12.

Canning, N. (2019a). How to create your own instagram stories filter (using spark AR studio), *Later*, viewed 1.10.2019, https://later.com/blog/create-instagram-stories-filter/.

Capcan, P. (2019). 6 Gestalt Principles, *UX Cheat*, viewed 30.09.2019, https://uxcheat.com/visual-ui-design/gestalt-principles/.

Chamberlain, L. (2016). GeoMarketing 101: What are geofilters?, *GeoMarketing*, viewed 1.10.2019, https://geomarketing.com/geomarketing-101-what-are-geofilters.

Cherry, K. (2019). What is gestalt psychology? *Very Well Mind*, viewed 30.09.2019, https://www.verywellmind.com/what-is-gestalt-psychology-2795808.

Christensen, S., & Pionke, J. J. (2019). Social media best practices: Implementing guidelines for disability and copyright. In *Social Media* (pp. 45–55). Hull: Chandos Publishing.

Dawkins, R. (1976). *The selfish gene*. Oxford, England: Oxford University Press.

DeFelice, K. (2019). How to write an effective design brief, *Canva*, viewed 1.10.2019, https://www.canva.com/learn/effective-design-brief/.

Duggal, E., & Verma, H. V. (2019). Relationship quality and customer demographics in Indian retail. In *Dynamic perspectives on globalization and sustainable business in Asia* (pp. 106–127). IGI Global.

Edwards, C., Stoll, B., Faculak, N., & Karman, S. (2015). Social presence on LinkedIn: Perceived credibility and interpersonal attractiveness based on user profile picture. Online Journal of Communication and Media Technologies, 5(4), 102.

Elliot, K. (2019). Should you be adding alt text to your social images? *KWSM Digital*, viewed 30.09.2019, https://kwsmdigital.com/should-you-be-adding-alt-text-to-your-social-images-2/.

Erton, I. (2018). The essence of semiotics as a mediator of communication and cognition. *International Online Journal of Education and Teaching, 5*(2), 267–277.

Facebook. (2019). About text in ad images, Facebook.com, viewed 30.09.2019, https://www.facebook.com/business/help/980593475366490.

Fox, A. K., Nakhata, C., & Deitz, G. D. (2019). Eat, drink, and create content: A multi-method exploration of visual social media marketing content. *International Journal of Advertising, 38*(3), 450–470.

Google. (2019). Add video thumbnails, *Google Support*, viewed: 29.09.2019, https://support.google.com/youtube/answer/72431?hl=en.

Gotter, A. (2019). The Best WordPress Featured Image Size & Post Thumbnail Tips, *Snappa*, viewed 29.09.2019, https://blog.snappa.com/wordpress-featured-image-size/.

Gretzel, U. (2017). The visual turn in social media marketing. *Tourismos, 12*(3), 1–17.

Hughes, J, (2019). How to change thumbnail size in WordPress and why you want to, *Elegant Themes*, viewed 29.09.2019, https://www.elegantthemes.com/blog/tips-tricks/how-to-change-thumbnail-size-in-wordpress-and-why-you-want-to.

Khamitov, M., Wang, X. S., & Thomson, M. (2019). How well do consumer-brand relationships drive customer brand loyalty? Generalizations from a meta-analysis of brand relationship elasticities. Forthcoming, *Journal of Consumer Research*.

Kliever, J. (2019). The complete social media image size guide: With awesome design tips [infographic], *Canva*, viewed: 24/11/2019, https://www.canva.com/learn/social-media-image-size/.

Kolowich, L. (2019). Your Bookmarkable Guide to Social Media Image Sizes, *Hubspot*, viewed 29.09.2019, https://blog.hubspot.com/marketing/ultimate-guide-social-media-image-dimensions-infographic.

Kolowich, L. (2017). Why Are Infographics So Darn Effective? [Infographic], *Hubspot*, viewed 30.09.2019, https://blog.hubspot.com/marketing/effectiveness-infographics#sm.00026qpk916kfeunwb11a31w9qelb.

Lepard, C. (2017). What are GIFs and how to effectively use them on social media, *WIX Blog*, viewed 1.10.2019, https://www.wix.com/blog/2017/11/gifs-in-social-media.

Long, B. (2011). *Complete digital photography*. Boston: Course Technology.

Manic, M. (2015). Marketing engagement through visual content. *Bulletin of the Transilvania University of Brasov. Economic Sciences. Series V, 8*(2), 89.

Medina, J. (2018). *Brain rules for ageing well: 10 principles for staying vital, happy, and sharp*. Victoria: Scribe Publications.

Microscope. (2019). Image resolution, size and compression, microbus, viewed 30.09.2019, https://microscope-microscope.org/microscope-info/image-resolution/.

Miltner, K. M., & Highfield, T. (2017). Never gonna GIF you up: Analyzing the cultural significance of the animated GIF. *Social Media + Society, 3*(3), 2056305117725223.

Morris, M. R., Johnson, J., Bennett, C. L., & Cutrell, E. (2018). Rich representations of visual content for screen reader users. In *Proceedings of the 2018 CHI conference on human factors in computing systems* (p. 59). Montreal: ACM.

National Geographic. (2011). *Complete photography - the one-stop creative photography reference that covers it all*. Washington DC: National Geographic Society.

News.com.au. (2016). Liberal Party slammed after launching Snapchat filter, News.com.au, viewed: 27/11/2019, https://www.news.com.au/national/federal-election/liberal-party-slammed-after-launching-snapchat-filter/news-story/9fad12389cd1a9fbcb7931b5aacec34d.

Orsow, A. (2017). 7 tips for designing awesome animated GIFs, *Inside Design*, viewed 1.10.2019, https://www.invisionapp.com/inside-design/7-tips-for-designing-awesome-gifs/.

Patel, N. (2019). Content Marketing Case Study: How 4 Infographics Generated Over 10,000 Social Shares, *Neil Patel*, viewed: 24/11/2019, https://neilpatel.com/blog/content-marketing-case-study-how-4-infographics-generated-over-10000-social-shares/.

Pinantoan, A. (2015). How to massively boost your blog traffic with these 5 awesome image stats, *BuzzSumo*, viewed 1.10.2019, https://buzzsumo.com/blog/how-to-massively-boost-your-blog-traffic-with-these-5-awesome-image-stats/.

Poulsen, S. V., Kvåle, G., & van Leeuwen, T. (2018). Special issue: Social media as semiotic technology. *Social Semiotics, 28*(5), 593–600.

Price, D., & Wells, L. (2009). Thinking about photography. In L. Wells (Ed.), *Photography: A critical introduction* (4th ed., pp. 9–64). Oxon: Routledge.

Robin, B. R., & McNeil, S. G. (2019). *Digital storytelling. The international encyclopedia of media literacy* (pp. 1–8). Wiley-Blackwell.

Rogers, S. (2014). What fuels a Tweet's engagement?, *Twitter*, viewed 1.10.2019, https://blog.twitter.com/official/en_us/a/2014/what-fuels-a-tweets-engagement.html.

Siricharoen, W. V., & Siricharoen, N. (2018). Infographic utility in accelerating better health communication. *Mobile Networks and Applications, 23*(1), 57–67.

Snap Marketing. (2015). Top 10 tips for a great graphic design brief, *Snap*, viewed 1.10.2019, https://www.snap.com.au/articles/top-10-tips-for-a-great-graphic-design-brief.html.

Sutherland, K. (2017). Marketing Food on Instagram, *Dr Karen Sutherland*, viewed 5.10.2019, https://drkarensutherland.com/2017/03/25/marketing-food-on-instagram/.

Thomas, K. (2013). Revisioning the smiling villain: Imagetexts and intertextual expression in representations of the filmic Loki on Tumblr. *Transformative Works and Cultures, 13*, viewed 1/10/2019, http://journal.transformativeworks.org/index.php/twc/article/view/474/382.

Trafton, A. (2014). In the blink of an eye MIT neuroscientists find the brain can identify images seen for as little as 13 milliseconds, *MIT News*, viewed 30.09.2019, http://news.mit.edu/2014/in-the-blink-of-an-eye-0116.

Triggs, T. (2017). Visual rhetoric and semiotics. In T. Triggs & L. Atzmon (Eds.), *The graphic design reader*. New York: Bloomsbury Visual Arts.

Ulanoff, L. (2016). The secret history of the GIF. *Mashable*, viewed 1.10.2019, http://mashable.com/2016/08/10/history-of-the-gif/#UgkIE3El7sqa.

Varis, P., & Blommaert, J. (2015). Conviviality and collectives on social media: Virality, memes, and new social structures. *Multilingual Margins: A Journal of Multilingualism from the Periphery, 2*(1), 31–31.

Vice. (2016). The Liberal Party Just Got Its Own Snapchat Filter, *Vice*, viewed: 24/11/2019, https://www.vice.com/en_au/article/xd3454/the-liberal-party-get-its-own-snapchat-filter.

WordPress. (2019). Gravatars, *WordPress support*, viewed 29.09.2019, https://en.support.wordpress.com/gravatars/.

Wright, T. (2016). *The photography handbook*. New York: Routledge.

Yates, L. (2019). What image size do you need for the world's 20 biggest social networks? [Updated For 2019], *Blogging dot Com*, viewed 29.09.2019, https://blogging.com/social-media-image-sizes/.

Further Reading

Canning, N. (2019b). How to create your own instagram stories filter (using spark AR studio), *Later*, viewed 1.10.2019, https://later.com/blog/create-instagram-stories-filter/.

Chandler, D. (2017). *Semiotics: The basics*. London: Routledge.

Cope, P. (2018). *The smartphone photography guide: Shoot* Edit* Experiment* share*. London: Carlton Books, Ltd.

Milner, R. M. (2016). *The world made meme: Public conversations and participatory media*. Cambridge: MIT Press.

Riley, S. (2018). *Mindful design: How and why to make design decisions for the good of those using your product*. New York: Springer.

Thompson, J. & Baird, F. (2019). How to Make a GIF: 4 Tried and True Methods, Hootsuite, viewed: 1.10.2019, https://blog.hootsuite.com/how-to-make-gif/.

Triggs, T., & Atzmon, L. (2019). *The graphic design reader*. New York: Bloomsbury Academic.

Helpful Links

Photography

Adobe Photoshop.: https://www.adobe.com/au/products/photoshop.html

Adobe Photoshop Lightroom.: https://www.adobe.com/au/products/photoshop-lightroom/edit-photos.html

GIMP.: https://www.gimp.org/

PicMonkey.: https://www.picmonkey.com/

Photographic Release Form (Template Lab).: http://templatelab.com/photo-release-form/#Photo_Release_Form_Templates

Snapseed.: https://snapseed.online/

Graphic Design

Adobe InDesign.: https://www.google.com

Adobe Spark.: https://spark.adobe.com/

Canva.: https://www.canva.com

Over.: https://www.madewithover.com

Infographics

Visme.co.: https://www.visme.co

Easel.ly.: https://www.easel.ly

Piktochart.: https://piktochart.com/

Memes

Imgur.: https://imgur.com/memegen

Livememe.: https://www.livememe.com

Quickmeme.: http://www.quickmeme.com/

GIFs

Image GIFs.: https://ezgif.com/maker

Video GIFs.: https://ezgif.com/video-to-gif

Giphy.: https://giphy.com/

Makeagif.: https://makeagif.com

Filters/Geofilters

Lens Studio.: https://lensstudio.snapchat.com

Snapchat Create.: https://www.snapchat.com/create

Spark AR Studio.: https://sparkar.facebook.com/ar-studio/

15

Producing Videos that Pop

Contents

© The Author(s), under exclusive license to Springer Nature Singapore Pte Ltd. 2021
K. E. Sutherland, *Strategic Social Media Management*, https://doi.org/10.1007/978-981-15-4658-7_16

By the End of this Chapter You Will

- Learn why social media video is such an effective way to communicate and engage with a target audience.
- Become familiar with a range of video formats that can work well in a social media environment.
- Understand the differences between vertical and landscape video and best uses of each.
- Know the video specifications for mainstream social media platforms.
- Gain an in-depth insight into the three phases of video production: Pre-Production, Production and Post-Production.
- Learn how to effectively brief a professional videographer.
- Learn the four important stages in the Post-Production process.

TLDR

- Video content has the capability to convey comprehensive details within defined time periods and encourages much greater rates of information retention and comprehension.
- Video is also a powerful tool to generate positive word-of-mouth and in building brand and organisational identity.
- There are many varieties of video formats such as 'How To' or interviews, but their selection must be aligned with the relevant stage in the customer journey.
- The orientation of a video (landscape, square or vertical) depends on the specifications of the social media platform.
- It is most effective to upload a video natively to a platform than linking through to a different website.
- Budget, time, equipment, purpose and expertise are all considerations when deciding to produce a video in-

house or appoint an external videographer.
- Providing a clear and detailed brief to a professional videographer improves the likelihood of a successful end product.
- The three stages of video production are: Pre-Production, Production and Post-Production.
- Planning is the most important component of the video production process.
- Risk minimisation and flexibility are the keys to a successful video shoot.
- There are four vital stages in the Post-Production process: 1. Gathering all required elements, 2. Loading elements into the video editing tool, 3. Arranging components in order, 4. Rendering.
- Closed Captions are an essential inclusion on any social media video.

16.1 Introduction

Video has become a fundamental form of strategic social media content. Annually, predictions are made in digital marketing blogs about the future trends of social media for the coming year and video is nearly always on the list (Ahmad, 2019; Goodwin, 2019; O'Brien, 2019). These predictions about video are incorrect. Video is not a future trend. Video has been an essential part of strategic social media for many years. This is why it is crucial from a strategic social media management perspective to understand the format and the process of creating compelling video content that connects with target audiences on behalf of clients or an organisation. If a client or organisation is not regularly producing videos for their social media platforms, they need to start now, and this chapter can help to make that happen.

▶ Chapter 16 explores the process of producing and editing engaging social media videos for a range of platforms and in a variety of formats. It also presents the pros and cons of video-related debates around vertical versus landscape video, posting natively or linking through to other sites, using a smartphone instead of a digital video camera and when to produce video in-house compared with appointing a professional video producer. The phenomenon and production of live video for platforms such as Facebook, Twitter, YouTube and Instagram will also be investigated with key principles imparted to plan and execute an effective livestream. Essentially, this chapter explains the process of video production, providing a detailed analysis of the pre-production, production and post-production process and the various tools and information required to make it a success. As you will discover with video production, it can be Murphy's Law during the production phase; anything can go wrong. This chapter will help to plan ahead to minimise the risks that are within your control. Careful planning is the key.

16.2 Why Video?

The popularity of video stems from its ability to convey significant amounts of information in an efficient way. Dr. James McQuivey of Forrester Research has been quoted as suggesting that "a one-minute video is worth 1.8 million words," (Harrison, 2016). While this statistic has been disputed (Audiohype, 2018), research studies have confirmed the power of video as an educational tool (Hung, Kinshuk, & Chen, 2018).

A study by Hung, Kinshuk and Chen (2018) found that video's capability to convey comprehensive details within defined time periods can encourage much greater rates of information retention and comprehension. Conveying information in a way that is both understood and retained by target audiences assists considerably when attempting to position a brand, product or service as top-of-mind as discussed in ▶ Chap. 3.

Additional studies have also suggested that video is also a powerful tool to generate positive word-of-mouth and in building brand and organisational identity (Sutherland, 2019a, 2019b; Smyth, 2011; Hung & Higgins, 2016; Hsieh, Hsieh, & Tang, 2012; Waters & Jones, 2011). It can be much easier to form a connection with the person or people behind a brand when they speak directly to the audience through a video. A brand can become three dimensional. Videos convey body language, movement, facial expressions and sounds that can build much stronger connections than those attempted through text and/or static images.

At time of writing, videos on the mainstream platforms such as Facebook, LinkedIn and Twitter seem to generate much greater reach if the content is compelling prompting users to engage with it. As we explored in ▶ Chap. 7 the algorithms of the major social media platforms tend to increase the reach of content that has generated a high degree of engagement within the first hour of posting (Barnhart, 2019). Taking a strategic approach to video production will help to support goals and objectives. Slapping together a video for the sake of it will result in it sailing past your target audience on their newsfeed without them taking notice (if it makes it to their newsfeed at all).

16

> ❝ Slapping together a video for the sake of it will result in it sailing past your target audience on their newsfeed without them taking notice (if it makes it to their newsfeed at all). ❞
>
> **Dr Karen Sutherland**

Another advantage of producing video for social media is that it can be repurposed and used as different content types for a range of platforms. This approach is also known as chunking (Handley & Chapman, 2010). Chunking is a practice used and promoted by digital marketing leaders such as Gary Vaynerchuk (2019) who even generously published instructions detailing *'How to Create 64 Pieces of Content in a Day'* which is listed in the Helpful Links section at the end of this chapter.

A simplified example of chunking is detailed below:

1. 20 minute video interview is recorded with an industry expert
2. The entire video is posted to YouTube.
3. The video is edited into smaller, platform-appropriate lengths to post on Facebook, LinkedIn, Instagram, IGTV and Twitter.
4. The video is transcribed and text reworked to use as a blog post and LinkedIn article.
5. Relevant quotes pulled out to create graphic content for Facebook, Instagram, LinkedIn and Twitter.

As demonstrated above, one 20 minute video can create multiple pieces of content that can be edited to suit the specifications of each platform. Therefore, as a content type, the versatility of video is evident.

This chapter will guide you on how to produce videos that support the achievement of the goals and objectives for a client or organisation as identified in ▶ Sect. 1 of this text.

16.3 Video Formats

A wide range of video formats exist that can assist in connecting with a target audience while conveying key messages and supporting the goals and objectives of a social media strategy.

Social media video fits within two broad categories: Live and Recorded as detailed below.

Live video is the broadcast (of livestream) of video in real-time across one or multiple social media channels (Rein & Venturini, 2018).

■ **Advantages**

Live video is a great way to capture attention from existing followers, because all receive a notification when a client or spokesperson begins a live video on their official social media profiles.

Live streaming can also generate engagement and live two-way interaction with audiences as they react or write questions and comments to the person live-streaming or to interact with other viewers. In fact, live video has been suggested to positively influence gift-giving and tourist opinions and behaviour as people perceived live video as providing a more authentic insight than recorded video (Huertas, 2018; Yu, Jung, Kim, & Jung, 2018).

■ **Live Video Reaps Its Rewards for TikTok Influencers**

For example, on TikTok users are provided with live video access once they have 1 k followers and those watching them have the ability to send monetary gifts.

Real currency is exchanged for virtual coins that are then used to purchase Influencers gifts (TikTok, 2019). Once the influencer receives a gift, it turns into a diamond.

The influencer can exchange these for real currency once the amount reaches $100 using a PayPal account (TikTok, 2019).

Turkish chef, Burak Özdemir (Czn Burak) has been reported to have earned more than $10 million on TikTok as a result of his live cooking demonstrations (Leskin, 2019).

▪ Risks

A disadvantage is that there is less control with live video in terms of what social media users can see. Live video cannot be edited. However, it can be downloaded and edited after it is broadcast, but this does not minimise the risk at the time it is being live-streamed.

▪ Officials Embarrassed After Facebook Live Goes Rogue

Canadian Police were deeply embarrassed when using Facebook Live during a press conference reporting on a double homicide, because a cat filter appeared on the police spokesperson during the broadcast (Vesoulis, 2019).

A similar incident occurred in Pakistan where Shaukat Yousafazi, a regional minister led a media conference using Facebook Live to discuss local issues and the same cat filter (cat ears, a blackshiny nose and whiskers) appeared on the vision of the Minister throughout the broadcast (Klar, 2019).

Both examples highlight the risks involved with using live video particularly when communicating about highly sensitive and serious topics. It can be challenging to be perceived as professional and credible with what is supposed to be an amusing filter distracting viewers from the message being communicated.

▪ Equipment

Live video requires a stable internet connection, a camera and a microphone (a smartphone, a laptop or a desktop with a webcam) will suffice for basic native live-streaming within Facebook and Instagram. However, some platforms (e.g. LinkedIn and Twitter) require third party tools to facilitate live-streaming. Third party tools are also required to broadcast live video simultaneously across social media platforms and can add extra features such as screen sharing and graphics to the video. Please see the Helpful Links section at the end of this chapter for a list of third party live-streaming tools.

Additionally, as mentioned in ▶ Chap. 6, the onset of COVID-19, video conferencing tools such Zoom, Google Meet, and Facebook Rooms rising in popularity to facilitate online events during the lockdown period. These tools are extremely simple to use and have free features (Google Meet and Facebook Rooms are free). Zoom also has recording functionality so that video can be later downloaded and edited for use as social media content. The Helpful Links section also includes a list of resources for these video conferencing tools.

▪ Tips for Broadcasting Live Video

The process for broadcasting live video is very similar to that of recorded video explored later in this chapter. Live video still undergoes pre-production and production processes, but post-production is optional (Stewart, 2017a). Careful planning is required for a successful live video experience. During the broadcast, interaction with viewers is important, but remaining focused on delivering the key messages requires much greater attention. People will switch off in a flash if the on-camera talent does not get to the point quickly and rambles instead. Respect an audience's time and give them something that is worth interrupting their day.

16

Recorded video is the footage gathered and edited before it is uploaded to one or more social media channels.

It allows for much greater control but can be more costly and take longer to produce. However, recorded video also allows for much greater flexibility in terms of format as listed in ▣ Table 16.1. The video formats listed in ▣ Table 16.1 includes a description of their approach and the stage of the customer journey for which they may be suitable (as explored in ▶ Chaps. 3 and 5).

In theory, these formats can be posted on most social media platforms that support video but must be configured to suit the specifications of each. In reality, some formats may be more challenging than others to execute effectively on particular platforms. For example, producing a 15 second or 1 minute 'How To' video for TikTok is not

▣ **Table 16.1**	Common social media video formats	
Video format	**Description**	**Customer journey phase suitability**
Explainer	These videos focus on communicating the 'why'. This could involve explaining why a client started their business, why a product was invented, why an event or nonprofit was created etc. For example, a video explaining why an annual CEO Sleepout event was created to raise money to assist people who are experiencing homelessness.	Awareness Interest
How to	An instructional video that teaches the audience how to complete a specific task to solve a common problem. For example, a personal trainer could teach the audience how to complete a deadlift without causing injury to the back.	Awareness Interest Desire Support
Product or service demonstration	A video that shows the audience how a specific product or service works. For example, a dishwasher manufacturer demonstrating what each of the settings do on a particular model.	Interest Desire Support
Interviews	A video that documents the discussion between two or more people. Usually there is an interviewer who asks questions of someone who is of specific interest to the audience. For example, a Facebook group for entrepreneurs interviewing Richard Branson.	Awareness Interest
Behind-the-scenes	These videos show the audience the inner-workings of a business or organisation that are usually not public facing. Do this provides the audience with a glimpse of the action that they do not usually get to see. For example, showing the happenings backstage at a gala charity ball or at a factory sharing the process of how a specific product is made.	Interest Support Loyalty
Q&A	These videos provide answers to the audience's commonly asked questions. They can take place as a live video so that it is highly interactive, or the questions can be collected ahead of time and their answers pre-recorded. If pre-recording, it is recommended that each video only contains one question and answer at a time to keep the content focused and easy to digest for the audience. For example, a florist may be regularly asked how to keep cut flowers fresher for longer and answer this question in a 1-minute video.	Awareness Interest Desire Support Loyalty

(continued)

Table 16.1 (continued)

Video format	Description	Customer journey phase suitability
Customer testimonials	Word-of-mouth remains as one of the most effective marketing tools. Videos with customers sharing their positive experiences with a client, organisation or product can really help a prospective customer decide whether to act and make a purchase. Rather announcing how good it is, a customer testimonial can provide that evidence by showing rather than telling (see ▶ Chap. 6). Customer testimonials should be brief and to the point. They should also specifically address a problem or pain point commonly experienced by prospective customers and explain how a client's product or service helped to overcome it. For example, a customer sharing their story of how a landscaping company designed a small backyard to be a comfortable outdoor area.	Desire Support Loyalty Advocacy
Product review	Product reviews can involve customers, or they can be presented by a client or other organisational representative. The goal of a product review video is not to review a client's products or their competitors. Instead they should be created to help customers to save time by providing general advice about a range of products on the market that are of interest to them that are still within the brand's expertise. For example, an interior designer could produce a video where they review a range of similar bathroom tiles on the market from least expensive to most expensive. This will establish their credibility and expertise in their field while providing the audience (home renovators specifically) with an overview of a range of tile products on the market.	Awareness Interest
Event Wrap Ups	Events Wrap Ups are also extremely helpful for people interested in a specific event. They provide an overview of the key take-aways for those who could not attend and also provide a document summarising the event as a reminder for the people who went. For example, as a Social Media Manager, attending an industry event such as Social Media Marketing World provides the perfect opportunity to create a video that communicates the key take-aways back to current and prospective clients. It also establishes you as someone who keeps their skills and knowledge up-to-date. This is the same for clients in any field who can take the same approach when attending conferences and other industry events.	Awareness
Staff introductions	Brief videos introducing the people who work for a business or organisation is a great way to build relationships with a target audience. It is challenging for the audience to build a relationship with a business or organisation without feeling a connection with the people who drive it. Staff introductions bring the heart and soul of an organisation into the light so that a feeling of connection can be cultivated. For example, a medical centre could make a 1-minute video introducing the new receptionist. This will help customers feel at ease by seeing a familiar face behind the counter when visiting the centre for medical advice.	Awareness Support Loyalty

16

▣ Table 16.1 (continued)		
Video format	**Description**	**Customer journey phase suitability**
Promotions/ Competitions/ Offers/Giveaways	These types of video must be handled cautiously to ensure that they comply with legal and platform requirements (see ▶ Chap. 4). Videos in this format explain the promotion, competition and giveaway. Competitions also require the announcement of the winners. For example, a video from a Japanese restaurant offering a 5% discount to customers who mention the code word from the video when they order.	Desire Loyalty
News & Announcements	These video formats relay important information or developments relating to an industry, a client, business or organisation that are of direct interest to the target audience. Remember, the audience must come first and sometimes just because a client thinks the information is extremely important, it may not be for the people they are trying to connect with and can cause them to disengage instead. Examples of video in this format may be if a business is moving, a new product being launched or a change in the law and how it will affect the target audience. For example, an accountant may create a brief video to announce a change to tax law and its potential impacts.	Awareness Support Loyalty

impossible, but definitely more difficult than producing a 3 minute 'How To' video for Facebook.

Therefore, please approach the video formats in ▣ Table 16.1 as genres and compare them with the social media platform video specifications in ▣ Table 16.3 to determine which formats best support a client's or organisation's goals, objectives and most importantly, their audience.

> ❝ The most important consideration when selecting a video format is how it can bring value to the target audience. What problem will it solve with the information it conveys? ❞
>
> **Dr Karen Sutherland**

In terms of video formats, it is also worthwhile to consider is Dennis Yu's 3 × 3 Video Grid Strategy as featured in ▣ Fig. 16.1, which provides a logical way to move target audiences through the customer journey stages of awareness, consideration (interest and desire) and conversion (action) using a series of nine 1 minute videos (Yu, 2019a, 2019b).

The 3 × 3 Video Grid Strategy recommends creating three formats of 1-minute videos with three different videos within each format. The first format is the 'Why' video similar to the Explainer video featured in ▣ Table 16.1. Creating three separate videos explaining a client or organisation's motivation behind three different aspects of

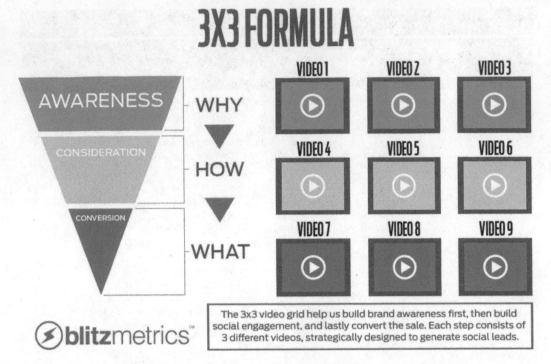

Fig. 16.1   Dennis Yu's 3 × 3 Video Grid Strategy (Yu, 2019a, p. 36)

their brand helps a target audience to learn more about them.

Why: For example, a restaurant owner could produce one video explaining where their love of food originated, another explaining why they wanted to open their restaurant and a third explaining why they selected the name of their restaurant.

How: The restaurant owner could produce one video of them interviewing the chef while they make a simple recipe from the menu, another interview with the Sommelier advising on how to match the correct wine with the dish made by the chef in the previous video and a third video sharing feedback from some customers after finishing the food and wine from the previous videos.

What: The final three videos are where the offer is made. The restaurant owner could produce one video promoting the new menu, another promoting the wine list and free tastings and a final video promoting a two-for-one deal on a particular day of the week.

This strategy is specifically Facebook-related and Yu (2019a) recommends sequencing the videos so that only those audience members who have seen the first will see the second, and only those who have seen the second will see the third and so on. This is to ensure that the target audience is moving through the customer journey and that only those audience members who have shown an interest will be retargeted. Please see ▶ Chap. 6 for more information and helpful resources about Facebook advertising.

There are many other video formats that can work on social media platforms. Those presented in ◘ Table 16.1 and ◘ Fig. 16.1 provide only an overview. There are links to further resources in the Helpful Links section at the end of this chapter. With an insight of video formats, the next step is to understand more about the social media platforms that can support them.

16.4 Social Media Platforms Supporting Videos

Presently, all mainstream social media platforms can support video content, which is a huge shift from the early days of social media (Lach, 2017). With the rapid evolution of smartphones, the ability to produce video content has been made highly accessible to anyone owning this technology, increasing the demand for social media platforms to be optimised for user generated video content.

While there is considerable choice in terms of social media platforms that support video content, as with other forms such as text and image-based content, video content is not one-size-fits-all. Each social media platform has its own specifications and characteristics in terms of audiences that are most suitable. However, with the platforms constantly changing, specifications and audience preferences continue to move with them.

▣ Table 16.2 provides details regarding video duration recommendations for each mainstream social media platform at time of writing, as reported by Chi (2019) and Bedrina (2018). These may be different by the time you read this, and it is always advisable to research video specifications for each platform from a range of sources as part of the pre-production process. The notion of 'measure twice, cut once' applies to more than building. Understanding platforms specifications before planning a video can greatly reduce the risk of having to reshoot it because it does not comply.

16.5 Ongoing Social Media Video Debates

There is much speculation surrounding various aspects of video production for social media which should be explored to provide guidance if they are encountered during the

▣ **Table 16.2** Video duration recommendations for mainstream social media platforms

Social media platform	Video type	Recommendations
Facebook	Recorded	1–3 minutes
	Live	15–19 minutes
	Stories	15 seconds
Instagram	Recorded	30 seconds
	Live	Not stated. Maximum length 1 hour.
	Stories	15 seconds
	IGTV	Not stated. Maximum length between 10 minutes and 1 hour.
YouTube	Recorded	5–7 minutes
Fleets 6 secs	Live	Not stated. Maximum length 8 hours
Twitter	Recorded	45 seconds
	Live	Not stated.
LinkedIn	Stories	15 seconds
	Recorded	30–90 seconds
	Live	10–30 minutes
Snapchat	Snaps	10 seconds
TikTok	Recorded	15–60 seconds Live (once you have 1 k followers)
WeChat	Video Calls	Unlimited
	Moments	15 seconds
Vimeo	Recorded	Not stated. Limits to file size depending on subscription type.
	Live	Not stated.
Pinterest	Promotion	15–30 seconds

day-to-day practices of a Social Media Manager. Debates, ongoing and new, abound in the social media management space, but some of the most prominent relating to video are explained below.

16.5.1 Vertical Vs Square Vs Landscape

The debate surrounding the effectiveness of vertical versus landscape video has raged for a number of years (Menotti, 2019; Voorveld, 2019). Traditionally, landscape (16:9) video has been considered industry standard because it resembled the broadcast quality content that we were used to seeing on our television screens or in movie theatres (Menotti, 2019).

With the widespread adoption of smartphones, the dimensions changed within which people most commonly consumed video content (Angova, Tsankova, Ossikovski, Nikolova, & Valchanov, 2019). This evolution resulted in video being consumed in less traditional dimensions such as square (1:1) and vertical (4:5) in feeds or (2:3) or (9:16) in Stories (see ◨ Fig. 16.2) (Forno, 2019).

Not only did these new dimensions disrupt traditional video production principles, they also sparked speculation as to which ones generated the greatest amount of engagement and reach.

Studies have indicated that square video (1:1) outperforms traditional landscape (16:9) video. One study found that "...square video resulted in 30-35% higher video views and an 80-100% increase in engagement," and it cost "7.5% less to get someone to engage with square video on Facebook" and "33% less to get someone to engage with square video on Instagram," (Peters, 2019a).

A similar study was conducted comparing the performance of vertical and square video and found that vertical video on a Facebook newsfeed cost up to 68% less per view and up to 38% less CPC (cost per click) than square video (Peters, 2019b). Yet, vertical video does not work well on every platform. ◨ Table 16.3 provides recommendations in terms of video dimensions for the mainstream social media platforms analysed in this chapter. The dimensions are listed in order of performance.

◨ Table 16.3 demonstrates the variations between platforms in terms of video dimensions. As will be explored in the pre-production and production phases further in this chapter, if planning to post videos across several platforms, it helps to record videos in more than one aspect ratio (vertical and square and landscape to ensure that it is possible. While there are editing tools that can alter dimensions it is a risk to rely on them to change this in the post-production phase. It is better to think ahead and record everything that you could possibly need rather than working out in the editing phase that you have to plan an additional shoot. The next debate analysed is whether it is more effective to upload videos natively to each platform or link to videos located on an external webpage.

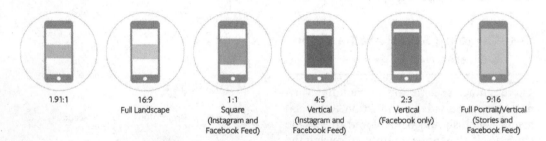

| 1.91:1 | 16:9 Full Landscape | 1:1 Square (Instagram and Facebook Feed) | 4:5 Vertical (Instagram and Facebook Feed) | 2:3 Vertical (Facebook only) | 9:16 Full Portrait/Vertical (Stories and Facebook Feed) |

◨ **Fig. 16.2**   Smartphone video ratios (Forno, 2019)

Table 16.3 Recommended video dimensions for the mainstream social media platforms

Social media platform	Recommended video dimension
Facebook (Peters, 2019a, 2019b)	Vertical (newsfeed and stories) Square (newsfeed) Landscape (newsfeed)
Instagram (Peters, 2019a, 2019b)	Vertical (newsfeed, stories and IGTV)
YouTube (O'Neill, 2019)	Landscape
Twitter (Jain, 2018)	Square and landscape
LinkedIn (Howard, 2019)	Vertical (organic posts) Landscape (advertisements)
Snapchat (Slade-Silovic, 2018)	Vertical
TikTok (Anastasia, 2019)	Vertical Landscape (permitted but not recommended)
WeChat (Rodriguez, 2016)	Vertical Landscape (possible but not recommended)
Vimeo (Social Report, 2019)	Landscape
Pinterest (Clayton, 2018)	Vertical Square

16.5.2 Native Vs Linked

The term "native video" refers to video that is uploaded directly to a specific social media platform. For example, producing a one minute 'How To' video for LinkedIn and uploading that video directly to my account.

The term 'linked video' describes the practice of including a link to a video located on a different platform within a social media post so that the target audience must leave the original social media site to view the video. For example, including a link to a YouTube video in a Facebook post.

As best-practice, it is always better to upload a video natively to a social media platform than to link to an external location. Native Facebook videos can achieve 86% greater reach than linking to an external site such as YouTube or Vimeo (Ayres, 2018).

Consider that social media sites want users to stay on their platforms as much as possible, therefore, it is of greater benefit to them to show users videos where they are rather than sending them to a competitor.

When curating video content (as covered in ▶ Sect. 2) it is better to find the original video post within the platform and sharing that than locating a video on YouTube and linking to it.

The only time it is viable to link to an external video is when it cannot be located within the platform. However, be prepared for minimal reach as a consequence.

16.5.3 In-House Production Vs a Professional Video Producer

A definitive answer does not exist when considering whether it is of greater benefit to produce video in-house compared with hiring the services of a professional video producer. There are pros and cons and variations associated with each. The term 'in-house' can refer to a range of set-ups depending on the business or organisation. For a sole-trading social media manager, in-house means directly producing video. However, for a large corporate, in-house could refer to an internal video production team employed by the organisation.

While definitions may vary, there are five key factors to consider when determining the feasibility of creating videos in-house or outsourcing the task:

1. **Budget:** External video production can be costly. Therefore, the budget will quickly stipulate whether outsourcing is a viable option.

2. **Time:** While in-house video production may seem a faster option, if the people undertaking the task are not experts in the process, it may take much longer than hiring a professional. If trying to meet a tight deadline, always ask how long the video will take to produce and be extremely honest about your expertise if producing it yourself. Estimate the time you think it will take then double it to allow for errors.

3. **Purpose:** If the video being recorded is going to be used for more than social media content, appointing an external supplier may be the best idea. For example, producing video interviews with award finalists with a smartphone can be acceptable quality to share on YouTube and Facebook, but may not work so well if projected onto a large monitor at the awards event. It is important to consider video quality when producing video for public and corporate events and to call in the professionals if a high standard cannot be attained in-house. Not doing this can result in poor quality video and/or inconveniencing subjects by having to re-record.

4. **Equipment:** The equipment required to produce quality video will depend on its purpose. As we will explore in the next section about pre-production, in many instances it is acceptable to produce social media video using a smartphone. At other times more advanced video production equipment may be required and it will be necessary to hire an external supplier if you, the business or organisation does not own the required tools.

5. **Expertise:** This chapter will provide the basic process and areas of consideration to produce a video for social media. However, it will not provide the practice. Video production is a process that must be perfected over time. Social Media Managers are strongly encouraged to learn as much as they can about this process to keep improving. It can take time to develop the skills to produce high quality social media content, so sometimes it can be a positive experience to pay professionals (if budget allows) and to learn from them at the same time.

The first step to learning how to produce quality video for social media is to understand the three stages of video content production: pre-production, production and post-production.

16.5.4 How to Brief a Professional Videographer

If a client has the budget to appoint a professional videographer, it does not mean that a Social Media Manager's work is done. While it may feel like the responsibility has shifted, it can increase in complexity depending on how well the video's vision and purpose are articulated to the videographer.

Sometimes it can be simpler to produce a video yourself when you have an in-depth understanding of a client's or organisation's brand and vision and how the video must support the achievement of strategic goals and objectives. Communicating this to someone who is unfamiliar can be both challenging and costly if ineffectively executed. This is why knowing how to brief a professional video producer is so important for both parties to avoid a lackluster end product.

Developing an accurate and articulate brief will be less cumbersome after undertaking the social media strategy development process outlined in ▶ Sect. 1, because brand, goals, SMART objectives, key messages, audience, platforms, tactics and measurement will have already been defined and any piece of content must align and support these strategic components.

A tight and detailed brief is the best way to communicate these to a video producer. Ben Amos, Online Video Strategist from Innovate Media recommends nine key components to address when briefing a videographer (Sutherland, 2019a, 2019b) (◻ Table 16.4).

Table 16.4 Important components of a video production brief

Brief component	Description
Clarity surrounding strategic alignment	Never present a social media strategy document to a videographer without a detailed face-to-face discussion to explain how it aligns with the video to be produced. A strategy may seem perfectly logical to the people who developed it but can be open to interpretation to an external supplier such as a videographer. It needs to be unpacked.
Creative approach	The goal of the video will determine its creative approach. A one-minute explainer will require less of a creative direction than a three-minute brand story. Articulating the level of creativity required from the outset helps to lay the plan for the entire video production process.
Video format	As detailed in ◘ Table 16.1 video can be produced in a range of formats and including clear instructions of the most appropriate video format in the brief will greatly assist a videographer to understand the vision and purpose of the piece.
Budget	As outlined in ▶ Chap. 5, budget is the most important component of a social media strategy because it dictates the tactics that can be included. It is the same case when producing a video. The budget determines what can be produced in actuality. It is essential to have realistic expectations when stating the budget on the brief to the videographer. Do not ask the videographer to suggest the cost of producing the video. It is up to the person commissioning the video to confirm the budget.
Deliverables	The deliverables refer to the outputs required for the different platforms where the videos will be uploaded and will already be identified in the social media strategy (see ▶ Sect. 1). As detailed in ◘ Table 16.2, each social media platform has different recommended specifications and uploading exactly the same video across platforms in not recommended. For example, a 'How To' video may be edited to be 4.20 for YouTube, 1 minute for Facebook and Instagram and 15 seconds for TikTok. A list of deliverables including length and platform must be included in the brief.
Timeframe	Providing a finite deadline within which the video must be produced is extremely important information for the videographer as it can determine what can be achieved within the specified timeframe.
Location	Providing a list of locations to feature in the video can greatly assist a videographer when planning a shoot. Furthermore, indicating if the videographer must arrange access to these locations is important as it will need to be included in the pre-production phase.
Talent	The brief must contain the names and contact details of who will be appearing in the video so the videographer can liaise with them directly. If professional actors are required, it must be stated in the brief whether casting will be the responsibility of the person commissioning the video or the videographer.
Branding guidelines	The videographer must be informed about how the finished product needs to comply with the client or organisation's branding guidelines and how brand voice can be brought to life. It is recommended that a copy of the branding guidelines is included with a video production brief along with a detailed discussion with the videographer so that mutual understanding of the brand can be achieved.

16.6   Pre-Production

Planning is the most important component of the video production process (Johnson & Radosh, 2017a). Careful planning in the pre-production phase can dictate how well the production and post-production stages will play out. This stems from having an extremely clear idea of the finished product and planning what is required to achieve it before going anywhere near a camera or smartphone.

This insight originates from the audience research and strategy development process as explored in ▶ Sect. 1. Every piece of social media content must support the goals and objectives of the strategy and communicate at least one key message and video content is the same.

Audience research, strategy development and data analysis should inform the following decisions relating to the video to be produced:

1. Audience segment to be addressed.
2. Strategic goal/s and SMART objective/s to be supported.
3. Key message/s to be communicated (including the call-to-action).
4. Social media platform to post the video.
5. Video format.
6. Video length.
7. Subjects (who will appear in the video).
8. Graphics.
9. Branding (including visual and personality).
10. Location where the video will be recorded most appropriate to the audience and the brand.

It is essential for Social Media Managers to have all of these components identified at the beginning of the video production process to ensure that the piece being produced is focused, aligned with the target audience and supports the overall social media strategy. Some of these elements may shift slightly during the production and post-production stages, but the core decisions relating to audience, strategic goals, objectives, key messages and branding should not. These must be consistent elements because they align directly to business goals and veering off course will be counterproductive.

With the key video components identified, the next step is to plot out the visual and audio elements of the video by developing a shooting script or a storyboard.

16.6.1   Video Shooting Script and Storyboarding

Plotting out a video using a shooting script, or a storyboard has many benefits. It further articulates the vision of the piece and allows amendments to be made before any recording takes place minimising the risk of wasting time, money and effort.

Additionally, it provides an insight into what the audience will see and hear when watching the video and assists in creating a list of items that will be required in the production and post-production phases such as props, wardrobe and music etc.

16.6.1.1   Video Shooting Script

A shooting script is a text-based list that states the shot number, visual and audio elements of the video in a table format (see ◘ Table 16.5). A copy of a Video Shooting script can also be found in Appendix 2.

◘ Table 16.5   Video shooting script example

Shot No.	Visuals	Audio
1	Mid-shot Restaurant Owner (RO): Title: *Jane Lewis, Owner Hello Halo Restaurant*	Jane: If I could breathe food instead of air, I would.

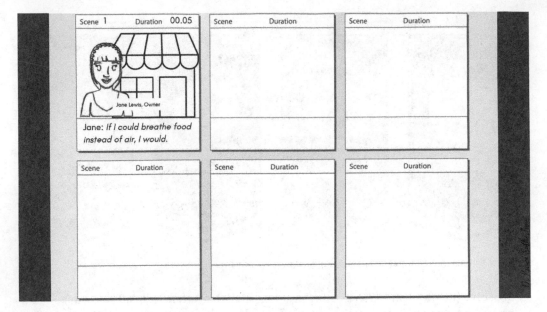

Fig. 16.3 Video storyboard

16.6.1.2 Video Storyboards

A video shooting script is extremely helpful to plot a video out on paper. However, a video storyboard helps the video come to life by drawing what will appear on the screen. It helps to visualise the look and feel of the video from the audience's perspective. Advanced drawing skills are not required to develop a storyboard, rough outlines and stick figures are also helpful in specifying the content of the video (see ▪ Fig. 16.3).

As demonstrated in ▪ Fig. 16.3, the storyboard provides the shot number and duration, space to draw what will be seen on the screen, then underneath the shot type and audio are written. Detailing all of these elements together organises the video ready for the production phase. However, there are other elements that can be considered in terms of what to include in a video, as suggested by Dennis Yu (2019b).

16.6.2 The Four Components of a One Minute Video

While Dennis Yu (2019b, p. 88) recommends the following four components to be included in a 1-minute video, they can be essential ingredients to a wide range of formats. As ▪ Fig. 16.4 details, these components consist of the:

1. **Hook (3 seconds):** Capturing attention without opening titles or introducing yourself. For example, the restaurant owner asking: *"Do you like wine?"*
2. **Ignite Pain/Pleasure (3–15 seconds):** Explain a common problem experienced by the target audience. For example, the restaurant owner saying, *"But wish you knew more about the differences between them?"*
3. **Describe the Solution (15–30 seconds):** How can your client's business or prod-

■ **Fig. 16.4**   The four components of a 1 minute video (Yu, 2019b)

uct solve the problem? *"To celebrate our new wine list at Hello Halo we're having a free wine tasting class so that you can learn more about wine and so we can show you what is on offer. We love wine too and we'd love to share some with you…"*

4. **Call-To-Action (50–60 seconds):** What do you want them to do? For example, The restaurant owner says: *"Go to our website to register your place and we'll see you there."*

> 66 The first three seconds of a video is referred to as the 'hook' because it must capture the audience's attention and inspire them to watch more of the video. 99
>
> **Dr Karen Sutherland**

16.6.3 The First 3–10 Seconds Are Crucial for All Videos

The first 3 seconds of a video is referred to as the 'hook' because it must capture the audience's attention and inspire them to watch more of the video. It is essential to carefully plan the action in those 3 seconds so that the video cuts through all of the other content in the target audience's newsfeed to command attention.

This is why Yu (2019b) recommends avoiding the traditional conventions associated with beginning a video such as titles or the person on camera introducing themselves. Get to the point immediately. There are only 3 seconds to attract attention and another seven where the audience decides whether they will continue watching. On average, 33% of the audience will stop watching a video after the first 30 seconds, 45% will drop off after the first minute and

16

60% of the audience will not continue watching after the 2 minute mark (Biteable, 2019).

These statistics further highlight the necessity to first attract the audience's attention in the first 3 seconds and include the most important information within 30 seconds. It is also important with the 'hook' to provide the audience with some incentive or reward to watch until the end, for example some free advice, a free offer or discount code.

16.6.4 Talent

Talent refers to the people who will appear in the video. It is recommended to use people associated with a client's business or organisation to add greater authenticity to video and to create a connection between the target audience and the people behind the brand. However, it may take some time before those who are not used to being in front of the camera become comfortable.

In the interview at the end of this chapter, global video influencer String Nguyen, suggests creating brief 'one-take' videos to help people to become comfortable and confident in front of the camera. Similarly, Dennis Yu (2019c) keeps the camera rolling continually to capture a more natural conversation once the talent feels more comfortable instead of stopping and starting. It is also essential for the talent to be thoroughly briefed well ahead of the production stage so that they know what the video aims to achieve and what they need to do.

Using real people instead of actors can return much greater results. Veena World Travel, a Mumbai travel company has experimented with both types of talent and has found that using staff members as the face of their video campaigns returns much higher rates of reach and engagement than when using actors. For example, a Facebook video about Diwali that featured staff members generated 53k views, 1.1k reactions and

25 comments (see ◘ Fig. 16.5) compared with an advertisement from around the same time featuring professional actors that generated 52 k views, 223 reactions and 1 comment (Veena World, 2018a, 2018b).

It is extremely important to assess the location of the video shoot before the production phase to ensure that it is a viable option. For example, the restaurant owner from the previous example, might plan a video shoot during the dinner rush, but in reality, noise will most likely be an issue. Testing the location before the production phase can save time, money, effort and frustration if it turns out to be unworkable. It also allows for a more suitable location to be sourced.

The best locations for a video shoot have bright lighting (natural light is excellent),

◘ **Fig. 16.5** Veena World's #AbGharDurNahi Diwali campaign featuring employees location

◘ **Fig. 16.6** The Rule of Thirds

are reasonably quiet and have an interesting and relevant background (but not so lively that it diverts attention away from the on-camera talent). As part of the planning process, it is important to preempt everything that could interrupt the video in this location and develop measures to completely eradicate or at least minimise the risk of such delays taking place.

16.6.5 Video Equipment

There are so many gadgets on the market that can assist with the video production process. However, there are only a few staple pieces of equipment that Social Media Managers should have in a kit, ready to go, if they ever need to produce video. These essential items are listed below and listed in the Helpful Links section at the end of this chapter.

- **A smartphone or a digital video camera:** As part of the pre-production process ensure that all batteries are charged, lenses are cleaned, and the camera is in working order. If using a smartphone, ensure there is enough space on the phone, and it is switched to Flight Mode before recording to avoid any calls or notifications during the shoot. It can be extremely worthwhile to buy a quality camera that captures both still images and video to also increase the standard of content being produced for customers. However, if starting out, the later models of iPhone or Android phones can capture quality content (Montgomery, 2018).

- **Lights:** Having access to three lights can help to increase the quality of videos being produced because the talent can be shown on camera without any shadows. ◘ Figure 16.7 demonstrates the three-point lighting technique that helps to light a subject up from every angle. While there are some reasonably priced video lights on the market, even having access

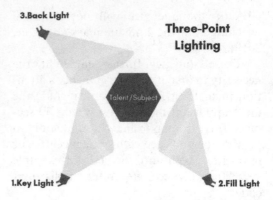

◘ **Fig. 16.7**   Three-point lighting

to the sun and some desk or floor lamps can work nearly as well. Also, make sure that any battery-powered lights are completely charged before a video shoot. Ring lights area popular choice with vloggers, however, the reflection of the ring can usually be seen in their eyes when on camera. It is worth testing before purchasing.

- **Microphones:** A lapel microphone is an essential item to have in a video kit. Even though a high percentage of people watch a video with the sound off, not capturing clear sound at the time of recording can ruin a video (Johnson & Radosh, 2017a). Lapel microphones can be reasonably inexpensive and can be plugged into an iPhone to ensure that the sound being recorded is clear. It is important to check batteries and adapters the day before the video shoot is going to occur.

- **A Tripod:** An unsteady video can lose an audience quickly. While camera steadiness can be achieved by propping up a camera or smartphone using books, it is much more convenient to have a tripod on hand rather than scrambling around on the day of a shoot looking for a makeshift one. There are many inexpensive options available both smartphones and cameras and they really make a difference to the quality of video being produced. If selecting between a desktop sized tripod

16

and a full-sized adjustable variety, it is better to invest in a piece of equipment that will be the most versatile.

With a strategic video concept storyboarded, the talent briefed and the equipment triple-checked, it is time to begin the video production stage.

16.7　Production

The main aim of a successful video shoot is to gather all planned footage and sound (of high quality) as efficiently as possible to produce the proposed video in the post-production phase. Extensive planning is instrumental in assisting this process to run smoothly. Controlling the environment where the video shoot will take place as much as humanly possible also plays a huge role.

For example, having the talent briefed and practiced in what they need to say and do on camera, all batteries charged, turning phones off or on silent, putting signs on doors so people do not knock or enter when recording, not scheduling a shoot outdoors at the time when planes or trains are due to pass all help with an efficient shoot. Like life, not everything can be controlled, but extensive preemptive measures can definitely assist.

The following actions as detailed in ▢ Table 16.6 will also assist in the execution of a successful and efficient video shoot:

16.7.1　Be Flexible

Even with the most comprehensive preparation sometimes a video shoot may not go to plan. The key is to be flexible. Rather than cancelling, think about the video that you could record instead. Sometimes gathering footage exactly how it is detailed in the shooting script or storyboard may not be possible on the day due to uncontrollable

circumstances such as weather or a location becoming unavailable etc.

Therefore, it is important to be agile and solution-focused in these moments. Rather than feeling defeated, ask yourself, if I cannot gather the shot I have planned for, what can I record instead? What can I record that is as close as possible to the original shooting script that will still work with the rest of the video?

16.7.2　Grouping Shots

If there are multiple locations planned for the video, gather all footage from each location according to the availability of the location and the talent. Recording a video in order is unnecessary and can be edited in the correct sequence during the post-production phase.

16.8　Post-Production

With the video shoot completed and footage gathered, the next phase involves editing to show the target audience a compelling story with the final product. There are a number of key stages in the post-production process that if followed closely will help to produce a video that supports the strategic goals and objectives for a client or organisation.

16.8.1　Step 1: Gathering all Video Components

Organisation is the key to an efficient edit. Before beginning the editing process, gather all necessary components together to avoid having to locate them while editing is underway.

These items generally include:

- *The video shooting script or storyboard*
- *Video files.* Ensure to select the best takes to save time, confusion and file space.

▣ **Table 16.6**   Important actions for efficient video production

Action	Description
Compositional alignment	The Rule of Thirds applies to video production in the same way as in photography (as explored in ▶ Chap. 15. See below). Remember, with the Rule of Thirds that it is better to have the talent, or the action occur off-centre where the lines intersect (▣ Fig. 16.6).
Camera angle	If recording the talent speaking directly to the camera position it slightly below eye level, so that the subject is looking slightly down and into the camera. Also, ensure that the talent looks directly into the camera when speaking to build a connection with the person watching it (Sutherland, 2019a, 2019b).
Sound check	Test the microphones and the clarity of sound at the beginning of the shoot. To do this, have the talent wear the microphone and practice their part with the camera recording. Play the footage back to check for sound, composition and anything out of place such as crooked clothing or jewellery etc.
Light check and arrangement	Check the talent, product or location in the video are well-illuminated and without shadows. As mentioned previously, Three-Point Lighting is commonly used to achieve this. ▣ Figure 16.7 demonstrates the position of each light source. Be resourceful. One light source could be an open window, others could be a desk lamp coupled with a reading lamp.
Shot length + 3–5 seconds buffer each way	It is extremely important for each shot to be held between 3–5 seconds at its beginning and at its end. This helps with the editing process and avoids cutting off important information at the beginning of the video or ending the video prematurely such as with the talent in mid-position. Ask whomever is on camera to smile, look into the camera and hold their position for 3–5 seconds before speaking and to do the same once they finish speaking.
Cutaways (aka B-Roll footage)	Not having ample visual video content is a common issue experienced in the post-production phase. Depending on the length of the video, it can be a better viewing experience for the audience if the shots are varied, particularly if someone is speaking directly to the camera. Gathering additional footage related to the audio being captured is extremely helpful. These shots are often referred to as "cutaways" or "B-Roll footage". For example, if the restaurant owner from the previous example is speaking on camera explaining from where the restaurant's name originated, cutting to a shot of the front of the restaurant with the name visible adds greater interest and depth to the explanation. Gathering additional footage can also help cover edits that occur within the middle of a shot. For example, if the talent makes an error during a piece to camera, often cutting out the error can be covered by a different piece of footage so the video flows smoothly for the audience. Also, ensure that footage is gathered of on-camera talent from a range of angles to have greater options when editing in the post-production phase.

16

- *Image files.* Avoid low resolution images.
- *Branding* (logos, brand colour codes etc.).
- *Music files.* Must be copyright/royalty free.
- *Names of people and positions of people appearing in the video* (if these details will be displayed on the screen).

16.8.2 Step 2: Load Video, Graphics and Music Files into the Video Editing Software

With all video components collected, the next stage involves loading these items into the video editing software. The specific functionality can differ between editing software packages, but generally involves selecting 'Import' to transfer files into the system.

16.8.3 Video Editing Software

There are many video editing options available and it can be extremely overwhelming when attempting to select the most appropriate tool. The following factors should be considered when selecting video editing software:

— **Cost:** Budget will be the leading factor in determining which video editing tool will be accessible.
— **Usability:** There are some extremely user-friendly video editing tools available, but there are others that require training to master. Avoid purchasing a tool that is too complex to use. Be realistic.
— **Functionality:** Ensure that the editing tool can do what you need it to, plus more. Can the tool provide captions, titles, music, and different sizes for a range of social media platforms? Refer to a client's social media strategy to check that it can be supported by the videos produced by this particular video editing tool.

▣ Table 16.7 provides a list of five editing tools commonly used to produce video for social media. The list is clearly not exhaus-

▣ **Table 16.7** Social media video editing tools

Video editing tool	Description
Adobe Premiere Rush	Smartphone app that supports video editing and posting straight to YouTube, Facebook, Instagram and Behance. Includes animated titles and audio editing functionality.
Adobe Premiere Pro	A more advanced editing tool that Adobe Premiere Rush. A desktop application that provides a full editing suite that integrates with a range of Adobe products such as After Effects. Facilitates footage captured from a range of devices and shared directly to social channels after the editing process.
Biteable	An extremely user-friendly video editing program that provides titles, templates, stock footage, and customisable themes to produce professional-looking videos.
Camtasia	A user-friendly interface that includes a wide range of features including screencasting, quizzes, titles, transitions, music and audio etc. Can upload directly to YouTube and Vimeo.
Final Cut Pro X	Mac-based editing software suite that includes advanced functionality such as 360° video editing and VR headset playback, 3-D titles and multi-channel audio. May require some training to become a proficient user.
Wave	Extremely user-friendly tool to edit video stories, posts and ads for social media. Includes templates, stock footage, stickers, gifs and the ability to upload footage and resize for different social media platforms.
WeVideo	Extremely user-friendly video editing software that outputs in a range of sizes including square and vertical. WeVideo provides a range of themes, titles, music and transitions to produce quality videos for social media quickly and without an extensive video editing knowledge required.

tive. Instead, it provides an overview of tools available at the time of writing. As with other areas of social media, video editing tools are constantly evolving, therefore, it is best to conduct further research to see what is currently available. Links to these tools are available in the Helpful Links section at the end of this chapter.

Most of the tools in ◘ Table 16.7 provide a free trial. It is highly recommended to test a range of editing tools before making the decision and the commitment to purchase one to produce videos for clients or organisations.

16.8.4 Step 3: Arranging the Video Components in Order

Quality editing is the key to effective storytelling and plays a vital role in producing a video that supports strategic goals and objectives (Johnson & Radosh, 2017a). Therefore, with all required video components loaded into the selected editing software tool, the next stage is to assemble these items in order so that they convey a compelling story to the target audience. The pre-production and production process should have provided a clear vision of the finished video in terms of how it will be edited together. However, Barrance (2018) suggests the following key principles to keep in mind throughout the editing process:

16.8.5 Key Editing Principles

- *Include only what the story needs:* Less is more. Only include what is necessary for the audience to understand the story.
- *Show something new with each edit:* Every shot should add something new to the story. Avoid repetition.
- *Vary shot sizes and angles:* Provide a range of perspectives for the audience. However, every shot must earn its place

and seem like a natural inclusion to tell the story. Avoid switching between shot lengths and angles just for the sake of it.

- **Use cutaways (B-Roll) to hide jumpy edits (also known as jump-cuts)** As mentioned in ◘ Table 16.6, gathering extra footage helps to cover shots that may not fit well together.
- *Use a long-shot for context:* Depending on the video format, beginning with a long-shot helps to establish location and context for the audience.
- *Get the pace right:* Each shot should be long enough for the audience to see what is happening (or to be able to read text on the screen). However, a shot should not be too long, or the audience will lose interest. It is a good idea to test the pace with members of the target audience before posting it on social media and tweaking shot length according to their feedback.
- *Use appropriate transitions:* Transitions join shots together. Most editing tools provide a range of transition options such as fade in, fade out, cross-fade, and dissolve. A transition should feel logical and seamless to the audience. It should not be jarring unless that is the result being aimed for.
- *Edit on the action:* A video will flow if a shot begins while someone or something is moving rather than at the beginning or the end of the action.
- *Do not cut from motion shots to still shots:* This can feel particularly jarring for the audience. Instead, the action in the shot should cease first before cutting to something static in the next shot.
- *Pay attention to the audio:* Audio can impact the mood of the story being told in a video. Ensure audio is clear and that music is used to evoke the mood, feel and theme of the story being conveyed without overpowering it.
- *Stay focused on the bigger picture:* Remember to look at the video as a

whole and keep revisiting how it aligns and supports the client or organisation's strategic goals and objectives.

Further considerations when editing social media video are:

> 66 Music can play a pivotal role in guiding the audience through the action of a story.
> It can help to create an emotional connection between a brand and its audience 99
>
> **Dr Karen Sutherland**

16.8.6 Music

Music can play a pivotal role in bringing along the target audience through the action of a story in a video (Johnson & Radosh, 2017a). It can help to create an emotional connection between a brand and its audience. As explored in ▶ Chap. 4 and ▶ Sect. 2, it is essential to only use content (including music) that its owner has approved. Using popular songs can prove to be costly, particularly when recorded by original artists. However, many editing tools and websites offer free access to music files (links included in the Helpful Links section at the end of this chapter). Even YouTube Studio has an audio library with free access to music. Research thoroughly to find the most appropriate fit in terms of music. An incorrect choice can take the video off in a very different direction.

16.8.7 Thumbnails

A thumbnail is a still image (a single frame) that is used to represent the video on social media channels. For example, a YouTube video has a single image (usually a combination of a photo and titles) that conveys what the audience can expect if they view it. A thumbnail can have a strong influence over whether the target audience chooses to watch a video. It should clearly (yet succinctly) convey the content of the video without resorting to 'clickbait' tactics to manipulate the audience to watch. As explored in ▶ Chap. 15, the rules around images and visual content apply directly to thumbnails. Canva and Adobe Spark can generate professional-looking thumbnails. Also, asking the talent to smile at the camera for 3–5 seconds before speaking also helps to generate a friendly, personable image for a thumbnail.

16.8.8 Closed Captions

Closed Captions are an essential inclusion in the post-production process, because they can positively impact viewer numbers. Aside from reports suggesting 85% of Facebook video is watched without sound, Closed Captions make social media video accessible to members from the target audience who are experiencing deafness, hearing impairment, cognitive and learning disabilities (Abou-Zahra, 2019; Patel, 2016). Closed Captions can also help increase understanding from target audience members who may be watching the video in a non-native language.

There are many different tools and methods to generate Closed Captions. For example:

- *Manual Transcription:* Depending on the length of the video, manually transcribing video can be time-consuming.
- *Paying for Transcription:* Services such as ► Rev.com can provide a speedy and reasonably inexpensive solution to creating Closed Captions.
- *Automation Natively within Social Media Platforms:* For example, YouTube can automate captions that facilitate editing and the ability to download a .srt (SubRip Text) file that can be uploaded with video to other platforms such as Facebook and LinkedIn. Facebook also generates automated Closed Captions, but it is essential to check them for accuracy and amend them accordingly to avoid miscommunication.
- *Automation using External Tools:* Non-native tools such as Otter.ai and ► Rev.com's automated feature are tools that can generate Closed Captions extremely quickly. However, their accuracy is still not 100% and all outputs must be reviewed before uploading live to social media channels.

Links to closed captioning tools and information can be found in the Further Reading and Helpful Links section at the end of this chapter.

16.8.9 Step 4 Rendering the Video and Preparing for it to Posted on Relevant Social Media Channels

The final stage of the post-production process is rendering the video using the preferred editing tool. Rendering describes the process that mixes together all video components into the specified video size and file format. Rendering time is dependent on the length of the video and its components. For example, a one- hour 3-D animated video would take a significantly longer time to render than a 1-minute piece-to-camera. It is strongly advised to check the rendered video for errors before posting it on social media and include an independent member from the target audience in this final check too. It is better to be cautious than to risk a client's brand or organisational reputation by posting something that is not a high standard.

16.8.10 Outsourcing Video Editing Is Also an Option

If appointing a professional videographer is not an option, outsourcing video editing may be within reach. Justin Brown from Primal Video suggests that video editing can be outsourced for a little as $3 - $7 per hour via websites such as onlinejobs.ph, but a thorough recruitment process is necessary to ensure a professional video editor is appointed including editing tests (Brown, 2018). More information about this process can be found in the Helpful Links section of this chapter.

Conclusion

This chapter explored how video can be a highly effective method to communicate and engage with target audiences. A range of video formats were presented and their relevance to the customer journey examined.

Debates surrounding video production (such as vertical versus landscape, in-house production versus outsourcing and native versus linked) were also analysed.

The journey through the Pre-Production, Production and Post-Production stages deconstructed in detail to provide a useful framework for Social Media Managers to produce and/or outsource video production for clients or organisations that support the achievement of strategic goals and objectives.

16.9 · Interview: String Nguyen, Global Video Influencer and Fo...

385

16

Previously in the chapter, we explored the risks associated with using live video when communicating serious and highly sensitive topics. In these cases, a rogue cat filter distracted the viewer away from the seriousness of the information being conveyed and may have been perceived as an insensitive handling of the issue.

The real-time unpredictability of live video can also expose when a social media user is being intentionally deceptive, as was the case with Chinese vlogger, Your Highness Qiao Biluo (Chapman, 2019).

Live streaming across platforms such as Weibo, YouTube and Bilibili, Qiao Biluo used a filter to present herself to audiences as though she was a beautiful young woman. Her 100,000 plus follower base believed her, often referring to Biluo as a "cute goddess" and revered for her "sweet and healing voice," (Shah & Allen, 2019). Biluo was reported to have amassed more than 100,000 yuan ($14,533, £11,950) from her loyal following (Shah & Allen, 2019).

However, her facade was exposed during a live stream where the filter malfunctioned, revealing her true identity, that of a 58 year old woman whose appearance was completely different to the one that she had been presenting to her fans.

Biluo only realised this when her VIP followers began exiting her live stream in droves and withdrawing the donations that they made to her. This incident cost Biluo her reputation and the trust that followers had instilled in her resulting in her suspending her Weibo account (Shah & Allen, 2019).

This specific case reinforces the power of social media video as it has been explored throughout this chapter. Video (and live video in particular) helps to facilitate a direct connection with an audience and this must be respected.

Live video can be an extremely effective technique to build relationships with current and prospective customers but any relationship must be built on trust. Biluo used technology to deceive her audience about her appearance to elicit monetary gifts, but the technology worked against her in the end.

The recommended approach is to use video to build trust and genuine connections with a target audience by providing interesting and helpful content.

1. How could Your Highness Qiao Biluo have avoided losing the trust of her audience?
2. Suggest some alternative topics that Your Highness Qiao Biluo could have used to connect with her audience?

16.9 Interview: String Nguyen, Global Video Influencer and Founder of the Trusted Voice, Australia

1. **Welcome, String. Can you please introduce yourself and what you do?**
   I'm a global video influencer and founder of The Trusted Voice, which is my new startup where we help small businesses and professionals be awesome on video and social media to help them build up their reputation online.

2. **What do you like most about working in the field of social media?**
   I use social media as a way to be innovative, be on the forefront, and be an early adopter. So, for example, LinkedIn invited me to be a beta user for video and for LinkedIn Live, and it's one of the reasons why it helped me grow my profile to become a channel. I went from zero to 30,000 in, like, 14 months.

3. **What do you think are some of the challenges working with social media?**

There are so many content creators out there. It's almost hard to stand out these days.

4. **How did you come to work in social media? Tell me your career story.**

It all started off with my friends kept on asking me to help them on social media. And 10 years ago, that's where social media is still quite new and innovative, and a lot of people don't know how to leverage it as channel amplifiers.

But I used social media to document my art projects, which is where StringStory came about. And then, over time, I knew that video was going to be the next big thing, so I jumped on to Meerkat, which was a live-streaming platform before Twitter and Periscope squished it. But that was where I jumped on to video, and that was like 4 or 5 years ago. So, it's been massive. However, being an artist is not sustainable.

I was successful for 2 years. But I realised I was making less than $20,000 a year just with grants and stuff. I realised that I needed to learn business. I moved to Sydney and got a job as a Community Manager, and also was running my business for the first time and thinking about it. So that's when Sydney and Meerkat happened at the same time for me.

5. **What are the three most important things you think a Social Media Manager needs to know when producing a video?**

We should have minimal viable videos or minimal viable content. Sometimes you need to go fast and do nasty, initially, to see what works and be comfortable with the production side of things. If you throw yourself in the deep end, you need to realise that the first 10 seconds is really important. How do you script your story out or use storyboarding to create an interesting story.

Learn the techniques of video or video production as well. I usually give exercises to my clients, to say, "Do one-take videos first." So, they develop their talent and learn the presence and, like, it's all about being yourself and being super comfortable. The more comfortable you are, the more authentic you are... Or be an actor and learn how to be really confident on camera. People really like it when you're awkward on camera. It's an interesting thing. But as long as you're passionate and awkward, you're okay.

6. **What do you think are the benefits of producing video?**

Producing video, just from a vlogging kind of perspective, or sharing information, you get to communicate better, you get to understand what your audience wants as well, and also you get to stand out really fast, and also it amplifies your messages. And, for rapid growth, if you become a channel, or act like a channel, you will grow an audience really fast, especially if you have on-point branding, vision, values, key messages down, and your content pillars down.

7. **What do you think are some of the challenges when producing video content?**

For social media people and busy entrepreneurs, it's just making time to create video and being consistent about it. Even I have moments when I pick up clients that I forget to create my own content. So, learning how to create batch videos is a good way of doing it. And making time to be a channel. Because if you become a channel, then that's where the most growth comes in.

8. **How can you help current or prospective customers with videos?**

It's just better retention, and if the video is really great, it's better retention and memory retention. I think that's the most important one. It stands out and seeds their memory of that brand.

9. **What are your favourite tools for producing video?**
Your mobile phone. Any short-form videos, like TikTok, Snapchat, and Instagram Stories is a great exercise to learn how to develop videos and storytelling. Because, you know, the Vine days, it's coming back. Frame.io to review and comment on videos, based on, like, timing. Canva for thumbnails, because everything's all about visuals these days, especially a lot of professionals don't know how to use visuals properly or know how to use visuals to stand out. ▶ Rev.com for captions. That's one of my favourite tools.

10. **What do you think of the current landscape of social media management as a profession?**
I feel like they're more like curators than original thinkers. And that's okay. And it's probably better to become a curator. But anyone who produces interesting content will stand out. Because to be acceptable you'd be a curator. To stand out, you'd need to be a full-weight, all-creative person just to, like, stand out.

11. **Where do you think the profession and social media is heading in the future?**
There are two halves. There's audience building and community building. I think community building is the next thing social media managers will do. That's a specialist skill set as well, because it's, doing more internal than external. With social media it's external, but we're going back to internal now. So, I feel like it's going to go towards more, like, retention than acquisition.

12. **What has been the best piece of advice that you've been given?**
Learn how to be confident. By being interesting, by being curious, and being more self-aware. The more self-aware

you are, the more that you can find your voice and understand where you fit in the world.

13. **What advice would you give to someone who's trying to actually work in the field of social media?**
Two things. You could either be a channel. Set up an Instagram and learn how to experiment to give you the foundations of understanding, how to create content for yourself and be a channel. Or work as an intern for someone else, so you can build up work experience. Both are important, because they're both about building competent skill sets.

❓ Questions for Critical Reflection

1. Why is video an important tactic to include in a social media strategy?
2. Why should video format align with the customer journey stage?
3. What are the differences, benefits and challenges between live and recorded video?
4. What are the three main stages of social media video production and why are each important?
5. Why are the first 3–10 seconds of a video the most vital?
6. What areas should be considered when deciding whether to produce a video in-house or to hire a professional videographer?
7. Why are closed captions necessary inclusion in a social media video?

❯ Practical Exercises

1. Using the steps outlined in the pre-production phase, plan a 1-minute video where you will explain why you are studying social media.
2. Using the process detailed in the production process, record a 1-minute video as you have planned in the previous exercise.

3. Implementing the actions recommended in the post-production process, edit the video recorded in the previous step and upload it to your preferred social media channel. *What did you learn from this process? What would you do differently next time?*

References

Ahmad, I. (2019). 7 video trends that will dominate in 2019 and beyond [Infographic], *Social Media Today*, viewed 16.09.2019, https://www.socialmediatoday.com/news/7-video-trends-that-will-dominate-in-2019-and-beyond-infographic/555092/.

Abou-Zahra, S. (2019). Video captions, *Web Accessibility Initiative*, viewed 15.09.2019, https://www.w3.org/WAI/perspective-videos/captions/.

Anastasia. (2019). The ultimate guide to TikTok videos, *Clipchamp*, viewed 07.09.2019, https://clipchamp.com/en/blog/2019/ultimate-guide-to-tiktok.

Angova, S., Tsankova, S., Ossikovski, M., Nikolova, M., & Valchanov, I. (2019). Mapping digital media content. In *International conference on applied human factors and ergonomics* (pp. 233–238). Cham: Springer.

Audiohype. (2018). A video is not worth 1.8 million words, *Replay Science*, viewed 07.09.2019, https://www.replayscience.com/blog/a-video-is-not-worth-1-8-million-words/.

Ayres, S. (2018). Study proves: Facebook native videos have up to 86% higher reach!, *Agorapulse*, viewed 07.09.2019, https://www.agorapulse.com/social-media-lab/facebook-videos-reach.

Barnhart, B. (2019). How the Facebook algorithm works and ways to outsmart it, *SproutSocial*, viewed: 06/08/2019, https://sproutsocial.com/insights/facebook-algorithm/.

Barrance, T. (2018). Basic editing principles for filmmakers, *Learn About Film*, viewed 15.09.2019, https://learnaboutfilm.com/film-language/editing/.

Bedrina, O. (2018). Ideal video length: How long should your social video be? [Infographic], *Socially Sorted*, viewed 16.09.2019, https://sociallysorted.com.au/ideal-video-length-social-video/.

Biteable. (2019). 55 video marketing statistics for 2019, *Biteable*, viewed 08.09.2019, https://biteable.com/blog/tips/video-marketing-statistics/.

Brown, J. (2018). How to hire a video editor, *Justin Brown - Primal Video - YouTube*, viewed 15.09.2019, https://www.youtube.com/watch?v=tc9FFfJJDao.

Chapman, A. (2019). Livestream glitch reveals Chinese vlogger was using a facial filter to appear younger, 7news.com.au, viewed: 20/11/2019, https://7news.com.au/entertainment/viral-weird/livestream-glitch-reveals-chinese-vlogger-was-using-facial-filter-to-appear-younger-c-375026.

Chi, C. (2019). How long should your videos be? Ideal lengths for Facebook, Instagram, Twitter, and YouTube [Infographic], *HubSpot*, viewed 16.09.2019, https://blog.hubspot.com/marketing/how-long-should-videos-be-on-instagram-twitter-facebook-youtube.

Clayton, C. (2018). How to upload videos to pinterest (and why you should do it), *Conversionminded*, viewed 07.09.2019, https://conversionminded.com/upload-videos-to-pinterest/.

Forno, S. (2019). Animated video production - Vertical video guide: Facebook, Snapchat, aspect ratios & more, *Idea Rocket Animation*, viewed 07.09.2019, https://idearocketanimation.com/17553-vertical-video-guide-2/.

Goodwin, D. (2019). 10 social media trends that will matter most in 2019, *Search Engine Journal*, viewed 16.09.2019, https://www.searchenginejournal.com/2019-social-media-trends/286029/#close.

Handley, A., & Chapman, C. C. (2010). *Content rules: How to create killer blogs, podcasts, videos, ebooks, webinars (and more) that engage customers and ignite your business* (Vol. 5). New Jersey: John Wiley & Sons.

Harrison, K. (2016). Is your company giving video the love it deserves?, *Forbes*, viewed 07.09.2019, https://www.forbes.com/sites/kateharrison/2016/03/31/is-your-company-giving-video-the-love-it-deserves/#7be19ee8464d.

Howard, A. (2019). The 2019 guide to social media video specs, *Vyond*, viewed 07.09.2019, https://www.vyond.com/resources/the-2019-guide-to-social-media-video-specs/#linkedinvideos.

Hsieh, J., Hsieh, Y., & Tang, Y. (2012). Exploring the disseminating behaviors of eWOM marketing: Persuasion in online video. *Electronic Commerce Research, 12*, 201–224. https://doi.org/10.1007/s10660-012-9091-y

Huertas, A. (2018). How live videos and stories in social media influence tourist opinions and behaviour. *Information Technology & Tourism, 19*(1–4), 1–28.

Hunga, Kinshuk, & Chen (2018). Embodied interactive video lectures for improving learning comprehension and retention. Computers & Education. 17 pp. 116–131.

Hung, Y. W., & Higgins, S. (2016). Learners' use of communication strategies in text-based and video-based synchronous computer-mediated communication environments: Opportunities for language learning. Computer Assisted Language Learning, 29(5), 901–924.

Jain, G. (2018). Twitter videos and video formats: A detailed guide, *Rocketium Academy*, viewed

07.09.2019, https://rocketium.com/academy/twitter-videos-guide/#What_is_the_best_Twitter_video_format.

Johnson, K., & Radosh, J. (2017a). *Shoot, edit, share: Video production for mass media, marketing, advertising, and public relations*. New York: Focal Press.

Lach, A. (2017). The evolution of video on social media, *Pierpont*, viewed 16.09.2019, https://www.piercom.com/news/insight/the-evolution-of-video-on-social-media/.

Leskin, P. (2019). These are the 32 biggest stars on TikTok, the viral video app teens can't get enough of, *Business Insider*, viewed: 19.11.2019, https://www.businessinsider.com.au/tiktok-most-popular-stars-gen-z-influencers-social-media-app-2019-6?r=US&IR=T.

Klar, R. (2019). Pakistani politician accidentally livestreams press conference using a 'cat filter', *The Hill*, viewed: 19/11/2019, https://thehill.com/homenews/media/448860-pakistani-politician-accidentally-livestreamed-press-conference-using-a-cat.

Menotti, G. (2019). Discourses around vertical videos: An archaeology of "wrong" aspect ratios. *ARS (São Paulo), 17*(35), 147–165.

Montgomery, R. (2018). *Smartphone video storytelling*. New York: Routledge.

O'Brien, C. (2019). 8 digital marketing trends to watch out for in 2019, *Digital Marketing Institute*, viewed 16.09.2019, https://digitalmarketinginstitute.com/en-au/blog/8-digital-marketing-trends-to-watch-out-for-in-2019.

O'Neill, M. (2019). Square or landscape? Choosing a format for your video, *Animoto*, viewed 07.09.2019, https://animoto.com/blog/business/square-landscape-format-video/.

Patel, S. (2016). 85 percent of Facebook video is watched without sound, *Digiday UK*, viewed 15.09.2019, https://digiday.com/media/silent-world-facebook-video/.

Peters, B. (2019a). Square vs. landscape video – $1.5K worth of experiments: Here's how they compare, *Buffer*, viewed 07.09.2019, https://buffer.com/resources/square-video-vs-landscape-video.

Peters, B. (2019b). Does vertical video make a difference? We spent $6,000 on tests to find out, *Buffer*, viewed 07.09.2019, https://buffer.com/resources/vertical-video.

Rein, K., & Venturini, T. (2018). Ploughing digital landscapes: How Facebook influences the evolution of live video streaming. *New Media & Society, 20*(9), 3359–3380.

Rodriguez, K. (2016). The rise of vertical video, *Singapore Management University*, viewed 07.09.2019, https://web.smu.edu.sg/spring/the-rise-of-vertical-video/.

Shah, D & Allen, K (2019). Chinese vlogger who used filter to look younger caught in live-stream glitch, *BBC Trending*, viewed: 20/11/2019, https://www.bbc.com/news/blogs-trending-49151042.

Slade-Silovic, O. (2018). Horizontal vs vertical videos: Which video format should I use?, *Covideo*, viewed 07.09.2019, https://www.covideo.com/horizontal-vs-vertical-videos.

Smyth, S. (2011). Enhancing learner-learner interaction using video communications in higher education: Implications from theorising about a new model. *British Journal of Educational Technology, 42*, 113–127. https://doi.org/10.1111/j.1467-8535.2009.00990.x

Social Report. (2019). Vertical video masterclass: How (and when) to use the increasingly popular video format, *Social Report*, viewed 07.09.2019, https://www.socialreport.com/insights/article/360018863471-Vertical-Video-Masterclass-How-And-When-to-Use-the-Increasingly-Popular-Video-Format.

Stewart, P. (2017a). *The live-streaming handbook: How to create live video for social media on your phone and desktop*. New York: Routledge.

Sutherland, K. (2019a). Chapter ten producing video to enhance digital communication. In S. Kelly (Ed.), *Computer-mediated communication for business theory to practice* (pp. 99–110). United Kingdom: Cambridge Scholars Publishing.

Sutherland, K. (2019b). How to brief a videographer, DrKarenSutherland.com, viewed 15.09.2019, https://drkarensutherland.com/2019/09/14/how-to-brief-a-videographer/.

TikTok. (2019). Virtual items policy, TikTok.com, viewed: 19.11.2019, https://www.tiktok.com/legal/virtual-items?lang=en.

Vaynerchuk, G. (2019). *How to make 64 pieces of content in a day*, viewed 10/05/2020, https://www.garyvaynerchuk.com/how-to-create-64-pieces-of-content-in-a-day/.

Veena World. (2018a). #AbGharDurNahi, Facebook.com, viewed 08.09.2019, https://www.facebook.com/VeenaWorldOfficial/videos/546881782401618/.

Veena World. (2018b). #IssSaalPakka, Facebook.com, viewed 08.09.2019, https://www.facebook.com/VeenaWorldOfficial/videos/2196808907044275/.

Vesoulis, A. (2019). Canadian police accidentally livestream double homicide press conference using Facebook's cat filter, *Time*, viewed: 19/11/2019, https://time.com/5631158/canada-police-cat-filter-homicide/.

Voorveld, H. A. (2019). Brand communication in social media: A research agenda. *Journal of Advertising, 48*(1), 14–26.

Waters, R. D., & Jones, P. M. (2011). Using video to build an organization's identity and brand: A content analysis of nonprofit organizations' YouTube videos. *Journal of Nonprofit & Public Sector Marketing, 23,* 248–268. https://doi.org/10.1080/10495142.2011.594779

Yu, D. (2019a). Dennis Yu's 3 × 3 video grid strategy, *BlitzMetrics Topic Wheel Micro Course.*

Yu, D. (2019b). The four components of a one minute video, *BlitzMetrics Topic Wheel Micro Course.*

Yu, D. (2019c). One minute video course, *BlitzMetrics,* viewed 16.09.2019, https://blitzmetrics.com/omv/.

Yu, E., Jung, C., Kim, H., & Jung, J. (2018). Impact of viewer engagement on gift-giving in live video streaming. *Telematics and Informatics, 35*(5), 1450–1460.

Further Reading

Burgess, J. E. (2011). *YouTube.* Oxford Bibliographies Online.

Diefenbach, D. L., & Slatton, A. E. (2019). *Video production techniques: Theory and practice from concept to screen.* New York: Routledge.

Gioglio, J., & Walter, E. (2014). *The power of visual storytelling: How to use visuals, videos, and social media to market your brand.* New York: McGraw-Hill.

Johnson, K., & Radosh, J. (2017b). *Shoot, edit, share: Video production for mass media, marketing, advertising, and public relations.* Focal Press.

Stewart, P. (2017b). *The live-streaming handbook: How to create live video for social media on your phone and desktop.* Routledge.

Helpful Links

BlitzMetrics One Minute Video Course: https://blitzmetrics.com/omv/

Engage Video Marketing Podcast: https://engagevideomarketing.com/podcast/

Justin Brown - Primal Video: https://www.youtube.com/user/EditMyClips0

How to Make 64 Pieces of Content in a Day: https://www.garyvaynerchuk.com/how-to-create-64-pieces-of-content-in-a-day/

16

Live-Streaming Video Tools

Be.Live: https://be.live/
Easylive: https://easylive.io/en/
Socialive: https://www.socialive.us/
StreamYard: https://streamyard.com/
Switcher Studio: https://www.switcherstudio.com/

Video Conferencing Tools

Facebook Rooms: https://about.fb.com/news/2020/04/introducing-messenger-rooms/
Google Meet: https://meet.google.com/
Zoom: https://zoom.us/

Video Production Equipment

The Ultimate Video Production Equipment Checklist: https://www.uscreen.tv/blog/video-production-equipment/

73 Ways to Create a Video Studio on Any Budget: https://www.socialmediaexaminer.com/3-ways-to-create-a-video-studio-on-any-budget/

Editing Tools

Adobe Premiere Pro: https://www.adobe.com/au/products/premiere.html

Adobe Premiere Rush: https://www.adobe.com/au/products/premiere-rush/youtube-video-editor.html

Biteable: https://biteable.com/
Canva: https://www.canva.com/
Camtasia: https://www.techsmith.com/video-editor.html
Final Cut Pro: https://www.apple.com/au/final-cut-pro/
How to Hire a Video Editor: https://www.youtube.com/watch?v=tc9FFfJJDao
Onlinejobs.ph: https://www.onlinejobs.ph/
WeVideo: https://www.wevideo.com

Closed Caption Tools

Otter.ai: https://otter.ai/
Rev.com: https://www.rev.com

Music

dig.ccMixter.: http://dig.ccmixter.org/
Mobygratis.: https://mobygratis.com/
SoundCloud.: https://soundcloud.com/
YouTube Audio Library.: https://www.youtube.com/audiolibrary/music?nv=1

Conclusion: Social Media the Only Constant Is Change

Contents

© The Author(s), under exclusive license to Springer Nature Singapore Pte Ltd. 2021
K. E. Sutherland, *Strategic Social Media Management*, https://doi.org/10.1007/978-981-15-4658-7_17

By the End of This Chapter You Will

- Understand how social media management as a profession has evolved and keeps evolving.
- Know how to stay at the forefront of industry changes to keep developing as a social media professional.
- Recognise the potential personal and professional risks associated with working within the field of social media.
- Gain an insight into some strategies to protect the health and well-being of social media managers.

TLDR

- One of the key skills a Social Media Manager must learn is to be nimble, fast and flexible in the face of the constant evolution of social media technology.
- The evolution of Social Media Management has included three key stages thus far: 1. It is Just Another Task, 2. The Social Media Generalists and 3. The Social Media Specialists.
- The concept of the T-Shaped professional suggests that employability is increased by having a broad understanding of the tasks required within an industry but in-depth knowledge in one or two skill areas.
- If working social media as a profession, a strong emphasis must be placed on attempting to stay abreast of the key developments in the field and regularly developing knowledge and skills.
- Working as a Social Media Manager can be a hugely rewarding experience, but there are some potential risks that can also be part of the profession.
- You are the only person responsible for your wellbeing and it is essential to put actions in place to maintain and

17

improve it. Never let work take away your health and happiness.
- The key takeaways from this text are: i. Know your audience, ii. Always align social media activities to strategic goals and objectives, and, iii. Use social media to help others and to provide value.

17.1 Introduction

The previous 16 chapters in this text have provided an overview of the key functions of strategic social media management.

In ▶ Section 1 we explored how to develop a social media strategy, including the importance of audience research, managing issues and risks, helping more than selling, selecting relevant tactics, plus the importance of storytelling, listening, monitoring, measurement and scheduling.

▶ Section 2 focused on strategic content curation, paying particular attention to ethical, processes and techniques.

Finally, ▶ Section 3 investigated strategic content creation providing a comprehensive insight into copywriting, visual content and video production in a social media context.

With the fundamental principles analysed, it is time to take a holistic view of Social Media Management as a career and how it can personally impact professionals working within the field as they cope with client demands and continual change.

The final chapter of this text is aptly named: *Social Media - The Only Constant is Change*, because it is the truth. One of the key skills a Social Media Manager must learn is to be nimble, fast and flexible in the face of the constant evolution of social media technology.

Staying across perpetual change can take considerable time and effort, but the knowledge and experience gained in the process is invaluable. It is a gift to participate in a profession that requires consistent learning and development. We are living in one of the most exciting times in history and working with social media means being at the absolute forefront of change.

This chapter has two key focuses. Firstly, it explores Social Media Management as a profession, how it has evolved, how to cope with change and continue to develop as a professional in the field.

Next, this chapter explores the potential risks (personal and professional) related to working in social media and recommend actionable strategies to help eradicate or minimise any possible negative impacts that may be associated with social media management.

Finally, the chapter concludes with an interview with Brian Solis, world-renowned digital analyst, speaker and author of the book 'Lifescale' who discusses the future of social media and ways to reduce digital distractions to lead a more creative, productive and happy life.

17.2 The Evolution of Social Media Management

Social media began purely with the intention of connecting people in an informal and social way (Van Dijck, 2013). It was not until approximately 2008 that social media was perceived as a potential tool for business (McFadden, 2018). Yet, even as recently as five years ago social media was still being discussed as a fad in academic literature (He, 2014). Luckily, perceptions regarding the importance of social media have evolved within some businesses and organisations in line with adoption rates and technological advances. Considering there are now 3.5 billion social media users around the world, the discussions surrounding social media as a passing trend should now be over and the need for social media professionals galvanised across industries (Kemp, 2019).

The stages of social media management presented have been gleaned from the interviews with social media professionals throughout this text and industry observations and provide an insight into how the profession is changing. While these stages seem to focus on in-house social media teams and agency contexts, they can also apply to freelance Social Media Managers.

17.2.1 Stage 1. It Is Just Another Task

In business and nonprofit contexts, social media was often viewed as a 'nice to have' rather than a necessity, particularly because its Return On Investment (ROI) could not be clearly measured (which is sometimes still an issue). As such, decision-makers at businesses and organisations adopting social media often allocated the task of its management to an existing staff member without formal training apart from experience with their own personal use of the technology. This scenario still occurs in some workplaces. For example, a study into social media use in non-profit organisations in Australia found that it was common for social media management to be allocated to a staff member already grappling with a heavy workload (Sutherland, 2015). There remains some business and organisations that still do not understand the value of social media. However, where this was once the norm, there has definitely been a shift.

17.2.2 Stage 2. The Social Media Generalists

The next stage involved businesses and organisations acknowledging the power that social media can have in attracting and retaining customers when used effectively. This realisation resulted in business owners and organisational decision-makers identifying the need to employ someone focused solely on social media management. This person had to complete all social media-related tasks. Depending on the size of the

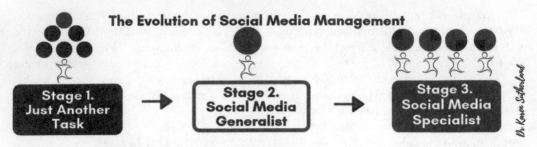

◘ Fig. 17.1   The Evolution of Social Media Management

organisation, its social media following and presence, this was a mammoth undertaking for one person, and many organisations are still in this phase.

In larger enterprises, a small team of social media managers were employed, each overseeing a different business segment. The same structure was also applied in some social media agencies where social media managers would work together in a team each providing services to multiple clients (◘ Fig. 17.1.).

17.2.3 Stage 3. Social Media Specialist Team

The next, and current stage in the evolution of social media management involves a social media team of specialists where each member focuses on one aspect of the process. For example, a team may consist of an advertising specialist, a strategist, a copywriter, a graphic designer, a videographer, a photographer and a data analyst who each provide their own area of expertise to provide services to clients. This current stage has developed after astute business-owners and organisational decision-makers have recognised the multifaceted and diverse nature of social media management. Rather than expecting social media professionals to perform every function, they acknowledge the range of skill areas required. This structure suggests that it is more effective to draw from the specific knowledge of a team of highly skilled specialists than to deliver outcomes that may not be of consistent quality

in every component of social media management. It can be unrealistic to expect a Social Media Manager to be equally as proficient in all aspects of their role. The shift to specialist teams is by no means widespread at time of writing, but it is exciting to witness social media management maturing as a valid and credible career option.

17.3 The T-Shaped Professional

The changes to social media management as a profession have increased the applicability of the T-Shaped professional as a concept of employability (Bierema, 2019; Demirkan & Spohrer, 2018). As demonstrated in ◘ Fig. 17.2. the theory of the T-Shaped professional suggests that employability is increased by having a broad understanding of the tasks required within an industry but in-depth knowledge in one or two skill areas (Korte, Hüsing, & Dashja, 2018; Davis, 2018).

It is theorised that a T-Shaped professional has both breadth and depth in their skills and knowledge, a combination that increases employability more than a person who is only a generalist or a specialist (Bierema, 2019; Demirkan & Spohrer, 2018; Korte et al., 2018; Davis, 2018).

In ◘ Fig. 17.2., the breadth of knowledge is symbolised by the horizontal section of the T and the deeper knowledge is signified by the vertical line.

For example, in the context of Social Media Management, this book has provided a broad overview of the key tasks associated

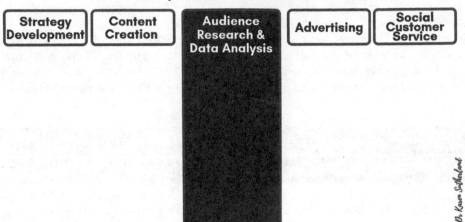

Fig. 17.2 The T-Shaped Social Media Professional

with the process. Applying a T-Shaped framework to social media management means that while having a working understanding of the key facets of the role and the process, you focus on building expertise in only one or two specific areas.

As a social media professional, you may understand the process of strategy development, but have advanced skills in copywriting and video production. Alternatively, while you have a broad understanding of content creation, your abilities and interests are focused on social media audience research and data analysis.

As this book has demonstrated, there are many facets to social media management and expecting to be highly proficient in every single one can be unrealistic. It is important to have a good breadth of understanding to be able to assist with any task if required, but to build a significant degree of knowledge in one or two areas that: 1. You enjoy and 2. Perform at a high level.

Approaching a career in social media as a T-Shaped professional also involves having a strong commitment and focus to continuous learning and skill development.

17.4 Fostering Continual Growth as a Social Media Professional

With social media's constant evolution, it can be challenging to maintain currency in terms of skills, knowledge and platform changes. This is why it is a stretch to call anyone a "social media expert". This is because social media is constantly changing, and nobody can be across every single change.

> 66 It is stretch to call anyone a "social media expert". This is because social media is constantly changing and nobody can be across every single change. 99
>
> **Dr Karen Sutherland**

However, if working social media as a profession, a strong emphasis must be placed on attempting to stay abreast of the key developments in the field and regularly developing knowledge and skills. ◱ Table 17.1. provides some techniques to support continual growth as a social media professional with links to examples in the Helpful Links section at the end of this chapter.

With Social Media Management as a profession examined, it is important to explore the potential impacts of working in the field to manage any potential risks.

◱ **Table 17.1**	Techniques to Remain Current as a Social Media Professional
Currency technique	**Description**
Follow social media commentators	Social media commentators seem to know first about platform changes and share these on their social media channels. Follow their profiles on Facebook, Twitter or LinkedIn (and other platforms if that is their main channel) to find out about news as it breaks
Follow the platforms media profiles	Most platforms share news via media releases and announcements via social media. Follow these accounts to stay on top of new developments
Read every day	Subscribe to social media-related blogs and check social media news sites every day as part of your morning ritual of beginning work for the day Also, read current social media books to gain further knowledge and be exposed to a range of perspectives
Set up a Google alert for social media	In ▶ Chap. 7 we explored how to set Google Alerts for social listening. It can also be a helpful practice to set up a Google Alert for the term "social media" or other related industry terms. This helps news about the industry be sent directly to your email inbox to help keep you informed and current
Complete online courses and certifications	There are some extremely helpful free and paid online courses and certifications available that can greatly assist in further developing practical skills and knowledge It is worth completing at least five relevant courses or certifications per year. In addition to increasing skills and knowledge, the completed courses and certifications can be included in your CV and LinkedIn profile to further increase your credibility with prospective clients or employers.
Join online groups for social media managers	Joining Facebook and LinkedIn groups for Social Media Managers and other related topics can also help to keep you across changes and can provide instant help and support if you need it The focus of many of these groups is for members to share a social media challenge or issue they are experiencing, and other members provide advice It can really help to feel connected to an online community if a sole trader or do not work closely with other social media professionals Also, relevant Twitter chats can be a great way to connect online with other social media professionals
Attend relevant conferences	Most countries have at least one social media-related conference every year. Attending can be a great way to meet other social media professionals and learn new techniques and approaches However, be aware that some of the conference speakers are there to sell their service, book or course so be prepared for heavy pitches as part of their sessions

17

Currency technique	Description
Attend relevant networking events	Local networking events with other social-media related professionals can also help build new connections, generate business leads and learn new knowledge and skills LinkedIn Local is a great example of a networking event that takes place in many countries around the world In response to the COVID-19 Pandemic, many localised networking events have moved online providing Social Media Managers with the ability to network with fellow social media professionals from around the globe
Join industry bodies	Social media-related industry bodies are now available in many countries around the world. For example, in Australia there is the Social Media Marketing Institute which provides support to its members and facilitates a professional community for those working in social media as a career
Subscribe to relevant podcasts and livestreams or create your own	Podcasts are a fantastic way to learn new perspectives, knowledge and skills about social media-related topics The best part about podcasts is that they can be listened to anywhere, at the gym, in the car, out walking so that you can build your knowledge wherever you are and whatever you are doing Another strategic approach is to create your own podcast or livestream show and interview industry leaders. Doing this will increase your knowledge, your networks and your personal brand as well as providing a service by sharing this knowledge with other social media professionals
Experiment with new platforms, tools and features	Wisdom is gained by turning knowledge into experience. As Mongezi Lupindo advised in ▶ Chap. 15, be the first to experiment with new tools, platforms and features. Do not be afraid to play and see what they can do. Do not wait for someone else to work it out. See new platforms, tools and features as new toys to be discovered and have fun learning by doing

Table 17.1 (continued)

17.5 Potential Risks Working as a Social Media Manager

Working as a Social Media Manager can be a hugely rewarding experience, but there are some potential risks that can also be part of the profession. These may not be experienced by everyone in the field, but it is important to be aware of the potential risks and possible strategies to navigate them from the outset to set you up for professional and personal success.

> 66 It is important to be aware of the potential risks and possible strategies to navigate them to set you up for professional and personal success. 99
>
> Dr Karen Sutherland

Table 17.2   Risks Associated with Social Media Management

Potential risk	Description
Digital distraction	Constantly monitoring multiple profiles for multiple clients can result in shortened attention spans and the inability to focus on specific tasks. "Ten years ago, attention shifted (on average) every 3 minutes, today attention shifts every 45 seconds," (Solis, 2019, p.16). Digital distraction can have a hugely negative impact on productivity Similarly, multitasking involving social media has been proven to be an ineffective approach to work. Brooks (2015) found that higher amounts of personal social media usage led to lower task performance, greater levels of technostress and lower happiness. Therefore, constantly checking personal social media accounts while trying to complete work tasks severely impacted the ability to complete the task
Viewing explicitly violent and disturbing content	The moderation of explicit content can be a requirement of the role for some social media professionals. In his article, The Trauma Floor, Newton (2019) provided a graphic insight into the work of a Facebook Moderator, the disturbing content they are required to assess on a daily basis and the psychological impacts resulting from it. Being required to be exposed to such explicit content can result in trauma and stress and other negative impacts to mental wellbeing
Being the victim of online bullying and abuse	Managing a client's, brands or organisation's social media profiles can result in online bullying and abuse from the public, particularly when dealing directly with social media users during times of issues and crises. Such negativity can take its toll on the mental health of a Social Media Manager.
Burn out	Burnout is a very real threat to the wellbeing of social media professionals because of the constant pressure to be online "Burnout is a state of mental, emotional, and physical exhaustion a person experiences in response to an excessive and prolonged stress," (Han, 2018, p.22; Maslach & Leiter, 2008). Social media burnout has been defined as the same state mentioned above but as a direct result of social media use (Han, 2018) Being constantly connected and ready to work at any time can have extremely negative impacts on the mental and physical wellbeing of a social media manager

◘ Table 17.2. lists some of the risks associated with working as a Social Media Manager.

17.6 Self-Care Strategies for the Social Media Manager

While there are potential risks associated with social media management, there are strategies that can minimise these risks or eradicate them completely. Remember, you are the only person responsible for your wellbeing and it is essential to put actions in place to maintain and improve it. Never let work take away your health and happiness. ◘ Table 17.3 provides a list of strategies to assist in addressing the potential risks of working in social media as a profession.

17

> 66 You are the only person responsible for your well-being. It is essential to put actions in place to maintain and improve it. Never let work take away your health and happiness. 99
>
> Dr Karen Sutherland

Table 17.3 Self-Care Strategies for Social Media Managers (Keemanovic, 2019; Brown, 2019; Sutherland, 2019)

Self-care strategy	Description
Regular breaks	Stepping away from the phone and computer can help to avoid burn-out by re-energising you. Even 10 minutes to make a cup of tea/coffee can really help
Turn on out-of-office email message and set phone to flight mode when focusing on a task	To avoid digital distraction and dive deeply into a task, set your out-of-office message to let people know when you will be available again and set your phone to flight mode to avoid attention being diverted by constant notifications. Experts recommend spending between 25 minutes and two hours focused on a specific task to complete it effectively (Solis, 2019; Goldhill, 2016). It can take more approximately 23 minutes to regain focus on a task after being distracted from it (Solis, 2019; Goldhill, 2016)
Avoid multitasking	Focus on completing one task at a time. Sometimes it may not be possible to complete an entire task in one sitting. Instead, chip away at a list of larger tasks by completing a small proportion of each one at a time. This allows progress to be made on each one. The key is to only focus on the task at hand
Report abusive social media users	Nobody deserves to experience abuse or online bullying under any circumstances. Always report abusive social media users and inform the relevant client or relevant manager about the situation so that they are aware. Also, keep screen shots of any abusive behaviour you are experiencing in case it is required as evidence in the future
Interact with other social media professionals regularly	Interacting with fellow social media professionals is more than a professional development activity, it can also help to feel supported and understood. Interaction can happen online or in-person. Remember, to be part of a community you must be a participant. It only works if you help each other
Get enough sleep and leave your phone in another room	Do not fall into the trap of "hustle culture", the idea that working excessively is the only way to be successful (Cochrane, 2018). Ample sleep is important and necessary to avoid burnout. It is also a good idea to leave your phone in another room to avoid checking it while in bed. Buy an alarm clock if you use your phone's alarm to wake you
Spend time in nature	Even 10 minutes standing barefoot on the earth can help to recharge you. Never underestimate the power of nature in reducing stress
Share quality time with friends, family and colleagues in person	Get away from the computer, put the phone away and spend time with people face-to-face. It can really assist with wellbeing and reduce feelings of isolation than can often be caused from spending excessive amounts of time online
Yoga, meditation and/or exercise	It does not matter which you prefer, the main aim is to calm the mind. Yoga, meditation or any form of exercise can boost serotonin in the brain that helps improve mood and feelings of wellbeing
Following intense periods of work with activities to help with recovery.	There are times when intense periods of work may be required. The body and the mind need assistance to recover from them. It helps to plan a massage or other well-being activity to help with recovery and to provide a reward to look forward to once the work has been completed

(continued)

Table 17.3 (continued)

Self-care strategy	Description
Helping others.	Volunteering has been proven to improve mental health (Lau et al., 2019). Focusing on someone else's needs is a great way to learn different perspectives and feel good about helping others
Speak to a mental health professional when necessary	It is perfectly acceptable to look after your mental health by debriefing with a mental health professional such as a qualified counsellor or psychologist. Social Media Managers can be the targets of abuse and bullying and/or required to view potentially traumatic content such as extreme violence as part of their everyday working lives. This can have a negative impact on mental health. Do not hesitate in unpacking this with a professional. It can make a profound difference compared with trying to cope on your own

Conclusion

This chapter provided an overview of the key topic areas covered in the book. Next, it explored social media management as a profession and provided advice to stay abreast of its continual evolution. Potential risks of the profession were also explored and strategies for self-care presented to protect or at least minimise any possible negative impacts.

As this is not only the conclusion for this chapter, but for the entire book, I hope that your reading experience was insightful, helpful and interesting. One aim of this text was to take the reader on the journey of social media management through the multidisciplinary lens of marketing, advertising and public relations; the other was to share my passion for this exciting profession.

The key takeaways from this text are:

1. Know your audience.
2. Always align social media activities to strategic goals and objectives, and,
3. Use social media to help others and to provide value.

Follow these principles and you will excel as a Social Media Manager. I wish you every success in your social media journey and feel privileged to have shared even a tiny part of it. Best wishes and thank you.

17.7 Interview: Brian Solis, Digital Analyst, Speaker, Author of 'Lifescale', USA

1. **Please tell me about your current role or what you're currently doing professionally.**

I spend my days studying disruptive technology and its impact on markets, businesses, institutions, and then further channel that into a variety of more tangible conversations, whether it's customer experience or innovation or a digital transformation or corporate culture or startup culture. I also spend a great deal of my time as a digital anthropologist exploring how that same disruption is affecting society and a variety of scenarios.

2. **What do you enjoy most about working in the digital space?**

There was a time where things moved much slower and the extent of which the impacts of these things weren't as far reaching. Nowadays it's almost as if things are not only changing in real time, but they're seemingly changing in real time because we're now just starting to realise the effects of all of the things.

There's a lot to make up for in terms of lost time in lost insights and so that it keeps me running, running really fast. And so, the enjoyment comes from at least trying to understand enough in order to deliver the types of observations.

3. **What are the greatest challenges that you experience working in the digital space?**

The irony of writing a book on the effects of technology on our own lives, on our brains, our bodies, and playing that out into a bunch of scenarios like work, or creativity, or learning, or love and relationships and friendships. It's just the irony of it is selling a book about that to a world or a market of people who don't realise that they are having any issues on those fronts, yet they are. We all are.

One of the biggest challenges is telling that or getting that more personal side of the story to those who don't necessarily realise that they need the help. It's also one of the things that drives my work.

4. **How did you come to work in this space? What is your career story?**

I've always been sort of a technologist. I've learned coding at a very young age and wanted to pursue a career in technology and moved to Silicon Valley from Los Angeles in 1996 to do so. Early on in my work I recognised that there was going to be real opportunities to humanise the evolution of technology. I tend to look at the more optimistic, more exploratory side of things.

That drove my work very early on. I started to share publicly a lot of this stuff that I was thinking, and some of the things that I was experimenting with. I started a company dedicated to that work in 1999 and that company became a big player in helping to launch not just a lot of the early internet companies, but also help develop a lot of the early consumer and business markets that helped tech change the world for better or for worse.

I would help to understand what it was going to take to shift a market from film photography to digital photography to change your market from keeping pictures as memories in shoe boxes and albums to actually posting their pictures on the internet for people to see. Which was massive shifts in behaviours and norms and values.

In the 90s I began working in digital anthropology and helped pioneer that space leading to the pioneering of a lot of other things like digital marketing, through peer-to-peer engagement, through consumer research, through influence, through becoming sort of a passionate thought leader in the technology that I was representing to help cultivate markets.

That was a long time ago, but it also seems like yesterday and that I'm literally on the same treadmill running faster, and faster, and faster, trying to always stay ahead of the curve to figure out how, not just what's happening in the world, but how to change it and, in much more positive directions.

5. **What are the three most important things that you would recommend for Social Media Managers (or those working in the digital space) to consider regarding their self-care in that profession?**

I think the biggest one is to get over yourself. I think the hardest thing about this is that we've all become accidental narcissists and some to greater degrees than others. We're bringing to that our own perspectives of what it means to be online as an individual and not necessarily understanding the unique perspectives, or challenges, or frustrations, or struggles, or aspirations of the people that you're engaging with or hoping to engage with. And that I think is a big, it's a big myth.

Where we are as a society is one that's having to help people understand two things. One is that you need self-care. And then too, we have to remove the stigma of it. And I guess there's a third and that third is it's actually our best way to personal growth and self-development and actually greatness, however you want to describe that, and happiness.

We need mentors and role models and peers who are all aware of all of the things that we deal with and the intellectual and psychological and even biological impacts of how technology is changing us. In order to recognise the opportunities for self-care isn't so much just about self-care, it's simply about self-love.

It's just giving ourselves the respect, but also the permission to love ourselves in a way that we don't even realise that we're not loving ourselves because we're so busy multitasking and scrolling and doing all of these things online and feeding the machine and trying to be fed by the machine and not recognising that we're actually draining and sapping our energy and that we're robbing ourselves of our creativity and our ability to love and be loved.

6. **What do you think are the benefits for people making self-care a priority?**
The benefits of self-care allow us to recognise the truth of self-awareness to grow up in paths that are much healthier and more productive and even creative. It unlocks the things we can't see or feel today because we just didn't notice, see or feel them.

7. **What are the benefits to customers if a business makes the self-care of its employees a priority?**
I believe that there is an energy in the world that when it's negative it's negative and when it's positive it's positive. Anything in between that is just not even worth feeling. But there is something to be said for super positive energy. If somebody's really happy around you, that's going to radiate on to you. It's just a reality and it's just when someone feels that you are in your best place, that's contagious. People notice that. People observe it. The same is true for when somebody recognises authenticity. It's noticeable.

8. **How do you practice self-care?**
Aside from writing a book to change my life. I'm someone who's hyper connected to some of the most well-known startup founders and entrepreneurs and engineers in the world. Even I wasn't immune to any of this. Even once I recognised it, I had a challenge. I didn't have access to what I needed to solve my own problems. It took me a good few years to recognise what those problems were beyond the symptoms and then more importantly, what to do about it. And that's where the birth of Lifescale came from was looking at what's happening in my life, but also why it's happening.

I control, alt, deleted my life to reset what those values and purposes are for an era where we have access to anything we want, when we want it. The first part was to get humble and recognise that I wasn't really actually living my best life. I was living my best life the way I wanted to see it. It's like that old David Foster Wallace commencement speech. This is water that we have to remind ourselves that we are surrounded by magical things and we have a place in it and then once we know what that place is in it we can do new things.

9. **How do you see the future of social media?**

People are too ready to believe what they see, and they soak their own cognitive biases and they seek that engagement that reinforces those biases. For anybody working in social media, they're already against the odds. At the same time, you're also dealing with people who are constantly distracted. We're at a point in time where we're, as individuals on average, distracted upwards of 200 or more times a day. Every time you're distracted, you're pulled away from wherever your attention or your focus was in the first place, no matter how strongly it was rooted in that focus.

I think what we really have to start doing is shifting attention into outcomes and those outcomes and sort of the, how does someone feel, how does someone think? Also, what somebody does. Two metrics that we aren't measuring enough today are affinity/loyalty and customer lifetime value or lifetime value. Those are much deeper meaningful metrics that will change how we look at data in order to think about how we think about engagement, content and community.

10. **What is the best piece of advice that you have been given?**

It's actually in the book, which is a friend of mine. He imparted a Western version of Eastern philosophy, which was three words. Be, do, get.

He said, "Figure out what it is you want to be and then go do the things that help you get what it is that you want to be."

It's sort of a much more practical but actionable version of the law of attraction. Don't just visualise what you want, put an action plan together and go get it. That was the advice that I still lean on today.

❓ Questions for Critical Reflection

1. Explain the three stages of social media management as a profession. Why do you think the profession has developed in this way? Please explain your answer.

2. What is a T-Shaped Professional? What do you think are the benefits of being T-Shaped? Share your responses with the rest of the class.

3. Why is it important for a social media professional to keep learning and developing their skills?

4. What are some of the key actions a social media professional can implement to remain current in terms of their knowledge and skills? Please explain your answers.

5. What are some of the risks associated with working as a social media professional? Which ones worry you the most? Please share your answers with your classmates.

6. What are some of the strategies that can be employed to help manage the risks posed to Social Media Managers? Which strategies interest you the most and why?

7. Now that you have finished reading Strategic Social Media Management: Theory and Practice what are the most important pieces of information that you have learned from this text? Why do you think they are the most important? Please explain your rationale.

▶ Practical Exercises

1. Go to the Contents page and refamiliarise yourself with the different components of social media management covered in this book. Select one or two topic areas that you most enjoyed learning about. Set up a Google Alert on this topic and subscribe to at least one blog and podcast devoted to this specific area of social media management. Explain the rationale for your selection with the rest of the class.

2. Go the Helpful Links section of this chapter, visit the LinkedIn Local webpage. Search to see if there is an event in your local area. If not, read the resources on how you can set up a LinkedIn event. Running an event can be an excellent way to build connections and credibility within your community. Share your findings with the class.

3. Considering the potential risks that can be associated with having a career in social media, develop a 5-point self-care plan to proactively minimise the impacts of being a Social Media Manager. Your self-care plan should contain relevant, realistic and achievable actions. Share your self-care plan with the rest of the class.

References

Bierema, L. L. (2019). Enhancing employability through developing T-shaped professionals. *New Directions for Adult and Continuing Education, 2019*(163), 67–81.

Brooks, S. (2015). Does personal social media usage affect efficiency and well-being? *Computers in Human Behavior, 46*, 26–37.

Brown, E. (2019). 7 ways for social marketers to avoid social media burnout. *Hootsuite,* viewed 2.10.2019: https://blog.hootsuite.com/ways-to-avoid-social-media-burnout

Cochrane, G. (2018). The #Hustle Myth. *Graham Cochrane,* viewed 2.10.2019: https://www.grahamcochrane.com/the-hustle-myth/

Davis, H. (2018). Connecting the dots for professional practice in higher education: Leadership, energy management, and motivation. *Professional and Support Staff in Higher Education*, 1–15.

Demirkan, H., & Spohrer, J. C. (2018). Commentary—Cultivating T-shaped professionals in the era of digital transformation. *Service Science, 10*(1), 98–109.

Goldhill, O. (2016). Multitasking is exhausting your brain, say neuroscientists. *World Economic Forum,* viewed 2.10.2019: https://www.weforum.org/agenda/2016/07/multitasking-is-exhausting-your-brain-say-neuroscientists

Han, B. (2018). Social media burnout: Definition, measurement instrument, and why we care. *Journal of Computer Information Systems, 58*(2), 122–130.

He, X. (2014). Is social media a fad? A study of the adoption and use of social media in SMEs. *SAIS 2014 proceedings.* Paper, 13.

Kecmanovic, J. (2019). 6 ways to protect your mental health from social media's dangers. *The Conversation,* viewed 2.10.2019: https://theconversation.com/6-ways-to-protect-your-mental-health-from-social-medias-dangers-117651?fbclid=IwAR0VQGTaXJEWQbkWqPN5I1pSVHWQCepb76bHuh-31gtaZ9FlVUF_KoJ0e_c

Kemp, S. (2019). Digital 2019: Global Internet Use Accelerates. *We Are Social,* viewed 2.10.2019: https://wearesocial.com/blog/2019/01/digital-2019-global-internet-use-accelerates

Korte, W. B., Hüsing, T., & Dashja, E. (2018). T-shaped professionals in Europe Today and in 2020. In J. Spohrer & H. Demirkan (Eds.), *T-shaped professionals: Adaptive innovators.* New York: Business Experts Press.

Lau, Y., Fang, L., Cheng, L. J., & Kwong, H. K. D. (2019). Volunteer motivation, social problem solving, self-efficacy, and mental health: A structural equation model approach. *Educational Psychology, 39*(1), 112–132.

Maslach, C., & Leiter, M. P. (2008). Early predictors of job burnout and engagement. *Journal of Applied Psychology, 93*(3), 498.

McFadden, C. (2018). A chronological history of social media. *Interesting Engineering,* viewed 2.10.2019: https://interestingengineering.com/a-chronological-history-of-social-media

Newton, C. (2019). The trauma floor – the secret lives of Facebook moderators in America. *The Verge,* viewed 2.10.2019: https://www.theverge.com/2019/2/25/18229714/cognizant-facebook-content-moderator-interviews-trauma-working-conditions-arizona

Solis, B. (2019). *Lifescale – how to live a more creative, productive, happy life.* New Jersey: Wiley.

17

Sutherland, K. (2019). Interviews; balancing the grind Dr. Karen Sutherland, Social Media Educator, Author, Researcher & Consultant. *Balance the Grind*, viewed 2.10.2019: https://www.balancethegrind.com.au/interviews/balancing-the-grind-dr-karen-sutherland-social-media-educator-author-researcher-consultant/

Sutherland, K. E. (2015). *Towards an integrated social media communication model for the not-for-profit sector: a case study of youth homelessness charities*, viewed 2.10.2019: https://monash.figshare.com/articles/Towards_an_integrated_social_media_communication_model_for_the_not-for-profit_sector_a_case_study_of_youth_homelessness_charities/4711576/1

Van Dijck, J. (2013). *The culture of connectivity: A critical history of social media*. London: Oxford University Press.

Further Reading

Eyal, N. (2019). *Indistractable: How to control your attention and choose your life*. London: Bloomsbury Publishing.

Quesenberry, K. (2018). Over 300 social media tools and resources for 2018. *Post Control Marketing*, viewed 2.10. 2019: https://www.postcontrolmarketing.com/300-social-media-tools-resources-2018/

Social Media+ Society: https://journals.sagepub.com/home/sms

Solis, B. (2019). *Lifescale – how to live a more creative, productive, happy life*. Wiley.

Spohrer, J., & Demirka, H. (2018). *T-shaped professionals: Adaptive innovators*. Business Experts Press.

Swallow, E. (2011). Top 10 Academic Journals for social media research. *Strategic Social Media Lab*, viewed 2.10.2019: https://strategicsocialmedialab.com/top-10-academic-journals-for-social-media-research/

Helpful Links

Social Media Commentators

Brian Solis: https://www.briansolis.com/category/articles/

Dennis Yu: https://www.dennis-yu.com/

Gary Vaynerchuk: https://www.garyvaynerchuk.com/blog/

Neil Patel: https://neilpatel.com/blog/

Matt Navarra: https://thenextweb.com/author/matthewnavarra/

Madalyn Skalr: https://madalynsklar.com/blog/

Mari Smith: https://www.marismith.com/mari-smith-blog/

Seth's Blog (Seth Godin): https://seths.blog/

Social Media Platform Newsrooms

Facebook: https://newsroom.fb.com/

Instagram: https://instagram-press.com/

LinkedIn: https://news.linkedin.com

TikTok: https://newsroom.tiktok.com/en-us

WeChat: https://blog.wechat.com/category/news/

Blogs

Digital Marketer: https://www.digitalmarketer.com/blog/

Social Media Examiner: https://www.socialmediaexaminer.com/

Social Media Today: https://www.socialmediatoday.com/

Google Alerts https://www.google.com.au/alerts

Courses and Certifications

BlitzMetrics Courses: https://blitzmetrics.com/menu/

HubSpot Free Social Media Courses: https://www.hubspot.com/resources/courses/social-media

Facebook Blueprint: https://www.facebook.com/business/learn

Facebook Ads Targeting: https://learn.fiverr.com/courses/facebook-ads-targeting

Google Digital Garage: https://learndigital.withgoogle.com/digitalgarage-au

Online Groups

Social Media Managers: https://www.facebook.com/groups/socialmediamanagers/learning_content/

Social Media Masterminds Group https://www.facebook.com/groups/1509722192640979/

The Social Media Geek Out https://www.facebook.com/groups/socialgeekout/

Tik Tok Marketing Secrets | Growth Hacks for Marketers and Influencers https://www.facebook.com/groups/tiktoksecrets/

Conferences

World List of Social Media Conferences: https://www.socialbakers.com/events

Social Media Marketing World: https://www.socialmediaexaminer.com/smmworld/

VidCon: https://vidcon.com/

LinkedIn Local

LinkedIn Local website: https://linkednlocal.com/

Industry Bodies

Social Media Club: https://socialmediaclub.org/

Social Media Marketing Institute: https://www.smminstitute.com.au/

Podcasts

Social Media Marketing

59 Podcasts That Will Make You a Better Social Media Marketer https://blog.hootsuite.com/social-media-marketing-podcasts/

Social Media Advertising

Digital Advertising Podcasts: https://player.fm/podcasts/Digital-Advertising

Public Relations

Public Relations Podcasts: https://player.fm/featured/public-relations

Twitter Chats

62 best Twitter chats for digital marketers: https://awario.com/blog/digital-marketing-twitter-chats/

Supplementary Information

Appendix 1 and 2 – 408

Appendix 1 and 2

Appendix 1. Social Media Strategy Template

Cover Page

Include Client's Logo with permission

Social Media Strategy

Prepared by:

Phone:

Email:

Background

The background section does not need to be lengthy. Instead it is a succinct statement providing the reader with a brief overview of:

- When and why the company began
- Its main products and services
- The customers it serves
- Its current social media presence
- Its competitors
- The purpose of the strategy

(See Chapter 3 to complete the following three sections)

Goals

1.

2.

SMART Objectives

1.

2.

3.

4.

Key Messages

1.

2.

3.

(See Chapter 1 for advice on how to complete this section)

Target Audience

Demographic and Psychographic Information

Demographic:

- Age
- Gender
- Cultural Background
- Nationality
- Marital Status
- Number of Children (if any)
- Education Level
- Occupation
- Annual Income
- Living Status (home owner, renting etc.)
- Religion
- Languages spoken
- Disabilities
- Political Affiliation

Psychographic:

- Personality
- Personal Values
- Interests and Hobbies
- Attitudes
- Lifestyle
- Preferences and Dislikes
- Traditional and Social Media Consumption

Customer Persona/s

[Persona name]

Details

Age	
Location	
Language	

Job title	
Average income	
Buying behavior	
Interests & activities	
Life stage	

Pain points and goals

Customer pain point	Customer goal	How your business / product can help?
Pain point #1	Goal #1	Your solution #1
Pain point #2	Goal #2	Your solution #2
Pain point #3	Goal #3	Your solution #3

Customer Journey/s

Stage	Description
Awareness	
Interest	
Desire	
Action	
Support	
Loyalty	
Advocacy	

Selected Platforms

Social Media Platform	Rationale

(Please see Chapters 4 and 5 to learn more about Content Pillars)

Content Pillars

1.

2.

3.

(Please refer to Chapter 5 for information about Tactics)

Tactics

Customer Persona:

Customer Journey Stage: e.g. Awareness

Goal:

Tactic Description	SMART Objective Supported	Content Pillar	Rationale
1.			
2.			
3.			

Customer Journey Stage: e.g. Interest

Tactic Description	SMART Objective Supported	Content Pillar	Rationale
1.			
2.			
3.			

Customer Journey Stage: e.g. Desire

Tactic Description	SMART Objective Supported	Content Pillar	Rationale
1.			
2.			
3.			

Customer Journey Stage: e.g. Action

Tactic Description	SMART Objective Supported	Content Pillar	Rationale
1.			
2.			
3.			

Customer Journey Stage: e.g. Support

Tactic Description	SMART Objective Supported	Content Pillar	Rationale
1.			
2.			
3.			

Customer Journey Stage: e.g. Loyalty

Tactic Description	SMART Objective Supported	Content Pillar	Rationale
1.			
2.			
3.			

Customer Journey Stage: e.g. Advocacy

Tactic Description	SMART Objective Supported	Content Pillar	Rationale
1.			
2.			
3.			

(Please refer to Chapter 5 for more information about Social Media Monitoring, Listening and Measurement)

Measurement

Provide a brief overview to your client of what this section is about

Social Listening Plan

Method

Topic Areas

1.

2.

Key Words

Key Phrases

Qualifiers

Exclusions

Sentiment

Positive	Negative

(Refer to Chapter 5 and select ONE of the following measurement frameworks)

Paid, Owned and Earned Social Media Measurement Framework

	EXPOSURE	ENGAGEMENT	PREFERENCE	IMPACT	ADVOCACY
PAID					
OWNED					
EARNED					

Program, Channel and Business Social Media Measurement Framework

	EXPOSURE	ENGAGEMENT	PREFERENCE	IMPACT	ADVOCACY
Program					
Channel					
Business					

Method

Please detail the tools, methods you will use (please include how you will measure conversion metrics or impact) and how often you will undertake this measurement.

(For further advice about Budgets, please see Chapter 3)

Budget

Strategic Phase Budget Category	In-house Expense (fixed/percent)	Outsource Expense (fixed/percent)	Total Category (fixed/percent)
Development Research (Audience Research, Client Research, Industry Research, Social Media Audit,, Competitor Analysis etc). Social Media Strategy Proposal	$ per hour per item	$ per hour per item or $ amount for each item.	$ (per item) %
Implementation *Content Curation* Tools Time *Content Creation* Writing Graphics Video *Social Advertising* (List each platform) *Promotions/Contests* (Prizes, discounts, promotions etc.) (List each platform) *Social Engagement* (Time to listen and respond to comments and questions) (List each platform) *Offline Tactics* (Events etc.) *Software/Tools* Monitoring Scheduling Analytics	$ per hour per item	$ per hour per item or $ amount for each item.	$ (per item) %

Strategic Phase Budget Category	In-house Expense (fixed/percent)	Outsource Expense (fixed/percent)	Total Category (fixed/percent)
Evaluation Measurement and Monitoring Framework Implementation Data Analysis Performance Report and recommendation development Implementation of recommendations	**$ per hour per item**	**$ per hour per item or $ amount for each item.**	**$ (per item) %**
Measurement and Monitoring Framework Implementation Data Analysis Performance Report and recommendation development Implementation of recommendations		**or $ amount for each item.**	
TOTAL	$ %	$ %	$ %

Conclusion

Please write a brief concluding statement to sum up the entire Social Media Strategy.

- Summarise the purpose of the strategy.
- Restate the overall strategic goals to be achieved.
- Briefly summarise the key tactics that will be used to achieve these goals.
- Thank your client for the opportunity.

(Please refer to Chapter 6 for more information about Social Media Content Calendars)

Social Media Content Calendar

Week No.			Day:		
Platform	Content Type	Image Link	Copy	Time

References

(Always remember to reference all sources that you have cited within your strategy as part of ethical practice).

Appendix 2. Social Media Video Shooting Script

(Please refer to Chapter 12 for guidance on how to develop a Social Media Video Shooting Script)

Shot No.	Visuals	Audio